HELP® 3–6 (2nd Edition)
Curriculum Guide

Edited by
Patricia Teaford, M.S.

Contributors
Jan Wheat, M.S. ECE
Tim Baker, Ph.D.

VORT Corporation
PO Box 60132
Palo Alto, CA 94306
http://www.vort.com

COPYRIGHT

Publisher's Note

We are pleased to have the opportunity to publish this important family support and information resource. It is concise and comprehensive, however, we cannot anticipate the circumstances under which a reader may apply its contents. We expressly decline liability for the techniques, activities, or results of conclusions you may reach about a child after reading and applying the contents of this book. Use the *HELP 3-6 (2ⁿᵈ Edition) Assessment Manual* for proper Instructions on how to use *HELP 3-6* as part of an ongoing curriculum-based assessment process.

Disclaimers

The developmental information contained in this book is intended for supplemental support and not a replacement for developmental or medical evaluation, advice, diagnosis, or treatment by healthcare or other developmental professionals. This book is intended to provide accurate information, however, in a time of rapid change it is difficult to ensure that all information is entirely accurate and up-to-date. It is the professional's responsibility to review each behavior and skill and procedures for appropriateness. The authors and publisher accept no responsibility for any inaccuracies or omissions and specifically disclaim any liability, loss, or risk, personal or otherwise, which is incurred as a consequence, directly or indirectly, of the use and or application of any of the contents of this book.

For Use by Professionals

These materials are intended for use by qualified child development professionals working with the child and the family. The child's doctor must be consulted under all circumstances if the child has special needs/health issues, or if there are any health or safety questions whatsoever. It is also important to remember that each child is unique and develops behaviors and skills at different rates and ages. No child is expected to demonstrate all behaviors and skills identified in *HELP 3–6 (2nd Edition)*. Age ranges listed are only a guide of the age range when a behavior/skill may typically emerge, <u>not</u> when a behavior/skill begins and ends.

Safety Guidelines

Although precaution and safety notes are included for behaviors and skills, there may be some which are not appropriate for some children, and some which have the potential for misinterpretation. It is your professional responsibility to carefully review the appropriateness of the information and activities for each particular child, and to alter the activity and/or add additional safety precautions as needed. It is extremely important to use caution with the child and to supervise the child carefully around sharp objects and utensils, appliances, small objects, scissors, hot water, etc. Be sure to check with the child's family/doctor regarding any food allergies or diet issues <u>before</u> providing or using snacks or food. Remind parents of these safety issues, and advise parents to always supervise their child. For example, the U.S. Consumer Product Safety Commission (CPSC) urges caregivers to be sure that toys and items used with or given to young children are safe and appropriate. Numerous toy safety guidelines and brochures are available through their website: www.cpsc.gov.

To be used as a reference

This book contains hundreds of activities and suggestions. For ease-of-use, <u>use this book as a reference</u>. Use the child's age as an approximate starting point, and use the assessment forms – *HELP 3–6 (2nd Edition) Strands* or *Checklist* or *Charts* – to identify the child's target behavior(s) and skill(s) to work on, and then look up the behaviors/skills in this book using the item ID number.

Contents

Introduction

The term "HELP" is derived from the product "Hawaii Early Learning Profile," which was first published by VORT in 1979. The original HELP materials consisted of a profile Chart and an Activity Guide for serving children, ages birth through three years (0-3).

In 1987, VORT published *Help for Special Preschoolers* (for serving children 3-6 years) which was adapted from the BCP (Behavioral Characteristics Progression) developed by VORT and the Santa Cruz County Office of Education.

To better link the 3-6 materials to the improved 0-3 materials, in 1995 VORT restructured the 3-6 year materials into *HELP for Preschoolers* to conform to the developmental Strand structure of HELP 0-3, thus offering a "seamless" birth-6 years HELP behaviors/skills continuum.

In 2010, a team of editors and reviewers completed a two-year revision of *HELP for Preschoolers* resulting in the new *HELP 3–6 (2nd Edition)* which includes an updating of the behaviors/skills (both text and ages and the removing of some skills; see page xi), and updating the assessment materials, procedures, and adaptations. To improve use of the materials, the assessment portion of *HELP 3–6 (2nd Edition)* was separated from the curriculum activities resulting in two new books, the *Assessment Manual* and the *Curriculum Guide*. These books parallel the two books for HELP 0-3: *Inside HELP* and the *HELP Activity Guide*. **See page xii for complete listing of What's New in this 2ⁿᵈ Edition.**

The *HELP® 3–6 (2nd Edition)* family of products includes:

> #659 – *HELP® 3–6 (2nd Edition) Assessment Manual*
> #652 – *HELP® 3–6 (2nd Edition) Curriculum Guide*
> #658 – *HELP® 3–6 (2nd Edition) Assessment Strands*
> #650 – *HELP® 3–6 (2nd Edition) Charts*
> #651 – *HELP® 3–6 (2nd Edition) Checklist*
> #656 – *HELP® 3–6 (2nd Edition) Activities at Home*

The combined HELP 0-6 materials cover over 1,250 unique behaviors and skills in six primary domains of: Cognitive, Language, Gross Motor, Fine Motor, Social, and Self-Help. The behaviors and skills (items) are linked by unique ID numbers to over 1,800 pages of assessment, curriculum, and family support materials. The six domains have been divided into 75 developmentally-sequenced strands. Each strand includes items which focus upon a specific underlying key concept and are hierarchical in nature; i.e., one item typically leads to or builds the foundation for the next item.

The HELP materials are not standardized. No child is expected to display all the behaviors or skills nor display all behaviors and skills for an age range. Be sure to consider individual, environmental, or cultural differences for each child. The age ranges reported in HELP are the ages at which a skill or behavior (for children who do not have disabilities) typically **begin to emerge** according to the literature. These age ranges are **not** when an item begins and ends. Some behaviors/skills are time-limited and emerge into more complex behaviors/skills, while others are lifetime skills.

Sometimes a behavior or skill stretches out over several months. This is not meant to imply that the item begins and ends within the age-range time frame. The age range reflects when the item typically emerges. Since there is not always agreement in growth and development literature, approximate age ranges are offered as a guide of when you can expect an item (behavior or skill) to typically be present. A child may develop the behavior or skill at any time within the age range to be "developmentally age appropriate." Descriptions of the child's behaviors and skills are more important than age levels for understanding a child's development and determining next steps in intervention or the child's educational plan.

Age ranges for HELP 3-6 are displayed in Months as well as Year.Month, e.g., 3.10-4.4 is 3 years 10 months to 4 years 4 months.

Note: The term "items" is used interchangeably to mean HELP 3-6 behaviors/skills.

Items listed on traditional developmental checklists and standardized tests, although generally listed in a developmental order according to age, are not generally hierarchical. Consequently, if a child "passes" one item it does not necessarily mean that he is ready to learn the next behavior or skill. Conversely, if a child "failed" an item, this does not mean that he cannot accomplish or is not ready to learn an item placed higher on the continuum. Without careful item analysis, it can be difficult to identify strengths and needs within a domain of development and difficult to identify "next steps" for planning. The *HELP 3–6 (2nd Edition) Assessment Strands* address these needs and provides an option for developmental assessment and monitoring.

Functional Outcomes

The HELP 3-6 curriculum-based assessment materials can be used to identify child needs and select a variety of activities designed to support the "Three Child Outcomes" presented by the U.S. Office of Special Education (OSEP).

The three OSEP Child Outcomes are:

1. Children have positive social-emotional skills (including social relationships)

2. Children acquire and use knowledge and skills (including early language/communication [and early literacy])

3. Children use appropriate behaviors to meet their needs

The outcomes are meant to be functional and "refer to things that are meaningful to the child in the context of everyday living" and "refer to an integrated series of behaviors or skills that allow the child to achieve the important everyday goals".

Functional means to refer to or include behaviors that integrate skills across domains instead of looking at a single behavior or skill and choosing just one item from the HELP 3-6 materials to achieve a single goal. In using the HELP 3-6 materials to develop functional child outcomes, you will want to consider the multiple domains associated with achieving the outcome.

For example, consider a child who does not play well with other children. All areas of development for this child should be investigated to help this child progress socially. A functional outcome for this child might be:

The child is to relate to adults and other children and follow rules related to groups or interacting with others.

For this sample outcome, you could use HELP 3-6 to help the child achieve success in play by:

1. Assessing the child on the items below using the *HELP 3-6 Assessment Strands* in conjunction with the *HELP 3-6 Assessment Manual*;

2. Using the *HELP 3-6 Curriculum Guide* for instructional activities linked by ID number;

3. Involving the child's family/parent by handing out and annotating the respective pages from the *HELP 3-6 Activities at Home* binder:

Cognitive:
   1.188…Works in small groups for 5-10 minutes
   1.239…Works in group for 10-25 minutes
   1.305…Role plays or organizes other children using props

Language:
   2.119…Carries on a conversation

Social:
   5.96…Plays with one or two others
   5.97…Exchanges items with another child
   5.98…Child engages in cooperative play with other children
   5.110…Looks at person when speaking
   5.112…Shares toys/equipment with another
   5.114…Stays with group during an activity

5.118…Takes turns
5.145…Obeys rules
5.163…Bargains with other children

All HELP 3-6 behaviors/skills are cross-referenced to the HELP curriculum materials and all HELP activities focus on the underlying concepts and skills that lead to functional child outcomes.

/*\ Safety First!

Although precaution and safety notes are often included for the activities, there may be some items or activities which are not appropriate for all children, and some which have the potential for misinterpretation. It is your professional responsibility to carefully review the appropriateness of the activities for each particular child, and to alter the activity and/or add additional safety precautions as needed. It is extremely important to use caution with the child and to supervise him carefully around sharp objects and utensils, appliances, small objects, scissors, hot water, etc. Be sure to check with the child's family/doctor regarding any food allergies or diet issues before providing or using snacks or food.

Involve families/parents

HELP 3–6 (2nd Edition) Activities at Home offers warm, at home suggestions for each item. These are written from the child's point of view and include an Introduction to the item, Materials in the home for teaching the skills, and Activities for the parent to follow to help the child develop the respective item. VORT products and publications are intended for use by and under the guidance of child development professionals. For example, families/parents interested in using the HELP materials must receive the materials through (ordered by) a qualified professional, and must work with and consult the professional on all procedures, including Gross and Fine Motor activities, Safety Issues, and any questions whatsoever. Be sensitive to, and adapt, the assessment items and procedures, and the instructional activities, as appropriate to the culture, customs, dress, appearance, and speech patterns of the child and his/her family.

Visit the VORT web site

The VORT web site (www.VORT.com) offers a wealth of current product information, training tips, instructions for use, and FAQs (answers to Frequently Asked Questions). Be sure to check out the web site, especially the FAQs, to supplement what is provided in the Introduction and Instructions in this book.

Purpose of HELP 3–6

HELP 3–6 (2nd Edition) is a curriculum-based assessment for use with both children who are exhibiting "typical" development and with those children who may have developmental delays. It is designed to be used by those working in early childhood settings and by those involved in a multi-disciplinary or transdisciplinary team approach. *HELP 3–6 (2nd Edition)* addresses the requirements for early childhood programs, including:

1. **Assessment and early identification**: Through family/parent interviews, observations, and exposure to different activities in all areas of development, individuals working with a child can get an overall picture of a child's skill levels. You can use the *HELP 3–6 (2nd Edition)* materials to document the child's growth and progress, both at home and in the educational setting. This can help you determine how a child is developing within and between developmental areas (strands). When there appear to be delays, mild or severe, it should be decided, with the family/parents involvement, whether the child needs to be referred for a more in-depth evaluation to determine eligibility for special services.

HELP 3–6 (2nd Edition) is a curriculum-based assessment, **not** a standardized test. The age ranges are provided to indicate when a skill "typically" emerges. You can use *HELP 3–6 (2nd Edition)* to record the child's development in a longitudinal manner from the age of three to six years. *HELP 3–6 (2nd Edition)* will **not** yield a definitive single age level or score. The primary purpose of *HELP 3–6 (2nd Edition)* as a curriculum-based assessment is to identify curriculum outcomes, strategies and activities, and to plan next steps. *HELP 3–6 (2nd Edition)* thus should not be used if your program requires standardized instruments to determine developmental delay. In addition, since *HELP 3–6 (2nd Edition)* cannot provide a single "score" or definitive developmental age, it should **not** be used to determine eligibility for children who may be experiencing mild developmental delays. In such cases, however, *HELP 3–6 (2nd Edition)* can be used to compliment standardized instruments to support "informed clinical opinion" requirements, and it can be used as an initial and ongoing assessment to help identify the child's unique strengths and needs, and the services appropriate to meet those needs. If your program does not require standardized instruments, *HELP 3–6 (2nd Edition)* can be used as an initial and ongoing assessment to help identify the child's unique strengths and needs.

2. **Program intervention and instructional teaching resource**: By recording a child's developmental progress using *HELP 3–6 (2nd Edition)*, strategies can be included in the curriculum to build and expand a child's skills. The child should be taught according to his rate and style of learning within the range of normal development. *HELP 3–6 (2nd Edition)* provides detailed instructional activities for each skill along with suggestions for adapting activities relative to the child's experience and abilities.

3. **Family/Parent involvement**: The parent/caregiver needs to be involved in the assessment and introduced to the teaching concepts that can be carried over into the home setting. As the parent becomes more involved, he or she will begin to feel more competent and effective in reinforcing skills at home that have been introduced in the educational setting. The *HELP 3–6 (2nd Edition) Activities at Home* binder provides practical, home-based activities that can easily be administered by the parents or the child's home-care provider. An introduction, a short list of easy-to-use materials and clear list of activities is included for most skills.

4. **Team approach and training guide**: Family members, the early childhood educator, and other school personnel, along with professionals such as audiologists, social workers and therapists, constitute the team that provides comprehensive services to meet the child's unique needs. *HELP 3–6 (2nd Edition)* can be used by the team to record growth and as a training guide for persons who are new to the field of early childhood education, particularly in working with young children who have a developmental delay or who may be considered to be at risk. *HELP 3–6 (2nd Edition)* can support early childhood teachers or administrator working with paraprofessionals, volunteers, or teachers' aides, and can be used to train staff in assessing the child's skill levels, as well as providing activities for teaching various skills. *HELP 3–6 (2nd Edition)* can be used as a resource for teachers whose classes include children with special needs.

Design of HELP 3–6

1. The *HELP 3–6 (2nd Edition)* (3-6) behaviors and skills are an extension of HELP 0-3. Thus, the item ID numbers for HELP 3-6 are based on domain (e.g., Cognitive = 1.0, Language = 2.0), and the 3-6 ID numbers start where the 0-3 ID numbers end. For example, Cognitive, 0-3 ends with item #1.159, and the first *HELP 3–6 (2nd Edition)* (3-6) Cognitive item is #1.160.

2. The age ranges provided with *HELP 3–6 (2nd Edition)* are based upon current literature. The age ranges are approximations as to when the behavior/skill "typically" emerges. The *HELP 3–6 (2nd Edition)* materials are **not** standardized, therefore, *HELP 3–6 (2nd Edition)* is not a formal "test" and you do not "score" a child. You use *HELP 3–6 (2nd Edition)* to credit a child's mastery of a behavior or skill and to plan next steps.

3. The activities in the *HELP 3–6 (2nd Edition) Activities at Home* binder are written from the child's point-of-view, which families/parents enjoy and which prevents any problems with gender. Some of the Instructions below are written using the male gender to avoid redundancy and confusion. No gender bias is intended.

4. *HELP 3–6 (2nd Edition)* covers 585 skills, ages 3 to 6 years. Activities and other content are written using both "he" and "she" to avoid gender bias. The references throughout this book to parents (in the plural) is meant to apply to all parents and caregivers, single, married, etc.

For each skill, this Curriculum Guide provides:

Unique ID number and text identical across all the HELP 3-6 family of products.

1.160 Counts orally to 3

Strand reference and Age range shown in both month-month(m), and year.month-year.month(y) formats.

Strand: 1-10 **Age:** 28-36m 2.4-3y

Definition

This clarifies the item; can be adapted to serve as a basis for criteria to determine mastery.

Instructional Materials

A list of the materials needed to conduct the assessment activity(s), including suggestions on how to make your own in-class materials or where materials may be purchased.

Instructional Activities

Step-by-step methods for teaching the item (behavior/skill).

5. The behaviors and skills in *HELP 3–6 (2nd Edition)* follow a "normal" developmental sequence and are applicable to all children. However, four of the Strands of skills are provided for use with children with special needs: 2-8 Sign Language; 2-9 Speech Reading; 3-8 Swimming; 3-9 Wheelchair skills. These strands require special instruction; thus, this *HELP 3–6 (2nd Edition)* does not provide parent/at home activities for these four strands.

Important Note: Instruction on some of the Self-Help items is not appropriate away from home. Follow proper local and agency guidelines regarding these items.

Note: Throughout this *HELP 3–6 (2nd Edition) Curriculum Guide*, sample words or sounds are identified in the activities, such as a, b, c, A, B, C. Normally these would be placed in quotes, but for consistency and ease of reading, the quotation marks have been omitted. Upon occasion this may make the grammar structure of the sentence appear awkward. Be sure to read the content carefully so these words/sounds are recognized as samples.

Structure and Link to HELP 0-3

The HELP 3-6 materials link directly to the HELP 0-3 materials according to the developmental strand structure of the 0-3 materials, thus offering a "seamless" Birth-6 continuum. The over 1,250 HELP 0-6 skills are grouped into 75 "concept-based Strands." There are some HELP 0-3 strands for which there are no 3-6 skills (e.g., 1-1 Symbolic Play), and likewise, there are some 3-6 strands that have no 0-3 counterpart (e.g., 1-8 Attention).

Following is the entire HELP 0-6 Strands structure: 0-3 Strands are shown as plain text, HELP 3-6 Strands are in **bold**, Strands that span *both* HELP 0-3 and HELP 3-6 in *italics*.

0.0 Self Regulation *(Regulatory/Sensory Integration 0-3)*	**4.0 Fine Motor:**
	4-1 Visual Responses and Tracking
1.0 Cognitive:	4-2 Grasp and Prehension
1-1 Development of Symbolic Play	4-3 Reach and Approach
1-2 Gestural Imitation	4-4 Development of Voluntary Release
1-3 Sound Awareness	4-5 Bilateral and Midline
1-4A Problem Solving/Object Permanence	*4-6A Pre-Writing*
1-4B Problem Solving/Means-End	*4-6B Blocks/Puzzles*
1-4C Problem Solving/Cause and Effect	*4-6C Formboard*
1-4D Problem Solving/Reasoning	*4-6D Paper Activities*
1-5 Spatial Relationships	4-7A Manipulating Pages
1-6 Concepts: A. Pictures B. Numbers	4-7B Pegboard
1-7A Discrimination/Classification:Matching/Sorting	4-7C Stringing Beads
1-7B Discrimination/Classification: Size	4-7D Scissors
1-7C Discrimination/Classification: Associative	**4-8 Perceptual Motor: Tactile**
1-8 Attention	
1-9 Reading Readiness	**5.0 Social:**
1-10 Math Readiness	*5-1 Attachment/Adaptive skills*
1-11 Writing Skills	*5-2 Development of Self Identification*
1-12 Dramatic Play	5-3 Emotions/Feelings
1-13 Time	*5-4 Expectations/Responsibility/Rules*
	5-5 Social Interactions and Play
2.0 Language:	**5-6 Social Manners**
2-1 Receptive: Understanding Words	**5-7 Social Language**
2-2 Following Directions	**5-8 Personal Welfare/Safety**
2-3 Expressive Vocabulary	
2-4A Communicating with Others: Gesturally	**6.0 **Self Help:**
2-4B Communicating with Others: Verbally	6-1 Oral-Motor
2-5 Grammar	*6-2A Dressing*
2-6 Development of Sounds	**6-2B Undressing**
2-7 Communication through Rhythm	*6-3A Feeding/Eating*
2-8 Sign Language Skills	**6-3B Drinking**
2-9 Speech Reading Skills	6-4 Sleep patterns and behaviors
	6-5 Grooming
3.0 Gross Motor:	*6-6 Toileting*
3-1 Prone	6-7 Household Responsibility
3-2 Supine	**6-8 Oral Hygiene**
3-3 Sitting	**6-9 Nasal Hygiene**
3-4 Weight-bearing	
3-5 Mobility/Trans. Movements	
3-6 A. Reflexes B. Reactions	
3-7A Balance/Standing	
3-7B Walking/Running	
3-7C Jumping	
3-7D Climbing	
3-7E Stairs (see 3-7B)	
3-7F Catching/Throwing	
3-7G Bilateral Play	
3-7H Balance Beam	
3-8 Swimming	
3-9 Wheelchair Skills	

Assessment/Instruction on some Self-Help skills may **not be appropriate outside the home.

How to Use the Curriculum

Be sure to use this Guide in conjunction with the procedures and alerts in the *HELP 3–6 Assessment Manual*.

Instructional Materials – Includes suggestions on how to make your own in-class materials.

Instructional Activities – Curriculum for young children involves two basic approaches:

• Curriculum based on children's interests—Supporters of creating instructional activities based on a child's interest generally believe that children from 3 to 6 learn through experience in their own way, style, and sequence. The aim of this approach is to provide opportunities for children to use real objects and explore in a stimulating setting. It allows children to interact with concrete items in an environment that is conducive to creativity and play. Because children in this age range have not yet fully developed abstract receptive/expressive language, users of this approach expose them to only a limited amount of teacher questioning and facts.

• Curriculum based on what children need to know—Supporters of creating instructional activities based on what a child needs to know, on the other hand, want a curriculum based on preparing children to function in their various real-life situations. This approach places the emphasis on a child's learning information and being able to use the acquired knowledge to operate in society.

The instructional procedures in *HELP 3-6 (2nd Edition)* have been designed to offer a combination of both approaches for use in early childhood programs and particularly for use with children who are at risk of developmental delays. The activities have been designed to keep the interest of children and to encourage them to create, explore, and interact, while at the same time providing teachers an opportunity to communicate knowledge and information. Preschool children need instructional strategies that are direct, concrete, and based on experiential interests along with planned directions and expected competencies. The instructional methodology offered through *HELP 3-6 (2nd Edition)* blends the two schools of thought and yields a very practical approach for meeting the needs of all preschool children. The following elements were emphasized in the development of the instructional procedures.

• Early learning should enhance self-awareness and positive self-concepts.

• Communication consists of expressive and receptive vocabularies; therefore, language learning leads to interpreting and expressing facts, thoughts, and feelings.

• The child's sensory perceptions and motor experiences exhibit his earliest form of cognitive development. Sensory/motor involvement and activities lead to pre-conceptual thinking.

• Social behaviors become functional as a child interacts with the environment and other people.

What's New in this 2ⁿᵈ Edition of HELP 3–6

Over the past two years, all materials related to *HELP for Preschoolers* were extensively reviewed and evaluated to determine if the behaviors/skills continued to be relevant, age ranges coincided with current literature review, present safety trends and procedures were being followed, and what additional behaviors/skills needed to be addressed. Behaviors/skills that were considered dated, or no longer appropriate, were either modified or removed. Behaviors and skills that were viewed to emerge prior to the age of three, or beyond the age of six, were removed. Some age ranges were modified when necessary. Items related to safety were updated, however, professionals are cautioned to determine the appropriateness of any given skill for each child being assessed. Where gaps in behaviors/skills were noted, new skills were written and incorporated. In addition, three new Strands have been developed.

Suggestions related to what type of grouping might be used to assess the different behaviors/skills have been added. Be mindful that informal observation is a very effective way of assessing a child's abilities because the behavior/skills are occurring in a natural context and in the environment where the task is typically performed. Informal observation should always be considered when the behavior/skill allows. The child is more at ease and their behavior is more natural during an observation. Additionally, an assessor can observe skills they won't necessarily see when conducting a standardized assessment that may require a certain protocol and procedure due to standardization factors. When informal observation isn't appropriate, or the child's skills make it more of a challenge to assess a behavior/skill, one-on-one assessment or small group assessments can often be used.

Another new feature is a section for each behavior/skill that addresses how to "credit" the item. Suggestions are offered regarding when a child should be given credit for demonstrating competency or mastery of each skill. This facilitates consistency across assessments and between children.

The *HELP for Preschoolers Assessment and Curriculum Guide* has been divided into two separate books for ease of use. *HELP 3-6 (2ⁿᵈ Edition)* materials maintain the integrity of the original materials. The breadth of information covered through the behaviors/skills continues to make *HELP 3-6 2ⁿᵈ Edition* a valuable assessment tool for assessing and planning programs for young children. It continues in the tradition of *HELP 0-3* by providing the assessor a broad view of the child's capabilities as well as a giving them a clearer picture of a child's unique areas of strengths and needs. *HELP 3-6 (2ⁿᵈ Edition)* continues to be a helpful resource for professionals to use in conjunction with *HELP 0-3* because of the seamless transition of covering behavior/skills from birth to age six.

Note: To incorporate changes in a manner that makes *HELP 3–6 (2ⁿᵈ Edition)* compatible with the prior version (*HELP for Preschoolers*), the item ID numbering has remained unchanged. For easier cross-reference to "look up an item," the items (behaviors/skills) are listed in this book in <u>ID number sequence</u>. In some cases this means that items do not appear in age sequence. The ID number is strictly for easy cross-reference between assessment and curriculum materials and should not be considered to represent developmental sequence.

After thorough review and analysis of current literature and information, the editorial team made the following changes to HELP 3–6:

A. Three **new Strands** have been added:

<u>0-0 Self-Regulation:</u> Self-regulation is the act of regulating oneself. This requires the child to demonstrate the ability to self-monitor, self-evaluate, and adjust behavior. As a child matures, he becomes more capable of regulating himself. With adult guidance a child can learn to tolerate some anxiety and not go from an impulse to an action by reacting too quickly. Developing a Strand for self-regulation helps the assessor identify a child's skills in this area, which can lead to planning and developing strategies to help the child stop and think before he acts.

1-12 Dramatic Play: Dramatic play was added because so much can be learned about a child's skills by observing them while they are engaged in pretend play. Play is spontaneous, enjoyable, involves interaction with other children, and gives the assessors an opportunity to see how children can assume the roles of others. How elaborate, or simple, a child's play themes or play sequences are can tell a great deal about their developmental level of functioning. In formal, standardized assessments we don't often get the opportunity to observe the child engaged in pretend play. Current literature suggests that when children are playing they are performing close to their optimal developmental level.

1-13 Time: Skills related to time were incorporated in the Strand – Math Readiness. While some of the skills associated with "time" focus on reading numbers on a clock, the abstract understanding of the concept of time (e.g., "today," "tomorrow," and "yesterday") and the days of the week seem to suggest skills outside the realm of math readiness. Therefore, a separate category for Time has been added.

B. Twelve **new** items (behaviors/skills) have been **added**.

ID	Strand	Age (Y.M)	Behavior/Skill Text
1.303	1-12	3.0-3.6	Uses imaginary objects during play
1.304	1-12	3.0-3.6	Uses dolls or action figures to act out sequences
1.305	1-12	5.0-6.0	Role-plays or organizes other children using props
1.306	1-11	5.8-6.8	Prints the numbers 1 - 10 correctly, in sequential and random order, when requested without the use of a model
2.224	2-4B	3.6-3.11	Answers questions logically
2.225	2-4B	4.0-4.6	Responds appropriately to "where" questions
2.226	2-4B	4.6-5.0	Answers "why" questions by giving a reason
4.128	4-6A	3.0-4.0	Holds paper with one hand while drawing with the other hand
4.129	4-7D	3.6-4.0	Cuts out a circle with scissors
4.130	4-6D	4.0-5.0	Places a paper clip on paper
4.132	4-6A	4.6-6.0	Holds pencil/crayon using a dynamic tripod grasp to draw
5.233	5-5	4.0-5.0	Engages in rough-and-tumble play

C. The **text** of the following items was changed, primarily to make the item more consistent with the literature or with HELP 0-3, or to replace/merge it with another item (behavior/skill). A few other items received minor wording changes to improve readability.

ID	Strand	Age (Y.M)	New Text
1.180	1-7C	2.7-3.6	Identifies objects based on appearance (color, shape, or physical characteristic)
1.207	1-11	4.0-5.0	Draws a square, copying model
1.210	1-11	4.9-5.9	Draws a triangle, copying model
1.211	1-10	4.0-5.0	Counts orally to 10, with one-on-one correspondence
1.212	1-10	4.0-5.0	Names penny, nickel, dime and quarter
1.224	1-11	5.9-6.9	Draws diamond, copying model
1.273	1-10	5.4-5.10	Finds group having more, less, or the same number of objects as a given group up to 10
1.292	1-10	5.0-5.6	Reads numerals to 19
1.293	2-7	5.6-6.6	Sings verse of a new song by rote
1.294	1-11	5.8-6.6	Prints all letters of the alphabet correctly, without models
1.298	1-9	5.0-6.0	Answers questions about a story related to the interpretation of the content (was 2.172)
1.308	1-11	4.4-5.0	Draws diagonal lines, copying model (was 4.114)
2.103	2-1A	2.8-3.2	Responds correctly with a non-verbal response or with a single word answer to a stated question
2.104	2-1A	2.8-3.6	Points to or places an object on top/bottom

2.114	2-1A	2.6-3.6	Provides objects as they are requested by name or referenced by function
2.139	2-3	4.0-5.0	Uses negatives in sentences
2.147	2-4B	5.0-6.0	Uses timed events appropriately when explaining a happening (today, yesterday, tomorrow)
2.157	2-2	3.6-5.0	Acts out at least two, but no more than five, commands in the same order they were presented
2.161	2-4B	4.0-6.0+	Uses four- to eight-word sentences
2.176	2-1A	5.4-5.8	Identifies order of sounds in a word and blends the sounds together to make meaningful words
2.182	2-1A	5.8-6.6	Repeats a poem when prompted by the title, a subject clue, or the first line
3.148	3-7A	3.0-3.8	Balances on each foot for 5 seconds, without support
3.163	3-7A	3.0-3.6	Kicks a large ball when the ball has been rolled directly to him
3.164	3-7B	3.8-4.7	Runs and changes direction without stopping, avoiding obstacles
3.170	3-7A	4.0-5.6	Stands up without losing balance after lying on back
3.175	3-7B	5.0-5.5	Walks up and down stairs carrying an object, without support
4.94	4-6B	2.6-3.4	Puts together simple inset puzzles
4.96	4-7D	3.0-4.0	Cuts across paper following a straight line 6 inches long and then a curved line 6 inches long
4.110	4-6D	2.6-3.4	Spreads paste/glue on one side of paper and turns over to stick it to another paper
4.111	4-6A	4.0-5.0	Draws a picture of a person
4.115	4-8	4.5-5.0	Matches or chooses through tactile cues like objects that are circular, triangular, rectangular, and square
4.120	4-7D	5.6-6.0	Cuts cloth with scissors
5.96	5-5	2.6-3.2	Plays with one or two other children
5.97	5-5	2.8-3.2	Exchanges items with another child during play
5.98	5-5	2.8-3.6	Engages in cooperative play with other children
5.99	5-8	2.10-3.5	Avoids hazards and common dangers
5.110	5-5	3.0-3.8	Looks at person when speaking/spoken to
5.116	5-1	3.0-4.0	Transitions from one activity to another at the request of an adult
5.129	5-7	3.6-4.6	Shows an emerging sense of humor by laughing at the appropriate time
5.133	5-6	3.8-4.4	Cleans up spills independently
5.135	5-5	3.6-4.6	Plays with group of 3 or more children
5.137	5-7	3.4-4.5	Uses appropriate manners to request an object
5.184	5-5	5.0-5.6	Waits appropriately for attention in group situation
6.94	6-2B	2.6-3.6	Pulls shoes off completely, including undoing laces, straps (*Velcro*), and buckles
6.100	6-2A	3.6-4.6	Puts on appropriate clothing depending on the weather
6.101	6-8	3.0-4.0	Puts toothpaste on brush and wets
6.115	6-2A	2.6-3.6	Puts shoes on the correct feet
6.121	6-2B	3.2-3.6	Removes pull-over clothing off both arms and starts over head
6.122	6-3B	3.2-3.10	Refills a glass using a container with a handle and a spout
6.153	6-3B	3.2-4.0	Holds container with one hand while sucking liquid through a straw
6.167	6-6	4.4-5.0	Uses toilet properly by self with no accidents
6.175	6-9	4.6-5.6	Covers mouth with tissue, hand or the bend of the elbow when sneezing or coughing
6.181	6-2A	5.0-5.8	Ties shoes, following step-by-step demonstration/support
6.190	6-8	5.5-6.6	Uses proper brushing strokes to clean teeth
6.193	6-2A	5.6-6.6	Ties shoelaces independently

D. Forty-eight items were **removed** for reasons including overlap with HELP 0-3, similarity to other items, or the updated age places the items below three years or above six years.

1.232	2.121	2.210	4.127	5.196	6.124
1.247	2.122	3.150	5.100	5.198	6.125
1.266	2.132	3.151	5.102	5.202	6.126
1.271	2.134	3.154	5.106	5.214	6.128
1.297	2.200	3.156	5.146	5.226	6.165
2.110	2.201	4.95	5.148	6.102	6.173
2.115	2.203	4.107	5.166	6.103	6.179
2.116	2.209	4.109	5.194	6.120	6.187

E. **Ages** were removed for the behaviors and skills in the Strands of 2-8 Sign Language, 2-9 Speech Reading, 3-8 Swimming, and 3-9 Wheelchair because the emergence and development of these behaviors and skills is more dependent upon when the child is exposed to or given an opportunity to learn in the respective environment, such as swimming.

F. **Updated ages** are shown for the following items:

ID	Age (Y.M)	ID	Age (Y.M)	ID	Age (Y.M)
1.180	2.7-3.6	5.107	3.0-4.0	6.101	3.0-4.0
1.192	3.6-4.6	5.108	2.8-3.6	6.104	3.0-4.0
1.194	3.8-4.8	5.113	3.6-4.6	6.107	3.6-4.6
1.203	3.8-4.8	5.116	3.0-4.0	6.113	2.6-3.6
1.210	4.9-5.9	5.124	3.6-4.6	6.115	2.6-3.6
1.224	5.9-6.9	5.125	3.0-4.0	6.118	2.4-3.2
1.241	3.0-4.0	5.128	3.0-4.0	6.119	2.6-3.4
1.292	5.0-5.6	5.135	3.6-4.6	6.127	3.0-4.0
2.111	2.0-3.4	5.137	3.4-4.5	6.131	2.6-3.8
2.112	2.6-3.4	5.138	4.0-5.0	6.133	3.4-4.4
2.114	2.6-3.6	5.142	4.0-5.0	6.135	3.0-4.0
2.120	2.6-3.2	5.143	4.0-5.0	6.139	2.6-3.6
2.130	2.6-3.8	5.145	4.0-5.0	6.144	4.6-5.6
2.139	4.0-5.0	5.164	4.0-4.10	6.145	3.0-4.0
2.147	5.0-6.0	5.165	4.0-5.6	6.147	3.6-4.8
2.155	3.0-4.6	5.167	4.0-5.0	6.151	3.0-4.6
2.156	3.0-4.6	5.171	4.0-6.0	6.153	3.2-4.0
2.157	3.6-5.0	5.172	4.0-5.0	6.154	3.0-4.0
2.161	4.0-6.0	5.178	3.0-5.0	6.156	4.8-6.0
2.173	4.0-5.6	5.179	4.0-5.6	6.157	3.0-4.0
2.177	3.6-4.6	5.181	4.6-5.6	6.161	4.0-5.6
3.153	3.6-4.6	5.182	4.6-5.6	6.166	5.0-6.0
3.157	3.0-3.8	5.183	5.0-6.0	6.169	3.4-4.6
3.160	3.6-4.4	5.186	4.6-6.0	6.174	4.0-5.0
3.161	3.6-4.4	5.189	3.6-4.6	6.176	4.6-6.0
3.163	3.0-3.6	5.197	4.0-5.0	6.177	4.0-5.4
4.94	2.6-3.4	5.199	5.0-6.6	6.178	4.0-5.6
4.110	2.6-3.4	5.211	3.4-6.0	6.184	3.4-4.4
4.120	5.6-6.0	5.225	5.0-6.6	6.185	5.6-6.6
5.98	3.0-4.0	6.97	2.6-3.2	6.188	5.5-6.6
5.101	3.0-3.4	6.100	3.6-4.6		

G. **Definitions** were rewritten and improved for many of the behaviors/skills.

H. These items were **moved between Domains**:

Old ID	New ID	Old ID	New ID
1.167	4.131	4.114	1.308
2.148	1.307	5.193	1.309
2.172	1.298	5.227	1.310

I. These items were **moved** to **different Strands** (with new item ID in bold)

ID	To Strand	ID	To Strand
1.167	**4.131** in 4-6A	1.243	1-7A
1.175	1-7B	1.244	1-7A
1.192	1-7B	1.256	1-7B
1.222	1-7B	2.148	**1.307** in 1-4D
1.233	1-7A	2.172	**1.298** in 1-9
1.234	1-7A	4.114	**1.308** in 1-11
1.237	1-7B	5.193	**1.309** in 1-4D
1.238	1-7A	5.227	**1.310** in 1-4D

1.160   Counts orally to 3

Strand: 1-10   **Age:** 28-36m 2.4-3.0y

Definition

Many children sing number songs long before the counting process takes meaning. Even though the songs do not develop concepts of quantity, they establish the auditory sequence of numbers which is the prerequisite to counting. The child will count up to 3 items upon request.

Instructional Materials

Construction paper and stickers or other assorted items to count. If the stickers are on a large sheet, cut out each individual sticker and put them in a bowl.

Instructional Activities

1. Tell the child they are going to make a picture using stickers. Show them the bowl of stickers.
2. Ask the child how many stickers they would like, "Would you like one, two, three, four or five stickers?"
3. Have the child count out the number of stickers they want for their picture.
4. Provide assistance, if needed.
5. If the child had difficulty counting, suggest that they take one sticker. Let them count out one sticker. If successful, suggest that they count out two stickers. Keep going to see how far they can count.

1.161   Draws circle, imitating adult

Strand: 1-11   **Age:** 28-38m 2.4-3.2y

Definition

Using a crayon or pencil at least ½" in diameter, the child will copy a circle. The circle needs to be at least two inches in diameter. The child may construct the circle by one continuous movement or by forming two half-circles and then joining them.

Instructional Materials

Cut a circle from tagboard at least two inches in diameter and retain the empty circle frame. Obtain a large sheet of paper, crayons, and short pieces of yarn.

Instructional Activities

1. Place the circle template on the paper and ask the child to choose a crayon.
2. Instruct the child to draw around the inside of the template to make a balloon.
3. Move the template, asking the child to choose another crayon and repeat.
4. Continue until 5 to 10 balloons are drawn.
5. Assist the child in gluing yarn pieces to the paper balloons.
6. Display the completed picture.

1.162   Completes task with some attention and reinforcing

Strand: 1-8   **Age:** 30-36m 2.6-3.0y

Definition

The child will complete a task, such as listening to a tape/CD, sorting blocks, or looking at a picture book for a specified period of time. It may be necessary to provide the child with a sequence of reinforcement activities to renew attention.

Instructional Materials

Six small toys, a tray and a towel to cover the tray.

Instructional Activities

1. Place the six small toys (such as a car, crayon, ball, doll, block and book) on a tray. Name and describe each item to the child as you place them one by one on the tray.
2. Tell the child that you are going to play a magic game. Then cover the tray with the towel. Have the child say "Abracadabra," with you. Remove the towel, and make one of the toys disappear in the towel as you remove the cover.
3. Ask the child what toy disappeared. Give them an opportunity to visually inspect the tray. If they are having difficulty, you can point to the place where the toy had been or even give one identifying piece of information about the toy (such as, it has four wheels).
4. Return the toy to the tray, once the child names it correctly.
5. If it is easy for the child to identify the missing piece, remove two pieces at once to make the game more challenging.
6. This can easy be done as a group activity. You may want to add more toys as the skills of the children improve to keep them motivated and interested in the game.

1.163   Repeats sequence by physical movements

Strand: 1-4D   **Age:** 30-40m 2.6-3.4y

Definition

When shown a series of at least two and not more than six different, concept-related movements, the child will repeat the series. The child needs to be asked to repeat the sequence immediately after the demonstration and encouraged to add to the sequence if appropriate. The physical movements can involve fine or gross motor responses.

Instructional Materials

Make a streamer for each child by attaching a two-foot length of crepe paper to a straw or a paper towel roll.

Instructional Activities

Note: Movement commands should match the child's age and developmental level. For these activities, more than one adult may be needed to observe the children and to record progress.

1. Place the children in a large area so they have adequate space for moving. Have each child select a streamer.
2. Show the children different ways they can move their streamers. Have the children practice moving their streamers. When the children are comfortable with their streamers and appear to have motor control of the paper wands, ask them to watch your movements. Request that the children give their wands a rest while they are watching you.
3. Demonstrate at least three different movements with your streamer.
4. Repeat the demonstration.
5. Ask the children to "wake-up" their streamers and to make them do the three different movements that they just observed.
6. Demonstrate another sequence of at least four different movements and ask the children to repeat these patterns.
7. As the children become skilled in repeating the sequential movements, add the following dimension: ask them to make their streamers go high, then low and round and round. To increase the verbal directions, tell the children to make their streamers fly like a bird, wave like a flag, make a figure eight, etc. After the children have followed the verbal directions successfully, request that they give their streamers a rest and listen carefully.
8. Say at least three movement directions, such as: high, round, and low. Tell the children to

"wake-up" their streamers and make them move to the directions just heard. Continue using other verbal clues, such as: bird, figure eight, and flag.
9. Before concluding this activity, allow the children time for some creative movement with their streamers.

1.164   Names an item when shown parts

Strand: 1-4D   **Age:** 32-42m 2.8-3.6y

Definition

The child is able to identify an object when only part of it is shown. This identification requires the child to utilize simultaneous thinking skills, by relating a part to a whole.

Instructional Materials

Prepare a series of six 8 ½ x 11 single item pictures, with parts missing. Examples: a boy's profile missing an eye and mouth, a cat without hind quarters and a tail, a car missing its wheels, and a sailboat without any sails, etc. Crayons, marking pencils, or other drawing material.

Instructional Activities

1. Place a picture and a marking tool in front of each child. Ask the children to look very carefully at the picture that was placed in front of them.
2. Explain that only a part of the picture is showing.
3. Call on one child. "(Name of child), tell me about your picture. What is it?" If the child is correct, ask him to use the crayons and to fill in what is missing.
4. If the child gives an incorrect answer, complete a small part of the missing visual. Example: put in the boy's eye, then ask the child if he can name the picture. Continue adding parts until the child can name the visual.
5. Have the child name each of the additional pictures, following the above sequence.
6. This activity can easily be modified to be a group interaction. Instead of individual sheets of paper with the partially displayed visual, place the visual on the chalk board for all to view. Keep adding lines until someone guesses what the completed picture would be.

1.165 Locates pictured analogy

Strand: 1-4D   **Age:** 32-44m   2.8-3.8y

Definition

The child will view and locate pictures that have like characteristics. The first level of difficulty will include sets of pictures with one odd color, shape or size. A more advanced level of analogy will include a picture that is different because of use or type.

Instructional Materials

A collection of single item picture cards. The cards should have pictures such as a fork, hat, shoe, boy, buttons, toothbrush, etc. Rewards (i.e., stickers, tokens, etc.)

Instructional Activities

1. Place the collection of pictures face-up on a table. Ask the children to sit around the table.
2. Point to each picture that is on the table and ask the children to name the item.
3. Tell the children that you are going ask them what things go together and they must find a picture on the table that goes with what you have asked for. Example: say, "A spoon goes with a _____."
4. The first child to select the correct picture and say the word receives a token. Allow the child an opportunity to explain her selection. She might say, for example, "You eat with them." or "They are both silver."
5. Continue until all the pictures have been matched and all tokens have been presented.
6. This activity can be modified by dealing out the cards and asking the children to hold the cards so no else can see them. Repeat the analogy statement, and instead of giving a token for a correct response, the child gets to discard the matching card from her hand. Have the children see who can get rid of their cards first.
7. As the children become skilled in analogy recognition, increase the difficulty of the pictured cards and the relationship statement.

1.166 Sings parts and phrases of familiar songs

Strand: 2-7   **Age:** 32-44m   2.8-3.8y

Definition

The child will sing a part, a phrase, or the chorus of a familiar song. His singing does not need to be intelligible speech if the melody can be determined. He may also sing only parts of the lyrics if the melody can be determined.

Instructional Materials

Recorded song with at least three sequences, such as *Old MacDonald Had a Farm*. Equipment to play the song.

Instructional Activities

1. Play the song and sing along with it at least twice.
2. As you reach the sequence part, pause to check whether the child will sing that part. For example, sing, "Old MacDonald had a farm" and then pause to see if the child will add in the chorus "E I E I O."
3. Continue singing the sequence song and increase the number of pause points. For example, sing, "Old MacDonald had a farm," pause waiting for "E I E I O." Then pause again after "and on his farm he had a . . ." Wait to see if the child names an animal on the farm.
4. Continue singing the sequences of the song and increase the pause points.
5. To modify this activity select a song that is not only sequenced but has hand and finger movements.

1.167 (Moved to Fine Motor, skill 4.132)

1.168 Names action when looking at a picture book

Strand: 1-9   **Age:** 36-42m   3.0-3.6y

Definition

The child will use verbs to explain what is happening in a picture. The action verbs the child might use are "running, jumping, the boys are climbing, riding a horse, the girls are playing with their dolls," etc.

Instructional Materials

A short picture book or a series of pictures that tell a story. The book or pictures needs to have action segments.

Instructional Activities

1. Seat the child at a table next to you. On the table, place the pictures or the book, title page up.
2. Explain that you are going to look at the pictures together.
3. Discuss with the child the illustrations on the cover, making sure that any action words are brought out in the discussion.

4. Turn the page and name the nouns in the picture. Example: "This picture shows a boy and his dog."

5. Point to the person or thing that is showing action and ask, "What is the boy doing?" If the child is unable to answer the question, ask them to "Show me what the boy is doing." Have the child demonstrate what the boy is doing in the picture. Then model the correct response by saying, "That's right, the boy is jumping. Let's look at some more pictures."

6. Continue with the other pages in the book or the picture cards.

7. After the story has been completed, tell the child that you are going to go through the story once more, and this time you are going to ask him what is happening in the pictures. Encourage the child to respond by saying, "The boy is _____."

1.169 Tells story when looking at a picture book that has been read many times

Strand: 1-9   **Age:** 36-42m 3.0-3.6y

Definition

The picture book should have many word repetitions and the illustrations should have a direct relationship to the story content. It should be a story that the child has not only heard several times, but one that the child would request to hear again. Using memory and picture clues, ask the child to tell the story.

Instructional Materials

A picture storybook that tells a story about making something (a step-by-step drawing that tells a story or a pictorial representation of how to make a peanut-butter sandwich). If you select a drawing story book you will need large chart paper, and a marker.

Instructional Activities

Note: There are many excellent books available that have stories with word repetition and illustrations that children will enjoy reading again and again. The books *The Napping House* by Audrey Wood and *In A Dark, Dark House* by David A. Carter are two such books. Stories such as these can be used in the same fashion as the made up story in the activity below.

1. Ask the child to sit next to you in full view of the chart paper.

2. Explain to the child that you are going to tell a story, and to help you tell this story, you are going to draw parts of it as you go along.

3. The name of the story is *A Springtime Walk*.

4. Once upon a time a little girl was taking a walk in early spring.

5. On her walk she looked up and there was a dark cloud above her (draw a picture of a cloud).

6. Next to where she was walking the little girl heard a voice coming from the ground. She looked down and there was a little hole in the dirt (draw a hole in the dirt right under the cloud).

7. The little girl heard a worm talking to the seed that was in the little hole (draw a picture of a worm talking to the seed in the hole).

8. The worm was telling the seed it was time to wake up and grow.

9. All of a sudden the little girl heard another voice. It was a voice coming from the cloud. She knew it was the voice of the Cloud Fairy. The Cloud Fairy was telling the little seed that she was going to drop a happy tear to help it grow (draw a tear shape drop coming from cloud).

10. As soon as the tear reached the seed, the seed began to grow (draw seed growing a stem).

11. The little girl looked up and another tear came and the plant grew more and more (draw the stem growing taller and some leaves beginning to appear).

12. The little girl looked up once more and the Cloud Fairy had a big smile on her face (draw a smile in the cloud).

13. The Cloud Fairy told the little girl to look at the plant (draw a tulip on the end of the stem).

14. The little girl was so surprised to see the first flower of spring, that she bent down and touched it very softly (draw a finger touching the tulip).

15. What a wonderful day for a spring walk.

16. Tell the story again, drawing the parts at the correct time.

17. Repeat the story again, but this time ask the child to point to the drawings when they are mentioned in the story. Assist the child as needed.

18. Ask the child what the story was about, who was in the story, what happened first, second, etc., and how the story ended.

19. Encourage the child to tell the story while you either point to the drawings or do a new drawing.

20. Depending on the child's motor skills, ask the child to draw the segments as the story is told.

1.170 Moves body to music
Strand: 2-7 **Age:** 36-42m 3.0-3.6y

Definition
When presented with live or recorded music, the child will move his body to the music. The child may sway, rock, tap, clap or do any physical movement that indicates a "feel" for the music. The child need not move in correct rhythm to the music. The musical rhythm may be fast or slow.

Instructional Materials
Live or recorded music that lends itself to hand movements.

Instructional Activities
1. Prepare to play the music.
2. Talk about different ways that hands can move. Demonstrate such movements as left to right across the body, up and down, wiggling of fingers, hands open and close, etc. Talk about different ways that the body can move. Demonstrate how you can sway your body from side to side, turn around in a circle, tap your feet, etc.
3. Play the music.
4. Encourage the child to move his fingers, hands, arms, legs and body to the music. Allow any movements and reward efforts.
5. Modifications can include putting names to the various rhythmic movements, such as: sway like a tree, galloping like a pony, finger talking, waves, etc.

1.171 Claps to music
Strand: 2-7 **Age:** 36-42m 3.0-3.6y

Definition
When the child is presented with live or recorded music, she will clap in imitation, but not necessarily in time to the music.

Instructional Materials
Prepare a simple song with the words that involves clapping.
Example:
O clap, clap your hands,
And sing out with glee
For playtime is coming,
And happy are we.
(Clap, clap, clap)
O clap, clap your hands,
And jump up with a whee
For treat time is coming,
And happy are we.

(Clap, clap, clap)
or
Clap, clap, clap your hands,
Clap, clap, clap your hands,
Clap, clap, clap your hands,
Clap your hands today.

Instructional Activities
1. Sit with the child and discuss clapping in time to music with them.
2. Demonstrate clapping her name with one clap (my name with two claps).
3. Clap other names and words, encouraging her to join you.
4. Sing the clapping songs and clap at the appropriate places. Repeat the song several times.
5. Invite the child to join in the singing and clapping.
6. Modify the beat and the rhythm of the clapping song.

1.172 Taps to the beat of music
Strand: 2-7 **Age:** 36-42m 3.0-3.6y

Definition
When presented with live or recorded music that has a precise, slow, simple beat, the child will mark time to the selection using his fingers, feet or an object (stick). The tapping activity may or may not generate a sound.

Instructional Materials
Recorded music that has a precise and simple beat. Rhythm sticks or dowels.

Instructional Activities
1. Provide each child with rhythm sticks or dowels.
2. Explain to the child that he is to listen carefully because you want him to tap his sticks together just like you.
3. First, tap your sticks slow. Have the children imitate you.
4. Next, tap your sticks fast. Have the children imitate you again.
5. Now tell the children to listen carefully because sometimes you will beat your sticks fast and sometimes you will beat them slow. Explain that you will tell them whether they should beat their sticks fast or slow and that they need to listen and follow what you are doing.
6. Once the children understand, put on some slow music and have the children tap their

sticks to the beat of the music. Then switch to fast music and have them tap along.

7. Continue to modify the music by playing both fast and slow songs.

8. Allow the child an opportunity to create their own tapping rhythm.

1.173   Marches to music
Strand: 2-7 **Age:** 36-42m 3.0-3.6y

Definition
When the child is presented with a repetitive marching musical selection, she will march to the music, but not necessarily with the beat.

Instructional Materials
Choose a musical selection that has a precise marching beat. Provide marching props such as a scarf, flag or pompom. Make sure there is ample space for the children to march.

Instructional Activities
1. Let each child choose the marching prop they would like to use.
2. Demonstrate marching and using the props correctly (holding the props in their hands while swinging their arms up and down).
3. Explain that we are going to march together. Let the children know when to start marching by saying, "One, two, three march." Remind the children to swing their arms as the march. Tell them when to stop by calling out "Stop!"
4. When the children seem comfortable marching, let them take turns being the leader and telling everyone when to begin marching and when to stop.
5. Now introduce music and encourage the children to march to the beat of the music. If the music is slow, they will march slowly. If the music is fast, they will march faster.

1.174   Identifies and counts quantities of one, two, three or four
Strand: 1-10 **Age:** 36-42m 3.0-3.6y

Definition
The child has been manipulating objects and gaining insight into the pre-symbolic concepts of size, form and quantity. The child must first assimilate and integrate his nonverbal experiences, and then he will associate the numerical symbol with that experience. Finally, the child will use the language of mathematics to express the value of the quantity. When shown one to four objects, the child will associate and verbalize the correct word for the quantitative value.

Instructional Materials
A collection of familiar objects (buttons, blocks, pencils, keys, spoons, etc.) Pictures of familiar objects on cards which also have a dot or represent the quantity (a picture of a button on a card with the two dots at the top of the card, a picture of a block on a card and one dot at the top of the card, a picture of a spoon on a card and three dots at the top of the card, and a picture of a key on a card and four dots at the top of the card).

Instructional Activities
1. Hide the familiar objects that are pictured on the cards. Example: hide 2 buttons, 1 block, 3 spoons, and 4 keys.
2. Explain to the child that you have hidden some objects around the room. Show him a card and tell him he must remember what he is looking for and how many.
3. After he has found the objects, have him match them with the cards and count them out loud.
4. Continue the above procedure with the other four cards.
5. After the child has become skilled at finding, matching and naming the amount, allow him to become the one that does the hiding.

1.175   Locates big and little objects in groups of 2
Strand: 1-7B **Age:** 36-42m 3.0-3.6y

Definition
The child needs to have an understanding and perception of different sizes in order to deal with such mathematical concepts as perimeters and areas. Without the basic notion of big and little, the child may find confusion in everyday activities, e.g., will this box fit into this drawer, will these keys fit into my pocket? By using models of two sizes, the smallest being at least 3 inches on a side or in diameter and the largest being 7 inches on a side or in diameter, the child will identify items according to size. The child will respond to the terminology large - big and small - little.

Instructional Materials
/*\ **Safety Note:** Provide scissors appropriate for the child. Remind the child of safety regarding scissors.
Magazines, catalogs, scissors, glue and paper.

Instructional Activities

1. Seat the child at a table.
2. Tell the child to cut out a picture of a person or object from the magazines or catalogs, and to then find the same kind of person or object, but smaller or larger than the first, and cut it out.
3. After the child has cut out several pictures, provide her with blank sheets of paper and glue.
4. Tell the child to glue the pictures of the objects or persons that are large on one page and the pictures of the objects or persons that are small on the other page.
5. Check the child's page when she is through mounting her pictures and print the word LARGE or SMALL by each object as she tells you what to write.
6. Continue, and put the pages together as a scrapbook.
7. Review the book with the child, asking her to identify the large, big, small, and little items.

1.176 Points to the same item in two different settings

Strand: 1-4D **Age:** 36-44m 3.0-3.8y

Definition

The child is expected to identify the same object even if the item has a modified spatial position, becomes distorted due to visual form change, or a different visual background.

Instructional Materials

Prepare a set of three pictures, large enough for a group to see. The set of pictures needs to follow a story theme and have the same cast of characters. Example: a girl putting water in a dog dish while the dog is sitting up waiting. The same girl bending over and putting the bowl of water on the floor for the dog. In the final picture the dog is drinking water and the girl is on her hands and knees watching. Another example: two children riding in a car. The car arriving at a park and the children jumping out of the car. The last picture showing the two children playing with other children at the park.

Instructional Activities

1. Arrange the three picture story cards on stands, a chalkboard railing, or on the floor for all children to view.
2. Call attention to the three pictures.

3. Ask the children to find the same item in each of the pictures. After all the same items have been located, select one item and talk about what it is doing in each picture, what it is wearing, where it is positioned, etc.
4. Repeat the discussion with each item that is viewed in the three scenes.

1.177 Plays on rhythm instruments

Strand: 2-7 **Age:** 37-42m 3.1-3.6y

Definition

When presented with a basic rhythm instrument (triangle, maraca, tambourine, cymbals, sticks, clappers, sand blocks, bells, drum) and background music, the child will play the instrument. She should be exposed to the following instruments first: sticks, clappers, sand blocks, bells, and drum. It is not necessary for her playing to be rhythmic or exact. (Note: Any item that is not too difficult to manipulate and that produces a distinctive sound may be used as a rhythm instrument.)

Instructional Materials

Rhythm band instruments such as sticks, clappers, sand blocks, bells, drums, cymbals, triangles, coconut half-shells, maracas and tambourines. (Any item that is not too difficult to manipulate that produces a distinctive sound may be used as a rhythm instrument. If the choice is limited, use drums, triangles, and sand blocks to provide a musical contrast.) A musical selection familiar to the child that has a distinct beat.

Instructional Activities

1. Place the selected instruments on a table. Have the musical selection and whatever is needed to play it available.
2. Allow the child an opportunity to experiment with the instruments (e.g., have her begin with the drum).
3. Discuss ways to play the instrument, and as she plays it, ask her whether she could play it another way. Encourage her to use different musical patterns.
4. Give her directions to play loud music, soft music, slow music, fast music, to hold long tones, and to try rapid/varying beats.
5. Ask her to play "conductor" and have her call for the different musical tempos, pitches, and rhythms.
6. Introduce other rhythm band instruments in the same manner.

1.178 Marches in time to the music

Strand: 2-7 **Age:** 40-44m 3.4-3.8y

Definition

When she is presented with a marching song, the child will march in time to a repetitious beat.

Instructional Materials

A recording of a march with a definite beat. Equipment for playing the march. Marching props such as hats, pompoms, flags, or scarves. A washable marking tool (chalk or water-based markers) or masking tape.

Instructional Activities

1. Draw or tape a path on the floor for marching. Prepare to play the musical march.
2. Point out the path on the floor to the child. Tell her the path is just called a "Marching Path" because it is for marchers only.
3. Let her practice walking or marching on the path without music.
4. Tell her to listen to some marching music. Remind her that because you have named it the "Marching Path," she must stay on the path, but that she can march on it anyway she wishes.
5. Play the music and encourage her to begin marching.
6. Set the marching props on a table. Invite her to pick one of the props to use as she marches down the "Marching Path" one more time.
7. Give her an opportunity to use as many of the props as possible.
8. You can modify this activity by changing the "Marching Path" to include curves, sharp rights and lefts, stops, and so on.
9. You can also play different marches to accompany her when marching.
10. Include several children to form a marching band.

1.179 Claps to beat of familiar songs or to speech patterns

Strand: 2-7 **Age:** 40-46m 3.4-3.10y

Definition

When he is presented with a familiar song or with speech cadence or patterns, the child will clap in time to the selection. He should clap the beat during the main musical theme or in cadence with the repeating phrases.

Instructional Materials

A few jingles, which may be parodies.
Example:
There was an old lady
Who liked to make stew,
Whatever she cooked
Just tasted like glue.
There was an old lady
Who liked to eat snacks,
Peanuts and popcorn,
Crackers and smacks.
Familiar rhythmic songs the child enjoys, for example, "Twinkle, Twinkle, Little Star" or "Old MacDonald Had a Farm." A pair of mittens or gloves, and finger cymbals. (If finger cymbals are not available, place flat clip earrings on the ends of the child's fingers, clips on the outside). Plastic sandwich bags. Tape recorder or CD/MP3 player.

Instructional Activities

1. Place the mittens or gloves, finger cymbals, and the plastic sandwich bags on a table. Play the recorded music on the tape recorder or CD player.
2. Tell the child to listen carefully to the music. As the music is played, begin to clap to its beat, and encourage him to join in the clapping.
3. Repeat the selection and the clapping.
4. At the end of the selection, ask him to choose one of the items on the table and put it on his hands/fingers.
5. Play the music again, and encourage him to clap with the mittens, the finger cymbals, or the plastic sandwich bags.
6. Talk about how different the sounds are with the mittens and other props.
7. Read him the jingles in a chanting style. Tap your foot to the meter of the jingle.
8. Ask him to clap to the meter.
9. Repeat the jingle a few times, and encourage him to say it with you.
10. As you say the jingle, clap its cadence.
11. To expand this activity, invite him to create his own jingle.
12. After he has made up a jingle, read it and clap to its rhythm.

1.180 Identifies objects based on appearance (color, shape, or physical characteristic)

Strand: 1-7C   **Age:** 31-42m 2.7-3.6y

Definition

The child will identify objects that are based on: (1) Color; (2) Shape; and (3) Physical characteristics. The child will identify these objects by verbal response or by manipulation. The first objects presented to the child should be concrete (an apple, a ball, a hat, etc.) The child should then be asked to identify by visual representation (single item pictures). If the child experiences success in identifying these items, ask her to identify an object based on a verbal description of its appearance.

Instructional Materials

A group of toys which are exactly alike or almost alike in appearance (two toy cars, two small balls, two dolls, two miniature animals, two stuffed animals, two blocks, etc.) A box with the words "Toy Box" written on it.

Instructional Activities

1. Randomly place the toys on a table with the Toy Box nearby.
2. Ask the child to name each toy that is on the table.
3. Tell the child that the toys need to be put in the Toy Box and there are many pairs of two toys that are alike or nearly alike.
4. Give the child one of the toys from a group that is alike.
5. Ask her to find the toy that matches and place the two toys in the Toy Box.
6. Continue until all the toys are in the Toy Box.
7. Take one of each of the pairs out of the Toy Box.
8. Place these on the table and ask the child to reach in the Toy Box and draw out a toy.
9. After the child has drawn a toy ask her to match it with one that is on the table.
10. Request that the child draw from the Toy Box until all of the toys are matched.

1.181 Identifies objects based on category

Strand: 1-7C   **Age:** 40-48m 3.4-4.0y

Definition

The child will identify objects based on category. The child will identify these objects by manipulation or verbally. The first objects presented to the child
should be concrete. The child should then be asked to identify by visual representation (single item picture). If the child experiences success in identifying these items, ask him to identify an object based on a verbal description of its appearance.

Instructional Materials

Manila folders (one per child); the outside should be divided in half with a line to designate the two parts. Pictures of two different categories, such as foods, animals, objects of same color, plants, objects of same shape, things that move, toys, etc. should be place on the cover and inside the folder.

Instructional Activities

1. Ask the children to sit around the table.
2. Place the folders on the table, making sure that there is one folder per child.
3. Take one of the manila folders and show the children the squares on the front. Then open the folder and take out the pictures.
4. Discuss the pictures with the children. For example, identify the object in the picture, talk about it, and allow the children to share stories about the pictures.
5. Explain to the children that some of the pictures go together. As a group, have the children match the pictures by category.
6. Give each child a manila folder and ask him to take out the pictures that are on the inside. Tell him to find the pictures that go together and place them on the correct square of their manila folder. Provide assistance as necessary.
7. Have the children exchange folders and repeat the activity.
8. The children can also work in teams to complete the sorting.

1.182 Identifies objects based on function

Strand: 1-7C   **Age:** 40-48m 3.4-4.0y

Definition

The child will recognize those objects that are used for the same purpose or have the same general performance qualities. The child will match items that carry things, things that clean, things that keep us warm, things that we play with, etc. It is important that the child understands that she is classifying items by what they do. When asked, the child should begin to state the function of the item with some prompting.

Instructional Materials

/*\ **Safety Note:** Provide scissors appropriate for the child. Remind the child of safety regarding scissors.

Magazines, catalogs, calendars, pictures, etc. Scissors and at least three boxes large enough to put cut-out pictures in.

Instructional Activities

1. Place the collection of print material in three boxes and the scissors on the table.
2. Conduct a discussion about the function of everyday objects. Select at least three functions that were discussed.
3. Using one of the print materials from the table, find an item that represents each of the functions that were selected. Cut out the pictures and place one in front of each of the three boxes. Ask the children to tell what each picture is and what function it illustrates.
4. Instruct the children to select a magazine, catalog, or any other print material available and look for pictures that would match the function of the pictures in front of each box. After they have located the picture, they are to cut it out and place it in the correct box.
5. At the end of the activity, take each box and display the pictures inside. Ask the children to name the item and explain why it was placed in that particular function box.
6. Repeat the activity by changing the functions in the beginning discussion and the function pictures on the front of the boxes. Then ask the children to look for pictures to match the new functional categories.

1.183 Tells a word that associates with another word

Strand: 1-4D **Age:** 40-50m 3.4-4.2y

Definition

For children to be able to associate words, they must have the ability to process the interpretation and the relationship of word meanings. The hierarchy of word association is important. For example, automatic word association (dog-cat, hot-cold, fire-warm, bath-water) is a primary task to stating functional similarities (places to live - houses, tents, nests, trailers, apartments) which is a lower level association activity than abstract concepts (does the child know that a table is a table, but it is also furniture; a pea is in a pod, but it is also food; a ball bounces but is also a toy).

Instructional Materials

Prepare groups of three words (of the three words, two go together). Example: red, blue, dog; apple, orange, doll; car, coat, truck; table, bird, chair. It is important that in the first two to three groups of words given to the child, the final word is the one that is different. It is also important that the discrimination at the beginning of the activity be broad and easily identified. As the child becomes more comfortable with integration and response, the discrimination can be narrowed.

Instructional Activities

1. Tell the children that they are going to hear three words. Explain that two of the words name things that belong together and one thing is different. Tell them to listen and think very carefully before answering.
2. Begin by saying the words in the group. If the children are having difficulty, provide a cue of a visual representation. As the children become skilled in responding, increase the difficulty of the word groupings.

1.184 Identifies missing parts of a picture storybook that has been read several times

Strand: 1-9 **Age:** 42-48m 3.6-4.0y

Definition

The child is read a story that he is very familiar with, and part of the story is left out on purpose. The child is able to identify the part that has been omitted and is able to retell the part correctly. This can also include the modification of the story content. The child is able to tell what has been changed, and what the original story-line was.

Instructional Materials

Select a large picture book that has language patterning such as word repetition and rhyming semantics. The book should be a story the child enjoys and wants to hear again and again. The large book should also have a duplicate in a child size.

Good Listener Awards.

Instructional Activities

Note: You may need to read the book you have chosen a number of times over many days.

1. Invite the child to story time. It is important that the environment be comfortable; perhaps the child would enjoy sitting on a rug or a pillow.

2. Explain to the child that you are going to read a story from a large book. Show the child the cover of the book and discuss the picture and title.
3. Ask the child to listen while you read the story.
4. Read the story again.
5. Read the story once more, and encourage the child to recite the parts of the story he knows.
6. Give the child the duplicate, smaller book and tell him to follow along while you read the story. Encourage him to look at the pictures and turn the pages correctly.
7. Read the story one more time and omit an obvious part of the story.
8. If the child identified the missing part, give him a Good Listener Award or a chance to pick out the next story for story time.

1.185 Starts a task only when reminded, some prompting
Strand: 1-8 **Age:** 42-48m 3.6-4.0y

Definition
One of the most important elements of not beginning an activity until prompted is determining the cause. Some causes are: lack of motivation, sense of inability to achieve, preoccupation, low self-image, inappropriate role model, etc..

Instructional Materials
Various fun activities which address a topic that is motivational to the child. The activities should include tasks such as drawing or completing a puzzle. A timer.

Instructional Activities
1. Place the variety of materials and the timer on a table. Ask the child to come to the table.
2. Discuss the subject of the various materials with the child. Explain each activity/task and explain the directions for interacting with the materials.
3. Tell the child he can select one of the activities.
4. Provide him with the necessary materials, and tell him to start the task within the next minute. Explain and demonstrate the timer.
5. Set the timer for one minute.
6. Tell the child to start, and start the timer.
7. Praise the child for getting a quick start, and help him if necessary.
8. Vary by introducing less desirable tasks.

1.186 Makes hand/foot rhythmic movements
Strand: 2-7 **Age:** 42-48m 3.6-4.0y

Definition
When the child is presented with a rhythmic selection, she will move to the selection using at least two different parts of her body, e.g., hands, fingers, arms, legs, feet, head, etc. The child needs to move her body parts in rhythm to the music.

Instructional Materials
Recording of a short rhythmic song with a steady beat that is simple to follow, such as *Clap Your Hands* or *Skip to My Lou*. Appropriate equipment to play the selection. Adequate area for rhythmic movement.

Instructional Activities
A. 1. Invite the child to the movement area. Tell the child you are going to play a song, and ask her to listen carefully.
2. If you use the song, *Clap Your Hands*, do as follows:
3. Clap your hands at the designated spots, for example, "Clap, clap, clap your hands. Clap your hands together. Clap, clap, clap your hands. Clap your hands together."
4. Play the tune again.
5. Invite the child to join you in the clapping activity.
6. Change the wording of the song, for example, "Tap, tap, tap your feet. Tap your feet together." Using the word "tap," repeat the above.
7. Change the wording of the song to include a hand and foot rhythmic movement, for example, "Clap, clap, clap your hands. Clap your hands together. Tap, tap, tap your feet. Tap your feet together."
8. Continue by changing the action words of the song, for example, pat, nod, and snap.
9. Encourage the child to create her own verses.
B. 1. If you use the song, *Skip to My Lou*, follow these directions:
2. Skip at the designated spots, for example, "Skip, skip, skip to my Lou. Skip, skip, skip to my Lou. Skip, skip, skip to my Lou. Skip to my Lou my darling."
3. Play the tune again.
4. Invite the child to join in the skipping activity.
5. Change the wording of the song to include a hand and foot rhythmic movement. For example: "Clap, clap, clap to my Lou. Clap, clap, clap to my Lou. Clap, clap, clap to my Lou. Clap to my Lou my darling."

6. Interchange the movements; for example, sing, "Skip, skip, skip to my Lou. Clap, clap, clap to my Lou. Skip, skip, skip to my Lou. Clap to my Lou my darling."

7. Continue by changing the action words of the song, for instance, to hop, jump, and dance.

8. Encourage the child to create her own movement verses.

1.187   Attends to task without supervision

Strand: 1-8   **Age:** 43-48m 3.7-4.0y

Definition

The child will stay on task without any prompting or any reinforcement. The number of seconds/minutes that the child is expected to stay on task is left up to the discretion of the adult. There are numerous variables that need to be considered when placing a specific time for on-task behavior. Those variables include: child interest, child's attitude at that particular time, level of difficulty of the task, level of motivation, distractions, child's physical condition.

Instructional Materials

/*\Safety Note: Provide scissors appropriate for the child. Remind the child of safety regarding scissors.

A collection of pictures for the children to color and cut (coloring books are an excellent source). A timer. A variety of fun activities, such as puzzles, parquetry blocks, building blocks, design patterns, and listening to audio stories. Crayons and scissors.

Instructional Activities

1. Place the pictures, crayons and scissors on a work table. Tell the children that they are to select one picture that they would like to color and cut-out. Tell them you will set a timer and that they are to keep working until they hear the timer ring.

2. Before setting the timer allow the children time to select their picture.

3. Set the timer for 3 minutes (the amount of time can be adjusted based on the entry level of the children, conditions, and motivation) and ask them to start.

4. Observe and covertly guide those who do not stay on task.

5. After all the children have had a chance to work on the task, repeat and increase the time (minutes).

6. Vary by using any fun activity that allows individual work and can be sustained for a given amount of time.

1.188 Works in small group for 5-10 minutes

Strand: 1-8   **Age:** 43-48m 3.7-4.0y

Definition

A small group refers to four or five children; the project that these children work on should be designed to be completed within the 5-10 minute period. The group does not work independently, and should receive supervision. The amount of supervision will vary, depending on the group structure and the activity.

Instructional Materials

Make up or find a story about a person who enjoys working together with her friends. Reference books are available that assist in locating specific titles that reflect behaviors.

Instructional Activities

1. Invite the children to the Storytime Place. Read the story to the children and point out how unhappy the person might be if they had no one to talk to, to share things with, to play with, or to help them do things. Discuss with the children how they would feel if they didn't have friends to help them with different tasks.

2. Discuss how to work together, how to help one another in a nice way, e.g., share materials, take turns, etc.

3. Have the children decide on some rules to follow when helping each other. Assist in this rule-making session. Try to limit the rules to two or three. They should be rules that are observable and action-oriented. Example: Follow directions, Take turns, Speak quietly, Keep hands to yourself, etc. It maybe necessary to Role Play the rules, for complete understanding.

4. Place the children in groups of 3 to 4.

5. Decide on a task for each group.

6. Tell them to start, and observe the activities for 5 to 10 minutes.

7. Praise the groups that are following the rules, are working together and staying on task. Praise the groups that are trying and improving. Provide those that are having difficulty with a reminder of the rules and a structure in which to function.

1.189   Remains on task when distractions are present

Strand: 1-8   **Age:** 43-48m 3.7-4.0y

Definition

The child is to remain involved with an activity when there is varied visual and auditory stimulation in the child's immediate environment. The activity the child is doing is an independent task, with no direct supervision. The recommended time for this on-task behavior is 5 minutes, however this is only a recommendation; the interest level of the child and the degree of the stimuli affect any timing.

Instructional Materials

An activity that takes about five minutes to complete, such as a puzzle, drawing a picture, a manipulation task, picture book, etc. Tangible reward and a timer.

Instructional Activities

1. Place the activity on the child's work area.
2. Tell the child that the activity should take about five minutes, and that there will be things going on in the classroom that he might be curious about, but he should not let the distractions stop him from completing his activity.
3. Offer a tangible reward if he can complete the task without interacting or being distracted.
4. Set a timer for five minutes and tell the child to start. Begin walking around the room, making noises, pointing out the windows, talking to someone else, sharpening a pencil, writing something on the chalk-board, etc.
5. If necessary, remind the child to complete his work.
6. When the timer goes off, review how he did, and discuss what distractions occurred and which ones were the hardest to ignore.
7. To increase the challenge, provide another activity, extend the time on the timer and intensify the distractions.

1.190   Places illustration in correct sequence

Strand: 1-4D   **Age:** 44-52m 3.8-4.4y

Definition

Placing pictures in the sequence in which they occur is a cognitive process. This process helps children discover relationships which increase the learning of new information. Sequencing is also a conceptualizing skill used in many school-related tasks.

Instructional Materials

/*\Safety Note:** Provide scissors appropriate for the child. Remind the child of safety regarding scissors.

White and black construction paper, template for cutting a 4 inch diameter circle, a 3 inch diameter circle, and a 2 inch diameter circle. Set of four index cards, marking pencils, crayons and scissors.

Instructional Activities

Note:: Each child needs their own set of index cards and cut out materials for this activity.

1. Out of the white paper cut a set of two 4 inch circles, two 3 inch circles, two 2 inch circles and two snowmen type black hats. Prepare a set of four index cards that show the following: card one shows a boy rolling a snow ball on a cloudy day; card two shows the same boy stacking the snow balls to make a snowman on a cloudy day; card three shows the snowman with the hat on his head, two eyes and a nose, and the boy completing the face by adding a smiling mouth; card four shows the snowman complete, but the sun is shinning and the smiling face has turned to a sad one.
2. Ask the children to come to the table. Give each child a set of circles and a black hat.
3. Ask the child to put all the large circles in a pile, the medium circles in another pile and all the small circles in a final pile.
4. After the children have made the piles of circles, request that they lay the large circles out on the table. Then put the medium circles above each of the large one and finally the small circle above the medium circle and put the hat on top.
5. Discuss what they have created and the need for facial features.
6. Explain that one snowman needs to have a happy face because it is a cold, cold day. Talk about why a snowman would be happy if it was cold. Tell the children to use the crayons and make a happy face on one snowman.
7. Explain that the other snowman needs to have a sad face because it is a warm, sunny day. Talk about why a snowman would be sad if it was warm and sunny. Tell the children to use the crayons and make a sad face on snowman number two.
8. After all the children have completed their snowmen, give each child a set of the

Snowman Building Sequence Cards and request that they put them in the correct order by themselves. Allow the children to do this activity independent of any instructions or cueing.

9. Repeat just the above Snowman Building Sequence Card activity at a later date.

1.191 Puts manipulative shapes together to form same design as illustrated model

Strand: 1-4D **Age:** 44-54m 3.8-4.6y

Definition

The child will be presented with a picture that has been made of different basic shapes. The child will then use tangrams, construction paper shapes, wooden beads or templates to reproduce the basic shape picture on the model.

Instructional Materials

/*\Safety Note: Provide scissors appropriate for the child. Remind the child of safety regarding scissors.
Heavy colored construction paper (different colors), scissors, glue.

Instructional Activities

1. From the various colored construction paper, cut different sized circles, triangles, squares and rectangles. Select one sheet of construction paper as the background for the shape figures. Place the cut-out shapes, glue, and the background construction paper on the work table.
2. Ask the children to come to the work table.
3. Discuss the different shapes, sizes and colors that have been cut out.
4. Select a large yellow circle and place it on a background sheet. Tell the children that this is the body of a chicken, and glue it in place. Add a small yellow circle for the chick's head, a small black circle for an eye, two triangles for the beak, two more triangles for the chick's feet and a triangle for a little wing. Other figures can be made using the different shapes and colors.
5. After the children have observed you making the model picture, ask them to make their own chick.
6. Assist the children by re-doing a chick in this step-by-step manner: say, "Everyone find a big yellow circle. Place the big yellow circle in the middle of your green sheet of paper." Assist them in attaching the yellow circle. "Everyone find a small yellow circle for the

chicks head. Put the little yellow circle where you want your chickens head to be." Continue with the other shapes until the children have completed their chickens.
7. Allow the children an opportunity to develop their own figure using the various cut-out shapes.

1.192 Sorts according to shape, size, and length

Strand: 1-7B **Age:** 42-54m 3.6-4.6y

Definition

The reasoning process for early quantitative conceptualization is largely based on visual interpretation; hence, the child must be able to observe general configurations of shapes, sizes, and lengths in order to determine how things are similar and to follow nonverbal operations. Use circles, squares, and triangles (at least two of each shape) which are at least three inches on a side or in diameter. Mix the shapes and the child will sort them when requested. Continue the procedure using shapes of different sizes and strips of different lengths.

Instructional Materials

Collect 3 or 4 balls of various sizes (for example, a ping pong ball, tennis ball, *Whiffle Ball*, playground ball, etc.), 3 or 4 square boxes of various sizes (for example, a ring box, baking soda box, cereal box), and 3 or 4 cylinders of various sizes (for example, a toilet paper roll, paper towel roll, salt box, oatmeal box, etc).

Instructional Activities

1. Place the items randomly on the table.
2. Invite the children to come to the table and look at the various items. Engage them in a conversation about the shapes, sizes, and lengths of the items.
3. Ask one of the children to put all the circles or balls together. Talk about the items being smooth and round.
4. Ask another child to put all the square/rectangular boxes together. Talk about the items having sharp corners.
5. Ask another child to put all the cylinders together. Talk about the items being able to roll on its side.
6. Mix the boxes up and now have the children sort by size. Have someone gather all the smaller items and another child gather all the bigger items, regardless of shape. Talk about the different sizes.

7. Finally, mix the items again and have the children sort by length. Have someone gather all the longest items and someone else gather all the shortest items, regardless of shape and size. Talk about the different lengths.

1.193 Draws square, imitating adult

Strand: 1-11   **Age:** 42-50m 3.6-4.2y

Definition

The child will use a crayon, marker or a pencil and draw a square equal or nearly equal on each side with all corners meeting at right angles. The child will draw a square after watching an adult draw a square. The child will reproduce the shape upon verbal request.

Instructional Materials

Draw a square on an 8 ½ x 11 sheet of paper. Place a line of white glue around the edges of the square. Let the glue dry and repeat so there is a thick line.

Instructional Activities

1. Give the child the square and a crayon.
2. Tell the child to run his finger over the square outline several times.
3. Tell the child to use his crayon and draw just inside the outline using the dry glue as a guide to draw a square.
4. Repeat, slowly fading out the sheet with the glue and using a sheet with just a faint outline in pencil for the child to copy.

1.194 Participates in singing songs with group

Strand: 2-7   **Age:** 44-56m 3.8-4.8y

Definition

The child will join in singing with a group. His singing does not need to be rhythmic or completely in tune and he does not need to sing the exact lyrics.

Instructional Materials

Songs in which the name of the child can be substituted or a song adapted to include his name. If these songs are not available, write lyrics to a familiar song.
Example:
<u>Kathy Green</u> (Use the tune of *London Bridge*.)
Kathy Green is nice and sweet,
Nice and sweet, nice and sweet
Kathy Green is nice and sweet
My fair lady.

Andy Jones is happy today
Happy today, happy today
Andy Jones is happy today
My fair gentleman.
Note: Substitute his first and last names as well as the descriptive adjectives. Two or more children.

Instructional Activities

1. Invite the child and his friends to sit in a circle. Explain that you are going to sing a song that has one of his friend's names or his own name in it.
2. Sing the song:
   BINGO
   There was a farmer,
   He had a son,
   And Bobby was his name--O
   B-O-B-B-Y
   B-O-B-B-Y
   B-O-B-B-Y
   And Bobby was his name--O
   or
   Paw-Paw Patch
   Where, oh where is pretty little Penny?
   Where, oh, where is pretty little Alice?
   Where, oh, where is handsome Frankie?
   They're sitting right over there, over there.
3. Sing the song several times, until you have substituted all the children's names.
4. Invite them to join in the singing.
5. Ask the child whose name is mentioned in the song to stand up.
6. Allow them a chance to put in names and the descriptions.

1.195 Determines which of 2 groups has more and less, many and few

Strand: 1-10   **Age:** 46-56m 3.10-4.8y

Definition

The ability to view two sets (one with more objects than the other) and be able to determine which set has more or less (without counting each item) means reaching a stage of knowing that change in groups does not occur simply because the objects in a group are rearranged. Select objects that are close to the same shape, size and color. Place the objects in two groups and ask the child to point to the group that has more, less, many and few.

Instructional Materials

Develop a game board by dividing a piece of tagboard into three vertical columns. Label the first column "more" and the last column "less." Illustrate the middle column with sets of common objects. Make several two inch square cards with sets of objects drawn on them.

Instructional Activities

1. Place the game board and cards on a flat surface.
2. Tell the child to draw a card and look at the number of objects on it.
3. Tell her to place a card on the "more" side of the board if there are more objects on the card than on the middle column of the game board or on the "less" side if there are fewer objects on the card than on the middle column of the game board.
4. Continue until the all the cards have been drawn and placed on the board.

1.196 Matches like items based on appearance

Strand: 1-7A   **Age:** 48-53m   4.0-4.5y

Definition

Using more than one identical object or picture, the child will match the ones that look alike. Using more than one object or picture the child will match the ones that almost look alike.

Instructional Materials

Duplicate sets of pictures or objects. Catalogs, post cards, wallpaper sample books, buttons, child drawings, or copied pictures are only a few of the sources to locate sets of like pictures or objects. The more sets collected the more varied and challenging the activity.

Instructional Activities

1. Select a set of objects or pictures and place them in a row on a table. Place the second set of like objects or pictures in a face down position on the table.
2. Ask the child to look at the items on the table. Discuss with the child what the items are, if there are any that are the same or how they look different.
3. Show the child the items from the second set and explain that these are just like the ones that are in the row on the table.
4. Select one item from the second set and place it beneath the item in the row that it matches.
5. Explain to the child what you are doing as you model the activity.
6. Request that the child place the rest of the pictures/objects from the second set next to the ones in the row that match.

7. When the child has completed the task, change the pictures and repeat the directions.

1.197 Matches like items based on function

Strand: 1-7A   **Age:** 48-53m   4.0-4.5y

Definition

The child will match objects based on functional use. The child will identify these objects verbally or by manipulation. The initial functional categories should be within the child's interest and experiences, such as: things that keep us clean, things that keep us warm, things that move, etc.

Instructional Materials

/*\Safety Note: Provide scissors appropriate for the child. Remind the child of safety regarding scissors.

At least two sheets of large paper, glue, scissors, magazines, catalogs and pre-cut pictures.

Instructional Activities

1. Place the large sheet of paper, the glue, a magazine, and the scissors on the table.
2. Tell the child that she is going to be looking in the magazine for everything she can find that will match a given categorical function (e.g., things that keep us warm, things that we cook with, things that we put clothes into, etc.)
3. Ask the child to name and discuss the characteristics of items that might be in the functional categories.
4. Following the discussion, tell the child to look through the magazine or pre-cut pictures to find any items that match the category.
5. Each sheet of paper is for a single functional classification. Place a functional title (things we play with) on the top of each large sheet of paper.
6. When a picture is found, the child should cut it out and glue it to the matching large sheets of paper.
7. After a number of pictures are attached, ask the child to name the item and tell it's function. Label the pictures after the child has given the correct name and function.

1.198   Points to a word in a story being read

Strand: 1-9   **Age:** 48-53m 4.0-4.5y

Definition

When asked, the child will point to a word that is being read, or anticipates the word and points voluntarily.

Instructional Materials

Select a finger-play that has the following qualities: word repetition, rhyming words and action sequencing.
Example:
I touch my head,
I reach my toes,
I shake my hands,
I scratch my nose!
I raise my arms,
I cross my feet,
I nod three times,
I take a seat.
Write the finger-play on chart paper or the chalkboard. Use a pointer.

Instructional Activities

1. Ask the child to sit in front of the chart. Read the fingerplay to the child, emphasizing the meter or rhythm.
2. Read the fingerplay again, demonstrating the actions.
3. Invite the child to say the fingerplay and to do the actions.
4. Repeat, pointing to the words, as the fingerplay is read. Ask the child to do the motions.
5. Repeat, but this time point to the nouns: head, toes, hands, etc. while the child points to the body parts.
6. Ask the child to become the pointer, as the teacher points to the body parts and the child points to the nouns.
7. Continue by having the teacher point to the verbs: touch, reach, shake, etc. while the child does the action.
8. Allow the child to have a turn.
9. Conclude the activity by having the child point to every word in the fingerplay, while others do the actions, then reverse the roles.

1.199   Repeats words that rhyme

Strand: 1-9   **Age:** 48-53m 4.0-4.5y

Definition

The child is expected to repeat the phoneme sound order of words. These words or syllables have the same patterns (usually CVC-consonant/vowel/consonant) and are presented to the child orally. The child is expected to say other words that have the same linguistic arrangement. Generally the words are said in rhymes or jingles (e.g., Little Miss Muffet - Sat on her tuffet) prior to isolation (e.g., Muffet - tuffet). However, an extended skill could include beginning consonant substitution (rat, cat, fat, mat, bat, spat.)

Instructional Materials

Locate a book of rhymes. Collect a series of words that rhyme. Example: hat, fat, pat - sit, hit, mit - can, ran, fan - sing, ring, wing - etc.

Instructional Activities

Note: When beginning to name words, maintain widely different sounds, such as m and p. Gradually work into the finer discrimination such as m and n.

1. The child needs to be seated near you, but does not have to see the pages in the book of rhymes.
2. Review with the child the meaning of words that rhyme. Provide the child with examples of rhyming words.
3. Tell the child that she is going to play a game called Tap-Clap Rhyme.
4. Explain that every time she hears words that rhyme, she is to clap her hands or tap her foot.
5. Begin by reading rhymes, pausing to allow the child time to realize she is to clap or tap.
6. After several rhymes have been read, and the child is comfortable with the response, begin to say a series of words, some that rhyme (hat-cat) and other that do not (man-day).
7. Continue by presenting three words to the child, of which two are alike. Have the child say the two that rhyme.

1.200   Colors within the lines of a circle

Strand: 1-11   **Age:** 48-53m 4.0-4.5y

Definition

The child will fill in at least half of a circle with a single color, showing no more than two lines outside the circle. The child should use a crayon that is comfortable for his grip.

Instructional Materials

Develop a sheet of paper with four circles drawn at the top. The circles are to represent balloons. On the paper draw a line at the bottom that indicates the ground. Pieces of different colored yarn. Crayons and glue. An inflated balloon.

Instructional Activities

1. Read a story or a poem about balloons.
2. Show the child the balloon and talk about its shape, color, how it goes up in the air, sometimes it has a string tied to it, etc. Discuss with the child all the things that you can do with balloon.
3. Give the child the paper with the four circles and the ground line. Explain to the child that he is to color the four balloons and he should try to stay inside the lines.
4. Also, tell the child that he is to draw something that is holding the strings of the balloons. The "something" could be anything the child wants, such as a person, an animal, a tree, a bike, etc. It is important to allow the child to be creative.
5. Demonstrate how to attach the yarn between the balloon and the person or thing holding the balloon.
6. Allow the child time to complete the picture.
7. Display the pictures.

1.201 Sings and does actions with songs

Strand: 2-7 **Age:** 48-53m 4.0-4.5y

Definition

The child will sing a song and do actions that accompany the words. These actions may be creative or instructional and require either fine motor skills or gross motor skills. The child may sing along with live or recorded music.

Instructional Materials

Alternate lyrics to the tune of *Row, Row, Row Your Boat* (see example), a finger play activity to accompany the new song.
Loo-lee, Loo-lee, Loo
Roll, roll, roll your hands
As slowly as you can (roll forearms)
Hoppity, hoppity, hoppity, hoppity (hop)
Loo-lee, Loo-lee, Loo.(creative movement))
Shake, shake, shake your hands
As slowly as you can (shake hands)
Hoppity, hoppity, hoppity, hoppity (hop)
Loo-lee, Loo-lee, Loo. (creative movement)

Tap, tap, tap your foot
As slowly as you can (tap foot)
Hoppity, hoppity, hoppity, hoppity (hop)
Loo-lee, Loo-lee, Loo. (creative movement)
Continue with other actions and verses.
Record the song *Loo-lee, Loo-lee, Loo* on tape/cell phone or be prepared to play it on a piano or guitar.

Instructional Activities

1. Invite the child to the music area. Explain that she is going to hear a fun new song called *Loo-lee, Loo-lee, Loo* ("Lou-lee" has a long e sound).
2. Ask her to say the title of the song after you. Repeat it several times.
3. Play the recording of the new song and sing along with the song.
4. Play the song again. This time sing along and do the actions too.
5. Play the song again. Encourage the child to sing along and do the actions.
6. Play the song again. Allow her to sing along and do the actions independently.
7. Tell her you are going to play the song again, ask her to sing along, do the actions, and when at the last line--"Loo-lee, Loo-lee, Loo," she may do any movement she wishes.
8. Repeat the song and continue playing as often as she sustains interest.
9. Provide a chance for her to make up new lyrics and actions to the song.

1.202 Locates which out of 5 objects or pictures does not belong in same class/category

Strand: 1-7A **Age:** 48-54m 4.0-4.6y

Definition

The child is presented with five objects; four of the objects will belong to the same category and one will not. The child will identify the different object (object that does not belong) verbally or by manipulation.

Instructional Materials

One set of five pictures; four of the pictures should belong to one obvious class/category while the fifth item belongs to a different category, e.g., adult bedroom slipper, cowboy boot, high heeled shoe, apple, and baby shoe. Of the four items that go together, one should belong to a different sub-category (in this case the baby shoe). Different sets of pictures can be used based on the varied levels of difficulty.

Instructional Activities

1. Remove two pictures from the group (e.g., lady's shoe and apple). Place the rest of the pictures face down on the table.
2. Show the child one of the pictures you removed (lady's shoe). Ask the child to tell you what it is and if he can name other things that belong to the same group. If the child is unable to respond, name some of the characteristics of the group as clues. Show the child the other picture (apple) and ask him what it is and if he can name other things that belong to its group. Provide clues as needed.
3. Place these two pictures and the rest of the pictures on the table in full view of the child.
4. Ask the child to look carefully and select the one that does not belong (apple).
5. Ask the child to look at the pictures (slipper, cowboy boot, high heeled shoe, and baby shoe).
6. Request that the child select the picture that is different (baby shoe).
7. Involve the child in a discussion about the pictures and why he selected the pictures that he did.
8. Continue the activity using different sets of cards.

1.203 Places 3 pictures in sequence

Strand: 1-7A **Age:** 44-56m 3.8-4.8y

Definition

The child is shown three pictures (in random order) depicting a sequence of events. The pictures/sequence should be of something that is familiar to the child. The child will put the pictures in the correct order and be given an opportunity to tell about each picture.

Instructional Materials

One orange per child (or banana or other fruit that a child can peel). Paper towels. Napkins. Three large pieces of chart paper and markers. Drawing paper and crayons.

Instructional Activities

1. Start to peel each orange.
2. Give each child an orange, paper towel and a napkin. Discuss with the children the virtues of oranges, how and where they are grown, and the ways that they are eaten.
3. Tell the children that one of the best ways to eat oranges is to peel off the skin, divide it into sections, and then eat the orange.
4. Tell the children they are to place the paper towel on the surface in front of them and peel the orange.
5. While the children are peeling their oranges, draw the activity of peeling an orange on a single piece of chart paper.
6. After all the children have their oranges peeled, show them the chart picture and discuss some of the things they were thinking about while they were peeling their orange, what happened to their fingers, and what the peelings looked like.
7. Ask the children what needs to happen next in order for them to eat their oranges.
8. Once a child explains that the oranges need to be divided, tell the group to divide their oranges into sections.
9. While they are dividing the oranges, illustrate this activity on chart paper.
10. After all the children have divided their orange into sections, show them the illustration on the chart paper.
11. Then have the children predict what will happen next.
12. Have the children eat their oranges. Illustrate this step on chart paper as everyone is eating their orange. After everyone has finished eating, place the three pieces of chart paper so the children can see them.
13. Mix up the three pieces and ask a child to put them in the right order. Ask another child to tell the story of eating an orange.
14. As a group, name your story.
15. Have the children divide a sheet of paper into three sections and illustrate the sequence of events in eating a banana or putting cheese on a cracker.
16. Provide the children with time to tell the story of their new three-part activity.

1.204 Matches like items based on category

Strand: 1-7A **Age:** 48-56m 4.0-4.8y

Definition

The child will match at least six objects or pictures according to a class/category. The initial classification categories should be within the child's interest and experiences, such as: things she plays with, things to eat, things to wear, etc.

Instructional Materials

Make at least two card sets, with five cards per set representative of a category (e.g., food, clothing or animals) and the other five cards represent a different category. Pictures can be located and attached to cards (index cards are a good size). Pictures can also be drawn on the cards to make up the set.

Instructional Activities

1. Shuffle the cards and place them face down on a table in two rows of five.
2. Discuss the two categories that are represented by the pictures on the cards.
3. Explain to the child that each of the cards that are face down match one of the categories that has just been discussed.
4. Then ask the child to turn over two cards and decide if they are pictures of the same category. If they are, the child gets to keep the set. If the child identifies that the pictures belong to a different category, the cards are returned face down.
5. The child continues turning over cards until all have been matched.
6. Change the category cards and repeat the activity.

1.205   Repeats sequence of words with meaning association

Strand: 1-4D   **Age:** 48-58m   4.0-4.10y

Definition

The child associates words in a meaningful way and interprets how the spoken word reflects relationships. The child needs to be able to use a series of words to express a sequence of activities, categorical events, expression of feelings, recreational purposes and creativity.

Instructional Materials

Pictures or symbols that represent a hot day, cold day, rainy day, sunny day, snowy day.

Instructional Activities

1. Ask the children to sit in a semi-circle grouping. Have the visuals ready for viewing. Conduct a discussion on playing outside. Include in the discussion that rainy cold days are not as much fun as warm, sunny days for outside activities. Identify inside and outside activities.
2. Tell the children that during the talk about outside play, you used some weather words. Explain and use examples of weather words.
3. Show to the children the visual that represents hot, and emphasize the word hot.
4. Show to the children the visual that represents cold, and emphasize the word cold.

5. Continue with the words wet, dry, sunny, and rainy.
6. Ask the children to say the word that represents the picture you are going to show to them.
7. Show the children the picture of hot, and pause for the children to respond with hot.
8. Show the children the picture of cold, and pause for the children to respond with cold.
9. Continue with the words wet, dry, sunny and rainy.
10. Challenge the children to say the sequence of words without the pictures. Assist the group in getting started. Hot - Cold, Wet - Dry, Sunny – Rainy.
11. Use the pictures for a cue as needed. Encourage the children to say the words in a chanting fashion and to clap their hands in rhythm to the syllables.
12. This activity can be easily modified, by using a different word category.

1.206   Points to pictures that represent sequence of events in a story

Strand: 1-9   **Age:** 48-60m   4.0-5.0y

Definition

When presented with not more than five pictures, the child is able to place them in a sequence that reflects the order of events in a story. When asked the child will point to the first thing that happened and when asked will point to the last thing that occurred.

Instructional Materials

A story that has definite sequential events. The story may be created from prepared large index card pictures (a girl greeting friends at the door, her friends playing party games, the girl and her friends eating birthday cake and ice cream, the girl opening presents). The story may be from a book, and the four large index card pictures should be based on that story. A clothesline and clip clothespins.

Instructional Activities

1. Attach the clothesline to two hooks so the pictures can be hung on it. Make sure that the line is within reach of the child.
2. Call the child to join you at the Storytelling Area.
3. Tell the child that you are going to read/tell her a story. State the name of the story and make sure the child is aware that she will be asked what happened first, second, third, etc.

in the story. Give examples of sequenced events.

4. Read/tell her the story.
5. Place the sequence pictures in random order in front of the child. Also place the clip clothespins within her reach.
6. Ask the child to think about the story that she just heard, and to look at the pictures.
7. Instruct her to select the picture that shows what happened first in the story. After she has made her selection, ask her to hang the picture on the clothesline.
8. Ask her to locate the picture that represents what happened next in the story and to hang it on the clothesline next to picture number one.
9. Continue with the last two pictures.
10. When all the pictures have been placed in the correct sequential order, request that the child retell the story using the pictures. Assist her in the retelling as needed.

1.207   Draws a square, copying model
Strand: 1-11   **Age:** 48-60m   4.0-5.0y

Definition
The child will be presented with a drawing of a square (3 inches) and upon request he will copy the picture of the square, showing four clearly defined sides that are nearly equal in length with the lines meeting or close to meeting at the corners to form the beginning resemblance of a right angle.

Instructional Materials
Prepare a piece of 8 ½ x 11 cardboard/poster-board by drawing a square on it. The shape should be 6 inches square. Using a punch, make holes on the lines of the square about 1 inch apart. Chalk, markers, paper and pencils.

Instructional Activities
1. Place the "holed" square paper on a chalkboard and take a chalkboard eraser and dust through the holes. Remove the paper. The eraser dust should create outline dots of the shape.
2. Have the child form the pattern by connecting the dots.

1.208   Identifies own name when printed
Strand: 1-9   **Age:** 48-60m   4.0-5.0y

Definition
The child will point to her first name when it is printed on a sheet of paper with no other printing. The child will point to her first name when it is printed next to another name. The child will point to her first name when it is printed in a row of four other names which do not start with the same first letter as the child's name. The child will point to her first name when it is in a list of four other names, of which at least one starts with the same letter as the child's. If the child is successful in the identification of her first name, the above should be repeated with her last name.

Instructional Materials
Prepare a list of first names and print them on a chalkboard or chart paper. Make sure that the child's name is included on the list several times. Flashlight.

Instructional Activities
1. Cover up the names on the board or paper and invite the child to join you.
2. Mention to the child that she is going to play a game called <u>Flash My Name</u>.
3. Explain that on the board/paper are a list of girl's and boy's names and that you are going to turn the lights down low, and use a flashlight to flash on each name. Say, "When you see your name in 'lights,' raise your hand."
4. Begin at the top and flash the light on one name at a time. Provide verbal reinforcement when the child is correct.
5. This game can be repeated by using first and last names.
6. If the child seems to have difficulty with the way the light illuminates the names, keep the lights on and have her point to her name from a list of names on the board.

1.209   Identifies number symbols of 1 - 5
Strand: 1-10   **Age:** 48-60m   4.0-5.0y

Definition
Shown numerical symbols 1 - 5, the child will verbally give the name of the number.

Instructional Materials
Make a set of cards 2 ½ x 4 inches. The set needs to have eleven cards. On two cards write the number 1. On two cards write the number 2. On

two cards write the number 3. On two cards write the number 4. On two cards write the number 5. On one card draw a Ladybug.

Instructional Activities

1. Shuffle the eleven cards and place the deck face down on the table. Invite the child to the table to play a card game called Number Ladybug.
2. Show the child the deck of cards and explain that he is to draw one card from the deck.
3. Tell him that after he draws a card he is to say the number that is on it, and that if he is right he can keep the card.
4. If he says the wrong number he must place the card face up next to the deck. Then it will be your turn to draw.
5. Show him the Ladybug card and explain that if he draws that card he loses a turn.
6. The player with the most cards wins the game.
7. Number Ladybug can be expanded to use numbers 6 - 10.

1.210 Draws a triangle, copying model
Strand: 1-11 **Age:** 57-69m 4.9-5.9y

Definition

The child will be presented with a drawing of a triangle (3 inches base) and upon request he will copy the triangle with three clearly defined sides with the lines nearly equal in length, meeting at the corners at approximate angles (45 degrees - 90 degrees).

Instructional Materials

Have available a chalkboard, chalk or poster board and markers. Provide paper, crayons and pencils.

Instructional Activities

1. Ask the child to sit in front of the chalkboard.
2. Ask the child if she can think of anything that looks like a triangle.
3. Tell the child that she is going to learn how to draw a triangle.
4. Demonstrate by drawing a triangle on chalkboard.
5. Ask her to draw a triangle in the air with one hand.
6. Request that she practice drawing the triangle in the air several times.
7. Tell her to draw a triangle on the board. Provide help if necessary.
8. Give the child a sheet of paper and crayons or a pencil.
9. Tell her to practice making triangles on paper.

1.211 Counts orally to 10, with one-on-one correspondence
Strand: 1-10 **Age:** 48-60m 4.0-5.0y

Definition

Many children learn to count verbally, but without attaining the concept that each number corresponds to one object. In order to establish the counting principle, the child should first be involved in a motor and tactile response (placing pegs in a peg board, clipping clothespins on a line, or stringing beads). The child should count aloud to ten, while pointing at one object at a time (point to a block and say "One").

Instructional Materials

/*\ **Safety Note:** Provide scissors appropriate for the child. Remind the child of safety regarding scissors.

Create three paper chains of ten paper loops per chain (constructions paper strips work well). When constructing paper chain one, make each loop a different color; when constructing paper chain two, each loop should be the same color; when constructing paper chain three, the loops can be either all one color or different colors. Provide the child with a pair of scissors and glue.

Instructional Activities

1. Place the paper strips, scissors and glue on a work table. Invite the child to work area.
2. Demonstrate how to make a paper chain (creating paper chain one first) and assist the child as he constructs the item.
3. Place the constructed paper chain one in a straight line on the table.
4. Instruct the child to point to and count each loop.
5. If the child has any difficulties, ask him to count the loops along with you.
6. Point out to the child that each loop is a different color and represents a separate number and that each loop is counted only once.
7. Assist the child in making paper chain two.
8. Lay paper chain two in a straight line on a table.
9. Repeat the above counting process.
10. Assist the child in making paper chain three.
11. Hang paper chain three in such a manner that the child can reach each loop.
12. Request that the child point to and count each loop on the chain.
13. Modify this activity by making a paper chain of more than 10 loops.

1.212 Names penny, nickel, dime and quarter

Strand: 1-10 **Age:** 48-60m 4.0-5.0y

Definition

When presented with one coin at a time, the child will name the coin. The first presentation to the child should be based on value amount and in the following sequence: a penny, a nickel, a dime and a quarter. The second presentation should be based on appearance (size, color, engraving) and in the sequence of dime, penny, nickel and a quarter. The third presentation should be random. Note: It is important to use the same side (head or tail) of the coin when doing the presentations. It is also important to use real coins when introducing money concepts.

Instructional Materials

A penny, nickel, dime and a quarter. Locate rubber stamps of the coins (penny, nickel, dime and a quarter). Four 5 x 8-inch cards for the child.

Instructional Activities

1. Place the coins (same side up as the rubber stamp visual) on the table. Place the coins and rubber stamps on the table and provide the child with one of the index cards.
2. Point to one of the coins and ask the child to name it.
3. Tell the child to find the rubber stamp for that coin.
4. Instruct the child to stamp as many nickels on a 5 x 8 inch card, without overlapping, saying the name of the coin as she is stamping.
5. Point to another coin and ask the child to name it.
6. Tell the child to find the rubber stamp for that coin.
7. Instruct the child to stamp as many dimes on a 5 x 8-inch card, without overlapping, saying the name of the coin as she is stamping.
8. Continue with the other coins.
9. Count the number of coins on each card and mount highest group on bulletin board as World Champion.
10. Encourage the children to attempt to challenge the World Champion.

1.213 Traces own name

Strand: 1-11 **Age:** 48-60m 4.0-5.0y

Definition

The child will trace her first name with her finger when it is printed in manuscript form on a lined sheet of paper. She will use a highlight marker/primary pencil and trace her first name. The child will trace (write-over) her first name which has been written on lined paper.

Instructional Materials

A 1 inch sponge and a dish of water. A chalkboard and chalk.

Instructional Activities

Note: It is not important that the child know all the letters of her name.
1. Write the child's first name on the chalkboard. The name needs to be written at a height that is comfortable for the child. Write the child's name at least four times on the chalkboard.
2. Explain to the child that the word on the board is her name.
3. Tell her that you want her to learn to write her name and that to help her learn how, you want her to trace the letters.
4. Wet the sponge and squeeze the water out into the dish.
5. Move the sponge over each letter.
6. Point out to the child that the water stays on the board and that it shows what letter was there.
7. Allow the child to take the sponge and trace over all the letters of her name.
8. Make sure that the water is frequently squeezed out of the sponge.
9. After the child has had several opportunities to "water trace" her name, allow her to write her name with the chalk.

1.214 Constructs set of objects

Strand: 1-10 **Age:** 48-60m 4.0-5.0y

Definition

Using objects at least 3 inches on a side or in diameter, the child will make a set by separating a requested number of items from a group. Example: the child is presented with ten blocks and is asked to separate three blocks from the group of ten. Construction of sets should begin at the concrete level, by establishing set boundaries (string circles, sheets of paper, lids of boxes) and determining if the members of the set belong together (blocks, buttons, chips, shape templates). The child will need to use her knowledge of classification by attributes and one-to-one correspondence in order to develop sets. The child's first experience at constructing a set should deal with objects that are alike and should allow the child to discover the meaning of equal items per set.

Instructional Materials

Obtain six 3 x 5 inch cards and place dots or stickers on each card. For example: on Card One place one dot/sticker, on Card Two place two dots/stickers, on Card Three place three dots/stickers, on Card Four place four dots/stickers, on Card Five place five dots/stickers, and on Card Six place six dots/stickers. On two 3 x 5 inch cards draw a happy face or place a special sticker. Six chips.

Instructional Activities

Note: When the child draws a card that she has had a problem with, provide additional instructions and assistance.

1. Place the cards face down on a table with the six chips.
2. Tell the child to draw a card.
3. Tell her to look at the card and the set that is illustrated.
4. Explain to her that she is to use the chips and make a set just like the one pictured on the card.
5. Tell her she can keep the card if she makes the chip set match the set shown on the card.
6. Request that the child place the card at the bottom of the deck if she is incorrect.
7. Give the child a special reward or a point if she picked one of the happy face cards.
8. Continue until all cards are drawn.
9. If the child received points for the happy face cards, reward her at the end of the game.

1.215 Locates first, middle, and last in group of objects

Strand: 1-10   **Age:** 48-60m 4.0-5.0y

Definition

The child will point to or place an object in the first position when asked. The child will point to or place an object in the middle position when asked. The child will point to or place an object in the last position when asked. The first group of objects should be completely different (e.g., a toy car, a ball, a block), the second group of objects should be different by only one attribute (e.g., color--a blue block, a red block, a yellow block) and in the third group each object should be alike.

Instructional Materials

Collect at least four pictures of different animals. The pictures of the animals need to clearly have a head area, a middle body area, and a rear area. Cut the animal bodies into three sections, the

head is piece one, the body is piece two, and the rear area is piece three.

Instructional Activities

1. Mix the animal pieces.
2. Place two head pieces, two middle pieces, and two end pieces on the table.
3. Select a head, a middle and an end, then place the pieces together to form an animal.
4. The parts do not have to be from the same animal; in fact part of the fun of the game is to have a new mixed animal.
5. After you have placed the animal together, ask the child to point to the first part of the animal, then the middle part, and then the last part.
6. Ask the child to use the three pieces that are on the table to make an animal.
7. Say, "The first part will be the animal's _____."
8. Say, "The middle part will be the animal's _____."
9. Say, "The last part will be the animal's _____."
10. Allow time for the child to put the puzzle together.
11. Ask the child to point to the middle part of the animal.
12. Ask the child to point to the first part of the animal.
13. Ask the child to point to the last part of the animal.
14. Mix up the pieces on the table and add the other six animal pieces.
15. Tell the child to make four animals.
16. Allow time for the child to put the pieces together.
17. It is not important if the child makes true animals or if the parts are from different creatures.
18. Say, "Change two middle parts of your animals."
19. Allow time for the change.
20. Record if the child selected the correct parts.
21. Say, "Change two end parts of your animals."
22. Allow time for the change.
23. Record if the child selected the correct parts.
24. Say, "Change two first parts of your animals."
25. Allow time for the change.
26. Record if the child selected the correct parts.
27. Compare the child's responses; note if: (1) The child responded to your animal puzzle and your pointing; (2) The child identified the parts prior to placement; (3) The child

generalized placements and completed another task.

1.216   Matches coins

Strand: 1-10   **Age:** 49-58m 4.1-4.10y

Definition

Initial instruction using money needs to be a very concrete experience and it is best to allow the child to manipulate real coins. A fundamental aspect of understanding money is to become familiar with the appearance (engraving), the size, the shape and the metal color of the coins. The child will match like coins, stack like coins, arrange coins by size, identify coins by sides (heads or tails) and begin to understand the value of a penny, nickel, dime and quarter.

Instructional Materials

Five pennies, five nickels, five dimes and five quarters. Pictures of a penny, nickel, dime and quarter (stamps work well).

Instructional Activities

1. Place the coins in a pile on a table. Invite the child to sit at the table.
2. Tell him to put all the same coins in separate rows, so the pennies are all lined up, the nickels are together, etc.
3. Give the child a picture of real coins.
4. Have him place the pictures next to the correct rows.
5. To increase the difficulty, make up cards representing the coin values, such as 5 cents, 10 cents etc., and have the child match these cards with the correct rows.

1.217   Starts task with no reminding or prompting

Strand: 1-8   **Age:** 49-60m 4.1-5.0y

Definition

The child will be assigned a task to start at a specific time, and when the appointed time arrives, the child will begin without any prompting. The assignment will be given verbally.

Instructional Materials

Divide one sheet of paper into two sections, titling section one the "List To Do", and section two "When To Do."

Instructional Activities

1. Seat the child next to you to discuss the "List To Do" and "When To Do" paper.

2. Make a simple "To Do" list with the child using simple pictures to illustrate the tasks. The list should consist of one task of two to five minute duration.
3. Make sure the child understands how to complete the task independently.
4. Set a general time period for completing the task, such as this morning after snack. Use a picture to indicate the time on the "When To Do" paper. Also, agree upon some form of reward for completing the task.
5. Observe the child's approach to recalling and completing the task.
6. If she has difficulty, discuss with her what had been agreed upon and how she might remember what to do.

1.218   Attends to task without supervision for 10 minutes

Strand: 1-8   **Age:** 49-60m 4.1-5.0y

Definition

The child will stay on task without any prompting or any reinforcement for ten minutes. The task should be something he is motivated to do and there should be a limited amount of distractions.

Instructional Materials

Activities that the child will enjoy and is capable of doing independently. A timer. A reward that the children will work for (free time, tokens, points, party, etc.)

Instructional Activities

1. Place the collection of various activities (puzzles, paints, crayons, books, games, etc.) and any supplies necessary to complete the activities on a table.
2. Invite the child to visit the table and select an activity he would like to do for ten minutes.
3. Assist the child in his selection, making sure it is within his capabilities, and that it is one that he will enjoy and feel good about completing.
4. Tell the child he will receive free time, earn points for a toy, receive a token to go to the snack party, etc. if he can work independently on his task for ten minutes.
5. Have the child start the task, and set the timer for ten minutes.
6. Reward the child for on-task behavior.
7. Discuss with the child how his attention span might change if the task was not quite as enjoyable.

1.219 Remains on task for 5 to 10 minutes when distractions are present

Strand: 1-8 **Age:** 49-60m 4.1-5.0y

Definition

The child is to remain on task with an assignment, while there are distractions in the child's immediate setting. The activity the child is doing is an independent task, one that is within the child's ability range and that she is motivated to accomplish. The assignment is done with no individual supervision. As children get older their attention span increases.

Instructional Materials

An activity that takes about five to ten minutes to complete, such as a puzzle, game, art activity, book, worksheet, etc. Tangible reward and a timer.

Instructional Activities

1. Place the activity in the child's work area.
2. Approach the child by explaining to her that it is time to play a game. Tell the child that the game is going to be really hard for her to win. Explain the rules - Rule 1: You have to work on your activity no matter what. Rule 2: I cannot answer any questions. Rule 3: I am going to do things to try to get you to pay attention to me. I might make noise or wave my arms. Rule 4: You need to keep working until you hear me say, "Stop."
3. Explain to the child that she will be the winner if she does not pay any attention to your distractions.
4. Say, "The winner gets to choose a game to play or a favorite story for Storytime."
5. Set a timer for ten minutes and tell the child to "Start." Begin creating a distracting environment. Talk on the telephone, open a window, sharpen a pencil, turn on a musical tape/CD, write on the chalkboard, etc.
6. If necessary, remind the child to ignore you.
7. When the timer goes off, tell the child it is time to "Stop."
8. Determine if she stayed on task and is the winner. Discuss with her the distractions that occurred and which ones were the hardest to ignore.

1.220 Draws line between 2 parallel lines

Strand: 1-11 **Age:** 49-60m 4.1-5.0y

Definition

The child will be presented with a sheet of paper that has parallel lines drawn on it. The lines need to be at least four inches in length and about 1-2 inches apart. The child will draw a line between the two parallel lines when asked.

Instructional Materials

Draw a maze with a dog at one end and his bone at the other end.

Instructional Activities

1. Give the child a pencil and the maze worksheet
2. Demonstrate with your index finger the path the dog has to take to reach his bone.
3. Tell the child it is his turn to guide the dog to his bone.
4. Have the child draw a line from the dog to the bone. Assist when necessary and remind the child to keep the dog's path "between" the walls (lines).
5. Reward the child if he guides the dog to the bone without making any wrong turns.
6. Increase the difficulty by changing the path and not demonstrating the correct trail to the bone.

1.221 Shifts body rhythm when music tempo changes

Strand: 2-7 **Age:** 49-60m 4.1-5.0y

Definition

When presented with a musical selection that includes various tempos, the child will move her body in rhythm to the music. The tempo change should represent either slow or fast beats. The musical selection may be live or recorded.

Instructional Materials

Musical selections that have light and heavy tempos. Props that are "light" such as balloons or scarves, props that are "heavy" such as small bean bags. Equipment to play music.

Instructional Activities

1. Place the props on a table near the child.
2. Ask the child to watch how the balloon moves when you toss it in the air.
3. Ask her to reach up in a stretching position to grasp the balloon as it descends.

4. Say, "Watch the balloon and move like it."
5. Give her a balloon and mention the way she moves, twirls and lifts.
6. Praise her movements, using words that convey the feeling of airiness and lightness, saying, for example, "Your arms moved in such a light way, just like the balloon in flight."
7. Ask her to watch as you twirl a scarf around your head in figure- eights.
8. Give her the scarf and ask her to swing the scarf, twirl with it, and make it flutter.
9. Praise her movements, using words that describe the open gigantic sweeping arm motions.
10. Demonstrate with the heavy bean bag by asking her to move it from one hand to the other.
11. Emphasize the movements by chanting in sad, low tones, saying, for example, "Daaaa-Da-Daaaa," "Booo-Bo-Booo," or "Maaaa-Ma-Maaaa."
12. Play the music selection that has a tempo like a floating balloon. Invite the child to move to the music as if she is a floating balloon.
13. Play the music selection that has a tempo like a twirling scarf. Invite her to move to it as if she were a twirling scarf.
14. Play the music selection that has a tempo of a heavy bag. Invite her to move to it as if she were a heavy bag.
15. To modify this activity, provide her with other props as she moves to different tempos.

1.222   Selects long, longer, longest from group of objects

Strand: 1-7B **Age:** 50-56m 4.2-4.8y

Definition

A child will develop the concepts of length and the idea of constant units of measurement by interacting with concrete objects. Understanding that the length of an object does not change if the item has been moved is established after active experiences with lengths and the rearrangement of items. The child will point to the longest of two or more objects, when requested. The child will point to the longest of the same two or more objects, after the objects have been moved.

Instructional Materials

Obtain 7 wood dowels one fourth inch by 30 inches.
Cut one dowel into 4 pieces that are 3 inches, 6 inches, 9 inches, and 12 inches in length.

Make an 18 x 36 inch placement mat from colored poster board and tape another 18 inch piece of dowel on the bottom of mat so the child may line up the bottom of the dowels for better organization.

Instructional Activities

1. Place the dowels and the placement mat at the child's work area.
2. Choose two pieces of doweling and ask which is longer.
3. Continue by comparing two pieces of the doweling until the child demonstrates mastery.
4. Choose three pieces of doweling and ask which is longer and longest.
5. Continue comparing three until child demonstrates mastery.
6. Ask the child to demonstrate the task of sequencing by length from the shortest to the longest (have the child try the following: put sequencing items by size is a higher-level skill).
7. Place the shortest dowel toward the left of the mat with the bottom end touching the added edge.
8. Place the next longest dowel in the same location on the mat but directly next the first dowel that was placed.
9. Continue until all the dowels have been placed on the mat.
10. Discuss the dowels' location, noting the longest one, and call attention to the fact that they look like steps, etc.
11. Remove the dowels from the mat.
12. Give the child the dowels and ask him to do the task alone. Let him experiment with it.
13. Question the child about his choice of placement, demonstrating and explaining the correct placement if necessary.
14. Ask the child to repeat the dowel placement once again.
15. If the child is unsuccessful after a second attempt, remove several dowels.
16. If the child is successful in the dowel placement, add more dowels.

1.223   Plays simple rhythmic patterns

Strand: 2-7 **Age:** 52-60m 4.4-5.0y

Definition

The child will play a simple rhythmic pattern--one steady beat with the music. A percussion instrument such as rhythm sticks, wood blocks, drums, rattles, or bells can provide the most effective way to create a steady beat.

Instructional Materials

An assortment of percussion instruments-- drum, rhythm sticks, blocks, bells. Several poems that lend themselves to chanting or nursery rhymes, such as *Hickory, Dickory Dock*. You may also use the following chant:

I Am

I am (one beat) skipping (one beat), skipping (one beat), skipping (one beat-- steady beats)
I am (one beat), skipping (one beat) down (one beat) the street (steady beats).
I am running, running, running
I am running down the street. (See above beat patterns)
I am walking, walking, walking
I am walking down the street. (See above beat patterns)
I am skipping, running, walking
I am skipping, running, walking down the street.(See above beat patterns)
A prerecorded march such as *Caissons Go Rolling Along*. Equipment to play recording.

Instructional Activities

1. Place the following instruments on the table: drum, rhythm sticks, wooden blocks and rattles. If the child has not had experience with rhythm instruments, allow him time to explore them. Let him choose one of the instruments.
2. Tell him to listen carefully as you say some names. Say his first and his last name. Clap the syllables of his name, for example: Steven (two claps) Parks (one clap). Ask him to use his sticks or drum to beat out the rhythm of his names, for example: Steven (two beats) Parks (one beat).
3. Continue with other names until he is comfortable in the manipulation of the instruments.
4. Tell him you are going to say a rhythm poem or chant, and ask him to use his sticks or drum to keep the word beat.
5. Repeat the process several times.
6. When he has become successful in the word-beat task, play the marching selection and encourage him to keep time.
7. Allow him to keep the beat and march around the room or display other creative expressions.

1.224 Draws diamond, copying model

Strand: 1-11 **Age:** 69-81m 5.9-6.9y

Definition

The child will be presented with a drawing of a diamond at least 2 inches in diameter and upon request he will copy the shape to display fairly close right angles and four straight lines of nearly equal length.

Instructional Materials

Chalkboard and chalk.

Instructional Activities

1. Ask the child to sit in front of the chalkboard.
2. Tell her that she is going to learn how to draw a diamond.
3. Demonstrate by drawing a diamond on the chalkboard. Discuss with the child the configuration of the diamond (the four sides are the same length, the points meet, etc.) and point to the each area you are discussing.
4. Ask the child to draw a diamond in the air with one hand.
5. Request that the child come to the board and draw a diamond.
6. If the child has difficulty, you can make four dots on the board to indicate the four tips of the diamond. Ask the child to connect the dots to make a diamond.
7. Instruct the child to go to the table. Distribute crayons or pencils and paper.
8. Ask her to draw a diamond on the paper.

1.225 Tells or draws a picture to provide a solution for a given problem

Strand: 1-4D **Age:** 52-66m 4.4-5.6y

Definition

When presented with a problem, the child will be able give a solution based on anticipated needs to a situation (You are invited to a birthday party, what will you need to do to get ready?), the anticipated next happening in a situation (You have accidentally spilled some milk on the carpet, what will you do now?), the anticipated outcome to a problem based on known information (The picnic basket is ready, the car will be here in a minute, when should I get ready?), and the anticipated cause and effect of a situation (What would you do if you lost your favorite toy?)

Instructional Materials

Select or prepare a short story and problem solving questions about the story. An example of a short story is: "Today it is raining. There are many fun puddles of water. They are the kind of puddles that are just right for splashing. Mother has said we can go out and play if we dress right. Oh what fun we will have playing in the rain."

Instructional Activities

1. Invite the children to join you at the story telling area. Prior to reading the story, explain to the child that he is going to hear a story and he is to listen carefully. Explain to the child that at the end of the story you will ask him some questions.
2. Read the story.
3. Ask the following type of questions: (1) What kind of clothes should we wear to play in the rain? (2) After you splash in the puddles, what other things can we you do in the rain? (3) If you wanted to throw rocks in the puddles, but the rocks are a long way from the puddles. What can you do? (4) What will happen when the sun comes out? (5) What should you do if you become all wet from playing in the puddles? (6) What should you do if a friend falls into the puddle? Encourage the child to respond verbally as well as illustrate his responses. The illustrations could be made into a class book to read and enjoyed many times. The questions asked need to be designed based on the hierarchy identified in the definition above.

1.226 Names item(s) that would assist with a problem-solving situation
Strand: 1-4D **Age:** 52-66m 4.4-5.6y

Definition

After viewing a concrete problem, the child will locate the object that is needed to solve the problem. Example: the child needs one more circle to finish the picture, one more block to finish the house, or a chair to get to the cookie jar. From the concrete problem the child will look at a picture of a problem and select another picture or name an object(s) that would solve the problem. Finally, after hearing about a problem, the child is able to name an item(s) that would assist in the solution.

Instructional Materials

Prepare a group of "I See" or "I Hear" situations. Example: "I see a Teddy Bear without an eye. What can we do?" "I see a

spilled glass of milk. What can we do?", "I hear a baby crying. What can we do?", "I hear a dog barking outside the door." What can we do?"

Instructional Activities

1. Invite the child to the story-telling area.
2. Explain to the child that you are going to ask some "I See" and "I Hear" questions. After she has heard the questions, she is to think of all the different ways that the "I See" and "I Hear" questions could be answered.
3. Give the child a point for each appropriate response.
4. Use visuals to cue if the child has difficulty in responding and the problem is related to the verbal presentation.

1.227 Selects an item based on appearance
Strand: 1-7C **Age:** 53-60m 4.5-5.0y

Definition

When the child is shown a group of items or a picture with multi-items in it, he will identify at least one item in the picture based on appearance. The child will identify the items after an oral description. The child will identify these objects by manipulation or a verbal response.

Instructional Materials

An assortment of items, such as pencils, a spoon, buttons, flat plastic figures, jewelry, puzzle pieces etc. Pencils, crayons, poster board or white construction paper.

Instructional Activities

1. Take the assorted items, place them on a sheet of paper, and trace around them. Take another sheet of paper, place the assorted pieces on that paper, trace around them, and color them.
2. Give the child the items and the sheet of outlines.
3. Demonstrate using one object and matching it to its outline, first by color/outline and then by outline only.
4. Have the child match the remaining objects by placing each on top of its color/outline and then outline only.
5. Request that the child locate items and trace around them on sheets of paper.

6. Ask the child to exchange sheets of paper and match items to outlines.

7. As the child becomes proficient at matching by color/outline and then outline only, remove the sheets of paper and ask the child to identify the item after listening to a verbal description.

1.228   Selects an item based on category

Strand: 1-7C   **Age:** 53-60m 4.5-5.0y

Definition

When the child is given a category (food), he is able to select, from objects or pictures, the item that meets the criteria of that category. Beginning categorical requests should be those that the child is familiar with within his environmental experiences. As the child becomes familiar with classifications and categories, the selection requests can become more abstract.

Instructional Materials

A set of at least twelve single item picture cards. These cards can be made by drawing an item on the card or by cutting pictures from various sources and placing them on the cards.

Instructional Activities

1. Place the cards face-up on the table. Ask the children to sit around the table.

2. Tell the children they will hear a word ("food") and that they are to look at the pictures and find something that goes with that word (apple). When they find the picture they are to pick it up and put it in front of them.

3. Before beginning the game have one practice turn.

4. For example, say, "(child's name), find a picture that goes with the word 'pet', and before you hear me say 'stop', find a picture of a pet or something that goes with a pet." Allow ample time for the child to find a picture of a dog, cat, dog house, bowl of milk, etc.

5. Make sure that the child places the correct picture on the table in front of him.

6. After the practice turn, and once everyone understands how to play the game, begin by saying a child's name and then the direction.

7. The easiest directions are those that can be matched with literal information. The most difficult are those directions that ask for knowledge that requires analytical thinking. It is important to set a response time that can be

changed from group to group, based on the skill levels of the children.

8. Continue until all the cards have been matched.

9. Count the number of cards in front of the children; the one with the most is crowned the winner.

10. The activity may be modified; hold up a picture that represents a category and have the child look at the pictures on the table to find a match.

1.229   Selects an item based on function

Strand: 1-7C   **Age:** 53-60m 4.5-5.0y

Definition

The child will select those objects that are used for the same function or have the same general performance qualities. The child will match items such as: things that carry items, items that clean, things that keep us warm, objects that we play with, etc. It is important that the child understands that she is selecting items by what they do (their function). When asked, the child will be able to state the item's function.

Instructional Materials

/***Safety Note:** Provide scissors appropriate for the child. Remind the child of safety regarding scissors.

One large piece of paper divided into four sections for each child, or four sheets of paper attached to make a large sheet. A pencil, crayons, glue, scissors, magazines/catalogs.

Instructional Activities

1. Place a sheet of paper on a working surface for each child. It is important that each child have easy access to the magazines, crayons, pencils, and scissors.

2. Explain to the children that the paper represents a house and that each of the four sections represents something one does in a house. The sections could represent such things as cooking, sleeping, cleaning, playing, etc.

3. Label each of the sections with the selected activity.

4. Discuss some of the things that are used to cook with, for playtime, to help one rest, and to keep clean. After the discussion, explain to the children that you want them to draw a picture or find pictures in the magazines of all the things they can that match the labeled function.

5. After the children have completed filling in their four-section picture, ask each child to tell what they placed in each category and how it helps to accomplish the function.

1.230 Selects items that are different from a set/group
Strand: 1-7C **Age:** 53-60m 4.5-5.0y

Definition
When presented with an established set of four items, the child will identify at least one object that is different from the rest of the set. The set should include at least two items identical in shape, color, size, appearance, function, object class, etc.

Instructional Materials
A large assortment of buttons and red paper circles about the size of the buttons.

Instructional Activities
1. Ask the child to sit at the table. Distribute a handful of buttons to him. Join the child at the table.
2. Explain to the child that he is to select a button from the pile and place it in front of himself.
3. Indicate what you are doing by saying, "I am sorting the red buttons and putting them together," "I am sorting the round buttons," "I am sorting the buttons with four little holes in them."
4. Discuss what a set means.
5. Ask the child to use his buttons and make a set of his own. After the child has made his set, give the child a chance to tell about the set he made.
6. Tell the child to make a set of red round buttons and add a red paper circle to each set of red buttons.
7. Discuss why the red paper circle is not part of the set.
8. Have the child arrange a set of buttons and add a button that does not belong. Ask him to tell why the button that has been added does not belong.

1.231 Tells suitable ending to a simple story
Strand: 1-9 **Age:** 53-60m 4.5-5.0y

Definition
After the child hears an unfamiliar story with a single plot and not more than four sequences, the child will provide an appropriate ending. The ending should include making inferences and drawing a conclusion.

Instructional Materials
A dramatization with no more than three characters. Three puppets that represent the three characters in the play. Hand puppets or stick puppets work effectively. Example of a dramatization:
The Parade Characters (a clown, a boy, and a balloon):
Boy - (speaking to the clown), "The Parade will start in a few minutes."
Clown - (speaking to the boy), "I am not ready."
Boy - (speaking to the clown), "You have on your funny face and big shoes. Why aren't you ready?"
Clown - (speaking to the boy), "My balloon sailed up into the air and I need a new one."
Boy - (speaking to the clown), "I will get you a new balloon" (Boy leaves).
Clown - (speaking to himself), "I hope the boy brings me a bright yellow balloon."
Boy - (returns with a red balloon), "Look what I have for you! A new balloon! Now you are ready for the Parade" (gives balloon to the Clown; Clown and Boy begin to march in the Parade).
Clown - (Running quickly to boy), "Something awful has happened! My balloon..."

Instructional Activities
1. Prepare the puppet theater area, prepare any backgrounds, etc. Invite the children to the puppet show. Introduce the puppets to the children. Tell the children that they need to listen carefully because they may have to help with the puppet play.
2. Present the play.
3. When the Clown speaks his last line ("Something awful has happened! My balloon...") ask a child to take the part of the Clown and to tell the Boy what happened to the balloon.
4. To complete the play, other children will need to take the part of the Boy puppet and the balloon puppet.
5. Allow the children to act out the play.

1.232 (Removed, see page xii)

1.233 Sorts 5 multiple-classed objects or pictured objects according to class/category
Strand: 1-7A **Age:** 54-60m 4.6-5.0y

Definition
Given five objects or pictures that represent different classification groups, such as doctor, barber, truck, car, and firefighter, the child will sort into two groups the pictures that represent people that help us and the pictures that represent a form of transportation. The child will sort these objects verbally or by manipulation. The first objects presented to the child should be concrete, then by visual representation. If the child experiences success in sorting these items, ask her to classify based on a verbal description only.

Instructional Materials
Pictures of fruit, vegetables, toys, clothes, pets or other categories. 2 x 2 inch cards and a 10 x 12 inch piece of tag board that has been squared off into 2 inch squares (much like a Bingo card).

Instructional Activities
1. Place the picture cards face down on the table. Give each child a piece of the squared-off tag board.
2. Discuss with the child that the pictures on the cards are about different categories of things. One group is _____, another group is_____, and the last group is_____. Write the name of the groups (e.g., Animals, Homes, etc.) or place a picture that represents each group on the top row of the tag board.
3. Explain to the child that she is to draw a card and place it in the square under the correct category on the tag board.
4. Have the children take turns picking cards and placing pictures under the correct category.
5. To win, a category column must be completely filled.
6. Name the category and ask the child to read the picture names under that particular group.

1.234 Names classes/categories of sorted objects
Strand: 1-7A **Age:** 54-60m 4.6-5.0y

Definition
When the child is presented with pre-sorted objects in at least two different categories, the child will name each of the categories. The child may determine his own criteria for classifying objects and naming the set. (e.g., This category is called "Toss Toys", because they are things to play with and throw.)

Instructional Materials
A large sheet of white paper and pictures of vehicles (e.g., truck, boat, airplane, horse, balloon, and a raft). Attach the pictures to index cards.

Instructional Activities
1. Divide the paper into three sections. Draw a picture of land in one section, a picture of water in another section, and a picture of sky in the last section.
2. Show the child the cards one at a time and have the child name what he sees on the card.
3. Ask the child to state the name of the class that the pictures belong to (vehicles, things that we ride in, things that take us places, etc.)
4. Show the child the paper and point out the three sections.
5. Suggest that the child sort the vehicles into the correct section according to where they are found.
6. After the sorting has been done, ask the child to give a name to each section of vehicles (things we ride in that fly, things that carry big loads).
7. This activity may be continued by changing the pictures to animals that walk on land, fish found in water, and birds that fly.

1.235 Identifies and counts quantities of at least 6
Strand: 1-10 **Age:** 54-60m 4.6-5.0y

Definition
As the child becomes proficient in counting out loud, she discovers numbers, both printed and stated. The child also realizes that these numbers represent a specific quantity and that a specific quantity can be expressed by the spoken symbol ("three"), by the number (3), and by the written word (three). The child will say the numerical word that represents a set of objects and she will match the written number that corresponds to a set of objects.

Instructional Materials
Prepare a set of 10 poster board cards. Each card should be 3 x 5 inches. Secure at least 10 colored chenille balls. Provide glue and a marker. Prepare a set of number cards. Card number one should have the number one on it, card two should have the number two on it, etc. Continue

until the number ten has been reached. A set of ten blocks.

Instructional Activities

1. Place the material on a work area. Invite the child to come to the area.
2. Explain to the child that you are going to show her a number card and that she is to select the correct number of chenille balls and glue them on one of the poster board cards to make that set.
3. Give the child six poster cards and six colored chenille balls.
4. Show the child the number one card and the one block. Say, "This is the number one (pointing to the card) and this is a set of one block."
5. Remove the number one card and the one block.
6. Show the child the number two card and the set of two blocks.
7. Say, "How many blocks are on the table? Point to the number two."
8. Remove the number two card and the two blocks.
9. Show the child the number three card and the set of three blocks.
10. Say, "How many blocks are on the table? Point to the number three."
11. Remove the three blocks.
12. Show the child the number four card and a set of four blocks.
13. Say, "How many blocks are on the table? Point to the number four."
14. Remove the four blocks.
15. Show the child the number five card and a set of five blocks.
16. Say, "How many blocks are on the table? Point to the number five."
17. Remove the number five card and the five blocks.
18. Show the child the number six card and a set of six blocks.
19. Say, "How many blocks are on the table? Point to the number six."
20. Remove all the number cards and the blocks.
21. Show the child the number two card.
22. Say, "Use the chenille balls and make this set" (pointing to the number two card).
23. After the child has completed the task, ask her how many chenille balls she has on her card.
24. If the child displays any difficulties in accomplishing this activity, place two blocks by the number card and ask the child to place the same amount of chenille balls on the card.

25. Fade the visual cue as soon as possible.
26. Show the child the number four card.
27. Say, "Use the chenille balls and make this set" (pointing to the number four card).
28. After the child has completed the task, ask her how many chenille balls she has on her card.
29. Continue the above until the child has made a set of 1 - 6 chenille ball cards.
30. Show the child one of her chenille cards and ask how many balls are on the card; when the child responds with the number, write the numeral on the card.
31. After all the numbers have been written on the chenille ball cards, ask the child to place them in order from 1 - 6.
32. Continue the above procedure for numbers 7 - 10.

1.236   Places 4 pictures in sequence
Strand: 1-7A   **Age:** 54-62m 4.6-5.2y

Definition
When the child is shown four pictures depicting a sequence of events, the child will put the pictures in the correct order and tell the picture story.

Instructional Materials
/*\Safety Note: Be aware of special diets and allergies before doing these activities.
A favorite recipe that uses no more than four steps (e.g., taking the skin off an orange to eat it, popping pop corn, baking a boxed cake, baking brownies, frying an egg, etc.) The steps in making the treat should be illustrated simply on four index cards. Collect the ingredients and utensils needed to make the treat.

Instructional Activities
1. Place the necessary ingredients and utensils on a table. Invite the child to the cooking area.
2. Explain to the child that you are going to cook something special.
3. During the discussion explain how food is prepared in a certain order and that recipes tell us in what order and in what way to put the various ingredients together.
4. Show the child the recipe cards in the correct sequence.
5. Take the first card and discuss what is happening. Do what is shown on the card.
6. Continue until all three or four cards have been displayed and the directions followed.

7. Mix up the cards and ask the child to put them in the correct order based on what happens first, second, third, etc.
8. Ask the child to tell about each picture in the sequence.
9. When the cards have been put in the proper order and the story has been told, enjoy the special treat.

1.237 Locates big, bigger, biggest and small, smaller, smallest in group of objects

Strand: 1-7B   **Age:** 54-64m 4.6-5.4y

Definition

The child will compare and contrast objects of different sizes, formulating the concept of big, bigger, biggest and small, smaller, smallest. . When the child is looking for the smallest item in a group, she will understand that this item is smaller than all the ones that she will select later. When the child is looking for the biggest item in a group, she will understand that this item is bigger than all the items she will select.

Instructional Materials

A big ball, a medium size ball, and a little ball.

Instructional Activities

1. Ask the child to sit on the floor.
2. Show her the three balls and ask her to point to the BIGGEST ball, the BIGGER ball and to the BIG ball. Show the correct size ball if the child is incorrect and have her try again.
3. Tell the child to roll the BIG ball to you.
4. Tell her that you are going to roll the BIGGER ball to her.
5. Tell the child to roll the BIGGEST ball to you.
6. Gather all the balls. This time show the child the balls and identify the balls as SMALL, SMALLER, and SMALLEST.
7. Continue rolling the balls, use terms such as bigger, biggest, smaller, and smallest. Example: "Roll me the biggest ball. Show me the ball that is smaller than this one. I want you to toss the smallest ball to me. Here comes a big ball. Here comes a bigger ball. Here comes the biggest ball."

1.238 Sorts items by category

Strand: 1-7A   **Age:** 54-65m 4.6-5.5y

Definition

When the child is given a category (e.g., food), he is able to sort objects or pictures which meet the criteria of that category. Categorical sorting should begin

with items the child is familiar with and which are within his experiences. After sorting objects into a single category, the child will be presented with additional categories and items, as well as an emphasis on subtle differences of the categories.

Instructional Materials

One set of three objects that are hard (e.g., wood, rock, steel). A set of three objects that are soft (e.g., foam rubber, cotton, velvet). A set of three objects that are rough (e.g., sandpaper, brush, dried starfish). A set of objects that are smooth (e.g., glass, gloss paper, plastic). Four containers, large enough to hold the objects. In a separate container place one representative of the four tactile categories (e.g., rock, cotton, etc.) A sack for all the remaining items.

Instructional Activities

1. Place the assorted objects in a sack and the four containers on a table.
2. From the separate container (containing one item from each of the four categories) pull out one item. Show the children the item and discuss its shape, color, use, and texture. Make sure that each child has a chance to feel the item. Decide as a group if it is hard, smooth, soft, or rough. After the group has decided the texture, place the object in one of the four containers on the table.
3. After each object has been handled, discussed, and placed in the correct container, continue with the other objects that have been placed in the sack.
4. Ask the children to take turns and select one object from the group, handle it, pass it around, and then place it in the correct container. The child sorting the object must tell if it is hard, soft, rough, or smooth.
5. Allow each child to have a turn selecting, naming, and placing an object.
6. When the children have sorted the items successfully, gather up the various things and place them back in the sack.
7. Repeat the activity, only this time the child must put their hand in the sack and without looking tell the texture of the item they are holding and then place it in the correct container.
8. Expand this activity to match things in the room that are rough, smooth, soft, or hard.

1.239 Works in small group for 10-25 minutes

Strand: 1-8 **Age:** 54-72m 4.6-6.0y

Definition

A small group refers to four or five children. The project that these children do should be designed to be completed within the 10-25 minute period. The group does not work independently, but receives supervision. The amount of supervision will vary, depending on the group structure and the activity.

Instructional Materials

Make up or find a story about a person who enjoys working with his friends.

Instructional Activities

1. Invite the children to the Storytime Place. Read the story to the children and point out how unhappy the person might be if they had no one to talk to, to share things with, to play with or, most importantly, to help them do things.
2. Discuss with the children how they would feel if they didn't have friends to help them with different tasks.
3. Discuss how to work together and how to help one another, e.g., share materials, take turns, etc.
4. Have the children decide on some rules to follow when helping each other. Assist in this rule-making session. Try to limit the rules to no more than two or three, and make the rules observable and action-oriented. Example: Follow directions, Take turns, Speak quietly, Keep hands to yourself, etc. It may be necessary to role play what the rules mean for complete understanding.
5. Place the children in groups of four to five. Decide on a task for each group. Tell them to start, and then observe how the children work on their task for 10 to 25 minutes.
6. Praise the groups that are following the rules, working together and staying on task. Praise the groups that are trying and improving. Provide those that are having difficulty with a reminder of the rules and a structure within which to function.

1.240 Tells as many solutions as possible for a given problem situation

Strand: 1-4D **Age:** 54-72m 4.6-6.0y

Definition

The problems presented to the child should be those that begin with such statements as "What are some of the things that could happen if_____?" or "If _____ happened, what are some of the things you could do?" Make sure that the problems presented are those that are within the realm of the child's experiences. Example: "What are some of the things that could happen if you lost one of your shoes?" or "If your ball got caught in the tree what are some of the things you could do to get it down?"

Instructional Materials

Collect three sequence pictures of problem situations. Example: set one, picture one, girl riding a tricycle; picture two, wheel on tricycle starting to bend; picture three, wheel falls off of tricycle, girl tips over. Set two, picture one, cat spying a mouse; picture two, cat chasing the mouse; picture three; mouse runs into hole, cat too big for the hole. Set three, picture one, a boy's pants hanging on a hanger; picture two; a boy getting ready to put on the pants; picture three, the boy with pants on (but they are very short), the boy looking at his short pants.

Instructional Activities

1. Select one of the sets of pictures. Tell the children that you are going to show them some pictures.
2. Place the three sequence pictures in view of the children, in the correct order. Point to picture one and ask questions, such as, "What do you see in the picture?", "Where do you think this is happening?" etc. Continue with pictures two and three of the set. Retell the story using pictures one, two and three.
3. After the retelling ask the children, "What do you think happened next?" or "What would you do next?" Be sure that the relative ideas and responses are accepted as solutions to the problem.
4. To assist the child in judgmental reasoning, select the solution that appears to be the best. Illustrate that solution and add it to the sequence of pictures.
5. Retell the complete story.
6. Continue the above procedure with sets two and three.

1.241   Draws recognizable face with eyes, nose, mouth

Strand: 1-11   **Age:** 36-48m 3.0-4.0y

Definition

The child will draw a face with eyes, a nose and a mouth when asked. The face needs to be recognizable and the features in approximate facial positions.

Instructional Materials

Collect four 6 x 6-inch pieces of construction paper. Secure four crayons in the following colors: orange, red, blue, and brown.

Instructional Activities

1. Give each child four 6 x 6-inch pieces of construction paper. Give each child the four crayons.
2. Tell the child to draw a face outline on one sheet of paper with the orange crayon.
3. Tell the child to draw two eyes with the blue or brown crayon.
4. Tell the child to draw a nose in the center of the face with the orange crayon.
5. Begin with a happy face and then go on to sad, mad, and surprised expressions. Have the child draw a smiling mouth for a happy face, a downward mouth for a sad face, a mouth with closed teeth for a mad face and a circular mouth for a surprised face.
6. Sing the following song after the child has drawn the four different faces and then have him point to or hold up the correct face as he sings:
   "If you are happy and you know it, clap your hands."
   "If you are happy and you know it, clap your hands."
   "If you are happy and you know it, then your face will surely show it."
   "If you are happy and you know it, clap your hands."
7. Sing the next verse substituting "happy" with "Sad", and "clap your hands" with "wipe your eyes."
8. Sing the next verse substituting "happy" with "mad", and "clap your hands" with "stomp your feet."
9. Sing the next verse substituting "happy" with "surprised", and "clap your hands" with "say Oh My."

1.242   Names capital and lower case letters when shown printed letters

Strand: 1-9   **Age:** 58-72m 4.10-6.0y

Definition

When shown a letter of the alphabet the child will be able to name the letter. The child will be shown one letter at a time, capital and lower case together. The letters should be printed on cards not less than 2 x 2 inches. Next present only the capital letters of the alphabet. Follow by presenting just the lower case letters of the alphabet. The letters in each group should be randomly presented.

Instructional Materials

Make three sets of cards at least 2 x 2-inches (index cards work well). Print the letters of the alphabet, upper and lower case, on cards (Set One). Print the capital letters of the alphabet on cards (Set Two). Print the lower case letters of the alphabet on cards (Set Three). The letters should be printed in one color and the capital should be first (Bb). For scoring purposes, a sheet needs to be prepared that has all the letters on it with three columns: column one for both the capital and lower case together, column two for the capitals only, and column three for lower case only.

Instructional Activities

1. Invite the child to sit across from you at a table. Explain to the child that you have a deck of <u>Alphabet Letter Cards</u>, and show her one of the cards.
2. Shuffle the cards.
3. Tell the child that you are going to give her a card and that if she can tell you the name of the letter on the card, she may keep the card. If she has a problem naming the letter, she needs to give the card back to you so you can add it back to the deck.
4. Continue the above, using the cards that the child has not seen and the ones that she has missed.
5. If the child misses five of the first cards shown to her, reorganize the cards in the cluster groups. Example: showing her the A card, the B card, the C card, and the D card, lay the cards side-by-side in front of her. Point to only one of the cards and ask the child to tell you the letter's name. If the child is correct allow her to keep the card.
6. If more than one child is involved in this activity, the child with the most cards is declared Today's Champ.

7. To assist in keeping track of the number of cards each child has and the letters named, make a chart with each child's name and spaces on it to mark cards earned and the letters named correctly.

1.243   Sorts items by appearance

Strand: 1-7A   **Age:** 60-65m 5.0-5.5y

Definition

Using more than one identical object or picture, the child will sort the ones that look alike. Using more than one object or picture, the child will sort the ones that look nearly alike.

Instructional Materials

Pictures of people of various ages and sexes, e.g., three pictures of infants, two of toddlers, three of 8-year-olds, three teenagers, three adults, and two seniors. These pictures can be secured from photographs, catalogs, or magazines.

Make sure that either one of the teenagers or an adult is bigger than either of the seniors or that one of the seniors is bigger than one of the other teens/adults.

Attach the pictures to index cards.

Instructional Activities

1. Shuffle the cards and place them face up in view of the child.
2. Discuss with the child differences in ages and the way people look. It is important during the discussion that the children understand that age and size don't always go together.
3. Say, "Give me the pictures of the youngest people (or little babies} on the table." Return the pictures to the table.
4. Say, "Give me the pictures of the oldest people (or the grandmothers and grandfathers) you see." Return the pictures to the table.
5. Say, "Give me the pictures of the smallest people (babies)." Return the pictures to the table.
6. Say, "Give me the pictures of the biggest people." Return the pictures to the table.
7. Continue by asking the child to sort the pictures based on different criteria.
8. Ask the child to sort the pictures according to where they are girls or boys.

1.244   Sorts items by function

Strand: 1-7A   **Age:** 60-66m 5.0-5.6y

Definition

Children begin by sorting objects that are of opposite function (e.g., things we wear and things that we cannot wear); gradually approaching sorting items by finer definition (e.g., things we wear to keep us warm and things we wear to keep us cool); and finally expanding the concept to the affective (e.g., things that I wear that make me laugh and things that I wear that make me feel special).

Instructional Materials

/*\Safety Note: Provide scissors appropriate for the child. Remind the child of safety regarding scissors.

A collection of magazines, catalogs, old picture books, etc. White paper large enough to fold in half to make at least two big books. Scissors, hole punch, and yarn or stapler.

Instructional Activities

1. Fold the paper in half to make the pages of the books (the number of books needed depends on the number of children involved). Each child should have two books to interact with. Attach the books at the side by stapling or punching holes and securing with yarn. Place the pictured material and scissors on the table.
2. Discuss with the children the fact that things do different jobs. Use examples such as stoves are used to cook our food, clothes are made to keep us warm, cars are made so we can go from one place to another, etc.
3. Name some items and ask the children to take turns and tell what the function of each item is (e.g., bread, nail, sacks, etc.)
4. Divide the children into groups of two or three.
5. Give each group two of the blank books.
6. As a group, decide what title (function) should be placed on the front of each book (e.g., Things That Move, Things That We Use to Keep Clean, Things That We Sit On, etc.)
7. Write the selected title on the front of the books and ask the children to look through the magazines, etc., to find pictures of items that do what the title indicates. These could also be illustrated by the child. After the books have been completed, ask each group to share their books with the class.
8. Save the completed books and add pages to them as new pictured items are located.

9. Continue making additional books using different, more selective, and creative titles.

1.245 Uses tactile terms to describe properties of items

Strand: 1-7C **Age:** 60-66m 5.0-5.6y

Definition

The child will describe an object by using such words as hard or soft, rough or smooth, round or flat, big or little, dark or light, large or small, and conclude by naming the object.

Instructional Materials

Cards with various textured surfaces attached. Ideas for different surfaces are sandpaper, different textures of carpeting, salt, tissue paper, slick plastic, granite, netting, bubble wrap, etc. A blindfold and some newspapers.

Instructional Activities

1. Spread the newspapers on the floor. Put the child's chairs around the newspapers. Place a sheet of paper with the textured surfaces in front of each chair. Gather the children in an area where they cannot see the circle of chairs or the textured papers.
2. Using two different textured surfaces (sandpaper and cotton), explain to the children that things often feel different and that there are words that describe how these things feel.
3. Have the children feel the sandpaper. After everyone has touched it, ask the children to use a word(s) to tell how the sandpaper felt. Encourage the children to mention a number of words, and ask if anyone can think of other things that feel rough, gritty, bumpy, etc. Continue with another item one that is soft (cotton).
4. Tell the children that there are words that describe how things feel. Say, "I am thinking of something that feels slick, what is it?" Let the children take turns naming things that fit the given category.
5. After the children have had the experience of feeling different textures and have named objects that have unique surfaces, explain the game called Feet Feel.
6. Tell the children to take off their shoes and that you are going to blindfold them. Then take them one at a time to a chair. They are to sit down on the chair and not to stand up until their name is called.

7. When their name is called they are to stand, take a step forward and their feet will feel something different.
8. Take the blindfolded children one at a time to the chairs.
9. After all the children have been seated, call on one child to stand, take a step forward. Wait for a few seconds and ask her to tell how her feet feel.
10. Repeat until each child has been called on and has responded.
11. Conclude the activity by having the children walk from one textured paper to the other. After the walk, ask such questions as, "How did the carpet feel? Did anything feel slick? Which feet feel did you like the best?"

1.246 Sings or dances to different songs

Strand: 2-7 **Age:** 60-66m 5.0-5.6y

Definition

The child will sing at least two different familiar songs (he will sing them mostly in tune and remember most of the lyrics). He will dance to at least two different musical selections. His dance may be either created or in a learned pattern.

Instructional Materials

/*\Safety Note: Provide scissors appropriate for the child. Remind the child of safety regarding scissors.

A song (prerecorded or live) that includes dance steps. (Examples: a circle dance, a simple polka, a square dance, a swing or rock song, or a simple folk dance.) Yellow and light blue construction paper, scissors, yellow and light blue stickers, tape.

Instructional Activities

1. Ask the child to put his left foot on the yellow paper, and draw around his foot. Cut out as many patterns as needed for the dance steps. Ask him to put his right foot on the light blue paper, draw around it, and cut out as many patterns as needed for the dance steps.
2. Tell the child to listen to some dance music. Play the music several times.
3. Demonstrate the dance steps and tape the foot patterns to the floor in the dance pattern.
4. Invite the child to dance to the tune, following the outlined feet (pattern on the floor). If left and right confuse him, place a yellow sticker on the top of his left shoe and the blue sticker on the top of his right shoe.

5. Give him several chances to practice the dance steps, using the floor patterns.
6. Remove the foot patterns, and ask him to dance to the music. Ask him to listen to the music again and to think about where the foot patterns should be placed.
7. Give him an opportunity to improvise dance steps.
8. If the music has lyrics, ask him to sing as he dances. If the music does not include lyrics, help him make up a song.

1.247 (Removed, see page xii)

1.248 Locates object of given number in group of 10

Strand: 1-10 **Age:** 60-66m 5.0-5.6y

Definition

The child, upon request, will select from a row of objects the item that is first, second, third, fourth and fifth. As an extension of this skill: the child, upon request, will select from a row of objects the item that is sixth, seventh, eighth, ninth and tenth. It is necessary that the child be able to count in cardinal order to five prior to using ordinal position to five. It is necessary that the child be able to count in cardinal order to ten prior to using ordinal position to ten. Special emphasis should be placed on first and second, because they are different contextual words than the number words one and two. Focus should also be on the words third and fifth as they are also contextually different from their counterparts three and five.

Instructional Materials

A sheet of drawing paper and a pencil or marker.

Instructional Activities

1. Provide the child with the drawing material.
2. Ask the child to place his hand palm-side down on the paper and explain that he must spread his fingers. Tell the child to draw around his right hand. If the child is right-handed, someone may need to help trace his hand for him.
3. Read the following directions to the child, pausing between each direction to allow the child time to respond (explain to the child that his thumb is finger number one).
4. Tell the child to draw a ring on the fourth finger.

5. Assist the child with the first direction if needed.
6. Tell the child to put red fingernails on the second and fifth fingers.
7. Tell the child to write the number 1 above the first finger (thumb).
8. Tell the child to write the number 3 above the third finger.
9. Tell the child to draw a blue ring on the fifth finger (little).
10. Tell the child to draw a *Band-Aid* on the second finger.
11. Allow the child to show his hand to others.
12. Increase difficulty by having the child trace both hands, and include directions for sixth through tenth fingers.

1.249 Matches groups having equal numbers of objects up to 10

Strand: 1-10 **Age:** 60-66m 5.0-5.6y

Definition

The child will match two equal groups of the same objects. When the child views objects in two sets of one, two sets of two and two sets of three, she will be able to point to the sets having the same number of objects upon verbal request. The presentation of sets should be done in clusters of one, two and three objects. Then in a cluster of four, five and six objects and in the final cluster of seven, eight, nine and ten objects.

Instructional Materials

At least two pictures of groups of objects or animals. Set One objects or animals should be in groups of one, two and three. Set Two objects or animals should be in groups of four, five and six. Set Three objects or animals should be in groups of seven, eight, nine and ten.

Instructional Activities

1. Ask the child to come to the table. Place Set One pictures on a table in front of the child.
2. Ask the child to put in one pile all the pictures that have, for example, two animals, and to place in another pile all the pictures that have two dolls, etc.
3. Repeat with Set Two.

1.250 Completes task with little prompting
Strand: 1-8 **Age:** 60-66m 5.0-5.6y

Definition
The child will complete an activity, with not more than two reminders. The reminders need to be of a positive nature. Such statements as "You have completed the hardest part of the _____(picture)! It is going to really look nice when you are done." or "I am really proud of the way you have been working, keep it up." The reinforcement prompt should be based on progress, not on accuracy. Continue the reinforcement strategies as described, then fading should begin.

Instructional Materials
Index cards and a marker. A reward that the child will want to receive. Gather at least three activities that are on the child's instructional learning level, plus something that the child will enjoy. This could be a game, a book, a favorite picture to color, a matching worksheet, an art project, a pattern for a peg-board, etc.

Instructional Activities
1. Ask the child to come to the table. Have the activities and any supplies needed on the table.
2. Tell the child that he can select one activity to do from the choices. Also explain that this is a game of I Can Do It By Myself and to help him do the activity by himself, you are going to place an index card by his place at the table. The child must understand the rules of the game, which are: "If you decide to get off task while you are doing the _____ and I have to remind you about that, I will make a mark on your card. If you complete the _____ and you have only two marks on your card, you will earn a special reward" (remember the reward is given for completing the task).
3. When the rules of the game are understood, tell the child to begin. Each time the child stops work, provide support such as saying "You have been working so hard! I'm proud of you." "Can I help you get started on the _____ again?" and make a mark.
4. If the child has two or less marks on his card, give him the reward.

1.251 Reads and writes numerals to 5
Strand: 1-10 **Age:** 60-68m 5.0-5.8y

Definition
When the child is presented with the written numerals 1, 2, and 3 he will read them. The numbers should be presented in the following manner: first present number 1, with a set of one object; after the child has responded, remove the number and object. Then present number 2, with a set of two objects; after the child has responded, remove the number and the set of two objects and present numbers 3, 4, 5 in the same way. The child should then say each number (1 - 5) when the number and set are presented randomly. Using pencil, crayon, marker and paper, the child will write the numerals 1, 2, 3, 4, and 5 when verbally presented in random order.

Instructional Materials
/*\Safety Note: Be aware of special diets and allergies before doing these activities, and supervise use of the clay.
Secure enough shoestring/rope licorice so that the child can create the numbers 1 - 5. Secure at least 15 pieces of licorice bits (small pieces). Develop a set of number cards 1 - 5. If licorice is a problem, substitute clay. Waxed paper.

Instructional Activities
1. Place a sheet of waxed paper on a table. Ask the child to sit by the paper.
2. Instruct the child to use the licorice bits and make a set of three.
3. Provide the child with the shoestring or rope licorice.
4. Instruct the child that when you say a specific number (3), they are to use the shoestring or rope licorice and form that number.
5. Tell the child to check their answers with the model number cards.
6. Reward the child by allowing him to eat correctly made licorice numbers and sets.
7. If clay is substituted, make sure the child makes a long thin snake form before attempting to create the numbers. Small clay pieces may be used for developing the sets. (Be careful the child does not eat the clay.)

1.252 Counts orally to 20
Strand: 1-10 **Age:** 60-68m 5.0-5.8y

Definition
The child will verbally count from 1 - 20. She will be asked to count by rote, count items, count in groupings (count 1 - 5, 5 - 10, 10 - 15, 15 - 20) and

count to 20 from a given number (start with 7 and count to 20).

Instructional Materials

20 clothespins and at least three containers with openings ranging from wide (like a laundry basket) to small (like a coffee can).

Instructional Activities

1. Secure a straight back chair and place the container with the widest opening on the floor behind the chair. Put the clothespins on a table near the chair.
2. Ask the child to sit on the chair facing the back and to rest her elbows on the top of the back of the chair. Show the child the container that is on the floor in front of her.
3. Ask her to take a clothespin and try to drop it in the container. Tell her that she is to count the clothespins as she drops them.
4. Give her a point for each clothespin that she puts into the container.
5. Increase the challenge by switching to a container with a smaller opening.
6. Tally her points at the end of the activity.

1.253 Names days of week in succession

Strand: 1-13 **Age:** 60-68m 5.0-5.8y

Definition

The child will name the days of the week in order, but it is not necessary to start with Sunday. When learning the days of the week the child should begin to respond with an activity that he does on a given day (Monday go to school, Saturday play at home, Sunday visit friends, etc.)

Instructional Materials

Prepare seven definition poems, writing a poem for each day of the week. Some examples are: Sunday is my day to help Dad fix breakfast. Monday is back to school day. Tuesday is my day to help Mom bring the recycling containers back into the garage. Wednesday is the day I go to story time at the library. Thursday is my afternoon with Grandma, etc. It is important that the definitions are meaningful to the child and that they involve something he can relate to doing on a specific day.

Eric Carle's book *Today Is Monday* would be a good book to read in conjunction with this activity.

Instructional Activities

Note: Definition poems provide a successful method to associate meaning with words.

1. Invite the child to join you. Read the definition poems that you wrote about the days of the week.
2. Explain to the child that you are going to name a day of the week and that he is to think of something that he does on that day. Say, "Sundays are for. . ." or "Sunday is. . ." or "On Sunday I. . ." Continue with the rest of the days of the week in sequence.
3. Repeat the definition poems that the child created.
4. Phase out the definition part of the poem as the child becomes familiar with not only saying the days of the week but also associating an activity with each day.

1.254 Relates "today," "tomorrow," "yesterday" to days of the week

Strand: 1-13 **Age:** 60-68m 5.0-5.8y

Definition

The child will respond when asked "What day is today? What day was yesterday? What day will tomorrow be?" by stating the day of the week or by indicating a visual representation of the day.

Instructional Materials

Prepare cards with questions concerning relationships of today, tomorrow and yesterday such as: two days from tomorrow, day after today or day before yesterday, today, tomorrow, etc. Markers, such as checkers, to be placed on the game board squares.

Prepare a game board for each child with squares representing the days of the week.

Instructional Activities

1. Discuss relationships of today, tomorrow and yesterday.
2. Ask the child questions about events that happened yesterday and what will happen tomorrow.
3. Identify the days being discussed on the game board.
4. Discuss child's answers.
5. Give the child a group of markers.
6. Read one of the prepared cards about today, tomorrow and yesterday.
7. Tell the child she is to place a marker on the correct game board space. Explain to the child that she may remain on the space if she is correct, but that if she is incorrect she must return her marker.

8. Indicate that the Calendar Champ for the day is the child who is first to complete their game board.

1.255 Prints own first or last name, copying model

Strand: 1-11 **Age:** 60-70m 5.0-5.10y

Definition

The child will print his first or last name when shown a model. The model needs to be in manuscript form and the letters should be on a base line. The child's letters should be recognizable, however the strokes need not be made in the correct sequence, the lines need not be constructed perfectly, the spacing does not need to be equal between the letters, and the density of the lines may be different.

Instructional Materials

Note: The letters should be in manuscript form. Sheets of paper with the child's first and last name on it. Under the complete printed first name (Tim), leave a blank for the first letter (_im) of his name and then print the rest of the letters. Under the "one blank" name, leave two blanks (_ _m) for the first two letters of his name and print the remaining letter. Finally, the whole name is made up of blanks (_ _ _). Under the complete printed last name (Adamson), leave a blank for the first letter (_damson) of his name and then print the rest of the letters. Under the "one blank" name, leave two blanks (_ _amson) for the first two letters of his name and print the rest of the letters. Continue as above until there are all blanks.

Instructional Activities

1. Place the sheet of paper on the table in front of the child. Point to each letter of the child's last name and ask him to identify the letters in his name.
2. Give the child a crayon or marking pen to trace over ALL the letters of his name.
3. Point to the child's last name that is minus the first letter.
4. Ask the child to write ALL the letters of his name, filling in the blank to complete it.
5. Initially, provide immediate direction and correction.
6. Present the name with two, three, or more letters replaced by blank lines.
7. Require the child to fill in all the blank lines beginning from left to right.

8. After the child has filled in all the blanks, remove the paper and give him a new sheet of paper.
9. Say, "Write your first name."

1.256 Arranges objects in order of size from smallest to largest

Strand: 1-7B **Age:** 60-72m 5.0-6.0y

Definition

In order to grasp the idea of numbers, the notion of relations is as important as classification and matching one-to-one. By providing the child with different sized objects and asking her to put them in order from the smallest (a 3-inch object) to the largest (an 8-inch object), she will understand the concept of order and position.

Instructional Materials

A board with 10 hooks all the same size in a horizontal row. 10 washers of different sizes.

Instructional Activities

1. Set the board on a table, in a position that is easily accessible to the child. Place the collection of washers by the board.
2. Ask the child to find the smallest washer and put it on the hook on the left side of the board (point to the starting place if needed).
3. Ask the child to find the next larger washer and place it next to the little washer.
4. Have the child continue until all washers are in the appropriate sequence.
5. Tell the child to place them on the hooks from left to right.
6. Point to a little washer and say, "This is little."
7. Point to the next washer and say, "Bigger;" then move to the next and say, "Bigger", etc.
8. Ask the child to remove them from the hooks, moving left to right, and place them in a container.
9. Allow the child to manipulate and perform the task independently.

1.257 Says the sound a letter makes when shown the letter

Strand: 1-9 **Age:** 60-72m 5.0-6.0y

Definition

The first letters shown to the child should be consonants in both capital and lower case. Vowels (short sound only) should also be shown to the child in both capital and lower case. The letters should be printed on cards (which are no less than 2 x 2 inches) and displayed to the child one letter at a time. The consonants can be presented in alphabetical order, with emphasis placed on the fine auditory discrimination between m and n, s and t, and v and w. At the beginning levels, with those phoneme/grapheme consonants (c, g, s, and x) that have two sounds, the initial and most frequently used sound should be presented to the child (c - cat, g - go, s - sack, and x - xylophone). When presenting the vowels (a,e,i,o,u), caution and emphasis needs to be placed on the e and i due to the fine auditory discrimination.

Instructional Materials

Secure or develop a set of sound, letter, and picture cards. These alphabet sound cards are available from commercial sources or can easily be made by gluing a picture of an object whose name has the same beginning sound as the letter printed on the card and the word that names the object. Example: a - apple, b - boat, c - cat, d - duck, e - egg, f - fork, g - goat, h - house, i - ice cream, j - jump, k - kite, l - lamp, m - man, n - nest, o - orange, p - pan, q - queen, r - ring, s - sack, t - tack, u - umbrella, v – violin, w - wagon, x - xylophone, y - yellow, z - zebra. Drawing paper and crayons.

Instructional Activities

1. Give the child three sheets of drawing paper and crayons. Choose three alphabet picture/letter/word cards (a, b, c).
2. Show the child the card for the letter A. Ask the child to look at the letter and name the picture (apple). Say, " The sound of A is _____as in _____."
3. Ask the child if he can think of another word that starts like apple (animal, anchor), and then ask the child to draw a picture of at least one other thing that starts with the sound like apple. Add the letter and word to the child's drawing.
4. Continue with the letters B and C. Each day add more letters. When the alphabet has been completed, staple the drawings together and make a title cover that says My Picture Sound Dictionary.

1.258 Matches (visually) identical letters in group of different letters
Strand: 1-9 **Age:** 60-72m 5.0-6.0y

Definition

The child will recognize all the letters in a row that are the same. The sequence of letters to match will be:

(1) Upper case open letters, (2) Upper case round letters (3) lower case open letters and (4) lower case round letters. It is not necessary that the child provide the letter name or the letter sound.

Instructional Materials

Prepare a worksheet that has six printed letters on the left side of the paper. On the right side of the paper print the same letters but arranged them in a different order.

Instructional Activities

1. Ask the child to come to the table. Give the child the worksheet and use the first letter as a demonstration. The child will need a crayon or pencil.
2. Show the child the first letter on the left side of the paper.
3. Ask her to point to the same letter on the right side of the paper.
4. When the child has made a match, ask her to draw a line from one letter to the other.
5. Instruct the child to look at each letter in the left list and draw a line to the identical letter in the right list.

1.259 Matches (visually) identical words in group of words
Strand: 1-9 **Age:** 60-72m 5.0-6.0y

Definition

The child will match words that are visually alike. The first matching the child is asked to do will be words that are grossly different in configuration. The second area of matching will be words that are similar in configuration. The child does not have to read the words.

Instructional Materials

A collection of cards (index cards work well) which have words printed on them (these words should be of various configurations. Example: "tell" (tall letter, short letter and two tall letters), "happy" (tall letter, short letter, three letters that go below the line), and "what" (short letter, tall letter, short letter, tall letter). The cards should be cut out to cover the linear design of the words. There should be at least two of each cut-out word card. Example: two cut-out cards that have the word "tell," two cut-out cards that have the word "happy," etc.

Instructional Activities

1. Place the cut-out word cards in a sack and shake the sack to mix up the cards. Seat the child at a table or work area.

2. Show the child a card and explain that there are more cards like that one in the sack.
3. Give him directions to draw a card from the sack and put it on the table. Ask him to draw another card from the sack and try to match the cards by word shape.
4. Continue until all the cards have been drawn and matched.
5. As the child becomes proficient in matching by configuration, allot a certain amount of time to complete the task. By setting a time, it not only increases the challenge but also encourages the child to look at the whole shape, rather than detail.

1.260 Prints letters and numbers, copying model

Strand: 1-11   **Age:** 60-72m 5.0-6.0y

Definition

When a letter or a number is demonstrated to the child, she will reproduce the letter's configuration. The letter/number should be recognizable. It should have a base and the lines, circles, etc. that form the figures should be made from left to right, and the child does not have to know the letter or the numbers. The letters need to be written in manuscript form and can be upper or lower case. Present only one letter (e.g., A) and one number (e.g., 7) at a time. The child will use a marker large enough to facilitate writing control.

Instructional Materials

Writing paper and pencils.

Instructional Activities

1. Sit at a right angle to the child. Place a piece of paper in front of the child and yourself.
2. Write a letter or number on your paper, shielding your work from the child, but exaggerating the hand motion.
3. Tell the child to watch the motion of your hand and pencil. Start with letters and numbers with simple strokes like L, C, O, 1 and 3.
4. Ask the child to guess what you have written.
5. Let the child write the next letter or number while you guess what she wrote.
6. Take turns guessing what letter or number has been written.
7. Modify the activity by using the "talk about" strokes approach. Example: t - tall line down, cross near the top; o - pencil down, circle around; i - short line, dot; a - pencil down circle around, line down; W - slant down,

slant up, slant down and slant up; B - line down, hump up and hump down, etc.
8. Give a point to the child when she correctly guesses a letter/number.
9. If the child is having difficulty with a letter or number, provide a dotted outline of the letter or number for her to trace.
10. After a pre-determined number of points, reward her.

1.261 Imitates actions in the order told

Strand: 1-9   **Age:** 60-72m 5.0-6.0y

Definition

When given not less than three verbal directions, the child is able to do the following: listen to the directions, recall the commands when requested, and perform the actions in the correct sequence. At the beginning, the child will be expected to perform the actions immediately after being instructed (short term sequential memory). Gradually the child will be asked to perform the tasks after a delay (long term sequential memory). The first sequential actions presented to the child should be related (stand up, turn around, sit down). As the child becomes more astute in responding, the actions need to become less related (The girl puts on her coat. The girl went to the door. The girl picked up a book.)

Instructional Materials

Drawing paper, pencil and crayons for the child.

Instructional Activities

1. Give the child a sheet of drawing paper.
2. Mention to the child that she needs to listen carefully because you are going to give her some directions. Explain that she is not to start drawing a picture, according to the directions given, until you give her a pencil and a set of crayons.
3. Provide the child a set of directions that require drawing a picture. Example: Draw a house. Put a door in the house. Put two windows in the house. Draw a chimney on the roof. Color the house red. Color the door yellow.
4. If the child has difficulty with the number of directions, repeat them in groups of three. Example: Draw a house. Put a door on the house. Put two windows on the house (stop for the child to respond). Draw a chimney on the roof. Color the house red. Color the door yellow (stop for the child to respond).

1.262 Scans letters of word left to right

Strand: 1-9 **Age:** 60-72m 5.0-6.0y

Definition

Beginning reading not only involves the differentiation of letters but the patterning of letters within a word. This patterning of letters requires left-to-right movement. The letters of cat are written in this left-to-right pattern, and cannot be written in any other order. The first step to establishing the concept of left-to-right sequencing is to make sure that the child comprehends that letters in a word need to be in a particular order.

Instructional Materials

Prepare a sheet of paper that has at least six rows across the paper. There needs to be a separate box at the beginning of each of the rows. Example: Row One: in the box write XXO; after the box, write OXO, XXO, OOX, OOO, XXO, XXO. Row Two: in the box write aba; after the box, write baa, aba, aba, bba, aba, abb. Row Three: in the box write dccd; after the box, write ccdd, dccd, dccd, dccd, ccdc, dccd. Row Four: in the box write "ten;" after the box, write "ten," "tan," "net," "not," "ten," "tin." Row Five: in the box write "made;" after the box, write "make," "made," "made," "dame," "name," "made." Row Six: in the box write "kitten;" after the box, write "kitten," "little," "kitten," "mitten," "kitten," "kettle." Place an arrow aimed at the beginning of each row to indicate where the child is to start. Place a green dot under the first letter in each box and a red dot under the last letter in each box. A pencil or marker.

Instructional Activities

1. Provide the child with the prepared sheet of paper and a pencil or marker.
2. Tell the child to look at the arrow at the beginning of each row, and explain that the arrow is a signal to show him where to start.
3. Tell the child to look at the green dot, and explain that the dot tells him which letter to start looking at and the red dot tells him were to stop.
4. Inform the child to draw a circle around every XXO in the first row moving from the left to the right.
5. Repeat with the other rows, asking the child to circle/identify the different letters or words that match with the letters/words in the first box.
6. Make sure the child moves from left to right.
7. Remember, the child does not need to read the letters or the words.

1.263 Identifies missing or incongruous element of picture

Strand: 1-4D **Age:** 60-72m 5.0-6.0y

Definition

Being able to locate those things that are not correct, proper, or logical, or things that are missing, is related to developing the ability to understand that everything that is seen is not always the way it is.

Instructional Materials

Sheets of light weight, 5 x 5-inch paper (tracing paper or tissue type), drawing paper, crayons and markers.

Instructional Activities

1. Draw a nose, an eye, an ear, a mouth and an eyebrow on separate 5 x 5-inch sheets of paper.
2. Draw five faces with each one missing a part, such as a nose, eye, ear, mouth or eyebrow.
3. Invite the children to come to the table.
4. Discuss with the children the parts of faces. Point to and identify each facial part. During the discussion, bring out the fact that people would look strange without a nose, with a mouth above our eyes, etc. It is important that this discussion period be humorous.
5. Explain to the children that they are going to see some funny faces.
6. Spread out the nose, eye, ear, mouth and eyebrow pictures in full view of the children.
7. Place the face pictures face-down in pile.
8. Have the children take a sheet from the top of the pile. After they have looked at it and decided what part is missing, tell them to place their pictures under the part that is missing from their face.
9. If a child makes a mistake, return that picture to bottom of the pile.
10. After the children have completed matching the faces with the missing parts, provide them with a sheet of drawing paper and tell them to draw a face with something missing or something in the wrong place.
11. Encourage the children to tell about their completed funny faces.

1.264   Makes judgments in time and speed

Strand: 1-7B   **Age:** 60-72m 5.0-6.0y

Definition

The child will make a determination as to which of three time periods is the longest/shortest and will determine which of three objects move the fastest/slowest. The child will indicate the different times and speed by physical involvement, visual conclusions and conceptual decisions.

Instructional Materials

Ribbons to be tied into bows and placed on a strip of material, a rope, or strips of paper to make a paper chain. A calendar. Glue or stapler to connect the strips of paper.

Instructional Activities

1. Select a special day, such as a birthday, the end of the week, the day of a field trip, the day of a special program, etc. On the table place a calendar and the ribbons, rope, or paper to make a chain.
2. Show the children the calendar and talk about the special day that is coming up. Discuss what is going to happen, who will be there, what there will be to see, etc. Hold up the calendar and point to the square that represents that special day. Ask the children to judge the amount of time before the special event. Use comparison concepts, (e.g., it is a shorter time than the first day of _____ or it is a longer time than _____).
3. Following the discussion, mark that special day and ask the children to help count the days until then.
4. Talk about how difficult it is to wait for special things to happen. Include in the group discussion things that one can do to make the time go faster or slower.
5. After the days have been counted, select the ribbons, rope, or paper chain and explain to the children that together you are going to make a different kind of calendar. Then to represent the number of days, tie the ribbon into bows, tie knots in the rope, or make a paper loop for each day.
6. Demonstrate the longest part of the visual calendar and point to the bow/knot/loop which indicate the shortest time to wait till the marked day.
7. Each day, ask a child to undo one of the parts (untie a bow, straighten a knot, or cut a loop) and count the remaining "parts" (days).

Review the terminology long time/short time and fast/slow.

1.265   Finds the incongruous/out-of-place/misdirected object

Strand: 1-7C   **Age:** 60-72m 5.0-6.0y

Definition

The child will first locate a part of a picture that is missing, such as a man's ear; then the child will find a part of an illustration that shows a misplacement; an example would be rabbit ears on a cat; finally the child will locate the part of a scene that is not relative, like a child dressed in swimming trunks with a winter cap and scarf on, about to jump into a swimming pool.

Instructional Materials

A set of "mixed-up" pictures. These may be secured from such sources as magazines, catalogs, children's books, commercial sources, or by illustrating your own. A collection of single item cut-outs such as animals, toys, foods, items of clothing, furniture, ears, feet, trees, flowers, outdoor play equipment, etc. Mounting materials, crayons, and glue/paste.

Instructional Activities

1. Ask the child to join you in a small group. On another table place the collection of single item cut-outs, the mounting material, the crayons, and the glue.
2. Tell the child that everything he sees and hears is not always the way it is. Ask if he has ever seen something that wasn't really the way it should be.
3. Tell the child a story about something that you saw or heard that wasn't the way it was suppose to have been. Encourage the child to tell about any funny things he has seen or heard.
4. Assist the child in finding the humor in the stories. Explain to the child that you have some pictures which show some pretty funny, mixed-up things, and that you are going to show them one at a time.
5. After he has looked at the pictures, ask him to tell you what is wrong and why.
6. When the set of pictures has been shown and discussed, tell the child he is to go to the area which has the cut-outs, mounting material, crayons, and glue.
7. Tell the child that he is to use the cut-items to make his own mix-up picture.

8. After he has selected the items he needs to make a funny picture, show him how to glue it on the mounting material and how to use the crayons to add to his picture.
9. After the child has completed his task ask him to share with the others and tell what is incongruent.

1.266 (Removed, see page xii)

1.267 Improvises body movements to follow tempo/rhythm

Strand: 2-7 **Age:** 60-72m 5.0-6.0y

Definition

The child will do creative movements to music. He does some rhythmical movements without direction. The musical selection prompts creative dance and creative expression--its tempo may be fast or slow. The child may also move to a percussion instrument such as a drum, a tambourine, shakers, sticks, or blocks.

Instructional Materials

A recorded selection in which the music changes tempo. Examples: *To a Water Lily* (MacDowell), *Bourree* (Telemann), *Aragonaise* (Massenet), *Dance of the Little Swans* (Tchaikovsky), *Clowns* (Kabalevsky). Pictures of familiar objects. Examples: a cat crawling up a tree, wind blowing grass, snowflakes fluttering to the ground, a horse galloping, splashing water, or a ball bouncing.

Instructional Activities

1. Ask the child to stand in a large, open area.
2. Show the child a picture. Discuss how the object in the picture would be moving. Tell him to move like the object in the picture.
3. Reinforce him for his interpretation.
4. Show him another picture. Discuss how the object in the picture would be moving. Tell him to move like the object in the picture.
5. Reinforce him for his interpretation.
6. Continue with at least two more pictures.
7. Review the four different movements.
8. Play the recorded music and encourage him to move to the tempo.
9. Play the music again and ask him not only to move to the tempo but also to move like one of the objects in the pictures.
10. Repeat with other pictures, using other music.

1.268 Prints simple words, copying models

Strand: 1-11 **Age:** 62-70m 5.2-5.10y

Definition

The child will copy at least three simple words (cat, bee, hot, if) when presented with a model. The child will write the words with a writing tool that is comfortable and easy to control. The words should be readable, but each letter need not be the correct angle, spaced consistently, constructed in sequence, or totally aligned on a line.

Instructional Materials

A separate sample page for each letter of the alphabet in manuscript writing. Include the letter on the first line (c), words beginning with that letter on the second line (cat, car, come), and a simple sentence using that letter more than once on the third line (Come here cat.).

Instructional Activities

1. Invite the child to the writing table and provide her with the prepared sample pages.
2. Tell the child to copy the letter, words, and sentences onto her own piece of paper.
3. Once the child becomes proficient with the first sample sheets, give her additional sheets with different letters, words, and sentences.
4. Extend this activity by providing the child a page of consonant-vowel-consonant words that rhyme and ask her to copy the words onto another sheet of paper.

1.269 Colors within heavy outlines/within faint outlines

Strand: 1-11 **Age:** 62-70m 5.2-5.10y

Definition

The child will color the inside of a circle that is outlined with a thick dark black line. The circle should be 4 inches in diameter. The child will color inside the line. The child will color the inside of a circle that is outlined with a thin faint black line. The circle should be 4 inches in diameter. The child will color inside the line.

Instructional Materials

Some simple pictures in a coloring book of people wearing different types of clothing. Outline only the articles of clothing with a thick marking pen. Begin with only one or two items. A set of crayons.

Instructional Activities

1. Place the outline picture and crayons on a table.
2. Ask the child to identify the specific article of clothing. For example, say, "Touch the hat," or "Where is the hat?"
3. Give the child the crayons and instruct him to color the article of clothing that has the thick marking outline.
4. Praise the child for coloring only that article of clothing.
5. Correct immediately any gross errors by allowing the child to move to another picture while you guide his hand.
6. Repeat using other pictures of articles of clothing.
7. Use a different color for each item.
8. Make copies of the pictures and allow the child to color independently.
9. Vary the activity by using story characters.

1.270   Prints own first name without a model

Strand: 1-11   **Age:** 62-72m 5.2-6.0y

Definition

The child will print his first name without looking at a model or without being told the letters to write, and without any verbal assistance, physical help, or tactile experiences.

Instructional Materials

Prepare a sheet of paper with the child's first name on it. Under the complete printed first name (Mark), leave a blank for the first letter (___ark) of his name and then print the rest of the letters. Under the "one blank" name, leave two blanks (___ ___rk) for the first two letters of his name and print the rest of the letters. Continue as above until there are all blanks. The letters should be in manuscript form.

Instructional Activities

1. Place the sheet of paper on the table in front of the child. Point to each letter of the child's name and ask him to identify the letter name.
2. Give the child a crayon or marking pen to trace over ALL the letters of his name.
3. Point to the child's name that is minus the first letter. Ask the child to write ALL the letters of his name filling in the blank to complete his name.
4. Initially provide immediate direction and correction.

5. Present the other names with 2, 3 or more letters shown by blank lines.
6. Require the child to trace ALL of the letters, beginning from left to right.
7. After the child has filled in all the blanks, remove the paper, give him a new sheet of paper.
8. Say, "Write your first name."

1.271   (Removed, see page xii)

1.272   Identifies an object that does not belong to a group based on one or more characteristics

Strand: 1-7C   **Age:** 62-72m 5.2-6.0y

Definition

The child will select an item that is different from a group, first based on one criteria and then on two. The characteristics may include size, shape, color, function, etc. or any combination of these.

Instructional Materials

Three sheets of white poster board, markers or crayons, tape, three cut-outs per child, (these cut-outs should relate to a theme. Example: if the poster board picture is a farm scene, then two cut-outs should represent something that you would find on a farm, and one cut-out that does not have "farm-like" characteristics).

Instructional Activities

1. Prepare three theme scenes on the poster board, prior to the activity, on which you can draw the scene when the children are grouped around.
2. Place the cut-outs for each scene in an envelope labeled with the theme name.
3. Group the children around one of the poster board pictures. Discuss the picture. Ask questions that will require answers that tell about things you would find in the scene, what those things do, how they are alike, etc.
4. After the discussion, give each child one of the cut-outs. Ask them to look at the cut-out carefully, and when they are called on they are to come and tape their cut-out to the picture.
5. They must also tell what their cut-out is, and how it fits into the poster board theme.
6. As the children place their items, encourage them to tell how their particular one is alike or different than others.

7. Include the child that has the cut-out that does not belong. When it is his turn, request that he tell why he is not placing his item, and why it is different.
8. Continue the above sequence with the other poster board theme and cut-outs.

1.273 Finds group having more, less, or the same number of objects as a given group up to 10
Strand: 1-10 **Age:** 64-70m 5.4-5.10y

Definition
Use objects such as blocks or shapes. Make 4 groups; two groups of two objects, one group of one object, and one group of 5 objects. The example group is one of the two object groups and the other 3 groups are control groups. When asked, the child points to the group having more objects in it than the example group. Repeat using less objects and using same amount of objects. Repeat the requests of more, same and less using different numbers in the groups. The control group can change with each example group.

Instructional Materials
A piece of tagboard or poster board that has been divided into 16 squares. Write the numbers 1 - 16 randomly in the corner of each square. Draw shapes in each square that represent a different amount than the number written in the corner. Example: One square has the number 2 in the corner and has three circles drawn in that square. Draw fewer shapes than the number written in eight top squares. Draw more shapes than the number written in the eight bottom squares. Markers.

Instructional Activities
1. Place the game board on a working surface next to the child. Tell the child that some boxes have too many shapes and that some don't have enough.
2. Ask the child to cross out or add shapes with the marker to make the shapes and the number in the square the same.
3. Vary by using stickers instead of shapes or stamps rather than shapes.
4. To modify this activity, take turns with the child equalizing the number and objects. If a child does not mark out or add the correct number of shapes, a turn is lost.

1.274 Reads hour and half-hour time
Strand: 1-13 **Age:** 64-72m 5.4-6.0y

Definition
The child will identify the hour and half-hours on a conventional clock (hour and minute hands). The child will specify the hour and half-hours by reading the clock, relating the hour or half-hour by activities or by setting a conventional clock to the hour or half-hour requested.

Instructional Materials
Develop a series of clock face drawings representing various hours and half hours. These drawings can be placed on index cards. (There are commercially available stamps that show clock faces and all that is needed is to put in the times.)

Instructional Activities
1. Give the child a set of clock face cards showing hours and half-hours.
2. Ask the child to lay the clock cards out face side up.
3. Explain that you are going to ask her to find the clock that says 11:00, 9:30, etc.
4. When she locates the clock that represents the time stated she is to hold it up.
5. Continue until all times have been identified.
6. To enhance this activity, you may wish to time the child to see if she can increase her speed of recognition.

1.275 Matches time with daily activities
Strand: 1-13 **Age:** 64-72m 5.4-6.0y

Definition
When an activity is stated to the child, he will say, point to, or set a clock to the time that the activity takes place. Example: "What time do you go to bed?" The child will say 9:00, point to a written 9:00 or set a clock to show 9:00.

Instructional Materials
A cardboard clock.

Instructional Activities
1. Give the child the cardboard clock.
2. Tell the child that you are going to name various daily activities, such as lunch time, story time, play time, TV time, etc., and that when he hears one of these activities, he is to move the hands on his clock to show the time when the activity happens.
3. Say, "Show me the time we have lunch."

4. After the child has moved the hands on the clock to show lunch time, say, "We have lunch at _____." Encourage the child to say the time.
5. As the child becomes more proficient in matching time with activities, include the writing of the sentence ("We have lunch at 12:00").
6. Continue with other daily activities.

1.276   Adds 1's and 2's in a story format

Strand: 1-10   **Age:** 64-72m 5.4-6.0y

Definition

The child will solve word problems involving adding 1's and 2's when no unnecessary information is given. The child will state or demonstrate the story problem answers.

Instructional Materials

Two small paper bags; one bag has the name "Cathy" written on it and the other bag has "Bob" written on it. Five suckers.
Create a simple story about Cathy and Bob's suckers. Example: Cathy and Bob each had a sack. Cathy had two suckers in her sack. Bob had three suckers in his sack. How many suckers did Cathy and Bob have together?

Instructional Activities

1. Place the two bags on a table in front of the child.
2. Tell the addition story problem to the child. "Cathy and Bob each had a paper sack (point to the respective sack as you say this sentence). Cathy had two suckers in her sack (open Cathy's sack and take out the two suckers, laying them on the table in front of the sack). Bob had three suckers in his sack (open Bob's sack and take out the three suckers, laying them on the table in front of Bob's sack). How many suckers did Cathy and Bob have together?"
3. Allow the child time to respond.
4. Replace the suckers in the respective sacks and draw two suckers on the outside of Cathy's sack and three suckers on the outside of Bob's sack.
5. Repeat the story problem.
6. Turn the sacks around and write 2 on the outside of Cathy's sack and 3 on the outside of Bob's sack.
7. Repeat the story problem.

1.277   Subtracts 1's in a story format

Strand: 1-10   **Age:** 64-72m 5.4-6.0y

Definition

The child will solve word problems involving subtracting 1's when no unnecessary information is given. The child will state or demonstrate the story problem answers.

Instructional Materials

Collect 12 items, such as pencils or blocks. Develop a set of 9 number cards. Card one has number 1 on it, card two has number 2 on it, etc. Develop a card with a minus sign and a card with an equal sign.

Instructional Activities

1. Place six of the items on a table and ask the child to join you.
2. Give the child the six items.
3. Ask the child to count the items.
4. Encourage the child to have a dialogue about the items. Example: "I have six pencils, etc."
5. Tell the child to give you one pencil.
6. Encourage a dialogue. Example: "I took one pencil from you. How many pencils do you have left?"
7. Ask the child to count the pencils that he has left.
8. Verbalize the problem. "You had six pencils, I took one away and that left you with five pencils.
9. Using the number cards, place the number six and six pencils on the table. Place the minus sign beside the 6 pencils, and place the number 1 card and 1 pencil on the table. Put the equal sign and finally the number card 5 and five pencils on the table.
10. As you point to the elements on the table, restate the problem.
11. Continue by using different objects and different story problems (6 - 2 = 4, etc.)

1.278   Reads numerals on clock face and associates time with routine activity

Strand: 1-13   **Age:** 64-72m 5.4-6.0y

Definition

The child will read the numerals on a clock face at least 5 inches in diameter. Numerals should be in Arabic. A working clock or a poster board clock face may be used. The child should be able to tell what time it is (i.e., time for lunch, time for play, time for bed, etc.) The child should read the clock at least three different times (hours and half-hours only).

Instructional Materials

Provide the child with a poster board or paper plate clock with movable hands.

Instructional Activities

1. Select an area of the room that has ample space for dramatic play.
2. Pantomime a day at home and at school, such as getting up at 7:00, eating breakfast at 7:30, going to school at 8:00, etc.
3. Ask the child to move the hands on the clock to the correct time for the activity (hour or a half-hour).
4. Act out daily activities, such as brushing teeth, catching the bus, or eating dinner.
5. Repeat, allowing the child to determine the schedule and to pantomime the activity.

1.279 Makes judgments in weight without being confused by the object's size

Strand: 1-7B **Age:** 64-78m 5.4-6.6y

Definition

The child will determine which of four objects, varying in size, is heaviest by lifting each one to feel its weight versus focusing on its size.

Instructional Materials

A number of items of similar shape and size that vary in weight: a Styrofoam ball and a baseball, a wooden block and a sponge cut the same size as the block, an opaque bag of cotton and an opaque bag of dirt, a sock stuffed with plastic packing filler and a sock stuffed with rocks. A scale for weighing objects.

Instructional Activities

1. Place the like items before the child and have the scale available. Tell him that the pairs of items on the table look alike in size, length and shape, but that there is something very different about each pair; when you pick them up one is much heavier than then the other.
2. Hold up the opaque bag of cotton and the opaque bag of dirt.
3. Ask the child which one he thinks is the heaviest. Let the child guess and then give the bags to him to see if he was right.
4. Guesses can be confirmed by placing the object on the scale.
5. Continue with the other pairs of objects.

1.280 Attends to task without supervision for 15 minutes

Strand: 1-8 **Age:** 64-78m 5.4-6.6y

Definition

The child will stay on task without any verbal or nonverbal prompting or any reinforcement for 15 minutes. The activity that the child is asked to do within the 15 minute span should be on her leisure level and something that she is motivated to do, with a limited amount of distractions.

Instructional Materials

Activities that the child will enjoy and is capable of doing independently. A timer. A reward that is motivating for the child (free time, tokens, points, a party, etc.)

Instructional Activities

1. Invite the child to visit the table and select an activity she would like to do for 15 minutes.
2. Assist the child in her selection, making sure that it is within her capabilities and that it is one she will enjoy and feel good about completing.
3. Tell the child she will receive a special treat (free time, points, a token, a snack party, etc.) if she can work independently on the task for 15 minutes.
4. Have the child start the task, and set the timer for 15 minutes.
5. Reward the child for on-task behavior.
6. If appropriate reward the child for accuracy.
7. Discuss with the child how her attention span might change if the task was not quite as enjoyable.
8. Challenge the child to select an activity that isn't as enjoyable or perhaps more difficult.
9. Set the timer for 15 minutes.
10. After the 15 minutes, discuss with the child how her attention span changed because the task was different.

1.281 Compares items by appearance

Strand: 1-7C **Age:** 65-72m 5.5-6.0y

Definition

The child will perceive significant differences and likenesses in the appearance of objects. It is important to avoid those visual discrimination tasks that require the child to seek minute details. The comparisons should be based on such visual appearances as size, color, designs, parts, etc.

Instructional Materials

A collection of paper with various designs, such as wallpaper books or gift wrap paper. A cardboard pattern for an item, like gloves or socks. The patterns should be of different sizes.

Instructional Activities

1. Using the cardboard pattern, cut out two items making sure they are the same paper design.
2. Use the pattern and the design paper to make ten pairs. Place the cut-out pairs in a box.
3. Gather the children at the table and explain to them that you have a box with some paper socks/gloves in it.
4. Explain that there are two gloves/socks that are just alike but they are all mixed up in the box.
5. Discuss what mixed up means and why it is important that they should be put in pairs.
6. Encourage the children to find the two that look alike to make a pair.
7. Place the box on the table and take out two items that do not match. Ask the children if they are a match, and why not.
8. Continue drawing items from the box and when a child identifies a match, he is to place the pair in front of him. He is also to tell why they are a match (e.g., "They have the same flowers on them", "They are the same color", "They are the same size", and "They have blue stripes on them.")
9. Keep drawing from the box until all the matches have been made and discussed.
10. The child with the most like pairs is the winner.

1.282 Compares items by category and function

Strand: 1-7C **Age:** 65-72m 5.5-6.0y

Definition

The child will compare at least two objects from different classes. The selection of the classes should be determined by the entry level of the children and the experiential background. The following are suggested categorical classifications: things that move versus objects that are stationary, clothing that keeps us warm versus clothes we wear for cooler weather, animals that live on a farm versus those that live in zoos, items that are used in the kitchen versus tools that are used to build things.

Instructional Materials

Pre-cut farm animals. Pre-cut animals that live in a zoo. Pre-cut animals that are typically pets. String or yarn. Coat hangers or dowels. Glue and a stapler.

Instructional Activities

1. Cut the string or yarn into different lengths and tie the pieces to three dowels or to the straight bar of three coat-hangers.
2. Place all the pre-cut animals in a box or basket.
3. Invite the children to sit around a table. Explain to the children that you have a box of cut-out animals, and that some of the animals live on a farm, some live in a zoo and some live in houses/yards because they are pets.
4. Explain that animals do different things, such as some work for us, some play with us, and some live in places we can visit in order to learn more about animals from all over the world.
5. Discuss how the three categories of animals are alike and how they are different. Encourage the children to enter into the comparison discussion.
6. Divide the children into three groups. One group is responsible for attaching the farm animals to the dowels/coat-hanger, another group has the job of making the zoo animal mobile, and the other group is in charge of connecting the animals that are our pets.
7. Demonstrate how the children are to attach the cut-outs, using glue or staples.
8. Ask a child to pick an animal cut-out from the box. The group is to identify the cut-out and name which category it belongs to.
9. The group that has been given that classification is to place the animal on the end of one of the strings.
10. After all the animals have been drawn from the box, identified and attached, hang the mobiles and continue a discussion on how they are different and how they are similar.
11. Modify this activity by using different subjects and categorical references.

1.283 Groups objects by two analogies

Strand: 1-7C **Age:** 65-78m 5.5-6.6y

Definition

The child will be able to identify likeness in things even though the objects are totally different. The child will determine the like relationships by using different criteria. An example: A mug and a glass are alike because a person can drink from them. A sweater and a stocking cap are alike because they keep us warm. An apple and a radish are alike because they are both red, plus you can eat them.

Instructional Materials

A collection of various materials such as: pencils, rocks, spoons, doll clothes, balls, old jewelry, paper clips, blocks, chips, pieces of cloth, etc.
(A junk type drawer is an excellent source for this collection)
A collection of single picture items.

Instructional Activities

1. Place the collection of materials in a shallow box, and place the collection of pictures face up on the table near the box.
2. Invite the children to sit around the table where the items and pictures are located.
3. Ask each child to select one item either from the box or from the picture cards.
4. Have the children take turns telling what their object is, what it looks like, what color it is, what it is used for, and any other facts that are meaningful.
5. After each child has had a turn describing their selected object, ask them to find another object that goes with the first one selected.
6. Provide time for the children to select.
7. When everyone has selected, ask each child to tell what he chose and why the two things go together.
8. Let the children determine their own criteria for selection, rather than telling them to find something small or green.
9. Provide prompting as needed, e.g., hold up a short red crayon and a long green pencil. Then say "This crayon is short and red." "This pencil is _____ and _____" "This crayon is used to color pictures." "This pencil is used to_____ ".
10. Complete the comparisons if a child does not respond.
11. Depending on the number of items, continue selecting "go-to-gethers", requesting that the criteria for matching be based on one or two attributes of the items.
12. Present different objects each time the activity is conducted, so that the children don't memorize combinations.

1.284   Determines realistically when task is done

Strand: 1-8   **Age:** 65-78m 5.5-6.6y

Definition

When given just one task to do, the child will decide when the task is completed. Examples: all the questions answered, colored all of the picture, reached the end of the book, put the last piece of a puzzle in, matched the peg-board design, etc. When given one task to do, the child will decide if the completed task is done correctly and is her best quality work.

Instructional Materials

A sheet of paper that the child will be able to complete easily, e.g., matching, doing a dot-to-dot, doing a maze, finding the items that are alike/different, completing a drawing, filling in what is missing, etc.

Instructional Activities

1. Ask the child to come to the worktable. Discuss what it means to finish an assignment, and include in the discussion the two parts of activity completion: doing all the tasks and doing them well (quality).
2. Have the child begin the task, and remind her to tell you when she is half way done (this may need to be marked for her), and when she feels she is completely done.
3. When the child has informed you that she is done, check for quality and completion in her work. Review the finished product with her.
4. Identify activities around the room the child can do, and discuss how long each might take.
5. Have the child select one of these activities.
6. Have her start the task and let you know when she is done.
7. Praise her for completing the entire job, and for doing the best she can.

1.285   Groups objects by at least two analogies

Strand: 1-4D   **Age:** 65-78m 5.5-6.6y

Definition

The child is expected to place objects in groups based on the objects being alike in two or more ways. The objects could be very dissimilar, but could be alike in function or position. Example: oranges and radishes are both round and are both edible.

Instructional Materials

A group of objects that can be sorted by two analogies, such as a pencil and a marker, two small toys that move (a toy with wheels and a toy that moves when activated), a hair brush and a toothbrush, a mitten and a glove, a marshmallow and a cube of sugar, etc.

Instructional Activities

1. Place the objects on the table in front of the children. Point to each object and name it, but do not discuss any of the characteristics.
2. Tell the children that they are going to play a Funny Matching Game.
3. Tell them that the reason this matching game is different is because the items are alike in funny ways. Select one object, name it, and ask the children to describe the object you are holding. If the children do not include in the description how the object is used and to which class the object belongs to, elicit those responses by asking questions.
4. After the object has been discussed, ask the children to look at the other items on the table, and find one that goes with the first object.
5. Continue the directive approach as above, with another object.
6. When the children begin to go beyond an item's appearance and start naming its function, class, or position, modify your approach by holding up one of the objects and asking the children to find one that would go with it.
7. After the match has been made request that they defend their selection.
8. This activity can be changed by using different objects, or substituting pictures.

1.286   Reads simple 3-letter words paired with pictures

Strand: 1-9 **Age:** 66-72m 5.6-6.0y

Definition

The ability to match and read simple words is one of the first skills in learning to read. This beginning level of word recognition closely follows the child's developmental stage of recognizing a particular word form as being the same each time she sees it, and being able to name two words that sound alike after hearing a series of words. It is desirable that the child's first reading experience with words be associated with pictures. The initial pictures recommended are those that the child is familiar with,

and the initial words should be of a consonant-vowel-consonant (CVC) pattern (cat, dog, man, cup, etc.) In presenting the word/picture models to the child, it is important to have only one picture and one word on the material.

Instructional Materials

Develop a set of domino-like cards (6 x 2 inches) and select eight pictures/words to be used (cat, boy, pin, box, pig, can, rug, leg). In the middle of each card make a line, dividing the card in half (3 inches) so that it looks like a domino. On one end place the word "cat," on the other end glue or draw a picture of a cat. Continue with the other picture/words, making a double for each picture/word plus all the combinations (word cat, picture of a pig). For eight picture/words, there will be 36 dominoes.

Instructional Activities

1. Seat the child at a table. Select one domino card for each of the eight picture/words.
2. Show the child one domino card (cat) and ask her to name the picture and read the word.
3. Correct the child if she makes an error.
4. Continue with the rest of the words.
5. Place all the domino cards in a deck, face down on the table.
6. Draw five domino cards from the deck. Ask the child to draw five domino cards from the deck.
7. Leave the rest of the domino cards face down.
8. Ask the child to place one of her domino cards on the table, saying the word and naming the picture after the domino card has been played.
9. From your hand, match the word or the picture, saying the word and naming the picture.
10. Anytime that a player cannot read the word or name the picture, she loses her turn.
11. Anytime the domino player doesn't have a match, she draws two cards from the deck.
12. Continue until one player uses all of her dominoes.

1.287   Blends letter sounds to say the word as a unit

Strand: 1-9 **Age:** 66-72m 5.6-6.0y

Definition

As soon as the child has learned some of the consonant sounds and the short sounds of two vowels (preferably short a and short i), he needs to receive instruction on how to blend these sounds into meaningful words. The blending must be done smoothly to prevent mispronunciation of words and distortions. It is often helpful to begin with words composed of nasal consonants with a short "a" so there are no sound pauses between the letters (man, nap, map, mat, etc.) Once the child is able to sound blend a few words (man), consideration should be given to initial consonant substitution and the forming of other words by sound blending (pan, fan, ran).

Instructional Materials

Select at least ten words to be used for a game of Word Puzzles. Examples: mat, man, cup, jug, bag, etc. Draw a picture illustrating each word on a 5 x 8-inch card or cut and glue pictures from magazines. Write the name of the picture at the top of the card, with each letter evenly spaced. Cut vertically down the entire card between the letters. If you have three letters in the word there should be three pieces to the puzzle.

Instructional Activities

1. Mix up the pieces of the Word Puzzle and give to the child.
2. Tell the child to put the puzzle together saying the letter sound as he goes.
3. Ask him to sound blend the whole word when the puzzle is complete.
4. Increase the difficulty by giving the child pieces of several puzzles that have been mixed up and see if he can correctly assemble them.
5. Make sure the child says the whole word when the mixed up puzzles are completed.

1.288   Fills in a word when read a passage with words missing

Strand: 1-9   **Age:** 66-72m 5.6-6.0y

Definition

The child is expected to use the meaning of words, phrases or sentences that she hears to fill in any missing word(s). Learning to use context clues to determine the unknown word should begin with an oral presentation with a visual cue to accompany it. This should be followed by showing the child a printed phrase or sentence; read the selection and provide a picture stimulus. Gradually, the picture needs to be phased out and the child's response based on the word that would fit in because of the meaning of the other words.

Instructional Materials

Write a four or five sentence story with a word in each sentence left out.
Example:
A Boy and his Friend
The boy's name is_____.
He has a little brown_____.
The_____likes to get wet in the_____.
They like to swim and_____.
They are very _____.
Drawing paper and crayons. Chart paper and a marker.

Instructional Activities

1. Invite the child to come to the work area. Have the drawing paper, chart paper, crayons and marker available.
2. Explain to the child that you are going to read her a story, but that some of the words are missing from the story.
3. Tell her that she needs to fill in the missing words.
4. Read the story and pause before the missing word, allowing the child time to complete the sentence.
5. Write the story on chart paper, but do not fill in the missing words.
6. Read the story again, pointing to the words as you read, and pause to allow the child time to complete the sentence.
7. After the story has been read, ask the child to draw a picture of the word that belongs in the missing blanks (this does not include the first sentence; a name needs to be placed in that blank). Example: He has a little brown _____ (picture of a brown dog).
8. Place the drawn pictures on the chart paper.
9. Reread the story using the pictures as the word clue.
10. Invite the child to read the story, or read along with you.
11. To extend this activity, replace the pictures with the correct word.
12. Read the story using the words, but always have the picture available as a resource.

1.289   Reads simple phrases/sentences

Strand: 1-9   **Age:** 66-72m 5.6-6.0y

Definition

The child will read a fictional story that he has not been exposed to before. The story should have less than 60 words. The child is allowed to read the story orally or silently. After not more than two readings, the child will retell the story.

Instructional Materials

Select a story of less than 60 words that the child has not read before. Paper dolls or puppets that represent the characters in the story.

Instructional Activities

1. Provide the child with the story. Ask the child to read the story, either silently or orally. Provide him with assistance if he encounters an unknown word.
2. After the child has finished the story, ask him questions that will set the stage for a dramatization. Example: "Who was the story about?" "How many people were in the story?" "What did they do?" "Where did the story take place?" etc.
3. Show the child the paper dolls/puppets that represent the characters in the story.
4. Tell him to match the dolls/puppets with the characters in the story. Ask him to describe the location and how it fit into the story.
5. Ask him to retell the story, using the dolls and describing the scene.
6. Allow the child to refer to the story or have a practice rehearsal.
7. Act as the audience during the presentation and reward the performance.

1.290 Identifies what number comes before and after a given number, or between 2 numbers

Strand: 1-10 **Age:** 66-78m 5.6-6.6y

Definition

The child will be presented with three numbers in sequence. The middle number will be the example number and the child will pick the number that comes before. The middle number will be the example number and the child will pick the number that comes after. When shown two example numbers, the child will pick the number that goes between.

Instructional Materials

On a sheet of paper write each number from 1 to 10 with a blank line before and after each number, for example _1_ _2_ _3_. Make poster board numerals (0 - 10). The numerals should be at least 2 inches high. The numbers can be either cut out or written on cards.

Instructional Activities

1. Give each child a copy of the sheet and a pencil.
2. Tell the child to look at each number, to say what comes before it, and to write the number in the blank, or place a number card in the correct position.
3. Tell the child to look at each number, to say what comes after it, and to write it in the blank, or place a number card in the correct position.
4. Assist when needed.
5. Check each child's paper when they have finished.

1.291 Makes judgments in distance

Strand: 1-7B **Age:** 66-78m 5.6-6.6y

Definition

The children will determine which of a given number of objects is closest to, or farthest from, them. As the child experiences judgments in distances relative to themselves, the skill should be transferred from one object to another.

Instructional Materials

/*\Safety Note: Provide scissors appropriate for the child. Remind the child of safety regarding scissors.
Colored construction paper, scissors, and pencils/markers.

Instructional Activities

1. Select a wall where the children can view the activity. Give each child two pieces of construction paper and tell them to draw around each of their shoes. The children may work in pairs, or take off their shoes and draw around them. After the children have outlined each of their shoes, tell them to cut out the patterns.
2. Request that the children gather around the selected wall. Tell them to watch very carefully as you place the "paper shoes" in just the right spot.
3. Demonstrate the following position by standing at a right angle to the wall with your arm outstretched to touch the wall.
4. Place your shoe patterns on the floor under your feet.
5. Ask the child to assume the identical position, to observe where his feet are, and the distance that his arms need to stretch to barely touch the wall.

6. Choose a child to place his shoe patterns on the floor where he thinks his feet should be, to allow him to just touch the wall with straight arms.
7. Instruct the child to discover if he is correct. If he did not judge accurately ask him if the patterns should be farther from or nearer to the wall.
8. Adjust the patterns and try again.
9. Allow each child to have a turn placing his paper shoes and determining if they are the correct distance.
10. Extend the activity by asking, "Where would you stand to touch your elbow to the wall?" or "Where would you stand to touch this ruler / yardstick to the wall?"

1.292   Reads numerals to 19

Strand: 1-10   **Age:** 60-66m 5.0-5.6y

Definition

The child will say a number between 0 - 19 when shown a number randomly.

Instructional Materials

On a chalkboard or on chart paper, draw a picture of a house, a pond with stepping stones (each stone with a different number 0 - 19), and a path leading from the pond to the house. Rewards (e.g., favorite food, free time, etc.)

Instructional Activities

1. Tell the children that they are going to play a game called Going to Grandmother's House.
2. Point to the pond in front of Grandmother's house.
3. Tell the children that they must cross on the stepping stones to get to Grandmother's house and that Grandmother has a surprise for them.
4. Tell the children that they must read the numbers on each stone before moving to the next stone.
5. Be sure to change the numbers often and request that the child put the numbers on the rocks.
6. Make Grandmother's surprise a favorite food, free time, or another reward.

1.293   Sings verse of a new song by rote

Strand: 2-7   **Age:** 66-78m 5.6-6.6y

Definition

The child will learn at least one verse of a new song by rote. Teaching a song by rote can be defined in two ways: (1) Teaching a song by singing one line at a time and repeating the lines as they are introduced. Note: Teaching every new song using the "line-by-line" approach may create a negative reaction because a child does not hear or learn a song as a total entity; therefore, learning a new song is fragmented and may become a dreaded process. Using the line rote approach is effective in teaching him how to pronounce the words and for putting the melody with the words; (2) Teaching a song by the whole method. This approach allows him to sing along with words or phrases that are easy to remember. The phrases become cumulative, and he learns entire songs with enthusiasm.

Instructional Materials

A song the child does not know, but one in which he can become quickly and naturally involved. The song should have a particular theme, such as farm, Western, playing, sports, or dance with words that can be dramatized. Present the song by using a prerecording or by singing it acappella.

Instructional Activities

Note: Make sure the music area you use is large enough to accommodate the children dramatizing the song. When you select new songs, consider action songs. They provide a physical involvement that supports initial learning.

1. Invite the child to join you in the music area.
2. Play the recording of the new song and act out the words in the song.
3. Sing and act out the song several times (do not necessarily use the same movements each time).
4. Tell the child to sing the song with you if he likes and to join you in acting out the lyrics.
5. Encourage him to do his own dramatization of the content while he is singing the new song.
6. At the conclusion of the activity, ask him to choose a song he wants to sing.
7. Review the new song at different times during the day.

1.294 Prints all letters of the alphabet correctly, without models

Strand: 1-11 **Age:** 68-78m 5.8-6.6y

Definition

The child will print all letters of the alphabet using lined paper and a comfortable writing tool. The letters will be both upper and lower case. The letters should be legible, positioned on the paper correctly, with correct stroke sequence and a common stroke pressure.

Instructional Materials

Twelve 2 x 2 inch squares on construction paper to make an Alphabet Mobile. Scissors, pencils or markers, a dowel, tape, and string. Sheet of paper divided into 26 squares. Rewards (i.e., stickers, playing a game, etc.)

Instructional Activities

1. Place the material on the work table.
2. Have the child cut out the squares.
3. Have the child print capital and lower case letters on each side of the squares.
4. Attach a string to the letters making sure that four cards have longer strings than the other cards.
5. Cut the dowel in half. Wrap the cut ends with tape to avoid the sharp edges.
6. Attach one long and two short strings to each half of the dowel and let the cards dangle.
7. Cross halves of the dowel over each other (to form a cross) and tape the two halves together at the center. Attach the string where the centers meet to hang from the ceiling.
8. Encourage the children to point to and say each letter.
9. Provide the child with a worksheet that has been divided into 26 squares.
10. Ask her to write a letter (upper case) of the alphabet in each square.
11. Repeat with lower case letters.
12. Ask her to repeat the alphabet aloud while crossing out the letters she has written. Let her see if she is able to cross out all 26 squares.
13. Provide her a reward if she has written each letter. Provide her with an additional reward if she can name each letter.

1.295 Prints simple words without a model

Strand: 1-11 **Age:** 68-78m 5.8-6.6y

Definition

The child will print in manuscript form at least three simple words. The words should not have more than three letters (cat, dog, run, it, to).
The words should be printed on lined paper with a pencil or similar writing tool. The words should be readable and based on a line. The strokes should be consistent and even, with appropriate spacing between letters, and the size/width of letters should be in proportion. The child will write the words on request.

Instructional Materials

Different words (not to exceed three letters) printed on ten 3 x 5 inch cards. Glue and sand.

Instructional Activities

1. Give the child the cards. Place the glue and sand on the table.
2. Tell the child to copy over each letter of the word with glue; then have him sprinkle it with sand and let it dry.
3. Give the child the words when they are dry and ask him to run his finger over each letter in the word.
4. Collect the cards and give the child paper and a pencil.
5. Tell the child to write the word, without looking at the card, as you say the word.
6. Give the child the cards again and ask him to match the words to see if he formed each letter correctly.
7. Repeat if he formed the letters incorrectly.
8. Vary by using yarn, alphabet noodles, or clay.

1.296 Plays rhythm instruments in various rhythm patterns

Strand: 2-7 **Age:** 68-78m 5.8-6.6y

Definition

The child will play an instrument that is familiar to her using a song that changes rhythmic patterns, and she will change rhythm patterns with the music.

Instructional Materials

An assortment of rhythm instruments. A recommended collection should include: (1) Wooden blocks; (2) Drum; (3) Rhythm sticks; (4) Shakers; (5) Clappers; (6) Bells. A song that involves the various rhythm instruments. The song should include the child either in singing or in moving to it while playing a rhythm instrument. Musical presentations are available from rhythm band resource materials or a familiar song can be modified.

Example:

Our Band (to the tune of *She'll Be Coming Round the Mountain*)

I'll be drumming on my drum, here I come.
I'll be drumming on my drum, here I come.
I'll be drumming on my drum, drumming on my drum,
Drumming on my drum, here I come.
I'll be shaking with my shaker, here I come.
I'll be shaking with my shaker, here I come.
I'll be shaking with my shaker, shaking with my shaker,
Shaking with my shaker, here I come.
I'll be belling with my bells, here I come.
I'll be belling with my bells, here I come.
I'll be belling with my bells, belling with my bells,
Belling with my bells, here I come.

Allow the child to contribute by making up other verses, using other instruments, or choosing another song and adapting it to rhythm instruments.

Instructional Activities

1. Place the rhythm instruments on a table, and set one of them in a predominant location.
2. Ask the child to join you at the rhythm table.
3. Introduce one instrument at a time.
4. Discuss each instrument, and allow her to handle and explore it.
5. It is important for her to hear, see, and play the instrument enough times so she can distinguish its sound and be familiar with its mechanics.
6. Introduce another instrument and repeat the steps above. This process takes time but it provides her with enough exploration time so she can use the instrument in creative ways.
7. Once she is proficient, introduce her to music that has been specially arranged to use with rhythm instruments. (This music may be prerecorded, live, or created from a familiar song.)
8. Ask her to choose an instrument.
9. Explain that you are going to play or sing a tune, and you want her to play her [wooden blocks] as if she is in a band.
10. Repeat the selection several times and allow her to change instruments.
11. If the music lends itself, ask her to play the instrument and march or play and sing along.

1.297 (Removed, see page xii)

1.298 Answers questions about a story related to the interpretation of the content
Strand: 1-9   **Age:** 60-72m 5.0-6.0y

Definition

After hearing a story, the child will be able to answer questions that relate to the interpretation of the content. Typically the questions are based on making predictions, inferences, comparisons and generalizations. A prediction type of question is one that requires the child to assimilate some details, think ahead and guess the outcome. (What do you think will happen next?) An inference type of question requires the child to use deductive reasoning.(If Jane did____what do you think Bill will do?) A comparison question requires the child to examine the things that are similar and the things that are different and draw conclusions. (At the beginning of the story Jean was not happy, what happened to change Jean's feelings?) A generalization question is one that requires the child to take bits of information and put them together to reach a decision.(Why did the lady decide to go?)

Instructional Materials

Select or write a story that is appropriate for the child and is a story that she has not heard before.

Example:

A Visit to Uncle Joe

Frank visited his Uncle Joe every summer.
Uncle Joe was a cowboy, he lived in a log cabin.
He herded cattle on a big grass field, called a high range.
Uncle Joe had two horses and two dogs.
During the first two days of his visit, Frank was concerned about the newly born calves, who did not have a place to go in bad weather.
One night, Uncle Joe took Frank out to the herd while it was blowing and raining.
Uncle Joe and Frank looked for the baby calves. They were nice and warm and protected by their mothers and the other cattle.
Frank agreed not to worry about the little calves again.

Drawing paper, pencil and crayons.

Instructional Activities

1. Ask the child to join you at the story telling area. Have drawing material close to the story telling area.

2. Begin by reading the story and discussing it. At the conclusion of the story ask the child to respond to some questions.

3. During the discussion be sure to ask questions that have no answers directly in the story (literal). The interpretive-type questions that you ask are intended to challenge the child.

4. Example: "You have just heard that Frank is going to visit his Uncle Joe and that Uncle Joe lives in a Log Cabin. What do you think the inside of Uncle Joe's log cabin looks like?"

5. Give the child a sheet of drawing paper and drawing tools. Ask her to draw what she thinks the inside of Uncle Joe's cabin looks like.

6. Allow the child time to discuss her pictures.

7. Continue the discussion of the story.

8. Ask "Can you think of something fun and interesting that Frank did after he arrived at Uncle Joe's?"

9. Give the child a sheet of drawing paper and ask her to draw something that she thinks Frank might have done at Uncle Joe's.

10. Allow the child time to discuss her pictures.

11. Continue the discussion.

12. "At the beginning Frank was worried about the baby calves. Why did he change his mind?"

13. Allow the child time to draw a picture of what Frank learned about baby calves and how they are taken care if.

14. Continue as time allows. The children will find it enjoyable to retell the story and add their own picture interpretations.

1.299 Names numbers that represent more than and less than

Strand: 1-10 **Age:** 70-78m 5.10-6.6y

Definition

When the child is presented with a number, he will say a number that is more than and less than that number. When presented with a group of objects the child will create more objects and create less objects. The child will identify the number of beginning objects, the number added that makes more and the number taken away that makes less.

Instructional Materials

Collection of buttons or similar objects, all uniform in color, shape, and size.

Instructional Activities

1. Place six buttons on the table in a random design. Invite the child to join you at the table.

2. Ask the child to look at the button design and to count the buttons.

3. Ask the child to close his eyes or to turn around.

4. Take one button away.

5. Ask the child to open his eyes and tell if there are more buttons or less buttons than before.

6. Modify the activity by adding buttons and then asking if there are less or more buttons.

7. Vary the activity by using more buttons and removing varying numbers, or sometimes leaving the same number.

8. If the child has difficulty with the task, place the buttons in a straight line rather than randomly.

1.300 Counts orally to 100

Strand: 1-10 **Age:** 70-78m 5.10-6.6y

Definition

The child will count orally from 1 - 100 when requested.

Instructional Activities

1. Ask the child to sit across from you. If dealing with more than one child, divide the children into teams of two.

2. Explain to the children that they are going to be Team Counters. Each team member will say one number, then the other team member will say the next number. For example, starting with the number one, the first member says "One", the second team member says "Two". They keep counting, alternating turns, going as high as they can, or until they reach 100.

3. Make sure the children understand the directions by practicing with the numbers one to 10. Verbally praise the children if they were successfully. If they need help, model and prompt them as needed.

4. When the team is ready, tell them "Ready, set, count."

5. Continue back and forth between teams until they reach 100.

1.301 Reads and writes numerals to 49

Strand: 1-10 **Age:** 70-78m 5.10-6.6y

Definition

Using paper and a marker, the child will write the numbers from 1 - 49. The child will say a number when shown in random order (e.g., point to 14, 26, and 9) upon request.

Instructional Materials

Divide 3 x 5-inch cards in half and write a different number on each half to make dominoes. Make duplicate numbers so sides of different cards can be matched.

Instructional Activities

1. Shuffle the cards and lay them face up in front of the child.
2. Tell him to build a road by matching up and saying the numbers on the domino cards.
3. This can be played with two or more children.
4. Ask them to take turns building the road.

1.302 Locates day of week on calendar

Strand: 1-13 **Age:** 70-78m 5.10-6.6y

Definition

The child will locate all the days of the week in correct sequence and will locate the days of the week when they are presented out of sequence.

Instructional Materials

Print one day of the week on each of seven 3 x 5-inch cards. Basket.

Instructional Activities

1. Select a child. Tell them that you are going to play a calendar game called the <u>Days of the Week</u>.
2. Tell the child that you are going to show them a card with a day of the week written on it and they are to name the day.
3. Show them the cards in random order. As they correctly identify the cards they get to place the cards in a basket.
4. Once the child has correctly identified all seven days, they are given the cards and asked to place them in order, starting with Sunday.
5. Vary the game by having two children play together. The first one to name the day of the week presented on the card gets to place the card in the basket. When they are finished with all seven cards, they work together to place the cards in order.

1.303 Uses imaginary objects during play

Strand: 1-12 **Age:** 36-42m 3.0-3.6y

Definition

The child begins to use imaginary objects during play. At first he may use one object in place of the actual object, for example he will use a banana for a telephone. He may also pretend to do something even though he does not have the props, for example he will pretend to serve and eat imaginary food.

Instructional Materials

A selection of household materials (i.e., plates, cups, spoon, etc) that can be used when playing house. A variety of dress-up clothing.

Instructional Activities

1. Invite the child to join you in the house area.
2. Suggest that you pretend to play house together. You tell the child that they are going to be the mother or father, and you are the child.
3. As you pretend to be the child, ask the mother/father for something to eat because you are very hungry.
4. If the child hesitates, tell him to pretend to make some food. If necessary, help him through the process of making and serving the pretend food.
5. Once you have been served some food, pretend to eat it. Continue the scenario by commenting of how delicious the food is while you pretend to eat it. Ask the mother or father how they made the food.
6. Encourage the pretend play by continuing down the path of pretending, whether there are props available or not.

1.304 Uses dolls or action figures to act out sequences

Strand: 1-12 **Age:** 36-42m 3.0-3.6y

Definition

The child uses dolls or action figures to create situations from real life that they act out. The situations should include multiple sequences or steps to the scenario being played out.

Instructional Materials

A variety of dolls, action figures, dollhouse, doll furniture, doll accessories, and miniature objects from everyday life.

Instructional Activities

1. Invite a small group of two or three children to join you at the dollhouse.
2. Have everyone pick out the doll or action figure they would like to be.
3. Pick a topic for the play scene, such as, "Who wants to go to the movies?"
4. Encourage the children to pretend to be their doll/action figure and respond to the question.

5. If the children hesitant, begin by having your doll/action figure say, "I want to go and I want to see *Toy Story*!"
6. Have the children act out what sequence of events they will need to go through to take their dolls/action figures to the movies.
7. After you are finished acting out your scenario, encourage the children to pick out another adventure for the dolls and action figures.

1.305 Role-plays or organizes other children using props

Strand: 1-12 **Age:** 60-72m 5.0-6.0y

Definition

While engaged in pretend play the child organizes other children to use props while they role-play some event they have previously observed or experienced. The child orchestrates the role-playing event.

Instructional Materials

Dramatic play area with dress-up clothing, a kitchen area, and props used in the kitchen.

Instructional Activities

1. Invite a small group of children to the dramatic play area.
2. Act out a sequence of events using the props, such as setting the table, pretending to prepare some food, serving the food, pretending to eat the food, and then cleaning everything up.
3. Ask one of the children to take charge of preparing a meal for the family.
4. Encourage them to have the other children dress-up for the meal.
5. Observe to see if they remember the sequence of events.
6. If necessary, verbally prompt them or show some item that will be needed in the next step to see if that helps them remember the sequence of events.
7. Suggest other events they may act out, such as: going to the doctors, preparing a cake for a birthday party, or acting out a familiar story like the *Three Little Pigs*.

1.306 Prints the numbers 1 - 10 correctly, in sequential and random order, when requested without the use of a model

Strand: 1-11 **Age:** 68-80m 5.8-6.8y

Definition

The child will print the numbers 1 – 10, in sequential and random order, when dictated by an adult without the use of models. The child will use lined paper and a comfortable writing tool. The numbers should be legible, positioned on the paper correctly, with correct stroke sequence and a common stroke pressure.

Instructional Materials

Construction paper worksheet divided into 10 squares, 2 x 2 inches, to make a NUMBER MOBILE. Scissors, pencils or markers, two dowels of equal length (approximately 10 inches), tape, and string. Rewards (i.e., stickers, playing a game, etc.)

Instructional Activities

1. Place the materials on the worktable.
2. Have the child cut out the ten 2 x 2 inch squares.
3. Have the child print numbers on the squares (1 – 10).
4. Attach a string to the numbers making sure that five cards have longer strings than the other cards.
5. Cut the dowel in half. Wrap the cut ends with tape to avoid the sharp edges.
6. Cross halves of the dowel over each other (to form a cross) and tape the two halves together at the center. Attach the string where the centers meet to hang from the ceiling.
7. Attach two or three strings with number cards taped on them to each half of the dowel and let the cards dangle.
8. Encourage the children to point to and say each number.

1.307 Locates left and right

Strand: 1-4D **Age:** 48-60m 4.0-5.0y

Definition

The child will indicate his right hand/foot upon request. The child will indicate his left hand/foot upon request.

Instructional Materials

Make Tic Tac Toe grid on the floor with tape. Prepare cards which say, "Stand in back of," "Stand to the left of," etc. Include a picture on each card to demonstrate positions.

Instructional Activities

1. Discuss the directions right, left, front and back. Start the child on one side of the grid.
2. Choose a card and read the instructions to the child.
3. Ask the child to stand in the position described on the card.
4. Continue reading the instructions from the cards.
5. Increase difficulty by having the child try to arrange himself with other children to make straight lines (i.e., three children in a row) as in *Tic Tac Toe*.

1.308 Draws diagonal lines, copying model

Strand: 1-11 **Age:** 52-60m 4.4-5.0y

Definition

The child will copy a right-to-left diagonal line from a model. Then she will copy a left-to-right diagonal line from a model.

Instructional Materials

At least 15 craft sticks 5 inches long (available at craft shops and teacher supply stores; or substitute straws, short dowel sticks, or plastic strips). Paper and pencils, chalkboard, chalk.

Instructional Activities

1. Lay the craft sticks, paper and pencils on a table.
2. On a chalkboard, draw left to right diagonal lines and then right to left diagonal lines.
3. Invite the child to make diagonal lines on the board.
4. Tell her there are sticks on the table. Give her time to experiment and play with the sticks.
5. After the exploratory time, tell her to put the sticks in a diagonal position.
6. After she has placed the sticks in a diagonal/zigzag position, ask her to place the sticks on a sheet of paper and then to trace one side of the sticks.

1.309 Locates self in relation to other objects

Strand: 1-4D **Age:** 60-78m 5.0-6.6y

Definition

When the child is asked to take a position in relationship to another object or person, he will move to that position. Examples: If he is asked to stand on

the left side of the chair, he will move to that position. If he is asked to turn right, he will make the correct turn.

Instructional Materials

/***Safety Note:** Provide scissors appropriate for the child. Remind the child of safety regarding scissors.

A cardboard box large enough to go around the child, a piece of fabric long enough to go through each side of the box (e.g., a narrow scarf, a wide ribbon, or a soft belt) and around the child's shoulders. Scissors, five paper plates, brads, markers, masking tape.

To make a child car, remove all the flaps from the box, except one top to use as the dashboard. On either side of the box, cut a hole about a third of the way from the front of the "car" large enough to put the fabric through. Thread the fabric through one of these holes, and make a knot on the inside of the box to secure the fabric. Adjust the length of the fabric to go around the child's shoulders, and thread the other end through the hole on the opposite side of the box, and knot it. (The length of the fabric should allow the box to be waist- or hip-high. Make sure the child's legs can move through the holes in the bottom of the box.)

Instructional Activities

1. Place the masking tape on the floor to form two streets that meet at a four-way intersection. The tape streets should be wide enough for two "child cars" to pass.
2. Discuss and show the child the street and the intersection. Explain to him that he is going to make a "Child Car" to go on the street.
3. Show him the box, invite him to put it on, and make any adjustments.
4. Explain to him that the Child Car is not finished as it still needs four wheels, a steering wheel, headlights, trim, doors, and mirrors.
5. Give him the paper plates, tell him to use the markers to decorate four of the plates to be tires. After he completes the four tires, attach them to the box with the brads. Tell him to use the other paper plate to make a steering wheel. Attach it to the dashboard with a brad. Let the child decorate his Child Car, using the markers.
6. After he decorates it, help him put it on and "drive" up and down the streets.
7. After the driving fun, explain to him that you are going to give him some directions. Say, for example, "Drive down the street (naming the

streets is not only a learning experience but fun), and when you reach the intersection, stop and turn left."

8. Continue giving directions, asking him to turn left and right, right, then left, etc., as he drives the Child Car.

9. Involve more children in their created Child Cars and place them on the street, to follow left and right directions.

10. You may easily modify this activity by adding more streets, using other cardboard boxes to make houses, stores, schools, and churches along the streets. Name each street, by using street signs, and put house numbers on the box homes.

1.310 Uses left and right to direct others in concrete situation

Strand: 1-4D **Age:** 68-78m 5.8-6.6y

Definition

The child will give others directions using the terminology "left" and "right." Example: "Go past the door, turn right, and go straight ahead; when you come to the window, go left." She will give directions that relate to concrete experiences and situations. The left and right directions will have to do with a person's relationship to the spatial world and her orientation to other objects and persons and not to sides of a body.

Instructional Materials

Masking tape to attach to the floor.

Instructional Activities

1. Using the tape, set boundary lines approximately 8 feet square.
2. Tell the children to sit quietly and be ready to play Navigator to Pilot.
3. Explain that the boundaries are the runways for an airplane.
4. Choose a child to be the pilot and another to be the navigator.
5. Put a blindfold on the pilot.
6. Explain to the navigator that she must help the pilot take off.
7. Ask the navigator to tell the pilot how to take off, using left and right directions.
8. Allow the children to take turns being pilot and navigator.

2.101   Names sounds heard in the immediate environment

Strand: 2-1A   **Age:** 30-42m 2.6-3.6y

Definition

When the child is presented with known voices or laughs (such as family members, a teacher, a friend, a care provider, cartoon characters, or favorite characters from TV, or a talking toy), the child will name the person. When she is presented with different sounds heard in her environment (the classroom, on a walk, at home, in the car, playing outside, on a picnic, in the park) and is asked to name what made the different sounds, she will be able to respond correctly. When the child is presented with an audio recording of different sounds (animals, transportation, weather, toys), she will name the object or thing that is making the sound.

Instructional Materials

Different noisemakers for at least four players. They may include a whistle, bells, a drum, a horn, chimes, or a rattle. A blindfold or scarf that will fit over the child's eyes. Small prizes.

Instructional Activities

1. Assign a large enough area for the child to stand in the middle of a circle of at least four children.
2. Explain to the group that you are going to put a blindfold or a scarf over the eyes of the child standing in the middle of the circle.
3. Show the group the noisemakers and allow the children a chance to play the various items.
4. Blindfold one child.
5. Give each of the other children a noisemaker. Place the players with noisemaker around the blindfolded child.
6. Explain that you are going to point to one of the children with a noisemaker and that child is to make noise with her instrument. When she stops, the blindfolded child is to tell what made the noise. If she names the instrument correctly, give her a special reward.
7. Continue until all the children with noisemakers have had a turn.
8. Select another child to be blindfolded. Ask the players with noisemakers to trade instruments or select a different one from the table.
9. Allow each child a chance to be the guesser.
10. To modify this game, instead of noisemakers, tell the players with noisemakers that this time they are to say something. Encourage them to change their voices, to make funny noises, or to talk differently.
11. The blindfolded player must guess who made the noise.
12. If she names the person correctly, give her a special reward.
13. Allow all players to have a turn being the guesser.

2.102   Performs appropriate action when self pronouns (me, my, mine) are used

Strand: 2-1A   **Age:** 32-36m 2.8-3.0y

Definition

Level 1 - When the child is shown an object that he owns, he will say, "Give me my ball." When he has an object that belongs to him and is asked, "Whose ball do you have?" he will respond by saying, "The ball is mine," or "It is mine."
Level 2 - When the child is shown at least two items, he will give one of them to someone else upon request e.g., the recipient says, "Give me the blue ball." After the recipient receives the blue ball, the recipient will say, "This is my ball." The recipient will then place the balls together and ask the child, "Point to the ball that is mine."

Instructional Materials

Short sentences using the pronouns me, my and mine. Examples: "Bring me the book," "Point to my cup," "The ball is mine," "Bring it to me." Objects to match sentences, for example, a book, a cup, a ball. Small prize.

Instructional Activities

1. Place the necessary objects--book, cup, ball-- on a table, and sit near the child.
2. Explain that this is listening game. Tell the child to listen carefully and do what you say.
3. Point to him and say a pronoun sentence. Provide time for him to do the stated direction.
4. Say a silly sentence occasionally such as, "Bring me a door."
5. Give him several opportunities to listen and respond.
6. Keep an individual count of his correct responses for a predetermined reward.
7. Give him an opportunity to be the "caller" as you become the "listener and doer."

2.103 Responds correctly with a non-verbal response or with a single word answer to a stated question

Strand: 2-1A **Age:** 32-38m 2.8-3.2y

Definition

When the child is asked a question concerning a particular concept, she will answer correctly with a nonverbal response (nodding head yes or shaking head no). When asked a simple question (what color is this?) the child will respond correctly with a single word answer.

Instructional Materials

A set of 10 to 15 prepared questions such as: Are you sleeping? Are you hungry? Are you happy today? Did you get hurt? Is the girl crying?

Instructional Activities

1. Seat the child next to you. Begin by asking questions individually using the child's name, for example, "Sarah, are you sleeping?"
2. Accept head shakes or nods, gesture responses, or yes and no.
3. Provide cues whenever possible such as, "You are right, Sarah, you are not sleeping. Your eyes are wide open, you are not sleepy."

2.104 Points to or places an object on top/bottom

Strand: 2-1A **Age:** 32-42m 2.8-3.6y

Definition

When the child is asked, she will point to an object that has been placed in a spatial position (e.g., "Point to the ball that is on top of the box.") When the child is asked, she will place an object in a spatial position (e.g., "Put your shoes at the bottom of the stairs.")

Instructional Materials

One chair for each child and a box for each chair. A table. A group of objects (blocks, toys, balls, books) to place on top of and at the bottom of a location.

Instructional Activities

1. Place the chairs so each child can walk around one without touching someone else. Place a box on the seat of each chair.
2. Place the items to be used on a table for the children to view.
3. Check to make sure that each child involved will have an item from the table to use during the activity.

4. Direct each child to select a chair. Make sure they have plenty of room to move around it.
5. Tell the children to walk around their chairs.
6. Ask if they see anything on the table.
7. Tell the children to pick one of the objects on top of the table and put it on top of the chair, in the box, at the bottom of the chair, out of the box, etc.
8. Ask who can think of another place to put her objects.
9. Record the child's responses.

2.105 Points to or places object up, down

Strand: 2-1A **Age:** 34-42m 2.10-3.6y

Definition

When the child is given a small object such as block or a ball, he will place it up on a box or down on the floor on command.

Instructional Materials

A 4-inch basketball drawn in felt-tip pen and cut out of colored poster board or a 4- to 6-inch ball.

Instructional Activities

1. Make sure that there is ample space for the child to move. Give the ball to the child.
2. Discuss what games are played with balls. Include the following in the discussion: how to score a point, what a coach does, what players do, the names of popular players, cheers.
3. Tell the child he will make a point if he follows his coach's directions. Ask him to pretend you are his coach and that you will give him some directions.
4. Tell him if he listens carefully, he will score and win the game.
5. Tell him to place his ball, "Up above his head."
6. Give him a score if he responds correctly.
7. If he does not put the ball above his head, repeat the direction and assist him physically to place the ball above his head.
8. When the ball is positioned above his head, say, "The ball is up above your head."
9. Continue with the words down, up, in, and out.
10. Examples: "Put the ball down on the floor." "Put the ball in the hoop." "Put the ball up on the table." "Roll the ball out of the room."
11. Give a point for each successful response.
12. After the child reaches a predetermined number of points, allow him to be the coach.

2.106 Carries out 2 simple unrelated successive commands in order

Strand: 2-2 **Age:** 34-46m 2.10-3.10y

Definition

The child will respond correctly to a two-step command in which the steps are not logically related.

Instructional Materials

Several items of different colors, such as a red ball, a green pencil, a blue book, a yellow scarf, a black sheet of paper. Small prize or reward.

Instructional Activities

1. Select a large area to play a directional seek-and-find game.
2. Tell the child this is a game to find certain colored objects, and that each time he locates an object correctly, he will win a point.
3. Explain that he is called the "Runner."
4. Say, "Runner, when I say the color you must find an object with that color and place it where I tell you."
5. Tell him where to put the colored object. Say, "Find the red ball and put it on the table."
6. Give a point to him each time he completes a task.
7. When he reaches a predetermined number of points, provide him with the agreed reward.

2.107 Uses noun plurals. Uses verb plurals

Strand: 2-3 **Age:** 36-38m 3.0-3.2y

Definition

When a child is involved with a verbal situation or with a visual picture, she will respond by using noun plurals (e.g., shoes, girls). When she is presented with a situation or picture, she will respond by using verb plurals (e.g., girls run).

Instructional Materials

Several like objects, e.g., marbles, pencils, buttons. A group of action pictures.

Instructional Activities

1. Select any opportunity when the child is involved in verbalization, conversation, telling about an experience, or discussing a picture.
2. Show the child one of the objects and refer to it in the singular form of the noun. Show her two objects and refer to them in plural form. Ask her to respond first to one object and then more than one.

3. Show her the action pictures, and point to elements in the pictures that represent verbs and refer to them in plural form. Ask her to respond to the verb visuals.
4. When the child is involved in any conversational setting, listen for her use of plural nouns and plural verbs. When appropriate, model corrections, using the imitation and expansion method.

2.108 Identifies sounds, words just spoken

Strand: 2-1A **Age:** 36-39m 3.0-3.3y

Definition

(1) The child will look at an object that has just been named; he will look at a person who has just been named. (2) When a sound is produced, he will answer the question, "What was that?" or when someone speaks, he will answer the question, "Who was that?"

Instructional Materials

Assortment of toy animals, musical instruments (whistle, drum, xylophone). A blindfold.

Instructional Activities

1. Set the toy animals and the musical instruments on a table. Have the child sit at the table.
2. Tell him you are going to play a guessing game so he will need to be blindfolded.
3. Tell him he will hear a sound after he is blindfolded and that he is to tell you what made the sound.
4. Pick up and play an instrument, or pick up and make the sound of the animal ("moo" for toy cow).
5. Ask the child what sound he heard and what instrument or animal made the sound.
6. Repeat with the other animals and instruments.
7. Trade places with the child.
8. Allow the child an opportunity to create sounds.

2.109 Identifies loud and soft sounds

Strand: 2-1A **Age:** 36-40m 3.0-3.4y

Definition

When the child is exposed to a loud and soft sound, she will identify each according to volume. She may identify a loud or a soft sound by a physical movement (raises arm high if the sound is loud, lowers arm if the sound is soft), by verbal expression (says "loud" to identify a loud sound or says "soft" to identify a soft sound), by visual representation (a tall line means a loud sound and a short line means a soft sound), or by looking at pictures of a loud and a soft sound maker (an airplane and a kitten) and pointing to the airplane when asked which one makes a loud sound and pointing to the kitten when asked which one makes a soft sound.

Instructional Materials

At least two sets of four cards. A marker to draw the following on the cards: Set One: Card 1--two short lines and one long line. Card 2--one long line, one short line and one long line. Card 3-- three short lines. Card 4--two long lines and one short line. Set Two: Card 1--a picture of a big drum being hit. Card 2--a picture of a lion roaring. Card 3--a picture of a tiny bell. Card 4-- picture of a faucet dripping.

Instructional Activities

1. Invite the child to sit across from you. Begin with the cards from Set One. Tell the child that the long line means a loud sound and the short line means a soft sound.
2. Tell her to choose a sound to make; suggest clapping, foot tapping, or singing one note.
3. Show her Card 1 and assist her to in decoding the two soft sounds and then the one loud sound.
4. Continue this with the other cards.
5. After she completes the cards in Set One, place the cards face-up on a table in front of her.
6. Without indicating which card, clap the loud or soft pattern on one of the cards.
7. Ask the child to find the card with the pattern you clapped on it.
8. Continue this with the other cards. Leave all four cards on the table as you complete this activity.
9. Collect the cards.
10. Get Card Set Two. Hold the cards in your hands so that the child cannot see them.
11. Explain to the child that you are going to show her one picture card at a time, ask her to look at the picture and tell you whether the object on it would make a loud or a soft sound,
12. Show her Card 1, and ask her if the item would make a loud or a soft sound.
13. Continue with the other cards in Set Two.
14. Give her a positive verbal feedback on her performance when she has shown you that she has been listening and paying attention to the activity.

2.110 (Removed, see page xii)

2.111 Uses noun with possessive
Strand: 2-3 Age: 24-40m 2.0-3.4y

Definition
When he is presented with a situation or a visual and a verbal prompt, the child will respond by using a noun with a possessive.

Instructional Materials
Objects that belong to the child. Similar objects that belong to another child. Make sure that the items are not identical.

Instructional Activities
1. Place the objects in a container.
2. Use the child's objects first. Say to the child, "Whose coat is this?"
3. The expected response is, "My coat." If further help is needed, repeat, "Whose coat is this?" and tell him to say, "That is my coat."
4. Go through all the objects that are his until he can readily answer "my" and follow with the name of the item.
5. Go through all the objects belonging to the other child until he can readily answer [Billy's] and then name the item.
6. Repeat, alternating the objects and asking the question each time.
7. Practice until he can discriminate his things from others' things verbally.

2.112 Uses verb with noun (see dog, push wagon)
Strand: 2-3 Age: 30-40m 2.6-3.4y

Definition
The child uses a verb with a noun.

Instructional Materials
Sheets of construction paper in five different colors. Cut a 7-inch circle out of each color. Staple each circle to an 8 ½ x 11 piece of poster board or tag board. Some action pictures, such as a girl sleeping and a boy eating.

Instructional Activities
1. Place the pictures face down on a table, and invite the child to come to the work area. Show her the picture and ask, "What is the boy doing?" Touch a circle for each word that the child says. For example, if she says "boy," touch a circle and place it in a row. If she

adds, "eats" touch a circle and place it next to the first circle.

2. Give her a turn to say the words and manipulate the circles.
3. Demonstrate how to answer the question by using four words: "The boy is eating." Touch and then place a circle for each word stated.
4. Encourage the child to use four words and to place four circles in a row.
5. When the child is involved in any conversational setting, listen for her use of verbs and nouns. When appropriate, model correction, using the imitation and expansion method.

2.113 Uses pronouns appropriately (him, he, his, her, she)

Strand: 2-3   **Age:** 36-40m 3.0-3.4y

Definition

When the child is involved in a verbal situation or presented with a visual, he will respond by using the correct pronoun. Consideration should be given to the use of subjective pronouns (I, you, he, we, she) before objective pronouns (me, him, her, us, them) or possessive pronouns (your, his, our, their).

Instructional Materials

Photos from home of the child, his family, friends, pets, and neighbors. If available, use a digital camera to take pictures of the child and his friends at school. Or extra school pictures.

Instructional Activities

1. Ask the child to sit opposite you. Tell the child that you are going to show him a picture of one of his friends and that he is to tell you whom it is.
2. Show him a picture. Ask questions such as, "Who is he? What is his name? Is this you?"
3. Ask him to use "his" in a sentence.
4. If necessary prompt the child by saying, "His name is _____." Ask the child to repeat what you said.
5. If he uses the correct pronoun, allow him to hold the picture.
6. Continue until all the pictures are gone.
7. Give him a turn to present the pictures and ask the questions.
8. When the child is involved in any conversation, listen for his use of pronouns. When appropriate, model corrections, using the imitation and expansion method.

2.114 Provides objects as they are requested by name or referenced by function

Strand: 2-1A   **Age:** 30-42m 2.6-3.6y

Definition

When the child is presented with several different known objects and a verbal cue, for example, "Give me the spoon" or "Pick up the comb," she will select the correct item. When she is presented with known objects that also have a function such as a hairbrush, a glass, a spoon, or a hat, she will respond to the request, for example, "Give me the hairbrush." She may respond to a request to demonstrate the function of the item, for example, "Show me which one you would drink from."

Instructional Materials

At least six objects that are familiar to the child. Shallow box. Pictures of the same six objects on large index cards (Card Set 1) illustrated or cut out of magazines or catalogs. Note: Card Set 1 pictures should resemble the actual objects as closely as possible. Pictures of the six objects on large index cards (Card Set 2) illustrated or cut out of magazines or catalogs. Card Set 2 pictures should not be exact likenesses. Example: different size and color of blocks, different size and position of a toy car, different design and size of a drinking glass, different color, design, and position of shoestrings. Small prize or reward.

Instructional Activities

1. Place the familiar objects in a shallow box. Place the cards of Card Set 1 face-up on a table. Invite the child to the table to play the game of Me and Match.
2. Show her the set of real objects. Hold up each object and ask her to name it.
3. Show her Card Set 1 on the table. Point to each card and ask her to name the object illustrated.
4. Tell her you are going to give some directions and she is to listen carefully.
5. Say, "Put the real block on a picture of a block." Allow her time to respond. Praise her for her response.
6. Say, "Put the real car on a picture of a car."
7. Continue with the remaining objects and pictures.
8. When she completes the matching, collect the pictures and place the objects back in the box.

9. Place the cards of Card Set 2 on the table face-up. Point to each card and ask her to name the card.
10. Say, "Put the real glass on a picture of a glass." Give her time to respond. Praise her for her response.
11. Continue with the remaining objects and pictures.
12. When she completes the matching, collect the objects and place them back in the box. Leave the cards from Card Set 2 face up on the table.
13. Get Card Set 1 and give her one card at a time. As you are handing the card to the child say, "Put this picture of a block on a another picture of a block." Allow her time to respond. Praise her for her response.
14. Continue with the remaining cards.
15. Take turns with her to be the caller and the placer.
16. Give points for each correct answer and provide a reward for earning a predetermined number of points.

2.115 (Removed, see page xii)

2.116 (Removed, see page xii)

2.117 Correctly answers questions concerning a message just spoken

Strand: 2-1A **Age:** 36-42m 3.0-3.6y

Definition

The child will answer a literal question related to a short story told, some factual information provided, an activity that is going to happen, etc.

Instructional Materials

A short story that is within the child's interest and is enhanced by the use of puppets. Puppets that go along with the story. Many fairytales stories are excellent for puppetry.

Instructional Activities

1. Read a structured short story to the child. Show him the pictures in the storybook as you read.
2. Ask literal questions during the story that emphasize names, places and activities.
3. Read the story again, using the puppets to help tell the story.
4. At the end of the story, give the child one of the story puppets.

5. Ask the puppet (child) literal questions about his character in the story. Example: "What did you do when... In the story you left...Where did you go..." Encourage the child when answering for the puppet to imitate the puppet's voice and actions.

2.118 Sequences a 3-picture story that has been read

Strand: 2-1A **Age:** 36-44m 3.0-3.8y

Definition

After the child has heard a simple story with three events, she will be given a set of pictures showing the story sequence, and she will arrange the pictures in the correct order. The set of pictures will clearly depict the sequence of the story.

Instructional Materials

A story that has three clear sequences and that can easily be represented by manipulatives, such as puppets, flannel board characters, paper-dolls, or masks. Example: "Once upon a time there was a little boy named Tom. He had his face painted like a clown. It was a sad face with a turned-down mouth. When Tom saw himself in the mirror, he changed his sad mouth to a happy smile."

Three paper bags to illustrate the above story prepared as follows: (1) Keeping the bags flat and using crayons or markers make the first bag look like the boy named Tom. By using the bottom of the bag as the top of Tom's head, add yarn for hair. (2) Keeping the bag flat and using crayons or markers, make the second bag look like a sad clown face, making sure the mouth is turned down. Change Tom's hair by braiding it with ribbons on the ends. (3) Keeping the bag flat and using crayons or markers, make the third bag look just like bag two, except that Tom's mouth is smiling. The bags should be opened so they will stand up on a table.

Instructional Activities

1. Place the open bag puppets on a table with the faces away from the child. Be sure the puppets are not arranged in the correct sequential order.
2. Tell the child that you are going to tell her a story. Tell her the story.
3. Turn the bag puppets around. Explain that the face puppets are all of Tom, but they show him with different faces.
4. Tell the child that you are going to tell the story again and tell her that she is to put the

different faces of Tom in the right order according to the story.

5. Tell the story again.

6. During or after the story, ask her to place the bag faces in the correct order.

7. Discuss the three face puppets with her. For example, point to the first bag and ask, "Who is this?" Ask about the second bag, "What does Tom look like?" And ask her about the third bag, "What happened to Tom's mouth?"

8. Encourage the child to tell the story and to move the puppets during the telling of the story.

9. Make up another story, using the same puppets.

2.119 Carries on a conversation
Strand: 2-3 **Age:** 36-44m 3.0-3.8y

Definition
The child will organize and verbally present his ideas to others, listen to ideas expressed by others, converse informally, engage in conversational give-and-take during interaction periods, make up and tell stories, talk about the interpretation of visuals, repeat sayings, and share experiences by oral expression.

Instructional Materials
At least four objects (e.g., fruits: apple, orange, banana, bunch of grapes) or four models of objects (four different plastic fruits). A puppet or a stuffed animal.

Instructional Activities
1. Place the fruit on a table in full view of the child. Point to the fruit, name each one, and discuss with the child each fruit's appearance, its different uses, and where it grows.

2. Ask him to close his eyes, and remove one of the pieces of fruit, for example, the apple.

3. When he opens his eyes, ask, "Which fruit is gone?"

4. After he names the missing fruit, conduct a conversation about the missing fruit.

5. Give him an opportunity to take away a fruit and lead the conversation about the absent item.

6. If more than one child participates, encourage communication among the other children.

7. Show the child the puppet or stuffed animal. Say, for example, "Mr. Mouse wants to talk to you!"

8. Using the puppet, start a conversation with the child, and encourage him to visit with the puppet.

2.120 Describes an action using a verb
Strand: 2-4B **Age:** 30-38m 2.6-3.2y

Definition
The child will answer questions about common occurrences related to a person involved in an action. He will state the action by using a verb.

Instructional Materials
Action directives written out that can be used to ask the child to dramatize and then state the activity. Examples: (1) Run after a ball; (2) Drink a glass of water; (3) Sweep the floor; (4) Jump over a puddle; (5) March in a band; (6) Brush your hair; (7) Hop like a rabbit; (8) Catch a ball.

Instructional Activities
1. Select an area in the room that will allow for ample physical movement. Explain to the child that you are going to ask him to dramatize some actions.

2. Say, "Show me how you would run after a ball."

3. After he has demonstrated running after a ball, say, "Tell me what you were doing."

4. Pause for him to say, "Run for ball," "Run get ball," "I run after ball," or "I was running after a ball."

5. If he does not make the verb statement, say, "Were you running after the ball?"

6. After the child says yes, say, "Charlie, you say, 'I was running after the ball.'"

7. Prompt him as needed.

8. Continue by saying, "Show me how you would drink a glass of water."

9. After he has demonstrated drinking a glass of water, say, "Tell me what you were doing."

10. Pause for him to say "drink water," "drink from glass," "drinking," or "I was drinking a glass of water."

11. Resume the dramatizations with directives 3 to 10, using the steps above.

12. If more than one child is involved, modify the above by having one child perform the action and the others guess what he is doing. After they guess, the child who did the action must say, "Yes, run after ball," "Yes, get ball," or "Yes, I was running after a ball."

2.121 (Removed, see page xii)

2.122 (Removed, see page xii)

2.123 Imitates common syllables (da, ka, wa)

Strand: 2-4B **Age:** 36-48m 3.0-4.0y

Definition

When the child is presented with a cue, she will say a correct imitation of the following syllables (either consonant + vowel (short) or vowel (short) + consonant): (1) (m + vowel) me as in meat, mi as in mitt, mo as in mop, ma as in mat; (2) (vowel + m) em as in hem, um as in hum, im as in him; (3) (t + vowel) te as in test, tu as in tub, ta as in tap; (4) (vowel + t) et as in get, ut as in cut, at as in at; (5) (p + vowel) pe as in pet, po as in pot, pa as in pat, pi as in pit; (6) (vowel + p) ep as in kept, up as in up, ap as in cap, ip as in tip; (7) (d + vowel) de as in depth, du as in dump, da as in dab, di as in did; (8) (vowel + d) ed as in wed, ud as in mud, ad as in add, id as in lid; (9) (n + vowel) nu as in nut, na as in nap, ni as in nip; (10) (vowel + n) un as in under, an as in fan, in as in pin; (11) (l + vowel) le as in sled, la as in lamb, li as in lit; (12) (vowel + l) el as in fell, al as in alley, il as in ill; (13) (s + vowel) su as in sum, sa as in sat, si as in sit; (14) (vowel + s) es as in dress, us as in bus; (15) (k + vowel) ki as in kick; (16) (vowel + k) uk as in luck, ak as in pack, ik as in pick; (17) (r + vowel) ri as in rip, re as in red, ro as in rod; (18) (b + vowel) bi as in bid, ba as in bad, be as in bed, bu as in bum: (19) (vowel + b) ib as in rib, ob as in rob, ab as in dab, ub as in tub; (20) (f + vowel) fe as in fed, fa as in fan, fu as in fun, fo as in fog; (21) (vowel + f) uf as in gruff, if as in if, af as in after; (22) (g + vowel) ge as in get, go as in got, gu as in gun; (23) (vowel + g) ig as in jig, ug as in mug, ag as in bag, eg as in peg, og as in jog; (24) (h + vowel) ho as in hot, ha as in ham, hu as in hum; (25) (w + vowel) wi as in wit, we as in wet.

The presentation of the verbal model will be done by an adult who will exaggerate the facial movements as she creates the sounds. The child will be instructed to watch the adult as the sound syllables are being presented. This is not a skill related to phonic or linguistic instruction in reading, but a skill to determine whether the child is developing her articulation (voice folds) in such a manner as to reproduce all vowels and those voiced consonants that are produced by vocal folds vibrations and those consonants unvoiced that are produced without vibration from the vocal folds.

Instructional Materials

A simple rhyme or chant that uses only consonant + vowel beginnings and blends the consonant + vowel (c + v) into a word.

Example:
I say m
I say mi
I say mitt
I say a
I say ap
I say cap
Continue with other consonant + vowel syllables and vowel + consonant syllables.
A tape or CD recorder or cell phone.

Instructional Activities

1. Place the tape recorder on the table ready to play and record. Explain to the child that you are going to say a Silly Sounding Saying.
2. Say, "I say m." (exaggerate the m sound)
3. "I say mi." (exaggerate the mi sound)
4. "I say mitt."
5. "I say a." (exaggerate the short sound of a)
6. "I say ap." (exaggerate the ap sound)
7. "I say cap."
8. Repeat the Silly Sounding Sayings, asking the child to repeat each line after you.
9. Tell her to say the Silly Sounding Sayings after you.
10. Say, "Listen." Pause and say, "I say m." Point to the child to indicate it is her turn.
11. After she has said, " I say m," say, "I say mi."
12. Point to the child to indicate it is her turn.
13. After she has said, "I say mi," say, "I say mitt."
14. Point to the child to indicate it is her turn.
15. Invite her to join you in saying the whole silly sound.
16. Add the beat of a drum, the clap of hands or a tambourine to the silly sound chants.
17. Add actions to the silly sounds. For example, say, "I say m"-- place one arm straight out in front of body. "I say mi"--place the other arm parallel to the outstretched arm. "I say mitt"-- place hands above head and clap. (These actions closely imitate a cheerleader's; by adding crepe paper pompoms, you can make it a delightful activity.)
18. Continue with other Silly Sounding Sayings.

2.124 Says a favorite rhyme

Strand: 2-4B **Age:** 36-48m 3.0-4.0y

Definition

The child will recite the words of a familiar rhyme correctly. If he has not memorized the rhyme, he may be provided with prompts, visuals, or motor activities, but then these prompts must be phased out, and he will recite the rhyme without any cues.

Instructional Materials

/*\ **Safety Note:** Provide scissors appropriate for the child. Remind the child of safety regarding scissors.

A nursery rhyme the child enjoys hearing and that creates an understandable visual image.

Example:

Banbury Cross

"Ride a cockhorse to Banbury Cross,
To see a fine lady upon a white horse;
Rings on her fingers and bells on her toes,
She shall have music wherever she goes."

Instructional Materials

To make a toy horse: one dowel stick about 36 inches long and 1 inch diameter, a white sock, felt pieces, fabric scraps, markers, yarn, stuffing (cotton, packing pop-corn foam, washed pantyhose), scissors, marking pens, nontoxic glue.

Instructional Activities

1. Lay the material to make the toy horse on a work area.
2. Ask the child to listen while you say the rhyme. Recite the rhyme, *Banbury Cross*.
3. Repeat it several times and encourage the child to join say it with you.
4. Discuss with him what a cock horse (rocking horse or hobby horse) is and what Banbury Cross (a place) is.
5. Talk about how the fine lady would look riding on her white horse.
6. Decide how many rings and bells she would be wearing.
7. Choose the kind of music she would have wherever she goes.
8. Say the rhyme again and invite the child to say it with you.
9. Encourage him to recite the rhyme by himself.
10. Invite him to the work area to make a cock horse.
11. Ask him to stuff the sock and place the end of the dowel stick through the sock opening and as far as the beginning of the sock heel.
12. Using yarn, tie the open end of the sock tightly around the dowel stick.
13. Use the rest of the yarn to make a rein by placing the yarn around the top of the heel and under the cock horse's chin. This will take several loops. Attach the rein to the top of the head with glue. Let the child use the scraps of felt and fabric to make ears, a mane, and eyes.
14. Add any additional features by using the markers.
15. After the child has completed his cock horse, allow him time to practice riding it.
16. As he is riding about, say the rhyme, Banbury Cross.
17. Tell him to ride to Banbury Cross and to say the rhyme as he is going.
18. Ask him to ride back from Banbury Cross and to tell you what he saw and what he heard.

2.125 Names common objects and actions

Strand: 2-4B **Age:** 36-48m 3.0-4.0y

Definition

When the child is presented with a visual model (a picture) of common objects (nouns) and common actions (verbs), she will name the objects and the action. The pictures should be of single items.

Instructional Materials

A set of 16 object cards. A set of 16 action cards. Cards should be 3- by 5 inches or playing card size. Each set should contain three joker cards. The object and action cards may be purchased or made by cutting pictures from magazines and mounting them on index cards.

Instructional Activities

1. Shuffle the deck of object cards and place the deck face-down on a table. This game may be for the child and teacher, or may involve more than one child.
2. Explain to the child that she is to take a card from the top of the deck, lay it face-up on the table, and name the object shown.
3. If she is correct, she may keep the card.
4. If she draws a joker card, she loses a turn.
5. If she is incorrect, she must place the card face-up next to the deck.
6. When a card is face-up next to the deck, the next player may say the name of the object, and if she is correct, she takes the card.
7. If there is no card face-up next to the deck, the next player draws from the deck, lays the card face-up on the table, and names the object shown.
8. If she is correct, she may keep the card.
9. If she draws a joker card, she loses a turn.
10. If she is incorrect, she must place the card face-up next to the deck.
11. The game continues until the deck is gone.
12. The child with the most cards wins.
13. Repeat the above, using the action deck of cards.

14. This card game may be modified to require the players not only to name the object or action but also to use the word in a sentence.

2.126 Uses past tense by adding "ed" to verb

Strand: 2-3 **Age:** 36-48m 3.0-4.0y

Definition

When he is involved in a verbal situation or presented with a picture, the child will respond by using a past tense verb, adding "ed". Examples: pushed, jumped, skipped.

Instructional Materials

Locate or prepare simple poems that use past tenses of verbs with "ed" endings. Examples:

Hopped
Hopped high,
Hopped low,
Hopped fast,
Hopped slow,
Hopped fat,
Hopped thin,
All hopped down and
Locked themselves in.

The Zoo
The birds twittered,
The bears growled,
The lions roared,
The seals barked,
The owls screeched,
The ducks quacked,
Everyone woke up today,
Making noises, ready to play.

Instructional Activities

1. Invite the child to the story time area. Tell the child that you are going to read him a poem.
2. Read the poem, Hopped.
3. Read the poem a few times.
4. Invite the child to join in with the words or the poetic meter. Say the poem together several times.
5. Invite the child to dramatize the poem. For example; say, "Hopped high," and ask him to hop high. Say, "Hopped low," and ask him to hop low. Continue with the other lines from "Hopped" in the same way.
6. Ask the child to dramatize the poem and to say it at the same time. Repeat the poem dramatization and recitation several times.
7. Read the poem, The Zoo.
8. Read the poem a few times.

9. Invite the child to join in with the words or the poetic meter . Say the poem together several times.
10. Invite him to dramatize the poem. For example; say, "Birds twittered," and ask him to pretend to be a bird and to twitter. Say, "Bears growled," and ask him to pretend to be a bear and growl. Continue with the other animals in The Zoo.
11. Ask the child to dramatize the poem and to say it at the same time.
12. Repeat the poem dramatization and recitation several times.
13. Create a poem with the child, selecting verbs and adding "ed" to make them in the past tense.
14. Use the same procedure with the made-up poem as you did with Hopped and The Zoo.

2.127 Carries out 3 simple related successive commands in order

Strand: 2-1A **Age:** 36-48m 3.0-4.0y

Definition

When presented with a three-step command in which the steps are logically related, the child will respond by completing the necessary steps in order.

Instructional Materials

An item to hide, such as a toy or a snack. An item such as new socks, a hair ribbon, or a T-shirt may also be hidden. A single item such as a rock could be hidden with the understanding that the item represents a special treat or could be exchanged for a reward.

Instructional Activities

1. Hide the item in the room.
2. Tell the child that a surprise is hidden in the room. Tell her if she finds it she may keep it, eat it, trade it in for a reward or whatever is appropriate.
3. Explain to her that you are going to give her some directions to find the surprise and that if she follows the directions in the proper sequence she may keep it, eat it, or trade it in for a reward. Stress following the directions in the sequence given.
4. Ask her to listen carefully.
5. Give the "Finding Directions." Example: "Walk to the chest," "Lay down on the floor," and "Look under the chest."
6. If she is unsuccessful, provide her with more specific directions.

7. Take turns with the child, allowing her to hide the item and give the directions.

2.128 Uses four to six words in a sentence

Strand: 2-4B **Age:** 36-54m 3.0-4.6y

Definition

The child will spontaneously say a four- to six-word sentence.

Instructional Materials

A series of six kernel sentences. Design the six kernel sentences so that a single word can be substituted.
Example: (1) The child is _____. (2) The dog has a _____. (3) I took my _____ off. (4) We went to the _____. (5) The flower is _____. (6) The _____ is in box.
A kernal sentence is a simple declarative sentence in the active voice from which both simpler and more complicated English sentences may be derived.

Instructional Activities

1. Tell the child that you are going to say some sentences and that you want her to make up a sentence like yours.
2. Say, "The child is jumping."
3. Say, "I want you to repeat the sentence, only do not use the word jumping, but use your own word to tell what the child is doing."
4. Say, "Your turn. The child is _____. " Pause to allow the child to fill in the last line.
5. If she is unable to complete the sentence and substitute a word, prompt her by saying, "I want you to say, 'The child is _____.'"
6. Pause to allow her to say the sentence.
7. If she is still unable to respond, say, "Remember, I said 'the child is jumping'; what do you want your child to do?"
8. Repeat, "The child is _____ ." Pause to allow her to fill in the last word.
9. After she has filled in the word, say, "Now say the whole sentence."
10. Observe her response.
11. Explain to her that you are going to say another sentence.
12. Say, "The dog has a red ball."
13. Say, "I want you to repeat the sentence, only do not use the words red ball. Use your own word to tell what the dog has."
14. Say, "Your turn. The dog has a _____ ." Pause to allow her to fill in the last line.

15. If she is unable to complete the sentence and substitute a word, prompt her by saying, "I want you to say, 'The dog has a _____ '"
16. Pause to allow her to say the sentence.
17. If she is still unable to respond, say, "Remember, I said the dog has a red ball; what do you want the dog to have?"
18. Repeat, "The dog has a _____ ." Pause to allow her to fill in the last word.
19. After she has filled in the word, tell her to, "Say the whole sentence."
20. Observe her response.
21. Continue the above procedures for sentences 3 through 6.
22. As the child is involved in conversations, discussions, and play activities, observe her use of sentences, not only as to length but also as to structure. Use the correction technique of model—response, if appropriate.

2.129 Uses pivot verb "is" to form kernel sentences

Strand: 2-3 **Age:** 37-40m 3.1-3.4y

Definition

When the child is involved in a verbal situation or presented with a visual, he will respond by using the pivot verb "is" to form a kernel sentence. Examples: That is a cat. The cup is broken. (A kernel sentence is a simple declarative sentence in the active voice from which both simpler and more complicated English sentences may be derived).

Instructional Materials

/*\Safety Note: Be aware of special diets and allergies before doing these activities.
An assortment of 3-inch circles cut from poster board to represent cookies. Small pictures of objects (e.g., a dog) mounted on the circles. A large tin can, cookie jar, or basket. Cookie for the child to eat.

Instructional Activities

1. Place the poster board "cookies" in the container.
2. Instruct the child to reach in and remove a cookie and to say the name of object pictured on it, using the following structure, "This is a dog cookie."
3. Continue until he remembers to state the picture name correctly, using the "is" verb.
4. Reward him with a real cookie for his efforts.
5. Vary this activity according to the holiday season by cutting out Christmas trees, pumpkins or Valentine cookies and mounting

pictures of objects on them. Have the child pick a cookie form the jar and then ask them to tell which kind of cookie he selected as well as naming the picture.

6. When the child is involved in any conversational setting listen for his use of "is" as a verb. When it is appropriate, model any corrections, using the imitation and expansion method.

See #2.152.

2.130 Combines noun phrase and verb phrase to form kernel sentences

Strand: 2-3   **Age:** 30-44m 2.6-3.8y

Definition

When the child is involved in a verbal situation or presented with a visual, she will respond by using a noun phrase with a verb phrase. She may express the phrases with an article, a noun, the verb "is," and a verb (e.g., The dog is barking). (A kernel sentence is a simple declarative sentence in the active voice from which both simpler and more complicated English sentence may be derived).

Instructional Materials

Four 7-inch circles cut from four different colors of construction paper, each stapled to an 8 ½-inch by 11-inch piece of poster board or tag board. A few action pictures mounted on heavy paper, such as a dog barking and a bird singing.

Instructional Activities

1. Place the pictures face-down on a table, and invite the child to come to the work area.
2. Show the child the picture and ask, "What is the dog doing?" Touch a circle for each word that she says. For example, if she says "dog," touch a circle and place it in a row; if she adds "barks," touch a circle and place it next to the first circle.
3. Allow the child to say the words and manipulate the circles.
4. Demonstrate how to answer your question by using four words ("The boy is eating.") Touch and then place a circle for each word she says.
5. Encourage her to use at least four words, and as she says them, place the appropriate amount of circles in a row.
6. Proceed with additional words, and touch the number of circles to match.
7. Continue to help her build sentence length and encourage proper sequencing patterns.

See #2.129.

2.131 Asks questions using "is" and "have" forms

Strand: 2-3   **Age:** 37-42m 3.1-3.6y

Definition

When the child is involved in a verbal situation or presented with a visual, he will respond by asking a question using either "is" (e.g., "Is that a dog?") or "have" ("Do you have the cracker?")

Instructional Materials

Assortment of objects or pictures from a specified category in a box. Examples: Set of toy zoo animals, small train cars.

Instructional Activities

1. Place the box on a table. Tell the child the category of the things in the box, for example, train cars.
2. Ask him to guess what is in the box by asking questions that begin with, "Is there a [caboose] in the box?"
3. Whenever he guesses correctly, he may hold the object until the end of the activity. Continue until all the objects are guessed.
4. Replace the objects in the box and repeat the activity as a memory exercise.
5. When the child is involved in any conversational setting listen for his questioning skills. When appropriate, model correction using the imitation and expansion method.

See #2.129.

2.132 (Removed, see page xii)

2.133 Uses predicate phrases with noun phrases

Strand: 2-3   **Age:** 37-43m 3.1-3.7y

Definition

When he is involved in a verbal situation or presented with a visual, the child will respond by using the correct predicate phrase with a noun phrase (The boy is my brother). Attention should be given to the basic sentence patterns used in our language. The basic sentence patterns fundamental for early language development are: noun phrases and verb phrases, noun phrases divided by a determiner and a noun; as well as subdividing a verb phrase. Beginning sentences are all simple, active, declarative and referred to as kernel sentences.

Instructional Materials

Three sets of pictures drawn or cut and glued on large index cards. Set One--four pictures of different animals. Set Two--four pictures of different foods. Set Three--four pictures of different articles of clothing.

Instructional Activities

1. Select Set One, and invite the child to join you at a work area. Show the child the pictures. Point to each picture and name it. After naming each picture, go through them again, only this time say, "Dog--This dog is an animal. Horse--This horse is an animal. "
2. Ask the child to point to each picture and to name the animal.
3. Then ask him to point to each picture and tell the name and also the category. Prompt as necessary.
4. After he completes Set One, repeat with Sets Two and Three.
5. Allow him an opportunity to discuss the pictures.
6. When the child is involved in a conversational setting listen for his usage of phrases. When it is appropriate, model correction, using the imitation and expansion method.

2.134   (Removed, see page xii)

2.135   Categorizes sounds

Strand: 2-1A   **Age:** 43-46m   3.7-3.10y

Definition

The child will be presented with a sound that can be associated with a category, for example, an animal sound, a transportation sound, a people sound, or a musical sound, and he will be asked to identify each of the sounds by category. He will be asked to say the category (animal) or to point to a picture that represents the category (a picture of several different animals). Note: When selecting the sounds for the tape category, use sounds that are within his realm of experience.

Instructional Materials

A list of sounds that can be: (1) Whispered in an ear; (2) Reproduced after being whispered.

Instructional Activities

1. Ask the child to join you. Whisper a sound in his ear, for example, "Mew-mew-mew."
2. Tell him to make the sound and to tell you who or what made the sound (kitten).

3. Respond by saying, "That is right, a kitten, and a kitten is an animal."
4. Exchange places with the child, allowing him to become the sound maker.
5. If more than one child is involved, allow the child who named the source to be the next sound maker.
6. This activity can be modified by whispering an animal and having the child give the sound that the animal makes. Example: The animal name whispered was "kitten" and the receiver says, "Mew-mew-mew."
7. Another modification is to whisper a category (animal) and ask the child to produce a sound that something from that category makes (Mew-mew-mew). If more than one child is involved, ask him to name not only the sound source but also the category. Allow everyone to have a turn as category giver, a sound producer and a source namer.

2.136   Describes action in a picture using the present tense

Strand: 2-3   **Age:** 43-46m   3.7-3.10y

Definition

When she is presented with a visual, the child will respond by using descriptive words. She will describe the action occurring in the picture.

Instructional Materials

Some small objects in a closed bag.

Instructional Activities

1. Sit in front of the child and tell her you have a surprise inside the bag.
2. Tell her to close her eyes and reach into the bag. Tell her she may keep the object on her table for the day if she can describe it to you.
3. Encourage her to use complete sentences.
4. Prompt her by asking questions regarding the object, such as who uses the object, where do they use it, when would they use it, etc.
5. Once a general description has be given, allow the child to remove the object and place it on the table. Ask them to describe what they see, giving more detail (color, shape, size, etc.)
6. If the object is a manipulative (e.g., toy car), ask her to make the object move and tell what it is doing.
7. Try the activity again with her at another time.
8. Change the object in the bag and repeat the activity.

9. If the child has difficulty, help her form some sentences, but then ask her to put the object back in the bag.

2.137 Repeats simple words in the order presented

Strand: 2-1A **Age:** 43-48m 3.7-4.0y

Definition

When he hears no less than three or more than four familiar related words, he will be able to repeat them in the order presented. When he hears no less than three or more than four unrelated words, he will be able to repeat them in the order presented.

Instructional Materials

Five puppets: a pig, a dog, a cow, a horse and a cat. Purchase or make the puppets by using a lunch-size paper bag or a sock. Blank tape and a tape recorder (or cell phone).

Instructional Activities

1. Ask the child to join you. If more than one child is involved, have them form a circle and remind them that they will each have to wait for a turn.
2. Introduce the pig, dog, cow, horse and cat puppets to the child (or children). Imitate the sound of each.
3. Choose one puppet and make the noise of that animal.
4. Give the child one of the puppets and ask him to make the sound of that animal.
5. Allow him time to practice.
6. Give him another one of the puppets, and ask him to make that sound.
7. Allow him time to practice.
8. Continue with the other puppets.
9. Put the puppets aside.
10. Tell the child that you are going to say the names of three of the puppets (dog, horse, cat) and ask him to repeat the names.
11. Next, tell him you are going to make some animal sounds ("Meow-meow", "Arf-arf," "Moo-moo,") and ask him to repeat the sounds.
12. Tape the child's animal sounds and play the tape.
13. Allow the child to have a turn naming animal puppets and animal sounds.
14. If more than one child is involved, give each one a turn following the same steps.
15. After everyone has had a turn, let them all make the animal sounds together forming a "barnyard chorus".

2.138 Uses noun with demonstrative (this dog, that car)

Strand: 2-3 **Age:** 43-48m 3.7-4.0y

Definition

When she is involved in a verbal situation or is presented with a visual, the child will respond by using a noun with a demonstrative pronoun. This demonstrative pronoun is used to indicate the one referred to and distinguishing it from other noun-related items during a conversation or in an illustration.

Instructional Materials

Several fish drawn and cut out from colored construction paper. A paper clip attached to the mouth of each fish. A small picture of a single-item glued to each fish. A magnet tied to the end of a string to act as a fishing line. Container to serve as a lake for fish.

Instructional Activities

1. Place the fish in the container.
2. Instruct the child to fish for a picture by dropping the magnet-end of the string into the container.
3. Say the name of the picture that is attached to the fish she catches.
4. Ask her repeat it and to make a complete sentence or a phrase using the word she "caught."
5. If the child uses the word correctly in a sentence, she gets to keep the fish. If she is unable, model what she should have said and ask the child to return the fish to the lake and to try again on her next turn.
6. If more than one child is involved, announce the one who catches the most fish to be the winner.

2.139 Uses negatives in sentences

Strand: 2-3 **Age:** 48-60m 4.0-5.0y

Definition

When the child is involved in a verbal situation or presented with a visual, he will respond by using negatives in sentences ("The car is not broken.") He may also start to use contractions in sentences ("The car isn't broken.")

Instructional Materials

At least six picture cards of objects and people, either purchased or easily constructed by cutting and mounting pictures from magazines.

Instructional Activities

1. Place the pictures face-down on a table. Show the child one picture at time.
2. Ask him questions that must be answered "no," such as, "Is this apple green?"
3. Instruct the child to respond by saying, "No, the apple is not green."
4. Reward him with one point.
5. Review the procedure if he has difficulty.
6. Proceed with other questions to which he must respond, "No, the [object in picture] is not."
7. Show him the other picture cards, using the same procedure.
8. Give him an opportunity to be the questioner.

2.140   Uses conjunctions in sentences

Strand: 2-3   **Age:** 43-48m 3.7-4.0y

Definition

When the child is involved in a verbal situation or presented with a visual, she will use a conjunction (e.g., and, but, or) in a sentence.

Instructional Materials

Yarn strands of different colors and lengths tied together and rolled into a ball.

Instructional Activities

1. Instruct the child to sit across from you. This activity may involve more than one child.
2. Begin telling a story and unrolling the ball of yarn as you talk.
3. Demonstrate passing the ball to the child on the right as you come to the end of first strand.
4. Ask her to tell the next part of the story and to unroll the yarn. When she reaches the end of the color, she must give the yarn ball back to you.
5. Continue the story as each of you take turns story-telling and passing the yarn ball.
6. Require the child to begin her part of the story with a conjunction (cue as needed) in order to preserve continuity in the story-telling.

2.141   Uses infinitive verb forms in sentences

Strand: 2-3   **Age:** 43-48m 3.7-4.0y

Definition

When the child is involved in a verbal situation or presented with a visual, he will respond by using an infinitive verb form in a sentence. ("I want to. . .")

Instructional Materials

Several small toys and a bag to put them in. Several samples of foods the child likes.

Instructional Activities

1. Place the toys on a table and allow the child to see you put several of the toys in the bag.
2. Ask him, "Which toy would you like to play with?" Expected response is, "I want to play with the toy dinosaur."
3. Prompt if needed.
4. Change the infinitive to "to eat," and show him some foods he likes.
5. Ask "Which one of these would you like to eat?" Expected response is, "I want to eat the corn chips."
6. Prompt further if needed.

2.142   Uses auxiliary verbs "am," "is," "are" with present participle

Strand: 2-3   **Age:** 43-48m 3.7-4.0y

Definition

When the child is involved in a verbal situation or presented with a visual, she will respond by using auxiliary verbs, "am," "is," "are," with present participle (e.g., is running).

Instructional Materials

A large action picture, such as a picture that includes a girl, a boy, and a group.

Instructional Activities

1. Place the picture in view of the child.
2. Tell the child that she must tell one thing about the picture and she must use the word "is."
3. Prompt, if necessary; for example, say, "The boy is _____ ."
4. Clap if she says something about the picture and uses the word "is."
5. Tell her to say another sentence about the picture and to use the word "am."
6. Prompt, if necessary; for example, say, "I am happy that the girl _____."

7. Clap if she says something about the picture and uses the word "am."
8. Ask her to tell one thing about the picture and to use the word "are."
9. Prompt, if necessary, for example, say, "The boy and the girl are _____ ."
10. Clap if she says something about the picture and uses the word "are."
11. Change the picture and repeat the activity.

2.143   Points to common objects according to function based on verbal cues

Strand: 2-1A   **Age:** 45-48m 3.9-4.0y

Definition

The child will be able to identify objects or pictures by their use and function.

Instructional Materials

/*\Safety Note: Provide scissors appropriate for the child. Remind the child of safety regarding scissors.

One large piece of paper divided into four sections or four sheets of paper attached to make one large sheet for each child. Pencil, crayons, nontoxic glue, child-safe scissors, marking pen, magazines or catalogs.

Instructional Activities

1. More than one child may be involved in this activity.
2. Place the sheet of paper on a working surface for each child. It is important that the children have easy access to the magazines, crayons, pencils and scissors.
3. Explain that the paper represents our home and each of the four sections represents something we do in our house. The sections could represent such things as cooking, resting, keeping clean, working, or playing. The child may choose the four functions, one for each section.
4. Help the child label each section with the selected activity.
5. Discuss some of the things used to cook, to play, to help us rest and to keep clean.
6. After the discussion, explain that you want the child to draw a picture or to find pictures in the magazines of all the things they can match to the labeled function.
7. After the children have completed filling in the four-section picture, ask each one to tell what they placed in each category and how it helps to accomplish the function.

8. This activity can be adapted to categorize other functions and subjects.

2.144   Identifies words that rhyme

Strand: 2-1A   **Age:** 48-52m 4.0-4.4y

Definition

The child will repeat the phonemic sound order of words. These words or syllables have the same patterns (usually consonant-vowel-consonant-CVC) and are presented to the child orally. She is expected to say other words that have the same linguistic arrangement. Generally the words are said in rhymes or jingles (Little Miss Muffet--Sat on a tuffet) prior to isolation (Muffet - tuffet); however, an extended skill could include beginning consonant substitution (rat, cat, fat, mat, bat, spat.)

Instructional Materials

A book of rhymes. Collect a series of words that rhyme.
Example: hat/fat/pat, sit/hit/mitt, can/ran/fan, sing/ring/wing.

Instructional Activities

Note: When the child is beginning to name words, maintain grossly different sounds, such as "m" and "p." Gradually work into finer discriminations, such as "m" and "n."

1. The child should be seated near you, but she does not have to see the pages of the book of rhymes.
2. Review with the child the meaning of words that rhyme. Provide her with examples of rhyming words.
3. Tell her that she is going to play a game called Clap Tap Rhyme.
4. Explain that every time she hears words that rhyme, she is to clap her hands or tap her foot.
5. Begin by reading rhymes, pausing to allow her time to realize she is to clap or tap.
6. After you have read several rhymes and the child is comfortable with the response, begin to say a series of words, some that rhyme (hat/cat) and others that do not (man/day).
7. Continue by presenting three words to the child of which two are alike.
8. Ask her to say the two that rhyme.

2.145 Carries out simple one-part commands that denote difference in sensory qualities

Strand: 2-2 **Age:** 48-53m 4.0-4.5y

Definition

The child will complete a command when presented with two items that are visually different, or two different volumes of sound, or two materials that have tactile differences, or two materials of different weight.

Instructional Materials

A bag of different size buttons. Masking tape to be used as a divider. A pre-recorded tape/CD of marching music. Equipment to play the tape/CD. Two round circles at least 4 inches in diameter cut out from heavy paper. On one circle draw a representation of something loud (person with mouth wide open or a balloon breaking), and on the other circle draw a representation of a soft sound (person with mouth closed in a humming position, with light rain falling). Attach the circles back-to-back to a stick (small dowel or balloon stick). A square box with a hole cut in the side just large enough for the child to put his hand inside. Several pieces of rough material and several pieces of soft material.

Instructional Activities

Note: Place the bag of buttons on a table and spread them out. Prepare the equipment to play the pre-recorded tape. Put the pieces of material inside the square box, and place it on the table.

Visual Directions:

1. Ask the child to look at the collection of buttons.
2. Select one button of medium size.
3. Place the selected button on top of the table.
4. Place a strip of masking tape in a position on the table to divide the table in half.
5. Tell the child to find all the buttons that are larger than the one at the top of the table and to put them on one side. Tell him to find all the buttons that are smaller than the one at the top of the table and to put them on the other side.
6. Reward him for completing the task.
7. Put the buttons away and remove the taped divider.

Auditory Directions:

1. Show the child the stick with the circles attached.
2. Explain that on one side of the stick is a picture of a loud noise, and on the other side of the stick is a picture of a soft noise. Discuss the pictures and what they represent.
3. Tell him you are going to make a loud noise and ask him to hold up the stick with the picture of a loud noise facing you.
4. Make a loud noise and watch for the correct sign.
5. Explain that you are going to play some music, and when it is loud, the child is to show his loud picture, and when it is soft, he is to show his soft picture.
6. Play the music, and assist as needed.
7. Record the child's responses.

Tactile Directions:

1. Place the square box on the table, put your hand inside, and take out at least two pieces of material, one rough and the other smooth.
2. Give the child the pieces of material to handle, ask him to give you the rough piece, and then ask him to give you the smooth piece.
3. Place the two squares back in the box.
4. Show him how to put his hand through the hole in the box to feel the material inside.
5. Say, "Find a smooth piece of material and put it on the table."
6. Continue with the rough piece, the silky piece, and the scratchy piece.
7. If he has a difficult time using just his sense of touch, remove the pieces of material from the box and place them on the table.
8. Repeat the requests.

2.146 Speaks with inflection when describing an event or action

Strand: 2-4B **Age:** 48-53m 4.0-4.5y

Definition

When he is telling about an exciting occurrence, the child will speak with voice inflections that indicate enthusiasm, surprise, and spirit. He may increase or decrease his volume and/or pitch to emphasize a part of the description, or he may imitate sounds or dialogue he heard for effect.

Instructional Materials

A folk tale or fairy tale that has different characters and provides an opportunity for verbal expression. Adapt the selected folk tale or fairy tale into a dramatization. This dramatization could be for actors or puppets. Example: *The Lion and The Mouse* by Aesop. Characters needed--a lion, a mouse, a dog, a cat.

Lion: Roar! (loud and fierce)

Mouse: Squeak. (tiny and weak)

Lion: (after catching the mouse) I will eat you. (gruffly)

Mouse: Please do not eat me, and someday you will be glad. (tiny and weakly)

Lion: Ha-Ha! (loud laugh) Okay, little Mouse, go on your way.

Lion: (walks along and is caught in a net) Help! Help! (scared, mad)

Dog: Hello, Lion. I will help you. (tries to pull the net loose with his teeth) Growl, growl! I am sorry. I can't help you.

Lion: Help! Help! (scared, mad)

Cat: Hello, Lion. I will help you. (tries to pull the net lose with sharp claws) Meow, meow. I am sorry. I can't help you.

Lion: Help! Help! (weakly) Sob, sob. (crying)

Mouse: Hello, Lion. Remember me? I will help you. (begins to gnaw the rope and soon sets the lion free)

Lion: I am free! I am free! (happily) Thank you! Thank you!

Mouse: We will always be friends.

Suitable props for actors, or puppets and backdrops for puppet show.

Instructional Activities

1. Set the stage for the production. This activity may involve more than one child.
2. Tell the folk tale or fairy tale to the child, being sure to use inflections in the dialogue.
3. Repeat the tale and discuss it with him.
4. Repeat it once more, encouraging the child to join in the dialogue.
5. Explain to him that he is going to act out the story.
6. Assign roles, giving the role of the lion to the child who needs to increase intensity and the role of the mouse to the child who needs to modify his pitch.
7. Provide the different characters with the necessary props.
8. Begin the production by giving an introduction: (1) Announce the title of the story; (2) Introduce each character, and ask each one to speak (e.g., Say, "Here is Mr. Lion" lion roars); (3) Set the stage by saying, " One day Mr. Lion was walking in the woods, and he saw a mouse. 'The mouse would be a good bite,' he thought.
9. Begin the production by cueing as follows:
10. Say, "The lion roared." Pause for the lion to roar.
11. Say, "The little mouse squeaked." Pause for the mouse to squeak.

12. Say, "The lion catches the mouse, and says, 'I will eat you.'" Pause for the lion to say, "I will eat you."
13. Continue the dialogue as described above.
14. At the conclusion of the production, allow different children to be different characters.

2.147 Uses timed events appropriately when explaining a happening (today, yesterday, tomorrow)

Strand: 2-4B **Age:** 60-72m 5.0-6.0y

Definition

When the child is presented with a question such as, "Tell me, what you are going to do today?", "What are you going to do tomorrow?" or, "What did you do yesterday?" her response will reflect the timed happening correctly.

Instructional Materials

A clothesline strung between two points within the child's reach. Seven cards that represent the days of the week, with the word and an illustration. Clip clothespins. Example: Card One--The word "Monday" and a picture of something that happens on Mondays.

Instructional Activities

1. On the pre-strung clothesline, clip the seven days-of-the-week cards.
2. Invite the child to the clothesline.
3. Point to today, and say, "This is today. This is the day we [an activity for the day]."
4. Point to yesterday and say, "This was yesterday. This was the day we [an activity that happened]."
5. Point to tomorrow and say, "This will be tomorrow. We will [expected activity]."
6. Ask the child to point to today.
7. Provide assistance if needed and repeat, "This is today. This is the day we [an activity for the day]."
8. Ask her to point to yesterday.
9. Provide assistance if needed and repeat, "This is yesterday. This is the day we [an activity that happened]."
10. Repeat with tomorrow.
11. Repeat the clothesline recognition activity daily, and change the illustrations as needed.
12. Allow the child to illustrate the pictures or assist in the drawings.

2.148   (Moved to Cognitive, skill 1.307)

2.149   Answers specific questions based on spoken material

Strand: 2-1A   **Age:** 48-60m 4.0-5.0y

Definition

After hearing a story, the child will be able to answer questions that relate to understanding the primary, direct, or "literal" meaning of the content. The questions are based on "who was it," "what did they do," "when did they do it" and "where did it happen," etc.

Instructional Materials

A picture book with a story content that has the following: a character who does something at a given time and place. It is important that the picture book you choose has pictures of the "who, what, when, and where's" of the story.

Instructional Activities

1. Invite the child to sit next to you so he can see the book as you read it. Explain to him that you are going to read a story, and then you will ask him some questions.
2. Read the story.
3. When you finish the story, turn back to the first page, and ask a "who" question about the story.
4. Tell the child to answer the question and to look at the picture. Ask him to point to the "who" in the picture.
5. Continue asking "what" questions, "where" questions, and "when" questions.
6. Encourage the child not only to answer the question, but also to point to the answer in the visuals.
7. As an extension of this activity, invite him to draw a picture to answer the questions. For example, say, "Draw a picture of who [got lost] in the story," or "Draw a picture of where the [bear] in the story went."
8. Encourage the child to discuss the story in the context of why something happened and what effect this different happening had on the story's outcome.

2.150   Points to or places object before, after, above, below based on verbal cues

Strand: 2-1A   **Age:** 48-60m 4.0-5.0y

Definition

When the child is given the prepositions before, after, above and below as a verbal direction, she will complete the activity/task correctly. Example: (1) Put your hat above the shelf; (2) Place the apple before the banana; (3) Take the ball and put it below the bat.

Instructional Materials

Five empty boxes from a local fried chicken franchise store. A set of six chicken legs about 4 inches long drawn and cut from brown construction paper. (Note: Each child participating should have a box with one set of six chicken legs in it.) A chicken head drawn and cut out from yellow poster board with eyes, a mouth, a beak, and a comb added to make a chicken head mask. If you use cardboard, cover it with construction paper or paint it yellow before you draw animal features on it.

Instructional Activities

1. Invite the child to the table and give her a chicken dinner box.
2. Ask the child to open her box and look inside.
3. Ask her to take the chicken legs out of the box.
4. Tell her that you are the, "Head Chicken."
5. Put your chicken mask up to your face, and tell the child again that you are the, "Head Chicken."
6. Tell her that you are going to ask her to do some things with her chicken legs.
7. Say, "Put a chicken leg before the box." Then say, "Put a chicken leg after the box." Next say, "Take a chicken leg from the box and hold it above the box." Then say, "Move the box so that a chicken leg is below it."
8. Repeat the commands, and demonstrate until the chicken legs are correctly placed.
9. Give the child an opportunity to be the "Head Chicken."

2.151 Uses past participle to form past tense

Strand: 2-3 **Age:** 49-54m 4.1-4.6y

Definition

When the child is involved in a verbal situation or presented with a visual, he will respond by using a past participle to form a past tense. (e.g., He had run to the car.)

Instructional Materials

A short story in which many of the participles in past tense are incorrect. Example:

My Teddy Bear

My teddy bear's name is Russ.

Russ comed to live with me last year.

Last year Russ rided in my wagon.

This year Russ rides in the basket of my bike.

Russ and I eated crackers yesterday.

Russ got sick, he eated too many.

Russ is my favorite friend.

Instructional Activities

1. Invite the child to join you at the listening area. Explain to him that you are going to read a story, and that the story has some silly words in it.
2. Tell him every time he hears a silly word, he is to say "Silly, Silly."
3. Read the story, My Teddy Bear.
4. Pause slightly after each incorrect verb tense, allowing him to say "Silly, Silly." ("Russ comed (Silly, Silly) to live with me last year.")
5. Ask him if he can make the sentence "unsilly." ("Russ came to live with me last year.") Prompt if necessary.
6. Continue with the rest of the story, pausing at the "Silly, Silly" responses.
7. Develop additional stories and repeat the steps of the activity.

2.152 Uses verb "have" to form past tense

Strand: 2-3 **Age:** 49-54m 4.1-4.6y

Definition

When the child is involved in a verbal situation or presented with a visual, she will respond by using the verb "have" to form past tense. (e.g., We have a new kitten. She has run far.)

Instructional Materials

Some simple riddles developed by naming three or four characteristics of a person, a place, or a thing. Example: (1) I have long pointed ears. I

have a puff for a tail. In the spring, I have a basket full of eggs. What am I? (2) It has a top and a bottom. It has a round inside. It has pickles and onions with it. It has a name that sounds like grandmurger. What is it?

Instructional Activities

1. Invite the child to join you at the listening center. Explain to the child that you are going to tell some riddles and that she is to guess who or what the answer is.
2. Tell the first riddle, and pause for her answer.
3. Ask her to repeat the riddle, assist her by saying one line, and ask her to restate it.
4. Allow her the opportunity to draw a picture of the answer.
5. Repeat the above with other riddles.
6. Invite the child to make up some riddles; assist her by: (1) Asking her to think of a person, a place or a thing; (2) Starting the first line of the riddle for her: "I have _____ . I have a _____ . I have _____ .What am I?" Guess the answer to the riddle.
7. As an alternative: (1) Ask the child to think of a person, a place or a thing; (2) Start the first line of the riddle for her: "It has _____ . It has a _____ . It has _____ . What is it?" Guess the answer to the riddle.

2.153 Repeats what happened in story previously read by another

Strand: 2-1A **Age:** 50-58m 4.2-4.10y

Definition

When the child is presented with a short story, he will be able to retell the story. The story will be read from beginning to end without pausing between pages or episodes to ask questions or to reinforce the actions. If the child has difficulty telling the story, the reader may break the story down to smaller units. The story selected should be within the child's experiences and interests. If needed, visuals may be used to assist him in story recall.

Instructional Materials

Flannel or magnetic board props purchased or made for a simple story or fairy tale.

Instructional Activities

1. Read the story to the child, not using the props.
2. Show him the representative props that accompany the story.
3. Discuss the props, for example, who they are, what they did in the story, where they went

or lived, how they helped another character in the story.

4. Ask the child to retell the story using the flannel board or magnetic pieces.
5. Hand him or point to the next prop as a clue if he has trouble with recall.
6. Tell him to try telling the story using fewer and fewer props.
7. Continue until eventually he uses no props at all.

2.154 Carries out 4 simple related successive commands in order

Strand: 2-2 **Age:** 50-58m 4.2-4.10y

Definition

When the child is presented with a four-step command in which the steps are logically related, she will correctly complete the required tasks in order.

Instructional Materials

Pictures of food from a supermarket, magazines, or from food packages. One paper plate, one plastic fork, one plastic spoon, one napkin.

Instructional Activities

1. Place the items on the floor, and ask the child to sit down next to them.
2. Ask the child the name of the items, providing assistance as needed.
3. Ask her if she would like to "go to lunch."
4. If more than one child is participating, tell the child who is going to lunch to choose a friend to go along.
5. Ask the child to pick up a plate, a fork, a spoon, and a napkin.
6. Tell her to pick up the food items she would like for lunch. For example, she chooses a bowl of soup, a glass of milk, a cookie, and an orange.
7. Tell her she may keep the soup, give the milk to a friend, put the cookie on the napkin, and bring the orange to you.
8. Give her time to carry out the four directives.
9. Tell her to return the items, and to let her friend choose her lunch.
10. Repeat the steps.
11. This activity may be varied by using real food or different pictures.

2.155 Points to or places object by, beside, behind

Strand: 2-1A **Age:** 36-54m 3.0-4.6y

Definition

The child will respond to one-part directions containing indefinite and instrumental prepositions. He will demonstrate an understanding of verbal directions such as: (1) Put the rock by the box; (2) Stand beside the chair; (3) Hide behind the tree.

Instructional Materials

Items that can be manipulated to show "by," "beside" and "behind." Examples: can, box, ball, rock, small toys, blocks.

Instructional Activities

1. Place the items on a table. Ask the child to come to the table.
2. Put aside all manipulatives except the box and the ball.
3. Tell the child to close his eyes. Place the ball behind the box. Ask the child to open his eyes and to tell where the ball is.
4. Say, "You are right; the ball is behind the box. Will you put the ball beside the box?"
5. Select another set of items.
6. Ask the child to close his eyes. Place the toy car beside the rock. Ask the child to open his eyes, and to tell you where the toy car is.
7. Say, "You are right; the toy car is beside the rock. Will you move the toy car behind the rock?"
8. Continue, using different items.
9. Exchange places with him, letting him move the items and request the verbal directions.
10. If more than one child is involved, modify the activity as follows:
11. Choose one child to be "It."
12. Ask the others to close their eyes.
13. Whisper a prepositional command such as, "Sit beside table" or "Sit behind desk" to the child who is "it" while the others close their eyes.
14. Ensure that the child who is "it" is in the proper position, then say, "Where is [Bradley]?"
15. Tell the children to open their eyes and to tell where the child who is "it" is and in what position.
16. Instruct the child who is "it" to answer the questions with simple phrase, including the target preposition.
17. Choose the child who is first to answer correctly to be "it" next.

2.156 Points to or places object in front, in back, around, through based on verbal cues

Strand: 2-1A **Age:** 36-54m 3.0-4.6y

Definition

When the child is given the prepositions "in front," "in back," "around," and "through" as verbal directions, she will respond correctly by completing the required actions. Example: (1) Place the pencil in front of the book; (2) Put the red block in back of the green block; (3) Move the box around the corner; (4) Push the string through the bead.

Instructional Materials

At least six different colored blocks or six different character stand-up toys. Small toy car.

Instructional Activities

1. Place the colored blocks or the stand-up toys in a straight line on a table.
2. Ask the child to come to the table.
3. Say, "Point to the block (or character) that is in front."
4. Pause for a response.
5. Say, "Point to the block that is in the back."
6. Mix the blocks up.
7. Set up the blocks in a line again. (To add to the challenge, do not make the line straight.)
8. Repeat the directions.
9. Allow the child to set up the situation and give the directions.
10. Using the blocks, build a structure, such as a house, a bridge, or a road.
11. Say, "Take the toy car and move it around the house."
12. Change the structure.
13. Say, "Take the toy car and move it around the road."
14. Allow the child to build a structure and to give the directions.
15. Using the blocks, build a tunnel.
16. Say "Take the car and move it through the tunnel."
17. Change the structure.
18. Say, "Take the car and move it through the tunnel."
19. Allow the child to build a structure and give the directions.
20. If more than one child is involved, use the following game activity:
21. Place the children in a straight line, all facing forward.

22. Ask them to point to the child who is in front and then to point to the child who is in back of them.
23. Place the children in a straight line, all facing forward, but have every other one squat down.
24. Ask them to point to who is in front and who is in back of them.
25. Place them in a straight line, shoulder to shoulder.
26. Ask one child to point to the child in front and in back of her.
27. Continue by placing the children in various different configurations.

2.157 Acts out at least two, but no more than five, commands in the same order they were presented

Strand: 2-2 **Age:** 42-60m 3.6-5.0y

Definition

The child will listen to at least two and not more than five commands. After the commands are issued, the child will act them out in the order in which they were presented.

Instructional Materials

Some directions that require the child to pretend to be different animals while acting out commands.
Example: (1) Bears--Walk on all fours. Climb a tree. Get some honey in the tree. Eat the honey. Curl up and go to sleep; (2) Caterpillar--Lie down. Wiggle to the bush (identified prior to the request). Wiggle inch by inch to a flower (identified prior to the request). The sun is shining so turn stomach-side-up; (3) Bird--Fly on tiptoes. Sit in the grass. Tip your head and listen for a worm. Catch the worm. Eat the worm. Fly back to your nest.

Instructional Activities

1. Select an appropriate area for the activity. If using the Caterpillar sequence, be sure to locate the bush and the flower earlier for the child. If using the Bear or Bird sequence, designate the tree and the ground area to be used.
2. Select one of the animal action sequences.
3. Explain to the child that he is going to be a bear.
4. If the child is not familiar with bear habits, discuss what walking on all fours means and how bears like honey, climbing trees, and sleeping a lot.

5. Ask him to listen carefully to what he is supposed to do as a big brown bear.
6. Say, "[Richard], you are now a big brown bear. Today, Mr. Big Brown Bear, you are to walk on all fours to the big tree. When you get to the tree, climb up. You will find some honey in the tree. Get the honey and eat it. Then you will become very tired, so climb down the tree, curl up, and go to sleep."

2.158   Names main idea after listening to a story

Strand: 2-1A   **Age:** 53-60m 4.5-5.0y

Definition

When the child is read a short selection, she will identify the main idea when asked. Her response may be expressed verbally, illustrated, or selected from a multiple choice grouping.

Instructional Materials

Collection of clothes for dress-up play (requests of parents, trips to thrift stores or garage sales will build up a supply. Request and look for items such as dresses, shirts, blouses, shorts, skirts, scarves, gloves, jackets, ties, T-shirts, formal gowns, hats, caps, uniforms, boots, high-heeled shoes, vintage clothing, jewelry, veils, purses, etc.) A suitcase or trunk for storing the collection of dress-ups.

Instructional Activities

1. Display the collection of clothing.
2. Ask the child to dress up to be anyone he wants to be, using the clothes that are available. Allow him time to select from the collection and to put the clothing on.
3. After he is dressed, ask him who he is. He may tell you he is a cowboy, or he may say his name is Jim Porter.
4. If he says he is a cowboy, decide on his cowboy name.
5. If he says he is Jim Porter, decide what is important about Jim and what he does.
6. With that information, make up a story about this new character. This story should be short, have a main thought, and be positive.
7. Example: (No Title)
   Once upon a time there was a cowboy named Tex.
   He was the best cowboy on the Double Deal Ranch.
   One day Tex was riding in from the range.
   He sat tall in his saddle to make sure he saw everything.

He saw a herd of cattle a-runnin' and a-chargin' his way.
   They had gotten out of the corral.
   Tex and his horse went very fast.
   Tex waved his blanket at the leaders of the herd.
   The cattle were afraid and turned quickly.
   Tex started to sing quietly, and the cattle stopped running.
   He soon had them back at the ranch in the corral.
   Everyone was so proud of Tex, the best cowboy on the Double Deal Ranch.
8. After telling the made-up story to the make-believe hero, ask the child questions about the story. Example questions: Detail--What is your name? Where do you live? What happened when you were going home? What did you use to scare the cattle? What did you do to make the cattle walk? How did everyone feel when you went back to the ranch? Main Idea--What shall we call your adventure of getting the cattle back home?
9. An enjoyable addition to this activity is to tape record the story and play it back, to video the dressed up character acting out the story while it is being told in the background, or to write the story down and make a book of it, allowing the child to illustrate the pages.

2.159   States the characteristics and attributes of an object or a place

Strand: 2-4B   **Age:** 53-60m 4.5-5.0y

Definition

The child will name the characteristics of an object or place when the situation is stated (e.g., when he hears the word "zoo", he will name as many words as he can that describe a zoo). He will not be given a situation that represents a place where he has never been or an object with which he can not associate.

Instructional Materials

A house drawn and cut out from a large sheet of poster board. Draw four windows and one door on the house, cutting all of them to open only on three sides. Behind window one, tape a picture of bedroom furniture; behind window two, tape a picture of two children playing; behind window three, tape a picture of an adult doing a creative task (painting a picture, sawing a board, stirring a pot on the stove); behind window four, tape a picture of a room with toys all over the floor and clothing strewn about; and behind the door, tape a picture of a dog sitting quietly.

Instructional Activities

1. Place the house on a bulletin board or wall, or lay it flat on a table.
2. Explain to the child that this is a busy, busy house and that he will get to peek inside.
3. Open window one, and ask him to describe what he sees. If necessary, use prompts such as: "What room are we looking at? Why is there a bed in this room? Why isn't there a refrigerator in this room?"
4. Open window two, and ask him to describe what he sees and what is happening. If necessary, use prompts such as: "What are the children doing? Tell me about the game they are playing. Do you think the two children are friends?"
5. Continue with the other windows and the door.
6. Windows three and four and the door require convergent and divergent thinking; hence, you may need to give additional prompting.
7. You can modify this activity by changing the environmental subject; instead of a house, make the setting a playground, a store, a school, or a party.

2.160 Describes attributes of objects or items in picture

Strand: 2-4B **Age:** 53-60m 4.5-5.0y

Definition

When the child is presented with a picture, she will describe an object or an item by telling about its properties, characteristics, or qualities, using at least three sentences. Example: She looks at a picture of an apple, and she may say, "The apple is red and round. It grows on a tree. Apples are good in pies." Begin the activity by using single-item pictures of objects (nouns) and then single-item pictures in which the object is involved in an action (verbs). After she has successfully responded to single-item pictures, show her a multi-visual picture.

Instructional Materials

A collection of fish drawn on heavy paper, such as cardboard or poster board, and cut out. A collection of single-item pictures, one attached to each fish. A paper clip attached to each fish's mouth.
A fishing pole made by attaching a string to a 1-inch dowel stick about a foot long with a magnet attached to the other end of the string. A backdrop made from blue poster board that represents ocean waves. Two chairs.

Instructional Activities

1. Prop the backdrop between two chairs, put the collection of fish "in the ocean," and lay the fishing pole on the bank.
2. Invite the child to "go fishing."
3. Talk with her about what you do when you go fishing, why people enjoy it, various kinds of fish, and so on.
4. Tell her that she will be the fisherman.
5. Show her the pole and the lake.
6. Explain to her that when she catches a fish, she must look at the picture on the fish and tell you about it in at least three sentences.
7. Tell her to go fishing.
8. Provide assistance with her first "catch."
9. If she describes the picture on the fish, let her keep her catch. If she is unable to describe the picture, she must throw the fish back.
10. You can easily modify this activity by: (1) Putting multi-object pictures on the fish; (2) Establishing a descriptive criteria, such as telling what the object looks like, what it is used for, and where it came from.

2.161 Uses four- to eight-word sentences

Strand: 2-4B **Age:** 48-72m 4.0-6.0y

Definition

The child will speak four- to eight-word sentences on the same subject. The sentences can be in response to a past experience, a present happening, a visual representation, participation in a conversation or a future expectation.

Instructional Materials

A short story that has an open-ended component designed to allow the child to say what he thinks could happen, who was involved, or how the events might unfold. If you create your own story, it will tend to be more relative for the child. The following is an example:
You are riding a horse on a trail in the woods.
Your horse is trotting along the trail.
You are riding up and down in the saddle.
Up and down, trotting along, up and down.
Your horse starts to move faster, and you hold the reins as you move up and down faster.
Up and down, faster and faster, up and down.
All of the sudden, your horse stops in the middle of the trail.
You sit up tall in the saddle.
In the middle of trail, there is a big, big box.
You jump off your horse and go to the box.

The lid won't come off.
You need to push harder and harder.
Suddenly the lid comes off.
You look inside and . . .

Instructional Activities

1. Ask the child to join you at the storytelling area.
2. Tell the child to close his eyes and make mind pictures while you read him a story.
3. Read the story very slowly with much enthusiasm and suspense.
4. At the end of the story, ask him to tell you what he saw in the big box.

2.162 Rephrases others' comments in a discussion

Strand: 2-1A   **Age:** 55-60m 4.7-5.0y

Definition

The child will rephrase another's comments and will retain the original meaning. In rephrasing, she may use synonyms, reorganization of words, substitution of words, and expanded statements. She may be asked to fill in a different word in a sentence. Example: You say, "The wind is howling." Ask the child to complete, "The wind is _____" by using another word for howling. Or she may be asked to reorganize words she heard. Example: Statement heard: "Sally put her doll, her stuffed rabbit, and her basket in the wagon. They took a ride." Rephrased: "The doll, the play rabbit, and the basket took a ride in Sally's wagon." The child may then be asked to substitute a word that has been heard. Example: Statement heard: "The girls and boys were playing." Rephrased: "The children were playing." The child may be asked to expand a heard statement. Example: Statement heard: "I could tell the boy was having a good time." Rephrased: "I could tell the boy was having a good time because he was laughing."

Instructional Materials

A pre-recorded tape (CD / MP3) that includes short statements or descriptions. Example: (1) The wagon went past me so quickly that all I saw was a red flash; (2) The bird was busy making a home in the tall pine; (3) That man drove straight through the red light; (4) Paul crept softly out of the little room and went up the cold, dark stairs; (5) Katie went upstairs, laughing very freely, and feeling happier than she had ever felt.
The above statements should be recorded by different voices and with appropriate intonation and emphasis. Allow for at least a 30-second

pause between each statement or description so that the recorder can be turned on and off. Equipment to play the tape. Marking pen, paper. Have the children bring items for show-and-tell.

Instructional Activities

Note: Approach this activity as a fun task and one to be enjoyed by everyone. More than one child may participate.

1. Invite the child to join you at the listening area. Have the equipment ready to play.
2. Explain to the child that you are going to play a tape on which some people are talking. Tell her to listen to the tape
3. Play the first statement or description.
4. Say, "Can you say what you just heard, using different words?"
5. If the child is having a problem, play the tape message again.
6. Say, "Try to say what you just heard using different words."
7. Let her illustrate the way she restated the taped message. Display the illustration with her wording printed next to the picture.
8. Continue with the other statements on the tape.
9. Another way to elicit the same skill is to ask the children to bring one item to share with the others.
10. Select one child to share her item, and when she is finished, ask if anyone can retell what she just heard about the item.
11. Continue until all the children have a chance to share and retell.

2.163 Uses "will" to form future tense

Strand: 2-3 **Age:** 56-62m 4.8-5.2y

Definition

When the child is involved in a verbal situation or presented with a visual, he will respond by using "will" to form future tense. (e.g., He will run far.)

Instructional Materials

A series of "will" sentences. Examples: He will run fast. She will go to the window. Bob will jump over the block. Sally will get a drink of water.

Instructional Activities

1. Invite the child to the activity area. More than one child may participate.
2. Tell the child you are going to play a game of the future.

3. Give him a sample sentence such as, "He will run fast."

4. Explain that you will say other "will" sentences, and when he hears his name, he is to do what is requested. Example: Point to the child named John and say, "John will run fast."

5. Explain that you will start a "will" sentence and point to one of the child(s) to finish it.

6. Use sentences that start with, "She will," "Bob will," or "He will."

7. After he has had a turn, discuss how the word "will" makes the sentence relate to the future, and explain what the future is.

8. Review past, present and future with the child.

2.164 Describes events of past and future experience in logical, sequential order

Strand: 2-3 **Age:** 59-64m 4.11-5.4y

Definition

After the child has heard a simple story with at least three occurrences, she will be given a set of pictures showing the story's sequence. When asked, the child will arrange the pictures in the correct order and tell the story. The set of pictures will clearly depict past and future events.

Instructional Materials

A story that has three clear sequences and that can easily be represented by manipulatives like puppets, flannel board characters, paper dolls, or masks. Example: "Once upon a time there was a little girl named Teresa. She had her face painted like a clown's. It was a sad face with a turned-down mouth. When Teresa saw herself in the mirror, she changed her sad mouth to a happy smile."

Three paper bags to illustrate the above story as follows: (Bag 1) Keep the bag flat and use crayons or markers to make it look like the girl named Teresa as her face is being painted. Use the bottom of the bag as the top of Teresa's head, and add yarn for hair; (Bag 2) Keep the bag flat and use crayons or markers to make it look like a sad clown's face, making sure the mouth is turned down. Change Teresa's hair by braiding it with ribbons on the ends; (Bag 3) Keep the bag flat and use crayons or markers to make it look just like bag two, except make Teresa's mouth smiling. Open up the bags so they will stand up on a table. Extra paper bags, crayons or markers.

Instructional Activities

1. Place the opened bag puppets on a table with the faces away from the child. Be sure that the puppets are not in the correct sequential order.

2. Tell the child that you are going to tell her a story. Tell her the story.

3. Turn the bag puppets around. Explain that the puppets are all Teresa, but they show her with different faces that match the story.

4. Explain that you are going to tell her the story again and that she is to place the different faces of Teresa in the right order, according to the story

5. Tell the story again.

6. During or after the story, ask her to place the bag faces in the correct order.

7. Discuss the three puppets with her. For example, ask about the first bag, "Who is this?" about the second bag, ask, "What does Teresa look like?" And about the third bag, ask, "What happened to Teresa's mouth?"

8. Encourage the child to tell the story and to move the puppets as she tells it.

9. Discuss with her what Teresa's face might have looked like before it was painted. Give her a blank paper bag and ask her to make Teresa's face before it was painted.

10. Talk with her about what Teresa's face will look like when she removes the clown make-up. Give her a blank paper bag and ask her to illustrate Teresa's face with part of the clown paint removed or streaking.

11. Using the two new face puppet bags and add them to the story content.

2.165 Distinguishes between spoken messages differing in tone

Strand: 2-1A **Age:** 60-63m 5.0-5.3y

Definition

The child will detect anger, joking, or calmness between two messages that are just alike except for the intonation (keep facial expression the same). He will identify the difference based on the voice tone. He will demonstrate the identification by using various response modes. Example: When he hears, "Put your sweater on now!" spoken in an angry voice, he will point to a pre-drawn angry face. When he hears, "Put your sweater on now," spoken in a calm manner, he will point to a pre-drawn calm face.

Instructional Activities

1. Select an area that is large enough for gross movement. Tell the child to stand in the area and to stretch his arms out to the sides. Make sure that his arms are not touching another child's or any objects.
2. Act as the leader.
3. Tell the child to move his arms rapidly up and down like wings when you name things that fly, but to stop his arm movements whenever you name something that does not fly.
4. Slowly say, "The airplane is flying, the bird is flying, the mouse is flying!"
5. Note whether he stopped his arm movements when you named something that doesn't fly (the mouse).
6. If necessary, remind him when to move his arms and when he should stop moving.
7. Tell the child to sit down if he continues to move his arms when you have named something that does not fly.
8. If more than one child is involved, the winner is the child who remains in the game longest. Reward the winner by allowing him to be the leader.
9. Vary this activity by having the children change gestures to include affective (happy, calm, angry) and make different statements.

2.166 Identifies differences in unlike speech sounds, m, g, t, p, when in isolation

Strand: 2-1A   **Age:** 60-65m 5.0-5.5y

Definition

When the child hears the m--"mummer sound," she will point to a picture that begins with the m sound. When she hears the g--"growner sound," she will point to a picture that begins with the g sound. When the child hears the t--"tippler sound," she will point to a picture that begins with the t sound. When she hears the p--"popper sound," she will point to a picture that begins with the p sound.

Instructional Materials

Pictures of items that start with "m," "g," "t" and "p."

Instructional Activities

1. Place the "m" pictures together, the "g" pictures together, the "t" pictures together and the "p" pictures together. Place the pictures face-down.

2. Tell the child she is going to hear words that have sounds of M--Mummer, G--Growner, T--Tippler and P--Popper.
3. Ask her to listen to a mummer sound, then a growner sound, followed by a tippler, and finally, a popper.
4. Point to the child and ask for a mummer sound word. Repeat by asking for a "g," "t," and "p" word.
5. Tell her you are going to show her a picture. After she looks at the picture, she is to give the mummer, growner, tippler, or popper sound. Example: Show the child a picture of a table. Say, "What is the sound?" Then ask her to say the name of the item on the picture.
6. Vary this activity by making the mummer, growner, tippler, or popper sound and asking the child to locate the picture of the item that begins with the sound.

2.167 Identifies differences in similar speech sounds, f, s, th, when in isolation

Strand: 2-1A   **Age:** 60-65m 5.0-5.5y

Definition

When the child hears the f --"fuffer sound," he will point to a picture that begins with the f sound. When he hears the s--"sassy sound," he will point to a picture that begins with the s sound. When he hears the th--"thather sound," he will point to a picture that begins with the th sound.

Instructional Materials

Pictures of items that start with "f," "s," and "th."

Instructional Activities

1. Place the "f" pictures together, the "s" pictures together and the "th" pictures together. Place the pictures face-down.
2. Tell the child he is going to hear words that have sounds of F-Fuffy, S-Sassy and Th-Thather.
3. Ask him to listen to a fuffy sound, then a sassy sound, and then a thather sound.
4. Point to the child, and ask for a fuffy sound word. Repeat by asking for an "s" and "th" word.
5. Tell the child you are going to show him a picture. After he has looked at the picture, he is to give the fuffy, sassy, and thather sounds. Example: Show him a picture of a fan. Say, "What is the first sound?" Then ask him to say the name of the item on the picture.

6. Vary this activity by making the fuffer, sassy, and thather sounds, and then asking the child to locate the picture of the item that begins with the given sound.

2.168 Identifies where sound differences occur in words

Strand: 2-1A   **Age:** 60-65m 5.0-5.5y

Definition

The child will identify the same sound when it appears either in the initial or in the final position of a word. She will be asked to listen for the sound, and she will be able to tell the sound position.

Instructional Materials

A list of words with the same sound in the beginning and final position of words. Chair(s).

Instructional Activities

1. Set up chairs for each child participating in the activity. Ask the children to sit on a chair.
2. Tell the first child to listen for the first sound of a word and the next child to listen for the last sound of word.
3. Tell the child the letter sound she is to listen for.
4. Tell her if she hears the sound in her position (first or final), she is to jump up.
5. Say the word.
6. Tell the child she will lose her seat if she forgets to stand or if she stands at the wrong time.
7. Use words with the same sound in the first or final position, or not in the word at all to play a fun trick on the child.
8. If only one child is involved, ask her to stand in front of two chairs and sit in chair one if the sound is heard first and to sit in chair two if the sound is heard in the final position of the word. Example: Say, "The sound is m-m-m, as in the word man. Sit in chair one if the sound of m-m-m came at the beginning of the word man, and sit in chair two if the m-m-m came at the end of the word man."
9. This activity may be varied by having the child do other first and last movements besides sitting in a chair. She could toss a ball into box one and box two, or she could raise her hands, using hand puppets named First and Last.

2.169 Describes the outcome of a sequence of actions

Strand: 2-4B   **Age:** 60-72m 5.0-6.0y

Definition

When the child is shown a picture that depicts sequential actions, he will identify the action, and he will answer questions relating to the effect of the sequence. The sequence will illustrate at least three actions. Allow him to tell about each sequence before he answers questions about the results of these actions.

Instructional Materials

A map showing the neighborhood, including streets, buildings, playgrounds, or a map that shows leaving a house and going to a grocery store, or a map of a path through a woods. Cardboard cutouts of a man, a woman, a boy, and a girl, all proportioned to the size of the map.

Instructional Activities

1. Post the map on a bulletin board or lay it flat on a table.
2. Explain to the child that you will move the boy paper doll to leave the house and walk to the playground. Walk the figure of the boy out of the house, stop, and ask the child what the boy would see or do as he leaves his house. Then walk the boy cutout down the street toward the playground, stop, and ask the child what the boy would see or do as he walks down the street. Walk the boy cutout in front of a toy shop, stop, and ask the child what the boy would see or do as he looks in the shop window. Walk the boy cutout past some of his friends, stop, and ask the child what the boy would see or do as he meets his friends. Walk the boy cutout to the playground, stop, and ask the child what the boy is going to do now.
3. If you use another map, follow the same procedures as outlined above, only with different characters and content.
4. Give the child a opportunity to move the boy cutout on the trip from the house to the playground.

2.170 Uses sentences that express logical relations between concepts

Strand: 2-4B **Age:** 60-72m 5.0-6.0y

Definition

The child will use sentences that express logical relations between concepts. These will include comparative and "if-then" sentence structures. Examples of sentences using logical relations are: (1) Whole-part relationships--Sky is to airplane as water is to ship; (2) Part-whole relationship--Comb is to hair as toothbrush is to teeth; (3) Part-part relationship--Tires are to a steering wheel as pedals are to handle bars; (4) Object-to-action--A pencil is to writing as a scissors is to cutting; (5) Action-to-object relationship--Kicking is to soccer as batting is to baseball; (6) Cause-effect relationship--Sadness is to crying as happiness is to laughing; (7) Purpose relationship--A tail is to a kite as a string is to a balloon; (8) Antonym relationship--Hot is to cold as up is to down; (9) Synonym relationship--Jump is to leap as crawl is to creep; (10) Familial relationship-- A sister is to a brother as a grandmother is to a grandfather; (11) Temporal relationship--Morning is to sunrise as evening is to sunset; (12) Sequential relationship--Monday is to Tuesday as first is to second. The child expresses the linguistic concepts in sentence format such as, "If it rains, I will wear my raincoat," "Smoke means there is a fire," or "Airplanes fly in the sky. Ships float on water." These are easier and more understandable formats than "Sky is to airplanes as water is to ships." These sentences require logical operations for interpretation and expression.

Instructional Materials

Create a five-item chart that consists of either five shapes (five squares in different sizes and colors) or five animals from the same class (five cats in different shapes, colors, positions) or five children doing the same action (five boys and girls jumping but in different styles --jumping over a box, jumping a rope, etc.)
Some prepared cause-and-effect visuals. These visuals are available from commercial sources or can be made. Examples: (1) A group of people having a picnic with a big dark cloud above them; (2) A child trying to put a plate on a counter and it is about to tumble to the floor; (3) A group of children just finished building a snowman and the sun comes out; (4) A boy getting on his bicycle, looking at his back tire and it is flat; (5) A girl trying to put on a jacket that is much too small.

Instructional Activities

1. Place the chart in the child's view. Show the child the five-item chart.

2. Point to the big squares, and say, "What can you tell me about these squares? How are they different from the other squares?" When you have established the concept that they are bigger, you have introduced the first part of logical relationship (analogy).
3. Say, "If these squares are big (point to squares), then these squares (point to squares) are what?" Allow her verbally to determine size by relationships.
4. Repeat the procedure, using the colors of the squares as the determinate.
5. Encourage the child to use two comparisons, such as, "This square is big and blue, and this square is little and red."
6. Present her with one of the cause-and-effect pictures, for example, the group having a picnic with a dark cloud above them.
7. Discuss what is happening in the picture. Ask, "What are the people doing? What is overhead? What does the dark cloud mean?" Ask her what the people will do if it does begin to storm.
8. Encourage her to respond in a complete statement, such as, "If it starts to rain, the people will have their picnic under the shelter," "If it starts to rain, the people will run to their cars," "If it starts to rain, the people will get their umbrellas," "If it starts to rain, the people will go home," or "If it starts to rain, the people will sit in the rain."
9. Continue with other pictures.

2.171 Names an object's parts and gives the function of the object

Strand: 2-4B **Age:** 60-72m 5.0-6.0y

Definition

When the child is presented with a picture of an object, he will name the parts of the object and tell what the object does. The first objects presented to him will have standard parts and have basically one function, such as a pan (to hold things), a chair (for sitting on), a stove (to heat things), or a sweater (to wear). The second objects presented to him will be items that have unique parts and varied functions; such as a plant (to eat, for decoration, to protect) or a building (to live in, for storing things).

Instructional Materials

At least five single-item pictures collected or assembled on 8 ½- by 11-inch paper. Examples: (1) A clown with arms outstretched, legs apart, hat on head, funny face; (2) A tree with branches, leaves, trunk and fruit; (3) A dog showing legs, a tail, ears, a "barking" mouth, and a nose; (4) A hand showing fingers, rings on fingers, a watch, a bracelet; (5) A snowman showing a hat, rocks for eyes, holding a broom, ball of snow for body and head. Instructions: Glue the pictures on cardboard or poster board, and cut each picture into puzzle pieces, making sure that the different parts of the object are on separate pieces. Example: One clown arm is one puzzle piece, the other clown arm is another puzzle piece, the clown's hat is another piece, and so forth. Drawing paper, crayons or markers.

Instructional Activities

1. Select one of the puzzles and place the pieces face-up on a table. Place the drawing paper and crayons or markers on the table.
2. Tell the child that he is going to put a puzzle together, but explain that this puzzle is different because he may put the parts together only after he names them.
3. Ask him to look at the puzzle pieces on the table. Ask him to choose a puzzle piece, but before he can take it, have him tell what part it is.
4. Continue with the other pieces, asking him to find and name a puzzle piece. After he collects a few pieces, encourage him to start putting them together.
5. After he completes the puzzle, provide him with a sheet of drawing paper and marking tools.
6. Ask him to draw a picture of something that the puzzle character does. Example: A clown does tricks in a circus.
7. If his drawing is not appropriate, ask him to tell all the things he can about the character in the puzzle.
8. Continue the above with the other puzzles.

2.172 (Moved to Cognitive, skill 1.298)

2.173 Describes parts of a movie, TV show, live event or other audio/visual presentations

Strand: 2-4B **Age:** 48-66m 4.0-5.6y

Definition

After the child views an audio/visual presentation or a live production, he will be able to describe the content, sequence of events, characters, and outcomes. He will respond to the presentation when he is asked questions (Examples: What is the story about? Who was the story about? What was the first thing that happened in the story?) or when he is prompted (Tell me about the movie you saw yesterday).

Instructional Materials

A selected audio/visual presentation that will be of interest to the child. Prepared audio/visual presentations are available from media centers, commercial outlets, and local sources, or locate a play for a child production in books, create a presentation or use the following example: My Favorite Story.

Characters - A story teller, two children (Jane and Steve), groups of children to play different storybook roles.

Create the scene by placing two comfortable-looking pillows in the center of the stage. Next to the pillows place a stack of storybooks. Surrounding the pillows with several bookcases, filled with various children's books.

Enter Jane, Steve, and the storyteller. The children sit down on the pillows and move about until they are comfortable.

The following dialogue takes place:

Story Teller: It is your turn, Jane, to select the story you want me to read to you and Steve.

Jane: It is so hard for me to choose a story. There are so many that we like.

Story Teller: Why don't you and Steve talk it over, and I will be back in a minute.

Exit Story Teller.

Jane: (looking at Steve) What story would you like to hear today?

Steve: (looking at Jane) It is really hard to pick a favorite.

Jane and Steve place their heads in their hands to think about stories.

Jane takes a book (*Dr. Seuss*) from the stack by the pillows and opens it. Just as she opens the book, four children enter: one child is dressed as a cat with a hat on, another as a fox with socks, the third with several apples on top of her head and the fourth dressed as a bug and "kachooing."

Cat with a hat child: Please read about me!

Fox with socks child: Share my adventures and you will see.

Apples on top of head child: Funny tales and silly bees!

Bug child: Just a big kachoo, kachoo, kachooeey!

Four Children: (in unison) Please, oh please, choose me!

Jane and Steve laugh and clap as the four children dance off the stage.

Jane: Those are such wonderful stories, it is hard to choose. There are so many that we like.

Steve - It is really hard to pick a favorite.

Jane and Steve place their heads in their hands to think about stories.

Steve takes a book from the stack by the pillows and opens it. Just as he opens the book a child enters dressed as a rabbit with another child dressed as a full moon.

Child dressed as a rabbit: I say goodnight, goodnight, goodnight.

Child dressed as a moon: And goodnight to my bright light.

Jane and Steve laugh and clap as the two children dance off the stage.

(Continue the above play using other favorite stories and books.)

Storyteller enters.

Story Teller: Jane and Steve, have you decided which story you would like to have me read to you?

Jane and Steve look at each other, and all of the sudden all the characters who appeared earlier to Jane and Steve are on stage.

Characters: "Choose me, choose me, choose me."

Jane and Steve look bewildered, and finally Jane closes her eyes and Steve lays all the books out. Jane moves her hand over the books, and suddenly she points to one. Steve picks up the book and hands it to the story teller. Jane opens her eyes and claps with delight.

Steve and Jane settle down for story time and the story teller begins to read.

Instructional Activities

1. Set up the equipment necessary to project the selected audio/visual production.
2. Remove any distracting objects or elements. Invite the child to become comfortable for viewing the show.
3. Allow time for him to see the entire selection.
4. After he has seen the show, ask him questions as to the content, sequence, characters, conclusions, opinions, expectations, and projections.
5. Let him view the selection again if requested or needed.
6. It is important to accept the child's opinions and responses.

2.174 Chooses previously specified details from spoken material

Strand: 2-1A   **Age:** 63-70m 5.3-5.10y

Definition

The child will be told what details to listen for before she hears the spoken material. After hearing the spoken material, she will answer questions based on the details she was directed to note. The selected details will be those that require detailed/interpretive responses only and will answer who, when, where, what types of questions.

Instructional Materials

Chalkboard or sheet of chart paper, chalk or marking pen. A familiar story or rhyme rewritten as the examples that follow.

Familiar Rhyme:
This little piggy went to market,
This little piggy stayed home,
This little piggy had roast beef,
This little piggy had none.
This little piggy cried, "Wee, wee, wee."
And ran all the way home.

Rewrite One:
This little chick had corn today,
This little chick had only hay,
This little chick had worms, they say
This little chick cried, "Peep, peep, peep."
This little chick had feather shoes;
He wore them out to get the news.

Rewrite Two:
This little calf eats grass,
This little calf eats hay,
This little calf drinks water,
This little calf runs away,
This little calf does nothing at all
But lie around all day.

A who, what, when or where detail to ask the child to listen for before you read the original selection. For example, ask: (1) What did the little pigs eat? (2) How many little pigs were there? (3) Where did the little pigs go? (4) What happened to the last little pig?

Instructional Activities

1. Ask the child to join you at the chalkboard or near the chart paper. Tell the child that you are going to read her a favorite nursery rhyme or story. Tell her that as you read her the rhyme, she is to listen for one thing: "What did the little pig eat?"
2. Read the selection
3. Ask, "What did the little pig eat?"

4. Tell the child you are going to read the selection again and she is to listen for where the first little pig went.

5. Read the selection. Ask, "Where did the first little pig go?"

6. Tell her you will read the selection again and she is to listen for: "What happened to the last little pig?"

7. Read the selection. Ask, "What happened to the last little pig?"

8. After she has listened to the nursery rhyme or story and answered all the pre-detail questions, explain that you and she are going to write a new nursery rhyme together.

9. Include the child in doing the following:

Decide on a new main character (e.g., chick or calf)

Write: This little calf had _____ .

This little calf had _____.

This little calf had _____, they say.

Decide what the calves will eat and put the words in the first sentence.

Decide how many calves will be in the new rhyme and begin the sentences with "This little calf. . ."

Discuss and write where the little calf will go.

This little calf runs away.

Make up the last sentence of the new rhyme by writing what the last calf did.

"This little calf does nothing at all but lie around all day."

10. Read the newly completed calf rhyme.

"This little calf eats grass,

This little calf eats hay,

This little calf drinks water,

This little calf runs away,

This little calf does nothing at all

But lie around all day."

11. Ask the child to listen to the new Calf Rhyme and to be ready to answer the following questions: (1) What did the little calves eat? (2) Where did the little calf go? (4) What happened to the last little calf? Give these questions as listening details one at a time.

12. This activity can be continued, using different animals and creating new rhymes.

2.175 Makes facial expressions appropriate to spoken material

Strand: 2-1A   **Age:** 63-70m 5.3-5.10y

Definition

The child will make a facial expression that reflects what he has heard. For example, he will smile at another person's joke, will look awed when he is told something surprising, and will scowl after he is told something unpleasant.

Instructional Materials

Set of index cards, with facial expressions of happy, angry, sad, frightened, curious, and sleepy drawn or cut out and mounted on them. The same expression cards that were used in the assessment may be used for this activity. Prepared sentences that relate to a specific feeling. Examples: (1) The boy is looking at the face of a big bear; (2) The lady gave Tom a cookie; (3) It was very late at night; (4) Sally looked down at her broken doll.

Ask the child to bring in photos of himself.

Instructional Activities

Note: If more than one child is involved, continue until each child has had an opportunity to tell about and place his picture.

1. Prepare a space on a bulletin board, and at the top of the board, attach the facial expression cards. Allow ample space so that the child's pictures can be placed under the correct pictured category.

2. Invite the child to join you in front of the bulletin board. Tell him to bring his photographs.

3. Show him the facial expression cards and discuss each card, including the feeling it portrays and the name of the feeling.

4. Place the expression cards on the bulletin board within his reach.

5. Tell him that you will read him a sentence and that he is to point to the card that best tells the facial expression that would be used. For example, say, "The boy is looking at the face of a big bear. Can you point to the card that shows the way the boy's face would look?"

6. Allow him time to identify the correct card and to tell what feeling it represents.

7. After all the cards have been selected, remove them and place them in a horizontal row at the top of the bulletin board.

8. Ask the child to look at the photograph he brought and to tell you what is happening, what his feelings were, and how his face looked. Prompt him with questions as needed.

9. After he has described his photo, ask him under which facial expression card the photo should go. Example: A photograph with a happy face should be placed under the happy facial expression card row.

10. This activity can be modified by having the child draw a picture of a situation and a facial expression.

2.176 Identifies order of sounds in a word and blends the sounds together to make meaningful words
Strand: 2-1A **Age:** 64-68m 5.4-5.8y

Definition
As soon as the child has learned some of the consonant sounds and the short sounds of two vowels (preferably short "a" and short "i"), she needs to receive instruction on how to blend these sounds into meaningful words. The blending must be done smoothly to prevent mispronunciation of words and distortions. It is helpful to begin with words composed of nasal consonants with a short "a" so there are no sound pauses between the letters. (man, nap, map, mat, etc.) Once the child is able to sound blend a few words (man), consideration should be given to initial consonant substitution and the forming of other words by sound-blending (pan, fan, ran).

Instructional Materials
At least 10 words to be use for a game of <u>Word Puzzles</u>. Examples: mat, man, cup, jug, bag. At least 10 cards 5- by 8-inches, with pictures illustrating each word (drawn or cut and glued from magazines). Write the name of each picture at the top of each card, with each letter evenly spaced. Cut vertically down the entire card between the letters. If you have three letters in the word, there should be three pieces to the puzzle.)

Instructional Activities
1. Mix up the pieces of the <u>Word Puzzle</u> and give them to the child.
2. Tell the child to put the puzzle together, saying the letter sound as she does it.
3. Ask her to sound-blend the whole word when the puzzle is complete.
4. Increase the difficulty by giving her pieces of several puzzles at once that have been mixed up to see if she can correctly assemble them.
5. Make sure she says the whole word when the mixed-up puzzles are completed.

2.177 Responds verbally and non-verbally to questions concerning abstract and factual concepts
Strand: 2-1A **Age:** 42-54m 3.6-4.6y

Definition
When the child is presented with questions, he will answer verbally or he will indicate an answer nonverbally (e.g., shaking his head no or nodding yes). Examples of questions are: How old are you? (factual), Do you like apples? (abstract,) Did you hear the dog bark? (may be answered by nodding or shaking his head), Where would you like to go in the car? (abstract), What color is the sweater you are wearing? (factual), Are you ready to go? (may be answered by nodding or shaking his head).

Instructional Materials
At least six different single-item colored pictures, purchased or cut out from magazines, catalogs, or newspapers and mounted on cards or drawn on cards. Example of single item pictures: car, ball, sweater, book, tree, dog, cat.

Instructional Activities
1. Spread the cards, picture-side-up, on the table. Tell the child to look at the cards and listen while you ask a question.
2. Say, "Which card is something that you ride in?" (factual).
3. Ask the child to select the card that answers that question and name what is on the card (car).
4. If he provides the right answer, let him keep the picture card.
5. Say, "Is there a card on the table that is something fun to climb?"
6. After he has said "yes" or has nodded his head "yes," ask him to point to the card and say the name of the object (tree).
7. If he provides the right answer, allow him to keep the picture card.
8. Say, "Which card shows your favorite pet?"(abstract).
9. Ask him to select the card that has his answer to the question and to name what is on the card (dog or cat).
10. After he has named his favorite pet, ask him to point to the card that shows an animal.
11. Allow him to add the picture of the animal to his card collection.
12. Optional: Ask him why his favorite pet is a [dog]. Continue the verbal exchange about the selected pet.
13. Continue until all the cards are gone.

14. To modify this activity, allow the child to be the person who asks the questions, or change the pictures.

2.178 Identifies initial sounds of words
Strand: 2-1A **Age:** 65-72m 5.5-6.0y

Definition
When the child is asked to listen to a list of at least three words, of which two start with the same sound, she will be able to say the two that begin alike.

Instructional Materials
Poems or rhymes in which the words begin with a single sound.
Example:
"B Sound"
Big boy,
Big boy,
Billy, big boy.
Big boy,
Big boy,
Billy, big boy.
Big, big Billy,
Big boy.
T Sound
Tiny tots,
Tiny tots,
Tickly tiny tots.
Tiny tots,
Tiny tots,
Tickly tiny tots.
Tiny, tiny tots
Tickly, tickly.
M Sound
Mighty mice,
Mighty mice,
Many, many mighty mice.
Mighty mice,
Mighty mice,
Many, many mighty mice.
Mighty, mighty many mice
Many, many mighty mice.

Instructional Activities
Note: To assist in the memorization, do the Sound Poems in a chant format, using a tambourine to beat the rhythm.
1. Select a comfortable setting for the child. Explain to the child that you are going help her learn some silly sounding poems. Continue to explain that the reason the poems sound silly is because all the words in the poems start with the same sound.

2. Say, "Listen to the first Silly Sounding Poem. It is called B-b-b Sound." (sound out the b sound.)
3. Say the B Sound poem.
4. Repeat it several times, and encourage the child to join in with the "b-b-b" words. Continue saying the poem until she has it memorized.
5. Continue with the other Sound Poems, using the procedure above.
6. When the child has memorized several Sound Poems, tell her that you are going to say a sound-"m-m-m," and that she is to say the M Sound poem. Provide assistance in saying the poem as needed.
7. Say another sound and pause for her to say the poem that represents the given sound.
8. A motivational and a positive learning experience is to include the child when you create the sound poems.

2.179 Uses compound sentences with more than one main clause
Strand: 2-3 **Age:** 65-78m 5.5-6.6y

Definition
When the child is involved in a verbal situation, he will respond by using a compound sentence. He will connect the main clauses using such words as "and", "but", and, "or." (e.g., "I ran to the store and came back in an hour." "Jane can bake some cookies or a chocolate cake.")

Instructional Materials
Selected main clauses that are compatible with pictures (illustrate or locate in magazines or workbooks) that represent these clauses. Examples: (1) Picture 1--A cat is running. Picture 2--A dog is barking; (2) Picture 1--A boy is washing his face. Picture 2--The boy is combing his hair; (3) Picture 1--A basket has an apple in it. Picture 2--A basket has an orange in it; (4) Picture 1--One child is crying. Picture 2--Another child is laughing.

Instructional Activities
1. Place all four of the Picture 1's randomly on one side of a table, mounted on a bulletin board, or mounted on a magnetic board. Place the Picture 2's randomly on the other side of a table, mounted on a bulletin board, or mounted on a magnetic board.
2. Tell the child to select one of the pictures, to tell what it shows ("A cat is running"), and then to locate another picture that goes with it

(the picture of the dog barking). He selects the picture of the dog barking, and tells what it is ("A dog is barking.") Ask him if he can put the two pictures together and join the clauses so they become one complete sentence. ("The cat is running, and the dog is barking.")

3. Continue by having him select different pictures and provide two clauses, and then make up a compound sentence with more than one main idea.

2.180 Identifies initial and final sounds of words

Strand: 2-1A **Age:** 66-72m 5.6-6.0y

Definition

When the child is presented with a list of words that have different beginning and ending sounds, she will identify the sounds. The following sequence is recommended for beginning and ending sound recognition: (1) Present words verbally that have the same beginning and ending sound (pip); (2) Begin initial sound identification by consonant substitution (nip, tip, lip, sip); (3) Deal with final sound identification by consonant substitution (pin, pit, pill, pic).

Instructional Materials

Prepare a list of consonant, vowel, consonant (CVC) words. Example: fat, man, had, sum, saw, pup, bad, dog. Two noisemakers, such as a bell and a buzzer.

Instructional Activities

Note: Include only ending sounds, not silent letters.

1. Place the two noisemakers on a table. Explain to the child that you are going to say a word: say, "cat."
2. Tell her to listen to the last sound in the word cat. Tell her she must say a word, which starts with the ending sound of the word cat.
3. Assist her as needed, by isolating the last sound (t) and sounding it: "t-t-t-t," by prompting her with a word that starts with a "t-t-t-t" sound. Be sure to allow her thinking time to come up with a word that starts with "t".
4. If more than one child is involved in the activity, require the next child to give a word that starts with the ending sound of the last word heard.
5. Each time the child makes a correct response, ring the bell. Each time she makes an incorrect response, hit the buzzer.

6. Tell her the correct answer if she is incorrect, and ask her to repeat your answer to check that she understood.

2.181 Repeats story just heard maintaining original sequence

Strand: 2-1A **Age:** 68-72m 5.8-6.0y

Definition

When the child is told a short, simple story, he will be able to tell the story back and repeat the original sequence. He should tell at least four ordered events that were included in the story. The story will be one he has not heard before, but one within his experience level.

Instructional Materials

Note: A repeat playette is a dramatization that is read by a narrator. The narrator reads certain statements, and the assigned character repeats the lines he heard. The narrator reads about an action that is taking place, and the character acts out the action he hears. A repeat playette involves no memorization.

A simple "repeat playette" or use the example that follows. It must include exciting sequential incidents and descriptions.

Example:

Going On A Picnic

Characters needed: Narrator, Mother, Father, Sam, Alice, Deer, and Bear.

Props needed: Chairs set up to represent a car. A table and chairs set up to represent a picnic table. Picnic props such as picnic basket with plastic dishes.

One summer day the Adams' family was going on a picnic to a nearby lake. The family had never been to this lake before so everyone was excited (Pause--characters act excited). Mother and Sam made the picnic lunch (Pause--lunch-making), and Alice and Father put things in the car (Pause--put things in car). Sam brought out the picnic basket, and everyone got into the car (Pause--get in car), and they drove away.

They got to the lake and found a picnic table under a big tree. The family unloaded the car (Pause--unload the car). Mother and Alice put the dishes and the food on the table (Pause--set up the picnic). Mother said, "The picnic is all ready, come and eat."

(Mother motions to come)

Alice and Sam wanted to explore the lake and the woods, but they decided to eat the picnic lunch and look around later. Everyone sat down at the table and ate the picnic (Pause--eat picnic).

After the picnic, they decided to walk on the path down to the lake. They walked and walked (Pause--walk on path). Sam said, "I don't think we will ever come to the lake." (Sam--repeat.) Soon they did come to the lake. The lake was very blue and very quiet.

The family sat down on the big rocks by the lake (Pause--sit down on rocks). Sam and Alice threw rocks into the lake (Pause--throw rocks into lake).

All of the sudden, something moved in the bushes (Pause--Deer moves in bushes). Alice said, "I wonder what is making the bushes move?" (Alice looks at the bush.) "Maybe it is a bear," said Sam (Sam--looks at bush). "Oh, oh, oh, let's go back to the car," said Mother (Mother goes to Sam and Alice).

At that very minute, a deer walked out of the bushes (Pause-Deer walks out of bushes), and he went to the lake to get a drink.

Sam said, "Look, Mother, it is not a bear, it is a deer."(Sam points to deer.)

Mother answered, "Be very quiet and maybe it will come to us." (Mother puts 1st finger to her lips.)

The family watched the deer for a long time. Soon it was time to go, so they walked back to the picnic table (Pause--walk back up path).

When the family got back to the table, they could not believe their eyes (Pause--look astonished). Father said, "Someone or something has gotten into our picnic." (Father points to the mess made around the table.)

The leftover food was all over the ground, the basket was in pieces, and all the dishes were broken.

The family began to pick up the mess (Pause--pick up mess),when all of a sudden, Sam looked up and yelled, "There is a bear!" (Sam points and begins to run away.)

The bear stood up on his hind legs and growled (Bear--growl and stand on hind legs).

Everyone ran quickly for the car (Pause--run for car). They jumped in (Pause--jump in car) and locked the doors. As they drove away, Sam and Alice looked back, and they said together, "Look, the bear is waving good-bye to us." (Bear waves good-bye.)

Home looked good to the family. Sam and Alice told all their friends about their picnic adventure.

(This is an excellent activity to video and show to parents and other audiences.)

Instructional Activities

Note: It is best if a group of children are involved in this activity; if only one child is available, assign him one role only.

1. Set up chairs for the car, and set up a table for the picnic table. Option: Identify the lake, the bushes by the lake, the tree by the picnic table, provide a picnic basket, paper dishes, plastic forks, clay made into the shape of rocks and any other playette items the physical setting allows.
2. The teacher should take the role of narrator.
3. Explain to the children that you are going to read a story about a family that went on a picnic and met some interesting animals.
4. Read the story.
5. Discuss the events of the story.
6. Ask a child to tell what happened first in the story.
7. Ask another child to tell what happened next.
8. Continue asking different children to respond to the sequences in the story.
9. Ask for volunteers or select children to play the various characters in the story.
10. Explain to the children that they will hear the story again. Tell them that there will be times when they will act out a part and times when they will speak a part.
11. Place the characters in their stage positions.
12. Begin reading the story, pausing when action or speaking is needed, and prompt as needed.
13. At the conclusion of the dramatization, ask one child to tell and act out the sequence of events in the story.
14. Allow the children to do the repeat playette again.
15. Select different children to play the various roles.
16. As the children become familiar with the story, allow one child to become the telling narrator. (The child narrator should tell the story, and not be expected to read it.)

2.182 Repeats a poem when prompted by the title, a subject clue, or the first line

Strand: 2-1A **Age:** 68-78m 5.8-6.6y

Definition

The child will repeat a poem that she has learned when prompted by the title, a subject clue, or the first line. She may say the learned poem with another person. The poem should be no more than 20 words in length.

Instructional Materials

A poem appropriate for the child.

Instructional Activities

1. Provide a comfortable setting for this activity. Tell the child you are going to read her a poem and ask her to listen carefully.
2. Read the poem again, asking her to say what she recalls. Repeat as necessary.
3. Continue reading the poem until she is echoing parts.
4. Continue until she can repeat the poem.
5. Keep in mind, poems that lend themselves to chanting are an excellent selection for this activity. Chant poems are easy to develop, as they are often in a question and answer format. Example:

Where's the Cow?
The cow is not here.
Where's the horse?
The horse is not here.
Where's the pig?
The pig is not here.
Where's the farmer?
The farmer is here.
Asleep in the hay, I fear.

6. With a chant poem, the narrator says the first line and the child says the second line; it is said in a cadence. Drum beats or tambourines are helpful in establishing the voice rhythm.
7. If more than one child is involved, have one group of children say the first line and a second group of children say the second line.

2.183   Chooses main ideas from spoken material

Strand: 2-1A   **Age:** 70-78m   5.10-6.6y

Definition

When the child is questioned about spoken material, he can tell the main idea from it. The material should have only one central thought without any subplots.

Instructional Materials

Pictures of people engaged in an activity mounted on cards. Chalkboard or sheet of chart paper, chalk or marking pen.

Instructional Activities

1. Display the pictures so the child can study the action.
2. Conduct a discussion about each picture. Ask questions about the picture in the following sequence: (1) Discuss the characters in the picture; (2) Discuss where the action is happening; (3) Discuss what is happening in the picture; (4) Discuss what might have caused the action; (5) Review the characters in the picture: where the action is happening, what is happening, and the cause of the action; (6) Ask the child whether he could give the picture a title.
3. After he has discussed the picture and given it a title, write the title on a chalkboard or a sheet of chart paper.
4. Allow him to tell a story about the picture and record exactly what he says on the board or chart paper.
5. Attach the picture to the completed story, read the title, and read the completed story to the child.
6. This activity can be expanded by using different pictures to create a storybook.

2.184   Watches face and body of speaker to get clues as to meaning signed communication

Strand: 2-8

Instructional Activities

1. Place five sentences on the chalkboard that require different facial expressions, such as for a sad look: "I am sorry your cat is hurt," and for a pleasant look: "I am happy today."
2. Have the child sit facing you and the chalkboard.
3. Sign and say one sentence, using appropriate facial and body expressions as clues.
4. Have the child indicate she understands the sentence by pointing to it on chalkboard. If she is below reading level, have pictures beside each sentence.
5. Let her try again until she gets correct sentence, if her first choice was wrong.
6. Try sentences the child knows first, and then move to sentences they do not know.
7. Have the child make up sentences for you and write them on the chalkboard.

2.185   Reads own name on lips when paired with clues

Strand: 2-9

Instructional Activities

1. Have the children sit in a semi-circle around you.
2. Model what they are to do.
3. Have a child look at your mouth.

4. Mouth her name.

5. Have her stand up.

6. Have everyone clap for her.

7. Move to the other children, and point to each one and mouth their name to help them all get the idea that they are to stand when their name is mouthed.

8. Practice several times.

9. Repeat, this time without pointing. This forces children to watch closely to see whose name you are mouthing.

10. Reward a child with a treat if she recognizes her name and stands on her own.

11. Repeat until each child has two turns.

2.186   Responds to single signs pertaining to own wants or needs when signed by another

Strand: 2-8

Instructional Activities

1. Invite two children to join you at a table for a snack.

2. Have them sit so they are facing you.

3. Point to the items you have for snack.

4. Look at one of the children and sign, "Eat?" Repeat the sign for "Eat," while gesturing toward the food.

5. Wait for the child to indicate his choice of food by pointing to it, shaking his head "yes" or "no", or signing a response.

6. Continue by asking the other child the same question and following the same format.

7. After they've chosen something to eat, sign "Drink," while gesturing toward the available beverages.

8. Wait for the child to choose the beverage they want by pointing to it, shaking his head "yes" or "no," or signing a response.

9. When the child finishes what you've served them, sign "Eat?" or "Drink?" to see if they would like more.

2.187   Imitates single signs expressing own wants or needs when signed by another

Strand: 2-8

Instructional Activities

1. Invite two children to join you at a table for a snack.

2. Have them sit so they are facing you.

3. Point to the items you have for snack and sign the word for each item (e.g., cracker, apple, water, juice, etc).

4. Look at one of the children and sign, "Do you want something to eat?"

5. Wait for the child to respond. If he points to the food or shakes his head, demonstrate the sign for the food items again and ask him to sign the word of the food item he wants.

6. Point to the beverages and sign to the child, "Do you want a drink?"

7. Wait for the child to respond. If he points to the beverages or shakes his head, demonstrate the sign for the drinks again and ask him to sign the word of the beverage he wants.

8. Vary this activity by using different and more difficult signs.

2.188   Reads own name on lips with no clues

Strand: 2-9

Instructional Activities

1. Seat the children in small chairs in a semi-circle facing you.

2. Show them some stickers.

3. Explain that each of them will get sticker after they watch and listen for their name.

4. Do not look at any specific child, and call a child's name.

5. Wait for him to respond. If there is no response, repeat by looking directly at the child.

6. Give him a sticker.

7. Repeat for all the children.

2.189   Locates orally requested object when identical object is offered as clue

Strand: 2-9

Instructional Activities

Note: The animals should be as real looking as possible with a variety of textures.

1. Gather several pairs of toy animals.

2. Place all the animals in a colorful bag, box, or other container.

3. Hold the bag close to your face and wait for the child to look at you. Ask, "What do you think I might have in this bag?"

4. Let her feel the contents of bag without looking into it.

5. Take out one of each pair as you talk about each one in short phrases or sentences.

6. Place each animal on the table.
7. Ask the child to take a specific animal from the bag.
8. Remove the animal that you specified from the table, and hold it up.
9. Wait for the child to choose that animal from the bag.
10. Repeat until the bag is empty.
11. Use this activity with any objects you want to introduce.

2.190 Produces single signs expressing own wants without a model

Strand: 2-8

Instructional Activities

1. Invite the children to a table for a snack.
2. Make sure the items you have for snack are items the child is familiar with and knows the signs for.
3. Make sure the children are facing you.
4. Sign, "What do you want for snack?"
5. Wait for the child to respond.
6. If he gestures or points, remind him again by signing, "What do you want?"
7. Pause and wait for him to sign his response.
8. If another child signs their response, acknowledge them and give them what they requested.
9. Go back to the child who didn't sign, and if necessary, demonstrate the correct sign for the item they want again.
10. Continue to encourage the children to express their needs and wants by using single signs.

2.191 Responds to sign for own name when signed by another

Strand: 2-8

Instructional Activities

1. Take pictures of each child in the class.
2. Show the pictures to the group and practice signing the names of all of the children while looking at the pictures.
3. Show the children that you have a board where everyone will place their picture when their name has been signed.
4. Let the children know that you are going to sign the names of everyone in the class. When they see their name signed they should come up, sign "Hello" or "Good morning" to you,

and then get their picture to place on the board.
5. Continue the process until each child's name has been signed and everyone has placed their picture on the board.

2.192 Imitates action, requested orally, when shown action as clue

Strand: 2-9

Instructional Activities

1. Seat the children in small chairs in a semi-circle facing you.
2. Tell them, "We are going to be singing a song called *If You're Happy and You Know It*, but first let's practice some movements.".
3. Ask if anyone remembers: "Stand up."
4. Looking at each child and holding each one's hands, repeat his name and sign, "Stand up," and help each one stand up.
5. Repeat with each child, the direction: "Sit down."
6. Ask, "Does anyone remember 'Clap Your Hands'?"
7. Repeat: "Clap Your Hands" to each child, encouraging him to imitate by clapping his hands.
8. Ask, "Does anyone remember 'Stamp Your Feet'?"
9. Repeat: "Stamp Your Feet" to each child, encouraging him to imitate by stamping his feet.
10. Repeat the song substituting "sit down," "clap your hands," and then "stamp your feet" in place of "stand up."

2.193 Locates orally requested object when picture offered as clue

Strand: 2-9

Instructional Activities

1. Place several objects in a large box painted to look like a treasure chest.
2. Draw pictures of the objects.
3. Show the pictures to the child.
4. Discuss the names of the objects.
5. Instruct her to: "Find the . . . " and name one of the objects.
6. Show the picture if she needs a clue.
7. Vary the game by changing objects.

2.194   Uses 1 sign for many related things or for similarly formed signs
Strand: 2-8

Instructional Activities
1. Gather several pictures of items, and separate them into stacks according to category type.
2. Place stacks on the table, write the name of the category on slips of paper, and place them by the appropriate stacks.
3. Review the signs, sorting for animals, food, clothes, and other categories for which you have stacks of pictures.
4. Hold a few pictures selected from each stack in your hand.
5. Place one picture on the table in front of the child, and ask him which category it belongs to.
6. If he is correct, let him place that picture in the appropriate stack.
7. If he is incorrect, model the correct sign, return picture to your hand, and let him try again later.
8. Repeat, using all the different pictures, but not in any order.
9. Mix up the pictures as you use them.

2.195   Uses face and body to give clues to meaning of signs
Strand: 2-8

Instructional Activities
1. Glue pictures on cards the child would be able to mime.
2. Locate pictures of mimes.
3. Collect dress-up clothes.
4. Invite the child to put on the dress-up clothes.
5. Choose one card and demonstrate a mime if the child seem unsure.
6. Give each child a card and a few moments to plan her mime.
7. Remind her to use both facial and body expressions to help define a picture or action.
8. Let the other children guess the activity either by selecting the correct card from those displayed or by writing or by signing the word.
9. Applaud each mime.
10. Let the child who guesses correctly have the next turn to be the mime.

2.196   Smiles/frowns for clue to meaning of signed communication
Strand: 2-8

Instructional Activities
1. Gather large photos or cut pictures from magazines that show an action and a feeling.
2. Write a simple sentence at the bottom of each picture that expresses a feeling such as being happy, sad, or mad, but do not actually use those words.
3. Show one picture to the child, and sign the sentence without expression.
4. Have one child sign the sentence showing appropriate facial and body clues to match the sentence.
5. Give each child a chance to sign and express facially one picture.
6. If the response is not appropriate, explain why.
7. Ask the child how he would feel if he were the person in the picture.
8. Use this activity as a language development activity, too.

2.197   Uses hands, arms, feet, shoulders to add expression of signs
Strand: 2-8

Instructional Activities
1. Glue pictures onto cards the child would be able to mime.
2. Locate pictures of mimes.
3. Collect dress-up clothes.
4. Invite the child to put on dress-up clothes.
5. Choose one card and demonstrate mime if the child seems unsure.
6. Give each one a card and a few moments to plan the mime.
7. Remind the child to use both facial and bodily expressions to help define the picture or action.
8. Let the other children guess the activity either by selecting the correct card from those displayed or by writing or signing the word.
9. Applaud each mime.
10. Let the child who guesses correctly take the next turn as the mime.

2.198 Imitates sign for own name when signed by another
Strand: 2-8

Instructional Activities

1. Make up a story mentioning each child's name several times.
2. Explain to the children that they must watch closely for their names to appear in the story as you sign it, and when a child sees his name, he must repeat it immediately.
3. Begin to read and sign the story, watching for any children to recognize their name and sign it back.
4. Mark on a board or give the child a token each time he correctly recognizes his name and signs it back.
5. Be sure to have even number of names appearing in the story, and count the tokens at end of story to see if each child recognized his name each time you signed it.

2.199 Imitates action, requested orally when picture offered as clue
Strand: 2-9

Instructional Activities

1. Attach action pictures to several cards.
2. Seat the children in small chairs in a semi-circle facing you.
3. Hold the cards facing you and ask a child to pick one.
4. Take the chosen card and tell him what you see happening on the card.
5. Ask: "Will you [name of action on picture] with me?"
6. Show him the picture.
7. Perform that action with him.
8. Repeat with a new picture for each child.
9. Clap for each child after he completes the action.

2.200 (Removed, see page xii)

2.201 (Removed, see page xii)

2.202 Uses speed and vigor of signing to express haste, fear, anger
Strand: 2-8

Instructional Activities

1. Glue pictures on cards of actions the child would be able to mime.
2. Locate pictures of mimes.
3. Collect dress-up clothes.
4. Invite the child to put on dress-up clothes.
5. Choose one card, and demonstrate mime if the child(s) seems unsure.
6. Give each child a card and a few moments to plan the mime.
7. Remind the children to use both facial and bodily expressions to help define the picture or the action.
8. Let the other children guess the activity either by selecting the correct card from those displayed or by writing or signing the word.
9. Applaud each mime.
10. Let the child who guesses correctly take the next turn as the mime.

2.203 (Removed, see page xii)

2.204 Produces signs for own name without a model
Strand: 2-8

Instructional Activities

1. Teach the children words to the simple song, "What Is Your Name? My Name Is . . ." and make up the tune.
2. Have the children sit in a circle and watch for you to point to one of them.
3. Stand in the middle of the circle, slowly turn around, sign, and sing the song.
4. Point to one child when you get to second "Is," and have her sign and say her name without a model.
5. Turn around again, sign, and sing the song again, pointing to another child at end of the verse.
6. Repeat until you have pointed to each child in the circle.
7. Give each child a chance to stand in middle, sing the verse and point to another child, and repeat for a couple of times.

2.205 Points to 5 familiar objects when shown their signs by another
Strand: 2-8

Instructional Activities

1. Explain to the children that they will get chance to play detective.
2. Tell them you have hidden some treats in secret places in the room.
3. Indicate the areas that they will cover.
4. Tell them each of them will receive a secret sign that will tell him where to look.
5. Sign "table" to one child and let him find a treat located there.
6. Continue until each child has a chance to look in at least one place.
7. Have the children leave the room while you hide more treats.
8. Continue again until each child has a chance to look in at least five places.
9. Vary the treats, using peanuts, raisins or popcorn.

2.206 Locates orally requested object with no visual clues
Strand: 2-

Instructional Activities

1. Sit facing the child.
2. Provide a colorful container in which to place objects that you will be collecting from around classroom.
3. Demonstrate by announcing: "We are going on a treasure hunt. I am going to get the [name an object]."
4. Get that object.
5. Show the object and announce: "I got the [name of object]."
6. Put the object in the container.
7. Ask the child: "Get the [name a different object]."
8. Vary by repeating in a variety of settings familiar to him.
9. Reverse the procedure by having the child return the object to its specific place.

2.207 Imitates action, requested orally, with no visual clues
Strand: 2-9

Instructional Activities

1. Glue action pictures to cards.

2. Obtain a pocket chart.
3. Seat the children in small chairs facing you.
4. Tell them, "We are going to watch and listen."
5. Call a child's name as you look at him, and wait for him to look at you.
6. Bring him up next to you.
7. Request that he does one action.
8. After he completes the action, give him the picture of the action and direct him to put it in the pocket chart.
9. Repeat until all the actions are exhausted or the children's attention wanders.

2.208 Points to orally described object when given pictures of object
Strand: 2-9

Instructional Activities

1. Obtain some pictures of animals.
2. Sit across from the child at a small table at eye level.
3. Talk about the pictures as you show them, such as: "Here is the dog. Dogs bark, 'Woof, woof.' The dog feels soft. This dog has a long tail."
4. Ask her to pick out the picture you talked about by saying, "Which one goes 'woof, woof' and has a long tail?"
5. Pick up the correct picture if she does not respond.
6. Repeat for all the pictures.

2.209 (Removed, see page xii)

2.210 (Removed, see page xii)

2.211 Imitates signs for 5 familiar objects when signed by another
Strand: 2-8

Instructional Activities

1. Sit facing the child.
2. Present a common object to the child, and show her sign for it.
3. Assist her in making the sign.
4. Reduce your physical prompts and then reduce the visual cue of your signing of the object gradually.
5. Introduce the second object, repeating the same steps when she can correctly sign after you show her the object.

6. Present the first and second objects randomly, and have the child discriminate between them by signing.

2.212 Pairs siblings, classmates, friends with their signs when shown their signs by another
Strand: 2-8

Instructional Activities
1. Collect photos of the child, his siblings, and his friends.
2. Place the photos in a slot chart in random order.
3. Glue a paper pocket to the bottom of the chart.
4. Instruct the child, "Put the picture in the pocket of [child whose name you sign]."
5. Point to the photo if the child needs an additional clue.
6. Award a point for the correct response.
7. Indicate the winner to be the child with the most points.
8. Vary the activity by changing or adding pictures and names.

2.213 Produces signs for 5 familiar objects without a model
Strand: 2-8

Instructional Activities
1. Obtain a fishbowl or similar container.
2. Find some pictures of a few basic single-item objects, and tape a small magnet on each picture.
3. Place the pictures inside the fishbowl.
4. Attach a string to a stick to serve as fishing pole.
5. Place a small metal object on the end of the string to "hook" the magnets.
6. Instruct the child to fish for a picture.
7. Instruct her to give the appropriate sign for each picture she fishes out of the container.
8. Reward her correct responses by allowing her to keep the picture.
9. Model the correct sign if she responds incorrectly, have her copy the sign and return the picture to the bowl.
10. Give each child one turn at a time.

2.214 Points to orally described emotion when facial expressions are given as clues
Strand: 2-9

Instructional Activities
1. Draw five faces, each with a different expression--happy, sad, angry, sleepy, funny-- on a 24-inch-square piece of tag board.
2. Place this Face Chart on a chart holder or attach it to the chalkboard.
3. Tell the children you are going to describe some events and you want them to show you how a person might feel if they experienced an event like that by pointing to the appropriate face on the Face Chart.
4. Remind them to listen to your words, and to watch your facial expression and body language.
5. Describe an event that made you happy, smile as you are telling the story.
6. Instruct the child to point to the face that matches what you were saying and feeling.
7. If he chooses the correct face, acknowledge that he was correct and praise him for listening and watching.
8. If he responds incorrectly, point to the correct face, and demonstrate the proper facial expression.
9. Repeat this activity for all five faces.

2.215 Points to 10 familiar objects when shown their signs by another
Strand: 2-8

Instructional Activities
1. Choose some objects for which the child is working on the signs.
2. Practice the signs for these objects with him.
3. Have him go outside while you hide the objects around the room.
4. Ask him to return, and then sign the object's name to him.
5. Have him hunt around the room for the object.
6. Continue until he finds all the objects.
7. Reward him for finding the correct objects by letting him hide them for next child.
8. Repeat until each child has a turn.
9. Be sure to use complete sentences while you are signing to him.

2.216 Reads and signs 2 word phrases
Strand: 2-8

Instructional Activities

1. Prepare a simple game board with dice and two team markers.
2. Make two sets of matching cards containing two-word phrases such as "Black cat" and "Little boy."
3. Place one set of cards in a pile face-down and spread the other cards face-up so they are all exposed.
4. Seat four children around a table, each facing her partner seated opposite.
5. Instruct the first child to draw a card from the pile, read it, and produce the appropriate sign to her partner.
6. Instruct her partner to review the face-up cards and choose one she thinks matches her partner's.
7. Let the partner roll the dice and advance the team marker, if correct.
8. If incorrect, have the team return the cards to the piles and do not let them roll dice or advance the markers.
9. Have the children take turns around the table so that each one participates as a signer and a reader.
10. Indicate winners to be the team whose marker reaches the finish first.

2.217 Produces name sign for siblings, classmates, friend, etc., without a model
Strand: 2-8

Instructional Activities

1. Prepare all-occasion cards by printing one child's name on the inside of a card and another child's name on outside envelope.
2. Give one child a hat and a mail bag to wear as props.
3. Have this child sign the name of each person as he delivers the addressed card to that child.
4. Model signing the name anytime a child is uncertain.
5. Allow the children to open the cards they receive.
6. Ask each child to sign the inside person's name who sent it and to thank that person.
7. Vary this activity by using the cards to help children learn signs for various holidays.
8. Instruct the child to sign whatever occasion the card is for.

2.218 Imitates signs for 10 familiar objects when signed by another
Strand: 2-8

Instructional Activities

1. Have the children sit in a semi-circle.
2. Make or obtain pictures of at least 10 familiar objects.
3. Lay the pictures face-up on table in front of the child.
4. Sign the words and have her choose the appropriate picture.
5. Respond by showing a happy face card if she is correct and a puzzled face card if she is incorrect.
6. Repeat with the other children.

2.219 Produces signs for 10 familiar objects without a model
Strand: 2-8

Instructional Activities

1. Obtain some colored socks, and place one small, familiar object or toy in each.
2. Place the socks on the table, floor or work area.
3. Have the child sign the color of the sock he wants.
4. Tell him to reach into the sock and remove the object.
5. Instruct him to sign the name of the object.
6. Sign to him if his sign is correct and let him keep the object.
7. If he was incorrect, model the correct sign, have him sign it again correctly and return the object to the sock and onto the table.

2.220 Pairs 10 adjective signs signed by another with appropriate objects
Strand: 2-8

Instructional Activities

1. Have the children sit in a circle.
2. Toss some chips of various colors into the air.
3. Sign to one child, "Your job is to locate five red chips."
4. Allow the child enough time to complete the job.
5. Correct her if necessary.
6. Continue until all the children have several jobs.

7. Reward the entire team with a small treat, extra points or a badge.

2.221 Produces 10 adjective signs without a model

Strand: 2-8

Instructional Activities

1. Pin a poster or a picture on a flannel board or a bulletin board.
2. Cover the picture with pieces of paper in various colors and shapes.
3. Instruct each child to take a turn signing the color and the shape of the paper they choose to remove.
4. Remove the colored paper shape and give it to the child if his signs were correct.
5. If his sign was incorrect, model the correct sign and then go onto another child.
6. Vary the activity by using number or letter cards or pictures of actions instead of shapes to cover main picture.
7. Indicate the winner to be the first child to guess correctly and sign what the picture or poster depicts or the child who earns the most shapes.

2.222 Pairs 10 action verbs signed by another with appropriate actions

Strand: 2-8

Instructional Activities

1. Prepare cards with stick figures depicting various action verbs.
2. Have the children stand in a semi-circle.
3. Face them and sign an action verb.
4. Choose a child to select the correct picture.
5. Reward her correct response by allowing her to lead all the others in that action while you sign it.
6. Repeat the sign if she is incorrect, and let another child locate the picture.
7. Continue through all action verbs.

2.223 Produces signs for 10 action verbs without a model

Strand: 2-8

Instructional Activities

1. Prepare 10 to 20 cards, each containing a picture displaying an action verb.
2. Attach a paper clip to each card.

3. Put all the cards into a box where they cannot be seen.
4. Prepare a fishing pole from a dowel and a string.
5. Tie one end of string to the dowel and attach a magnet to other end to serve as a hook.
6. Instruct the child to put the hook into the box.
7. Have him pull up a card, remove it from the pole, and sign the action portrayed.
8. Allow him to keep the card if his sign was correct.
9. Return the card to the "pond" if his sign was incorrect.

2.224 Answers questions logically

Strand: 2-4B **Age:** 42-47m 3.6-3.11y

Definition

When asked a question, the child will respond by giving a logical answer.

Instructional Materials

Select a picture book with a story content that has one or more characters (the characters should do something at a given time and place). It is important that the picture book chosen has pictures of the "who," "what," and "when" of the story.

Instructional Activities

1. Invite the child to sit next to you so that he can see the book as you read it. Explain to him that after you read the story you will be asking him some questions.
2. Read the story.
3. When the story is completed, turn back to the first page and ask a "who" question about the story.
4. Tell the child to answer the question and to look at the picture. Ask the child to point to the "who" that is in the picture.
5. Continue asking "what" questions and "when" questions.
6. Encourage the child to not only verbally answer the question, but point to the picture in the book that goes with their answer.
7. Encourage the child to ask questions about the story too.

2.225 Responds appropriately to "where" questions

Strand: 2-4B **Age:** 48-54m 4.0-4.6y

Definition

When asked a question starting with "where", the child responds correctly.

Instructional Materials

Index cards. Glue or paste. Pictures from old magazines depicting people, places, and things. A large piece of poster board.

Instructional Activities

1. Have the children glue or paste the pictures of people, places, and things on the index cards to make a set of picture cards.
2. Take the large piece of poster board and label it the "WH" chart. Make three separate columns, and label the columns: "Who," "Where," and "What."
3. Show the child a picture card and ask her to place the card in the correct column. For example, a picture of a man would go in the "Who" column; a picture of an apple would go in the "What" column; a picture of a park would go in the "Where" column.
4. Continue with each of the pictures until each card has been placed correctly.

2.226 Answers "why" questions by giving a reason

Strand: 2-4B **Age:** 54-60m 4.6-5.0y

Definition

When asked a "why" question, the child will respond by stating a reason.

Instructional Materials

Select a picture book with a story content that has one or more characters (the characters should do something at a given time and place). It is important that the picture book chosen have pictures of the "who," "what," "when," "where," and "why" of the story.

Instructional Activities

1. Invite the child to sit next to you so that he can see the book as you read it. Explain to him that after you read the story you will be asking him some questions.
2. Read the story.
3. When the story is completed, ask a "who" question about the story.
4. Next ask a "what" or "when" question.

5. Continue asking "where" questions and "why" questions.
6. Encourage the child to answer the questions to the best of their ability and let them know that there is more than one answer to many of the questions you will be asking.
7. Encourage the child to ask questions about the story too.

3.147 Catches a large ball thrown from 5 feet using hands/arms

Strand: 3-7F **Age:** 30-42m 2.6-3.6y

Definition

The child will catch a ball at least 10 inches in diameter when it is thrown from a distance of 5 feet. The child will catch the ball using both hands and arms. The ball should be tossed gently, using an underhand motion. When the ball is tossed, it should be aimed in a curve peaking from above the child's head and following a downward path into the child's outstretched hands and arms at chest height.

Instructional Materials

A bubble-blowing liquid and blower. (If the commercial liquid is not available, you can make it by mixing ¼ cup dishwashing liquid, ¼ cup water, 1 teaspoon of sugar and 1 tablespoon of glycerine. Add food coloring and mix well. The bubbles can be blown by using a plastic straw, bending a thin wire coat hanger to make a giant bubble blower, or by attaching a string to a plastic straw and swoop it in the air after dipping it in the liquid. To create a giant bubble, thread a yard of string through two plastic drinking straws. Place the string and straws in the bubble mixture. Gather the soap film across the strings and pull the straws apart to stretch the film open. Pull up on the straws to form a giant bubble. Then relax the string and straws and snap the bubble free from the frame.) Several large balloons. Large ball.

Instructional Activities

1. Ask the child to stand in an outdoor area that can be used to blow big bubbles.
2. Create large bubbles for the child to pop or catch.
3. Encourage the child to hold her arms forward with elbows bent and to move toward the bubbles as they float.
4. If the child has difficulty catching the bubbles, place her either in a sitting position or on the ground where she does not have to be concerned about balance.
5. Blow a large bubble and ask her to catch it.
6. Repeat the above steps using a balloon instead of bubbles.
7. Have the child first stand to catch the balloon and then to do it from a sitting position.
8. Use a large ball and repeat activities above.

3.148 Balances on each foot for 5 seconds, without support

Strand: 3-7A **Age:** 36-44m 3.0-3.8y

Definition

The child will stand on one foot holding onto a support for at least one second. He will then stand on the other foot holding onto a support for at least one second. He will stand on one foot for at least five seconds, with his eyes open and his arms outstretched for balance. He will then stand on the other foot for at least five seconds, with his eyes open and his arms outstretched for balance. He will stand on one foot for at least five seconds with his eyes open and his arms in any position except hanging onto a support or outstretched. He will then stand on the other foot for at least five seconds with his eyes open and his arms in any position except hanging onto a support or outstretched.

Instructional Materials

At least six balloons and six strings, 10 to 12 inches long.

Instructional Activities

1. Inflate and tie a string to each balloon. Tie the balloon around the child's ankle on the outside of his leg. If other children are involved, tie a balloon around their ankles also, making sure the balloons are positioned on the outside of the legs.
2. Explain that the children are to pop one another's balloons by stepping on them. Demonstrate that one way to prevent a balloon from being popped is to stand on one foot and raise the foot with the balloon attached.
3. Tell the children that if their balloon is broken, you will replace it so they can play the game again.

See #3.149.

3.149 Balances on one leg with hands on hips

Strand: 3-7A **Age:** 36-44m 3.0-3.8y

Definition

The child will balance on one leg for at least five seconds with her eyes open and her hands on her hips. She will then balance on the other leg for at least five seconds with eyes open and hands on hips.

Instructional Materials

A modified hopscotch grid on a flat surface outside prepared by using chalk and a rectangle at least 6 feet long and 4 feet wide.

Instructional Activities

Note: If this activity is being conducted inside, use tape for the modified hopscotch grid, and tape small pictures of the item in the sections. It is important that the picture does not interfere or create a safety issue as the child moves within the grid.

1. Divide the rectangle in the following manner: (1) Measure the rectangle into 1-foot sections, and divide each section by drawing a line horizontally from one side to the other; (2) Divide every other section in half vertically. In the three undivided rectangles draw a simple picture (ball, tree, hat), and in the three divided rectangles draw a simple figure (wagon, cat, bottle, birthday cake, candle, apple).
2. Point out the pictures in the sections to the child. Make sure she is familiar with the name of each object.
3. Invite her to step into the [apple] section. When she gets to the correct section, ask her to put her hands on her hips and balance on one foot.
4. Then ask her to step into the [tree] section. When she gets to the correct section, ask her to put her hands on her hips and balance on one foot.
5. Continue with the other sections.
6. Give her the opportunity to name the sections for another child to step into when she calls.

See #3.148.

3.150 (Removed, see page xii)

3.151 (Removed, see page xii)

3.152 Bounces and catches a large ball

Strand: 3-7F **Age:** 36-44m 3.0-3.8y

Definition

The child will bounce a 10-inch ball at least once and catch it on the upward movement. She will begin the bounce-and-catch activity by standing in one spot and bouncing the ball; as she progresses, she may walk forward and bounce the ball.

Instructional Materials

A 10-inch rubber ball. A rhythmic poem or chant; example:
Bounce the Ball
Billy Bug, bounce the ball (Give the child the ball)
Bounce, bounce, bounce (Bounce the ball three times)
Bumpy Bat, bounce the ball (Hold the ball)
Bounce, bounce, bounce (Bounce the ball three times)
Buzzy Bee, bounce the ball (Hold the ball)
Bounce, bounce, bounce (Bounce the ball three times)
Billy Bug (Bounce the ball)
Bumpy Bat (Bounce the ball)
Buzzy Bee (Bounce the ball)
Billy Bug, Bumpy Bat, Buzzy Bee,
Bounce, bounce, bounce.

Instructional Activities

1. Allocate a large enough space for the child to bounce the ball.
2. Give the child the rubber ball.
3. Ask her to bounce the ball; begin a counting and clapping beat that matches the sound the ball makes as it hits the floor.
4. Tell the child to listen and to bounce the ball to the chant.
5. Encourage her to make up her own chant as she bounces the ball.

See #3.147.

3.153 Walks down stairs using alternate feet without holding railing

Strand: 3-7B **Age:** 42-54m 3.6-4.6y

Definition

When the child approaches stairs, she will walk down at least five regular-size steps alternating her feet, without holding railing.

Instructional Materials

A stairway, red and green stickers, masking tape in different colors, a small prize for the child.

Instructional Activities

Note: Make sure the child is aware of the colors red and green.

1. Bring the child to the stairway.
2. Demonstrate the method of alternating feet, placing only one foot on each step. Watch and work through the movements with the child so she gets a feel of the task.

3. Expect the use of alternating feet. If necessary, she can hold on to the railing until she is more comfortable.
4. If the child does not use alternating feet after the demonstration, put a red sticker on the top of her right foot/shoe and a green sticker on the top of her left foot/shoe.
5. Place colored tape on the stairs. Be sure it is securely fastened with no loose edges and that the tape is off to the sides of where the child will be walking.
6. Tell her that when you say red, she is to put her foot with the red sticker on the first step (point to the step with the red tape), and when you say green, she is to put her foot with the green sticker on the next step (point to the step with the green tape). Tell her that holding onto the handrail is okay.
7. After the color and auditory cueing, ask her to walk down the stairs.
8. Observe whether she uses alternating feet as she descends at least five steps and whether she holds onto the railing.
9. Give the child a prize when she reaches the bottom of the stairs.

3.154   (Removed, see page xii)

3.155   Stands on tiptoe for 10 seconds
Strand: 3-7A   **Age:** 38-42m 3.2-3.6y

Definition
The child will rise on her tiptoes when requested and will balance on her toes for 10 seconds. She may place her hands and arms in any position. If her heels touch the floor and she rises again on her toes, the timing must start over.

Instructional Materials
A large ball (tumble balls 26 or 38 inches in diameter), a play barrel, or a cylinder form.

Instructional Activities
1. Make sure that the selected ball/cylinder will roll.
2. Place the child in a prone (stomach-down) position over a large ball (hold her carefully).
3. Gently roll the ball so only her toes touch the floor. Have her bounce or "spring" repeatedly on her toes. Do not let her heels touch the floor.
4. Remove the ball and ask her to stay on her toes. Replace the ball and let her bounce, then roll the ball away and have her stand on her tiptoes.

5. Provide her with necessary support. See #3.148.

3.156   (Removed, see page xii)

3.157   Walks 10 feet on 4-inch wide line
Strand: 3-7H   **Age:** 36-44m 3.0-3.8y

Definition
After a demonstration, the child will walk in a straight line on a 4-inch wide line of tape. The child may hold her arms and head in any position. (Prerequisite skill to walking on a balance beam.)

Instructional Materials
An umbrella, several artificial flowers or colored paper flowers made from tissue paper, masking tape, music on cassette tape or CD/MP3 player.

Instructional Activities
1. Decorate the umbrella with brightly colored artificial or paper flowers. Attach the masking tape to the floor in a straight line not more than 10 feet in length.
2. Give the child time to practice walking on the "tightrope" (tape), using a heel-toe-heel step. Demonstrate this, if necessary.
3. Hand her the decorated umbrella and tell her to pretend she is a circus tightrope walker. Tell her the umbrella will help her keep her balance. Tell her to imagine she is high above the crowd and that everyone is looking at her.
4. Ask the child to begin her tightrope act as soon as she hears the music.
5. Applaud after each of her performances.
6. Encourage her to do other tricks on the tightrope.

3.158   Walks 20-foot diameter circle staying on path
Strand: 3-7B   **Age:** 38-44m 3.2-3.8y

Definition
The child will walk on a line of tape at least 4 inches wide in a circle 20 feet in diameter. The child's feet must touch the line, and he must use a heel-toe-heel-toe step alternating feet without physical assistance.

Instructional Materials
Floor-marking material, such as chalk.

Instructional Activities
1. Draw two parallel circles to make a large circular path on a flat surface.

2. Invite the child to play *Follow the Leader*; tell him he must copy whatever you do. Tell him to stand behind you.

3. Begin by walking like a duck around the circle, putting one foot on each side of the double line. Continue the duck walk with your hands on your waist, then hands in the air, then arms out to side and then hands on your head. Stop, turn around, and repeat in the opposite direction.

4. Continue the game by walking around the circle using alternate feet in a heel-toe-heel-toe step. Vary your walk by putting your hands on your waist, waving with one hand, placing your arms straight out and clapping your hands.

5. As long as the child stays interested, modify the manner of walking around the circle. For example, walk like a rabbit, walk on tiptoes, walk like a monster, walk like a cat, etc.

6. Give the child a turn to be the leader, and practice until staying on the path becomes a simple task for him.
See #3.157.

3.159   Kicks a stationary ball using a 2-step start

Strand: 3-7A   **Age:** 38-48m 3.2-4.0y

Definition
Place a stationary ball (soccer or rubber playground) on a flat surface approximately 2 to 4 feet away from the child (a distance of two steps for the child). The child will kick the ball, using a two-step start, any distance or any direction.

Instructional Materials
A 10-inch ball (soccer, rubber, plastic), a goal post (can be set up by putting two chairs back-to-back to represent the uprights of a miniature goal post; the space between the backs of the two chairs should be about 30 inches). Masking tape.

Instructional Activities
1. Place the miniature goal posts 6 feet in front of the ball. Attach a short strip of tape to the ground for a starting line where the child will stand. Place the ball at least two steps in front of the starting line.

2. Ask the child to stand on the starting line.

3. Tell her to kick the ball and to try to make it go through the posts.

4. She may use her right or left foot.

5. Give her one point if she kicks the ball through the posts.

6. Allow her to continue in an effort to improve her total points.

3.160   Rides tricycle with pedals to maneuver around obstacles, turn, stop and start

Strand: 3-7G   **Age:** 42-52m 3.6-4.4y

Definition
The child will get on a tricycle and pedal forward without touching his feet to the ground, and negotiate a turn without bumping into any obstacles.

Instructional Materials
Tricycle that fits the child. Objects to use as obstacles such as cardboard boxes, cones, large balls. Watch with second hand.

Instructional Activities
/*\ **Safety Note:** For safety, children should always wear a helmet when riding a tricycle.

1. Locate an area to set up a tricycle track--large enough for riding a tricycle forward, turning it around and maneuvering it through several obstacles. Place the obstacles on the return path after the turnaround area.

2. Explain the tricycle track to the child, showing him different places where he can turn around. Discuss what the tricycle track is and what can happen on it.

3. Show him the obstacles and explain that he is to ride the tricycle around them, beside them, or anyway he wants, but that he must avoid touching the obstacles.

4. Tell him to start when he hears the word "Go!"

5. To add to the challenge of the tricycle track, time the child as he pedals to the turnaround, turns around, and dodges the obstacles back to the starting point.

6. Encourage him to beat his own time.

7. Involve other children in racing against the clock on the tricycle track. For a racing atmosphere, hang numbers on the tricycles, decorate the tricycles, and present small awards to the winners.

3.161   Jumps forward 2-foot distance, feet together

Strand: 3-7C   **Age:** 42-52m 3.6-4.4y

Definition

The child will jump forward at least 2 feet and will land with her feet together. She may take as many consecutive jumps as she wants. She will complete this jump without physical assistance and without falling.

Instructional Materials

A standard-size pillowcase, string or narrow rope, tape.

Instructional Activities

/*\Safety Note: Supervise carefully and support her if she is not steady with the pillowcase around her legs.

1. Mark a 3- by 3-foot square with tape on a carpeted or soft floor.
2. Hand the child a pillowcase (sack). Ask her to put both feet in the case.
3. Ask her to take a jump with the pillowcase around her legs while she holds the rim of the case.
4. Ask her to jump into the center of the square.
5. Ask her to jump out of the square.
6. Ask her to jump from one side of the square to the other side.
7. Ask her to jump around the square.
8. Give the child several practice turns jumping.
9. Once she has learned how to jump with her feet together and to remain standing, have her try to jump without the pillow case, to see how far she can go.

3.162   Step-hops for five feet

Strand: 3-7C   **Age:** 40-50m 3.4-4.2y

Definition

After a demonstration the child will step-hop for 5 feet. He will step-hop-stand on one foot, maintaining balance without assistance for at least three seconds. Then he will step-hop-stand on the other foot for at least three seconds.

Instructional Materials

A poem, finger-play, chant or rhyme that involves the child in a step-hop activity; e.g., the movement chant that follows:
Steppity Step and Hoppity Hop
(To be said in a chanting style)
Step, step, step. (Child steps three times.)

Hop, hop, hop. (Child hops three times on either foot.)
Step-hop, step-hop, step-hop. (Child steps and hops three times.)
Step, step, step. (Child steps three times.)
Hop, hop, hop. (Child hops three times on either foot.)
Step-hop, step-hop, step-hop. (Child steps and hops three times.)
Step, step, step. (Child steps three times.)
Hop, hop, hop. (Child hops three times on either foot.)
Step-hop-hold, step-hop-hold, step-hop-hold. (Child steps, hops, and holds on one foot for a short time.)
Repeat as needed or as long as the child is motivated.

Instructional Activities

1. Identify a large area for movement and dancing. Ask the child to watch carefully as you do the Steppity Step and Hoppity Hop dance.
2. Do the movements in the chant while you say the selection.
3. Encourage the child to join you in the chant movement.
4. Assist him in the three steps--stepping, hopping, holding.
5. Invite him to move and say the chant at the same time.
6. Give him ample practice time.
7. He may begin to improvise the flow and direction, plus he may add different creative movements.
8. To modify this activity, add a musical beat to the chant or play a recording to accompany the rhythm of the words.

3.163   Kicks a large ball when the ball has been rolled directly to him

Strand: 3-7A   **Age:** 36-42m 3.0-3.6y

Definition

The child will kick a moving ball as it is rolled directly to him.

Instructional Materials

At least four kick balls (soccer, rubber, utility), masking tape.

Instructional Activities

1. Attach 6 feet of tape to the floor to mark the boundary line.

2. Invite the child to stand behind the boundary line. Explain that you will roll a ball to him and that he is to kick it after it crosses the boundary line.
3. Roll a ball toward the boundary line and encourage him to kick it back.
4. After he has successfully kicked the ball, increase the challenge by rolling one ball, and after a pause rolling another ball.
5. Continue rolling the balls, asking the child to kick the balls after they cross the boundary line.
6. To modify the kickball activity, increase the speed at which you roll the balls.

3.164 Runs and changes direction without stopping, avoiding obstacles
Strand: 3-7B **Age:** 44-55m 3.8-4.7y

Definition
When the child is running, she will change directions without coming to a complete stop, and she will dodge obstacles and corners.

Instructional Materials
Items to set up an obstacle course, such as boxes, cones, barrels, saw-horses. Also, a drum or other noise-making instrument.

Instructional Activities
1. Set up an obstacle course using the items, making sure that the course contains corners and curves.
2. Ask the child to stand in an area away from the obstacle course.
3. Tell her that she is to run to you when she hears the drum. Tell her that when the drum stops, she is to stop running.
4. Show the child the entrance to the obstacle course, and ask her to run through the course, stopping only when she doesn't hear the drum.
5. You can modify this activity and increase its difficulty by asking the child to: (1) Hold her arms straight out from her body like airplane wings as she runs through the course; (2) Run through the course in time to the drum (to run quickly if the drum beat is fast and to run slowly if the beat is slow); (3) Run through the course on her tiptoes.

3.165 Runs a 20-foot distance, breaking stride/rhythm
Strand: 3-7B **Age:** 44-55m 3.8-4.7y

Definition
The child will run 10 feet in one direction, stop, and then turn around and run 10 feet back.

Instructional Materials
Tape in several colors that can be attached to the floor, large sheets of green, yellow, and red construction paper.

Instructional Activities
1. Attach the two strips of different colors of tape in lines on the floor 5 feet apart.
2. Ask the child to stand on the first line.
3. Hold up a large green piece of paper and say, "Green light," while you stand on the second line.
4. Tell the child to run from one line to the next.
5. Take his hand and run the course with him if he has difficulty. Start over with him on the first line and repeat the process, holding up the green paper and saying, "Green light, run!" until the child can run independently from line one to line two.
6. Add a third line of tape in another color 5 feet from the second line.
7. Start the child on the second line.
8. Hold up the large yellow piece of paper and say, "Yellow light."
9. Instruct him to walk to the third line.
10. Repeat the process from the beginning at the first line with a green light and then at the second line with the yellow light.
11. Add a fourth and a fifth line 5 feet apart from each other.
12. Alternate the green and yellow lights, ending with holding up the red paper and saying, "Red light" for Stop.
13. Work with the child until he is able to move through the 20 feet without stopping until he reaches the last line of tape.
See #3.164.

3.166 Performs a complete forward roll (somersault)
Strand: 3-7G **Age:** 45-60m 3.9-5.0y

Definition
The child will do a forward somersault without assistance and without falling to either side. She will place her hands, palms down, on the floor. Her hands

will be placed on either side of her knees. She will lower her chin to her chest and put the back of her neck and her shoulders on the floor. She will give her body a forward push, roll over and land sitting up on the floor. She may also do a forward roll by beginning in a squat position, placing her arms in front of her body in a start position and her right foot in front of her left foot. She should then lean forward, tucking her head between her feet, roll and land sitting up.

Instructional Materials

/*\Safety Note: The forward roll should be done on a mat or a soft, carpeted surface. Supervise carefully. Exercise mat.

Instructional Activities

1. Place the mat on the floor. Ask the child to take off her shoes. Demonstrate a forward somersault or ask someone else to demonstrate.
2. Ask the child questions about the somersault, such as, "Did you see how I stayed curled up when I did my somersault?" "Did you see how she stayed curled up when she did her somersault?" "Where were my hands before I went over?" or "What do you think my chin was touching?"
3. Repeat the demonstration again, explaining each action.
4. Tell the child to stand at one end of the mat.
5. Tell her to squat, and assist her if necessary.
6. Tell her to put her hands on the mat outside her legs with her fingers pointing forward.
7. Tell her to tuck her chin into her chest and to roll until her feet touch the mat.
8. Assist her when necessary and allow time for her to practice.
See #3.179.

3.167   Maintains momentum on swing

Strand: 3-7G   **Age:** 46-54m 3.10-4.6y

Definition

When placed on a regular swing in a sitting position, the child will swing by himself. He may be started by someone giving a backward or forward push. He should maintain momentum on the swing by doing a pumping motion, which consists of knees bent, feet under the seat, elbows bent and body forward in a pushed-back position at the rear of the swinging arc; and knees straight, feet pointed forward, arms straight and body in a pulled-out position at the front of the swinging arc. The child should keep the swing in motion for at least 30 seconds.

Instructional Materials

A swing, large playground ball.

Instructional Activities

/*\Safety Note: Attempt this task only if the child shows interest, has experience sitting on a swing, and is stable sitting on and making the swing move. Supervise carefully.

1. Position the child correctly on the swing, his buttocks comfortably back in the seat and his hands holding the swing chains or rope.
2. Stand behind the child and push several times until a strong swinging momentum is achieved.
3. Walk around and stand in front of him.
4. Hold a large playground ball. Tell the child to push against the ball with his feet as he swings forward.
5. Repeat until he masters swinging with the aid of the ball.
6. Repeat the swinging action without the use of the ball.

3.168   Walks 10 feet carrying object blocking view of floor

Strand: 3-7B   **Age:** 48-54m 4.0-4.6y

Definition

The child will walk at least 10 feet carrying a large ball or empty box in her arms/against her chest, preventing her from seeing her feet.

Instructional Materials

Several patterns of feet cut out from sandpaper (that is not too abrasive). The feet should be smaller than adult-size feet but slightly larger than the child's feet. A box, ball, cube or related object large enough to block the view of the floor.

Instructional Activities

1. Lay the sandpaper feet on the floor with masking tape in any desired pattern. Ask the child to remove her shoes and socks.
2. Ask the child to follow the feet patterns.
3. Give her an object that will block her view of the floor.
4. Ask her to follow the feet patterns without looking down as she carries the object.
5. You can modify this activity by changing the feet pattern or by attaching the sandpaper feet to a large sheet of paper to be used again.

3.169 Gallops forward

Strand: 3-7B **Age:** 48-60m 4.0-5.0y

Definition

The child will gallop for at least 10 feet. A gallop is a movement in which the same foot is always the lead foot, and the trailing foot comes up to meet but never passes the lead foot. The lead foot strides forward, and the body weight is on the lead foot. When the trailing foot meets the heel of the lead foot, the weight is shifted to the trailing foot, enabling the lead foot to repeat the action.

Instructional Materials

Several cardboard boxes or cones.

Instructional Activities

1. Set up an obstacle course by lining up cardboard boxes or cones, leaving approximately 1 foot between each one. Explain the obstacle course to the child and ask him to walk through it.
2. After he has walked through the obstacle course, ask him to gallop through it, being careful not to knock down any boxes or cones.
3. Give him a few practice turns.
4. Time him as he gallops through the obstacle course, avoiding the boxes or cones.
5. Rearrange the boxes or cones to create a different course.

3.170 Stands up without losing balance after lying on back

Strand: 3-7A **Age:** 48-66m 4.0-5.6y

Definition

The child will rise from a horizontal (prone) position to a vertical position, by sitting up, placing his feet flat on the floor, pushing his body up with his hands while maintaining his balance as he comes to an upright stance.

Instructional Materials

A large sheet of paper, at least 4 feet wide and 1 foot longer than the child is tall; a marker.

Instructional Activities

1. Place the sheet of paper flat on the floor.
2. Ask the child to lie on the paper face up. Use the marker and draw around him.
3. Ask him to stand up: whenever he places a part of his body on the paper in an attempt to get up, draw around that body part with a marker. Example: The child puts his feet down, draw around his feet. If he places his hands on the paper for balance, draw around his hands.
4. Ask him to lie on the paper within the body model. Tell him to stand up and challenge him to use the same hands and feet positions that are indicated on the paper.
5. To modify this activity, ask him to lie down on the paper by placing his hands and feet in the patterns on the paper.
6. Cut out the body image and if you wish, let the child draw and color in body parts, clothing, hair, etc.

3.171 Walks 4 feet on 4-inch wide beam without stepping off

Strand: 3-7H **Age:** 52-64m 4.4-5.4y

Definition

After your demonstration, the child will walk at least 4 feet on a 4-inch wide balance beam without stepping off or holding onto another person or object. The balance beam should be placed securely on the floor.

Instructional Materials

About 10 right and left footprints made of tag board, large enough to accommodate the child's feet. Paint the right footprints red and the left footprints blue, using nontoxic paint. Red and blue stickers, tape, and a balance beam (no more than 6 inches off the floor–Supervise carefully). Mat to place under the balance beam.

Instructional Activities

1. Invite the child to play a game called Match Footprints. Place the balance beam on the mat. Securely tape the footprints in normal walking positions on the balance beam.
2. Place a red sticker on the child's right foot and a blue sticker on the child's left foot.
3. Show the child the footprints on the balance beam. Ask the child to walk on the floor next to the balance beam matching her stride with the footprints on the balance beam.
4. As the child is walking beside the balance beam, say, "Left, right, left, right, left, right". Encourage the child to join you in the "left-right" chant.
5. Invite the child to mount the balance beam and match her feet to the footprints on the beam.
6. As the child walks on the balance beam, say, "Left, right, left, right, left, right". Encourage the child to join you in the "left-right" chant.
See #3.157.

3.172 Throws a ball ten feet overhand

Strand: 3-7F **Age:** 53-65m 4.5-5.5y

Definition

When the child is provided with a ball that is easily held and manipulated with one hand, he will throw the ball overhand, not aiming at any specific target.

Instructional Materials

A hanging noisemaker such as a bell or wind chimes, a ball, and a string to hang the noisemaker from. Masking tape.

A hanging noisemaker can be made by attaching different size cans or spoons from a stick using different lengths of string.

Animal cookies, bite-sized crackers, or stickers for rewards.

/***Safety Note:** Be aware of special diets and allergies before doing these activities.

Instructional Activities

1. Suspend the noisemaker on a rope in midair. Put a piece of tape on the floor or ground to indicate where the child will stand.
2. Tell the child to stand on the tape and explain that he is to try to hit the hanging bell or chimes with a ball. Touch the bell or chimes to let him hear the noise, and hand him the ball.
3. Give him several tries to hit the target. Give him a point or a small reward (animal cookie, bite-size cracker, or sticker) each time he hits the mark.
4. If more than one child is playing, divide the group into teams and give each player one turn. The team that earns the most points wins.

3.173 Hangs from bar using overhand grip

Strand: 3-7G **Age:** 54-66m 4.6-5.6y

Definition

The child will hang from an overhead bar using an overhand grip for at least five seconds. An overhand grip is one in which the child's knuckles are on top of the bar and her fingers are wrapped down around the bar. Her feet should be off the ground, and her mount could be assisted.

Instructional Materials

An overhead bar. Mat to place under the bar.

Instructional Activities

Note: If the equipment is too low for adult demonstration, arrange for another child to model this skill.

1. Ask the child to stand near the overhead bar. Demonstrate an overhand grip on the bar.
2. Assist the child in reaching the overhead bar. Help fit her fingers over the bar in a grasping position.
3. Tell her to hang while holding the bar. Place your hands over hers and hold in position.
4. As she becomes successful and comfortable in the hanging position, modify this activity by beginning to count once she has reached the grasping-hanging stage.
5. Record the last number before she dismounts. Encourage her to beat her own number in future hanging attempts.

3.174 Hops forward ten feet on either foot without assistance

Strand: 3-7C **Age:** 54-68m 4.6-5.8y

Definition

The child will stand on her right or left leg and maintain her balance without support or help. She will hop forward ten feet on either leg, the other foot suspended without assistance. The child does not have to hop in a straight line.

Instructional Materials

Note: The blue paint should be thin so the child will not have a slippery solution on her foot.

A large sheet of white paper (10 feet long by 3 feet wide), masking tape, a pan with one half inch of washable nontoxic blue paint in it, a pan of soapy water, a towel.

Instructional Activities

Note: Do this activity only if the child is comfortable having blue paint on her foot. Tell her it will wash off easily.

/***Safety Note:** Safety is a concern during this activity because you do not want the child to slip and fall. Hold the child's hands as she walks across the paper.

1. Tape the large sheet of paper to the floor. Set the blue paint pan at one end of the paper and place the soapy water pan and towel at the other end of the paper.
2. Tell the child to take off her shoes and socks.
3. Ask her to put one foot in the blue paint pan; help her put her foot gently in the pan and make sure her foot is covered with paint.

4. Tell her to walk all the way across the paper so that she leaves several blue footprints on the paper. Hold her hand or spot her as she walks across the paper.

5. When she walks to the other end of the paper, help her wash her foot in the soapy water and dry it with the towel.

6. Allow the paint to dry thoroughly.

7. This time have her hop on the foot she used to make tracks across the paper.

8. Repeat the above activity using the opposite foot.

3.175 Walks up and down stairs carrying an object, without support

Strand: 3-7B **Age:** 60-65m 5.0-5.5y

Definition

The child will walk down the stairs carrying an object in one hand and using his other hand for support. He will walk up the stairs carrying an object in one hand and using the other hand for support. He will then walk up and down the stairs carrying an object by using one or two hands and no support.

Instructional Materials

Available stairway with at least five steps, construction paper in two different colors (one color to represent left and the other color to represent right), masking tape, stickers or ribbons in the same colors as the construction paper, a soft object, such as a small pillow or stuffed animal.

Instructional Activities

1. Cut out footprints from the construction paper, one color for left and the other for right; with masking tape attach them securely to each step - to the side, out of the direct path the child uses to go up and down the stairs.

2. Ask the child to stand at one end of the stairs.

3. Put a sticker or ribbon that matches the color of the left footprint on the child's left shoe and put a sticker or ribbon that matches the color of the right footprint on the child's right shoe.

4. Give the child the soft object to hold.

5. Tell him to put his right foot on the step that matches the right foot color, and repeat this with his left foot.

6. Remind him that the sticker on his foot should be the same color as the footprint on the step.

7. Tell him to keep walking without dropping the soft object.

8. Increase the difficulty and the motivation of this activity by removing the color-coding and

giving the child an object that requires more attention.

3.176 Runs through obstacle course avoiding objects

Strand: 3-7B **Age:** 60-68m 5.0-5.8y

Definition

The child will run a 20-foot course between two lines, 5 feet apart. Obstacles are placed at varied intervals (large box, cone, chair, foam blocks, etc.) The child will stay between the two lines and avoid making any contact with any obstacle.

Instructional Materials

Cut out planets, moons, stars, and space stations from heavy chart paper (the child may enjoy helping to make these space-oriented items). Some large cardboard boxes, stapler or glue, stopwatch.

Instructional Activities

1. Attach the space objects to the large cardboard boxes by stapling or gluing them to the sides of the boxes. Conduct this activity in a large room or outdoors. Position the boxes decorated with space objects around the open area.

2. Tell the child to pretend she is a rocket ship, and that she must crouch down very low for the Blast-Off.

3. Explain that when she hears the countdown and "Blast-Off," she is to jump up and run around each of the space boxes and then run back to the starting point.

4. Tell her that if she touches one of the space boxes, she must go back and start again.

5. Give her two practice runs.

6. Use a stopwatch to time the child as she makes her "space-run" and encourage her to beat her own time.

7. Give her one point for each planet, moon, or star that she does not touch when she runs around it.

3.177 Skips forward

Strand: 3-7C **Age:** 60-72m 5.0-6.0y

Definition

After the child has seen a demonstration, she will skip forward, using alternate feet, leading with the left or right foot at least four times. Example: Skip left-skip right, Skip left-skip right, Skip left-skip right, Skip left-skip right. Distance is not important.

Instructional Materials

A water-base marker (washable).

Instructional Activities

1. Using the marker, draw at least 10 squares in a path on the floor. The squares may be drawn in a straight line or with a corner or curve. The direction of the path should depend on the skipping skills of the child--the lower the entry level of the child, the less complex the path should be.
2. Ask the child to stand on the first square and explain that when she hears the word "go," she is to step-hop (one foot skip) to the next square in the path, and from there she is to step-hop (other foot skip) to the next square.
3. If necessary, model the step-hop on one foot and then step-hop on the other foot.
4. Tell her when she gets to the end of the path she may start over, or offer to make another path for her.
5. After she has been successful in skipping down the path, ask her to skip the path to a chant. A suggested chant might be: (1) Skip, skip, skip, skip (said at a normal speaking rate); (2) Ski-i-ip, ski-i-ip, ski-i-ip, ski-i-ip (said at a slow speaking rate); (3) Skip, skip, skip, skip (said at a rapid speaking rate); (4) Skip, skip (spoken at a normal rate), Ski-i-ip, ski-i-ip (spoken slowly), skip, skip (rapidly spoken).
6. Replace this spoken chant with a drumbeat or clap, and finally with a skipping musical selection such as *Pop Goes the Weasel* or *Spanish Dance* that you play or hum.

3.178   Maintains balance on a movable platform (balance disc, etc.)

Strand: 3-7G   **Age:** 60-78m 5.0-6.6y

Definition

The child will stand (both feet) on a movable platform holding on to a support (both hands) for at least 30 seconds. The child will stand (both feet) on a movable platform holding on to a support (one hand) for at least 30 seconds. The child will stand (both feet) on a movable platform holding on to a support when needed for at least 30 seconds. The child will balance on a movable platform for at least 30 seconds, arms in any position. The child will balance on a movable platform for at least 1 minute (In extending the time, the child may need to repeat the support steps as outlined above.)

Instructional Materials

A balance disc.

Instructional Activities

/*\Safety Note: Supervise this activity carefully to avoid the child falling off the platform / disc.
1. Place the balance disc on a firm surface.
2. Allow the child an opportunity to "walk around the surface" (one foot on the firm surface and the other foot is on the disc).
3. Provide the child time to explore different movements on the disc.
4. Ask the child to go from one side of the disc to the other without touching the ground.
5. Continue with other "stunts" using the disc. Allow the child to experiment with various activities and demonstrate.

3.179   Completes a backward roll (somersault)

Strand: 3-7G   **Age:** 70-72m 5.10-6.0y

Definition

/*\Safety Note: *The backward roll must be done on a padded floor mat.*
The child will do a backward somersault without assistance and without falling to either side. He will begin by lying on his back, clasping his fingers behind his neck with elbows out to his sides, with his knees next to his chest and his chin on his chest. He will appear to be in a tucked-in position. He will rock back and forth until he achieves momentum and then will push out with his arms on the floor and roll completely over backwards, taking the weight of his roll on his forearms.

Instructional Materials

A padded mat large enough for the child to roll backward.

Instructional Activities

/*\Safety Note: Make sure the child know how to place his hands behind his head as he rolls over to protect his neck.
1. Place the mat on the floor. Ask the child to take off his shoes.
2. Demonstrate a backward somersault, or ask someone else to do it.
3. Ask the child questions about the somersault, such as, "Did you see how I stayed tucked-in when I did my somersault?" "Did you see how she stayed tucked-in when she did her somersault?" "Where were my feet before I went over?" or "What do you think my chin was touching?"

4. Repeat the demonstration again, explaining each action.

5. Tell the child to stand at one end of mat.

6. Tell him to lie on his back, and assist him if necessary.

7. Tell him to put his hands behind his head with his fingers clasped.

8. Tell him to tuck his chin into his chest, bend his knees, place his feet flat on the mat, and to get himself into a tucked-in position.

9. Encourage him to begin a rocking motion.

10. Provide a gentle push to begin the roll over backwards.

11. Assist when necessary and allow time for the child to practice.

See #3.166.

3.180 Lifts torso from ground to complete one sit-up

Strand: 3-7G   **Age:** 70-78m 5.10-6.6y

Definition

The child will lie on her back with feet flat and knees bent at a 45-degree angle, arms crossed on her chest, hands in opposite directions. Her feet may be held, if needed. The sit-up is done to a two-count pattern. A two-count pattern is up on one and down on two.

Instructional Materials

An incline exercise board (if unavailable, make one by covering a board 32 inches by 48 inches by 2 inches with foam and a washable fabric. Place the constructed board on bricks, blocks or a 4-inch by 6-inch board). Make sure the board is stable.

Instructional Activities

1. Adjust the incline exercise board so that the raised end will place the child's head above her feet.

2. Place the child on the incline board so that her head is higher than her feet.

3. Hold her feet down in position while another adult holds her hands.

4. Pull gently and slowly on the child's hands and say, "Pull."

5. Repeat until the child can pull herself up on the incline.

6. Scoot her down so that only her head is elevated on the incline.

7. Hold her feet down and pull up on her arms until she can sit up independently.

8. Have her lie in a complete horizontal position without the incline board and repeat the above steps.

9. If she still has difficulty, gently push her up while you support her under her shoulders.

10. Advance by asking her to put her hands behind her head for a sit-up or ask her to try to do a specific number of sit-ups.

11. An option is to have her do sit-ups to music.

3.181 Lifts body off the floor to complete one push-up

Strand: 3-7G   **Age:** 70-78m 5.10-6.6y

Definition

After a demonstration, the child will lie flat on the floor, face down, with his palms flat on the floor. He will push his body straight up once, his toes on the floor and his arms extended (girls should start push-ups with their knees staying on the floor). He will then lower his body until his chest is 3 inches from the ground, straighten his elbows, and then raise his body once again. The child's head should be up and his eyes should be forward as he raises himself.

Instructional Materials

Colored stickers, two cutout hand prints (made by tracing around the child's hands on paper and cutting them out), tape. A padded floor mat large enough for the child to lie on face down.

Instructional Activities

1. Place the two colored stickers on the floor, and tape the two cutout hand prints about 12 inches or more from the stickers.

2. Ask the child to place his knees on the stickers and his hands on the handprints.

3. Tell him to keep his knees on the stickers while he lowers his body to the floor.

4. Provide assistance as necessary, especially in pushing back up.

5. If he has difficulty, have him lower himself only halfway to the floor, and then try to push back up so his arms are straight (elbows locked).

6. Modify this activity by moving the stickers and handprints, or by asking the child to put his toes on the stickers instead of his knees.

/*\ **Important Water Safety Note:**

Instructional Activities for Skills 3.182 through 3.228 require constant and close supervision.

3.182   Sits on steps of pool and kicks in water

Strand: 3-8

Instructional Activities

/***Safety:** Provide constant, close supervision.

Level One:

1. Fill a dishpan with water from the pool and set it on the pool deck near the stairs. Let the child become familiar with the pool water in the dishpan; look, smell, and feel the water with her.
2. Give her a plastic doll and ask her to set it in the dishpan, make the doll kick its feet, take it out and dry it.
3. Help the child stand in the dishpan and splash her feet.
4. Put the dishpan on the first step in the pool. Have the child sit on the deck and put her feet in the dishpan. Tell her to kick her feet in the dishpan to make splashes.
5. Move the dishpan down to the second step. Tell the child to move to the first step. Place her feet in the dishpan and have her splash.
6. Remove the dishpan and have the child kick in the pool.
7. Help her dry off when she indicates she doesn't want to continue.
8. If she is hesitant at any given step, go back one step and repeat.

Level Two:

1. Seat the child on the first step of the pool with her feet on the second. Ask her if she can touch her toes, thus getting her arms and chest wet.
2. Mark the third step with a rubber ring. Ask her if she can touch the ring with her toes.
3. Show her how to sit sideways on the second step next to her feet. Help if necessary.
4. Have her stretch her legs while sitting sideways on the second step and kick in water.
5. Turn her and have her put her feet on the rubber ring.
6. Instruct her how to make nice easy kicks.
7. Do not force any given step.

3.183   Allows self to be carried about in water

Strand: 3-8

Instructional Activities

/***Safety:** Provide constant, close supervision.

1. Seat children on the pool's edge with their feet dangling in the water.
2. Explain that you will carry each child in turn for a "merry-go-round" ride around the pool.
3. Instruct the child to put his legs around your waist and his arms around your neck.
4. Tell him you will hold him around his waist.
5. Taking turns, walk with each child in the pool, holding him so his shoulders do not go below the water.
6. Twirl around in water, and bob up and down.
7. Sing songs if the child is tense.
8. Take each child on as many trips as time permits.
9. Try to get each one to point out where he trusts you to take him; this will help him relax in water for success with later swimming instruction.

3.184   Stands in water up to waist

Strand: 3-8

Instructional Activities

/***Safety:** Provide constant, close supervision.

1. Ask the child to enter the pool slowly, standing up, walking down the steps one at time.
2. Put your foot on the step so she can feel it and stand next to it if she hesitates.
3. When she reaches the last step, place a rubber ring on the pool floor so she can see the pool floor.
4. Have her hold onto the edge of the pool and step onto the pool floor next to the rubber ring.
5. Allow her to stand on your feet if she is hesitant and step to the pool floor when she feels more confident.
6. Give her a few minutes of free water play after the lesson.

3.185   Blows bubbles in water

Strand: 3-8

Instructional Activities

/*\ **Safety:** Provide constant, close supervision.
1. Have the children stand in the water.
2. Talk about how a motor boat makes bubbles.
3. Demonstrate by putting your lips in the water and then blow bubbles.
4. Let the children pretend to be motor boats.
5. Challenge them to find out which motor boat can run longest.
6. Vary the activity by asking children to walk across the pool blowing bubbles.
7. Announce the winner as the first one to reach the other side.

3.186   Walks across width of pool with help

Strand: 3-8

Instructional Activities

/*\ **Safety:** Provide constant, close supervision.
1. Tell the child she is going to play a game with you. Have her stand in the shallow water. Stand facing her with your back facing the direction you wish to go.
2. Have her grasp your hands. Slowly take a step backward, allowing her to follow.
3. Sing or say, "Tugboat Tillie is towing [Samantha], Watch out ahead!" Have her say, "Toot-toot!" or something similar to help her overcome any fears.
4. Praise her when she reaches the opposite side.
5. Turn around and return to the starting point.
6. Move into deeper water as she gains confidence, but do not go above her midriff.

3.187   Walks across width of pool unassisted

Strand: 3-8

Instructional Activities

/*\ **Safety:** Provide constant, close supervision.
1. Have two children line up next to the pool wall in shallow water.
2. Place three rings behind each child.
3. Explain that the object of the game is to see who can get all three rings to the other side first by taking one ring across the pool at a time.
4. Start the race by saying, "Go.".

5. Tell each child to carry a ring across the pool, put it on the opposite edge, and return to retrieve another ring.
6. Assign an adult to stay close to each child to shout encouragement and steady him in case of a slip.
7. Announce the winner as the first one to get all three rings across the pool.
8. Move into deeper water as they gain confidence.

3.188   Puts face in water

Strand: 3-8

Instructional Activities

/*\ **Safety:** Provide constant, close supervision.
1. Ease the child into the water. Kneel in the shallow end with her and hold onto the steps.
2. Have her blow bubbles in the water.
3. Have her pretend to be washing her face by cupping water in her hands and splashing it on her face.
4. Tell her you are going to play a game that requires everyone to put their face in the water.
5. Sing the song *Ring Around the Rosie* and when you get to the line, "We all fall down," change it to, "We all put our face in the water."
6. Repeat the game until she gains confidence in submerging her face in water.

3.189   Enters and exits pool safely

Strand: 3-8

Instructional Activities

/*\ **Safety:** Provide constant, close supervision.
1. Explain safety rules for around a pool, such as not running on wet cement, no pushing, etc.
2. Explain safety rules for getting into water, such as making sure an adult is watching, no jumping on other people in the water, and making sure the pool is deep enough for diving in.
3. Explain safety rules for the water, such as no splashing other people, no dunking other people under the water, and how to call for help.
4. Add up the number of different rules you have explained. Ask the child if he can list all the rules you mentioned.
5. Make a memory game of it, emphasize the important need for safety, and discuss the consequences of not following the rules.

3.190   Bobs in and out of water 5 times, holding breath

Strand: 3-8

Instructional Activities

/***Safety:** Provide constant, close supervision.

1. Organize children in a circle holding hands in waist-high water.
2. Take each child, one at a time, and hold their hands helping them practice taking big breaths and bobbing in and out of water.
3. Continue until each one has had a turn with you.
4. Instruct the children how to play and sing *Ring Around the Rosie*.
5. Tell them that when they sing, "We all fall down," everyone is to hold hands, take a big breath and bob their heads under water.
6. Increase the number of bobs after, "We all fall down" until all of them have bobbed in and out of the water five times in row.

3.191   Ducks head underwater, holding breath for 10 seconds

Strand: 3-8

Instructional Activities

/***Safety:** Provide constant, close supervision.

1. Have the children walk to the 3-foot depth of the pool. Have them form a circle by joining hands.
2. Tell them to drop hands and to stand still. Instruct them to listen to a rhyme but not to move.
3. Repeat the rhyme twice so the children have an opportunity to hear what you will be saying:
   Jack-In-The-Box, Oh so still.
   Won't you come out? Yes, I will!
4. Tell them to duck slightly under the water at the count of three as you say the rhyme.
5. Tell them to stay underwater until they hear "Won't you come out?" and then to jump up, saying, "Yes, I will!" (lean close to their heads and shout so they hear you).

3.192   Opens eyes underwater

Strand: 3-8

Instructional Activities

/***Safety:** Provide constant, close supervision.

1. Laminate large bright pictures to waterproof them (or use plastic place mats).

2. Have children go in the water.
3. Place a picture in the water with its backside to the children.
4. Instruct the children to put their heads in the water and look at the picture.
5. Turn the picture to face the children.
6. Take turns choosing a child to describe the picture.

3.193   Retrieves object underwater

Strand: 3-8

Instructional Activities

/***Safety:** Provide constant, close supervision.

1. Show the children several small "treasures"-- small items such as pennies, buttons, plastic prizes-- on the edge of the pool.
2. Pass out individual "treasure boxes," or divide the group into two teams and have two larger boxes.
3. Tell the children they are going on a treasure hunt and they are to bring treasures back to fill their boxes.
4. Scatter treasures around in the pool.
5. Have all children get in the water at the side of the pool. Once they are all in the pool and ready, give them the prompt, "On your marks! Get set! Go!"
6. Announce the winner to be the child or team who retrieves the most treasures.
7. Vary the game by using different sized items for treasures, or by having children cover their eyes while you scatter them.

3.194   Bobs in and out of water 5 times, breathing rhythmically

Strand: 3-8

Instructional Activities

/***Safety:** Provide constant, close supervision.

1. Obtain a Jack-In-the-Box toy. Show the child how Jack pops out from the box.
2. Have the child get into the pool.
3. Ask her to pretend to be Jack-in-the-Box and to sink into the water and then pop out five times in a row.
4. Remind her to exhale and inhale as she pops out.
5. Let her play with the Jack-in-the-Box at the end of the lesson.

3.195   Performs jelly-fish float. Recovers to standing position
Strand: 3-8

Instructional Activities
/*\Safety: Provide constant, close supervision.
1. Instruct children to open and close their hands to resemble an octopus. Tell them they are to take an octopus for a walk to the bottom of the sea.
2. Have them stand with their octopuses (hands) on their thighs. Explain to them how they will walk the octopus from their leg planks to the bottom of the sea.
3. Tell them to bend at the waist and walk the octopus down the planks.
4. Praise those who try to make it to the bottom.
5. Repeat the activity in water chest-deep.

3.196   Performs turtle float and recovers
Strand: 3-8

Instructional Activities
/*\Safety: Provide constant, close supervision.
1. Have the children stand in a large circle in the pool.
2. Demonstrate a turtle float by lying on your stomach and pulling your knees up to your chest.
3. Show the children a large hoop.
4. Have one child demonstrate getting into a turtle float while you move the hoop so their body floats through it.
5. Have each child try the turtle float.
6. When they seem comfortable with the turtle float, have them take turns performing the turtle float as you take the hoop and make their bodies pass through it.

3.197   Performs dog paddle
Strand: 3-8

Instructional Activities
/*\Safety: Provide constant, close supervision.
1. Have the child spread his fingers apart and move his hands through the water to experience the sensation of water through his fingers.
2. Explain to him how a dog will paddle with his paws in order to keep his head above water.
3. Have the child practice paddling his hands like a dog would.
4. Instruct him to paddle and keep his head above water.
5. Have him paddle through the water.

3.198   Performs front float
Strand: 3-8

Instructional Activities
/*\Safety: Provide constant, close supervision.
1. Instruct the child to walk to the 3-foot depth of the pool.
2. Tell her to squat until water covers her shoulders.
3. Stand face to face and take her hands.
4. Instruct her to lean forward with her legs floating in a horizontal position, keeping her face out of water, as you pull her around the pool.
5. Have her hold her breath and put her face in water for two or three seconds at a time, then longer as her confidence builds.
6. Continue until she floats and feels secure, holding your hands. Do not exceed five minutes at each practice time.

3.199   Performs back float
Strand: 3-8

Instructional Activities
/*\Safety: Provide constant, close supervision.
1. Instruct the child to sit down on the second step of the pool, staying in a sitting position.
2. Tell him to lean back on the top step as if to lie down on a bed, letting his legs and feet float to the top of the water.
3. Tell him to lean way back and to rest his head on the top step in the water, letting his legs remain in a floating position and bracing himself with his hands.
4. Ask him to pretend to be asleep until you tap him awake with a magic wand.
5. Ask him to stay in a sleeping position for a count of ten.

3.200   Recovers to standing position from front and back floats
Strand: 3-8

Instructional Activities
/*\Safety: Provide constant, close supervision.
1. Place the child in the pool.
2. Have her float on her front.

3. Instruct her to pretend she is a balloon deflating and to let her feet sink until they touch the pool floor.
4. Tell her to stand as soon as her feet touch the bottom.
5. Assist as needed.
6. Use the same procedure for back float.

3.201   Performs front glide from 2 feet, 5 feet

Strand: 3-8

Instructional Activities

/*\ **Safety:** Provide constant, close supervision.
1. Have the children get in the pool at the 3-foot depth facing you about 4 feet from the steps.
2. Place a small floating toy for each child on the edge of the pool.
3. Instruct them to squat until their shoulders are underwater.
4. Tell them to extend their arms in front of their body on top of the water and to lock thumbs with fingers closed side-by-side.
5. Tell them to take a deep breath, put their head down between their arms, to face underwater with eyes looking at the bottom of pool, and to lean forward and push off the bottom of the pool with their feet, letting their legs and body float on top of the water.
6. Tell them to aim for the steps and the toy.
7. Allow them to play with the toy for a few seconds before repeating the activity.

3.202   Performs front glide with flutter kick for 2 feet, 5 feet

Strand: 3-8

Instructional Activities

/*\ **Safety:** Provide constant, close supervision.
Set up opportunity to demonstrate skill, model and observe, and point out correct techniques.

3.203   Performs back glide for 2 feet, 5 feet

Strand: 3-8

Instructional Activities

/*\ **Safety:** Provide constant, close supervision.
1. Have the children walk to the 3-foot depth of the pool.
2. Tell them to stretch their arms out like a butterfly.

3. Tell them to squat until the water is at shoulder level.
4. Tell them to lay their head back in the water, with their chin pointing to the sky, and arms stretched out like a butterfly.
5. Instruct them to keep leaning back until their legs are floating horizontal on the water, arms stretched out, shoulders back, chin pointing to the sky with face out of the water.
6. Assist by standing behind the child, grasping his chin with your right hand and placing your left hand under his head, pulling gently backwards until his legs are floating.
7. Repeat until children are able to float for at least 30 seconds.

3.204   Performs back glide with flutter kick for 2 feet, 5 feet

Strand: 3-8

Instructional Activities

/*\ **Safety:** Provide constant, close supervision.
Set up opportunity to demonstrate skill, model and observe, and point out correct techniques.

3.205   Jumps into water from deck with legs apart so head does not become submerged

Strand: 3-8

Instructional Activities

/*\ **Safety:** Provide constant, close supervision.
Set up opportunity to demonstrate skill, model and observe, and point out correct techniques.

3.206   Jumps into water from deck with legs together, pushes off bottom and glides

Strand: 3-8

Instructional Activities

/*\ **Safety:** Provide constant, close supervision.
Set up opportunity to demonstrate skill, model and observe, and point out correct techniques.

3.207   Performs front glide with kick and stroke

Strand: 3-8

Instructional Activities

/*\ **Safety:** Provide constant, close supervision.

Set up opportunity to demonstrate skill, model and observe, and point out correct techniques.

/*\ Important Safety Note:

Instructional Activities for Skills 3.208 through 3.228 require close supervision.

3.208 Stops wheelchair in any manner
Strand: 3-9

Instructional Materials

Masking tape, toy bowling pins or plastic bottles.

Instructional Activities

1. Place two tape marks on the floor about 18 inches apart.
2. Place a bowling pin on each taped line.
3. Tell the child to move in her wheelchair towards the tape line.
4. Instruct her to stop the wheelchair before it knocks over the pin.
5. Praise each safe stop she makes.
6. Keep score of perfect stops, and challenge her to beat her record.

3.209 Moves wheelchair forward using 1 push forward and release
Strand: 3-9

Instructional Materials

Masking tape, chalk, whistle.

Instructional Activities

1. Lay out a race course in the gym or on the playground with masking tape or chalk.
2. Mark a starting and a finishing line at one end of the area with tape or chalk.
3. Use chalk to define four racing lanes at least 10 feet apart.
4. Line up children who have equal ability in wheelchairs at the starting point.
5. Explain the push-and-release method to go forward.
6. Tell the children they must each follow their racing line.
7. Blow the starting whistle.
8. Assist children as needed.

3.210 Moves wheelchair backward using 1 pull back and release
Strand: 3-9

Instructional Activities

1. Place or have the child get into wheelchair and make sure her seat belt is fastened.
2. Instruct her to put her hands on the wheelchair rim in front of her.
3. Instruct her to hold onto the rim and to move her arms to her back (backwards).
4. Instruct her to release the rim when her arms are as far back as they can go.
5. Vary the activity by getting a slide whistle and blowing along with the children stretch forward and pull backward.
6. Stop blowing if the child stops prematurely.

3.211 Turns wheelchair in a circle to the right
Strand: 3-9

Instructional Materials

Several traffic cones or other objects.

Instructional Activities

1. Set up traffic cones or other objects in a circle.
2. Position the child with his right side toward the cones.
3. Instruct him to go around the cones without hitting them.
4. Demonstrate the best turning procedure.
5. Praise the child if he makes it all the way around the circle without touching the cones, regardless of his time.
6. Vary the activity by changing the size of the circle or by timing the child to see if he can beat his previous time.
7. Set up a maze or an obstacle course so the child must make right and left turns in order to get to the end.

3.212 Turns wheelchair in a circle to the left
Strand: 3-9

Instructional Materials

Several traffic cones or other objects.

Instructional Activities

1. Set up traffic cones or other objects in a circle.
2. Position the child with her left side toward the cones.

3. Instruct her to go around the cones without hitting them.
4. Model the best turning procedure.
5. Praise the child if she makes it all the way around the circle without touching the cones, regardless of her time.
6. Vary the activity by changing the size of the circle or by timing the child to see if she can beat her previous time.
7. Set up a maze or an obstacle course so the child must make right and left turns in order to get to end.

3.213   Sets brake on wheelchair to stop or remain stationary

Strand: 3-9

Instructional Activities

Set up an opportunity to demonstrate this skill, model, observe, and point out correct techniques.

3.214   Releases brake on wheelchair to resume movement

Strand: 3-9

Instructional Activities

Set up an opportunity to demonstrate the skill, model, observe, and point out correct techniques.

3.215   Travels forward 10 feet in wheelchair

Strand: 3-9

Instructional Activities

Set up an opportunity to demonstrate the skill, model, observe, and point out correct techniques.

3.216   Travels backward 10 feet in wheelchair

Strand: 3-9

Instructional Activities

1. Mark a starting and a finishing line for a race course, and place plastic bowling pins to make two lanes.
2. Instruct the child how to do the activity.
3. Place her in the wheelchair at the starting line with her back facing the course.

4. Ask her to wheel backwards between the bowling pins without knocking them down.
5. Award a badge to the child if she avoids hitting all the pins.
6. Vary this activity by timing the child and having her race against her record.

3.217   Travels length of classroom in wheelchair

Strand: 3-9

Instructional Activities

Set up an opportunity to demonstrate the skill, model and observe, and point out correct techniques.

3.218   Travels length of classroom in wheelchair in one minute

Strand: 3-9

Instructional Activities

Set up the opportunity to demonstrate skill, model and observe, and point out correct techniques.

3.219   Travels using wheelchair in roomy areas to go forward, backward, and to turn at will

Strand: 3-9

Instructional Materials

Cones made from construction paper or poster board, tape for floor or cement, green and red marking pens, stopwatch.

Instructional Activities

1. Set up an obstacle course in a room or on blacktop with cones made from construction paper or poster board.
2. Place tape on the floor in a path for the children to follow.
3. Color the beginning tape green for "Go" and the end tape red for "Stop."
4. Demonstrate how to move a wheelchair through the obstacle course without touching any cones.
5. Give each child a few practice turns.
6. Tell the children you will time them as they move through the obstacle course and that you will note how many cones they hit or if they went off course.

7. Record each child's time, number of cones hit, and when they went off course on a chart. Let them know when their scores have improved and praise them for the hard work they are doing.

3.220 Travels using wheelchair in compact areas to go forward, backward, and to turn at will

Strand: 3-9

Instructional Activities

1. Set up an obstacle course in a room with furniture.
2. Place yellow tape on the floor in the path you wish the children to follow.
3. Make a green palace from construction paper and stand it up at the end of the path.
4. Tell the children that in this activity they will follow the yellow brick road and try to get to the Emerald Palace to see the Wizard of Oz.
5. Explain that to get to the palace each child must follow your directions and stay on the path.
6. Demonstrate how to move a wheelchair through the obstacle course and follow directions without going off the path.
7. Give each child a practice turn.
8. Tell the children the Wizard of Oz will award a prize to those who successfully make it to the Emerald Palace.

3.221 Travels forward through doorway

Strand: 3-9

Instructional Activities

Set up the opportunity to demonstrate skill, model and observe, and point out correct techniques.

3.222 Travels backward through doorway

Strand: 3-9

Instructional Activities

Set up the opportunity to demonstrate skill, model and observe, and point out correct techniques.

3.223 Opens door, travels through doorway, and closes door

Strand: 3-9

Instructional Activities

Set up an opportunity to demonstrate skill, model and observe, and point out correct techniques.

3.224 Places foot rests in down position

Strand: 3-9

Instructional Activities

Set up an opportunity to demonstrate skill, model and observe, and point out correct techniques.

3.225 Places foot on rest

Strand: 3-9

Instructional Activities

Set up an opportunity to demonstrate skill, model and observe, and point out correct techniques.

3.226 Takes foot off rest and places foot rests in up position

Strand: 3-9

Instructional Activities

1. Put wheelchair brakes on.
2. Seat the child in the wheelchair.
3. Have the child lift one leg and put it next to the other on the other foot rest.
4. Use your hands to move her leg if necessary.
5. Bend over and push the heel loop forward if necessary.
6. Fold the foot rest up.
7. Take both feet off the other foot rest.
8. Bend over and push the heel loop forward if necessary.
9. Fold the other foot rest up.
10. Demonstrate the procedure, explaining all the tasks involved.
11. Have her try to raise the foot rests with your assistance.
12. Gradually reduce your assistance.

3.227   Transfers from wheelchair

Strand: 3-9

Instructional Activities

/*\ **Safety Note:** Check with the specialist or therapist working with the child on wheelchair skills before attempting this skill.

1. Place the child on the floor.
2. Bring the wheelchair to him.
3. Show him the timer.
4. Tell him you will time how fast he gets into his chair.
5. Do not allow him to rush. Stress the importance of moving safely.
6. Protect his back as he transfers positions.
7. Give him praise for moving safely.

---

1. Position the wheelchair for the child if he is unable to do it.
2. Put the wheelchair as close to bed as possible and in position so he turns toward his stronger side.
3. Swing away the foot rests and remove the armrests, if possible.
4. Make sure the brakes are on.
5. Assist or have him roll to edge of the bed.
6. Assist or have him sit on the edge of the bed with his legs over the side.
7. Assist or have him stand.
8. Block his knees with your knees if necessary.
9. Turn him toward the wheelchair.
10. Assist or have him sit in the wheelchair.
11. Assist or have him push back into the wheelchair.
12. Replace the armrests and foot rests.
13. Put his feet on foot rests.
14. Fasten the seat belt.

---

1. Position or have the child position his wheelchair as close to the bed as possible and in position so he turns toward his stronger side.
2. Put the brakes on.
3. Take his feet off the foot rests.
4. Swing the foot rests away and remove the armrests if possible.
5. Unfasten the seat belt.
6. Pull or have him slide to the edge of the wheelchair.
7. Assist or have the child stand.
8. Hold him by his pant tops or belt, if necessary.
9. Block his knees with your knees if necessary.
10. Turn him toward the bed.
11. Assist or have him sit on the edge of the bed.

12. Lower or have him lower himself onto the bed.
13. Swing his legs onto the bed.
14. Have a small treat on or under the pillow for him to have when the task is completed.

---

1. Seat the child in his wheelchair.
2. Position or have him position the wheelchair as close to the chair as possible and in position so he turns toward his stronger side.
3. Put the brakes on.
4. Put the foot rests up.
5. Pull or have him slide to the edge of the wheelchair.
6. Assist or have him stand.
7. Hold him by his pant tops or belt if necessary.
8. Block his knees with your knees if necessary.
9. Turn him toward the wheelchair.
10. Assist or have him sit in the chair.
11. Assist or have him push back into the chair.
12. Encourage his independence.
13. Repeat often, gradually reducing your assistance.

3.228   Follows safety rules using wheelchair

Strand: 3-9

Instructional Activities

/*\ **Safety Note:** Set up an opportunity to demonstrate skill, model and observe, and point out correct techniques.

4.94 Puts together simple inset puzzles

Strand: 4-6B **Age:** 30-40m 2.6-3.4y

Definition

When the child is presented with a four to six-piece inset puzzle, he will put it together.

Instructional Materials

Five inset puzzles with four to six-pieces.

Instructional Activities

1. Place a puzzle on the table. Talk to the child about the images in the puzzle.
2. Ask the child to remove the pieces and randomly place the pieces on the table.
3. Have the child pick up a puzzle piece, but before they place it back in the puzzle board, ask them to point to the place the puzzle piece will go just by looking at the puzzle shape.
4. Provide verbal prompts if necessary.
5. If he appears to be unsure about this task, put the puzzle pieces on the table and demonstrate how you take and examine an individual puzzle piece, then you examine and point to the place where the puzzle piece will fit.
6. As he becomes skilled in putting the puzzle together, place all five puzzles on the table. Remove all the pieces, scramble the pieces up, and have the child determine where each piece goes on the five different puzzle boards. (You can start with fewer than five puzzles and build up to doing all the puzzles at once.)

4.95 (Removed, see page xii)

4.96 Cuts across paper following a straight line 6 inches long and then a curved line 6 inches long

Strand: 4-7D **Age:** 36-48m 3.0-4.0y

Definition

When she is shown how to cut across a paper following a line, the child will cut along a straight line 6 inches long and not more than ¼ inch wide. She will then cut along a curved line 6 inches long and not more than ¼ inch wide. She will cut with appropriately sized scissors, and she will hold the paper correctly, not deviating from the line more than ¼ inch. She will do this cutting task without assistance.

Instructional Materials

/*\ **Safety Note:** Provide scissors appropriate for the child. Remind the child of safety regarding scissors.

A sheet of paper on which you have drawn funny faces, ghosts, snakes, or other figures using curved lines. Child-size scissors.

Instructional Activities

1. Provide the child with scissors that are appropriate for her and the sheet of paper with the curved line drawings.
2. Demonstrate cutting along the curved lines.
3. Ask the child to imitate you, being careful to follow the curved lines.
4. Encourage her to glue the cutouts on another sheet of paper.
5. Display her finished project.

4.97 Builds tower of more than nine blocks without assistance

Strand: 4-6B **Age:** 36-48m 3.0-4.0y

Definition

The child will build a tower of at least ten blocks without assistance. The child will make continued attempts on his own even if the tower topples over.

Instructional Materials

The inside core from a roll of paper towels, a core from a roll of gift-wrap paper. From 20 to 40 one-inch building blocks.

Instructional Activities

1. Stand the core from the paper towel roll upright on a table. Put the box of blocks on the table.
2. Pick up a block and drop it into the standing core, and then ask the child to drop three blocks into it.
3. After he has dropped the blocks into the core, carefully remove the core without knocking the blocks over.
4. Set the core upright again and drop in more than three blocks.
5. Before removing the core, tell the child to build a tower of blocks next to it. Let him use the core as a support for the outside tower.
6. Carefully remove the core, trying not to knock down either tower of blocks.
7. Place the gift-wrap core on the floor and drop blocks into the roll.
8. Ask another child to participate, and ask one child to remove the core very slowly while the other child aligns and steadies the tower.

9. Ask the child to build a tower without the core. Encourage him to use at least 10 blocks in his construction.
10. Suggest that the children try to establish records for building the tallest tower either inside a roll or outside it.

4.98 Strings small beads, cubes, cylinders (based on a simple shape pattern)
Strand: 4-7C **Age:** 36-48m 3.0-4.0y

Definition
When presented with a pattern/model, the child will string at least eight small beads. The beads should be ½-inch to 1-inch wooden spheres, cubes, and cylinders in different colors; the string should have a hard-tip or use a shoelace.

Instructional Materials
Food coloring in two or more colors, small bowls, small sponge or brush, paper towels, pasta in various shapes and sizes (large enough to string easily), a shoelace.

Instructional Activities
1. Tie a knot at one end of the shoelace to keep the pasta on the lace. Mix the food coloring with a small amount of water until reaching the desired shade.
2. Explain to the child that she is going to make a necklace out of pasta.
3. Tell her that first she will color the pasta. Provide her with a small sponge or brush. Give the child a piece of pasta and tell her to paint it.
4. Tell her to lay the painted pasta on a paper towel to dry.
5. Once the pasta is completely dry, she may sort the pasta according to color.
6. Next, show her how to string the pasta. Let her make a necklace, a bracelet, or chains.
7. Provide assistance as needed.
8. Tell her she may keep the necklace and wear it if she wishes.
9. Invite her to make other items with the pasta following a pattern that has been presented to her.

4.99 Folds paper three times
Strand: 4-6D **Age:** 36-48m 3.0-4.0y

Definition
When the child is given a demonstration of how to fold a piece of 8 ½ x 11 inch paper in half, in half

again, and in half again, he will fold his paper in the very same way. The edges of the paper will be nearly even.

Instructional Materials
/***Safety Note:** Provide scissors appropriate for the child. Remind the child of safety regarding scissors.
Several sheets of 8-inch square white or brown paper, markers, crayons, pencil, child-safe scissors, small ruler.

Instructional Activities
1. Place the paper and the material on a table or work area. Tell the child he is going to make a paper puppy by folding a sheet of paper three times.
2. Talk about a name for the puppy, fun things that puppies do, and the care a puppy needs.
3. Give the child a sheet of paper.
4. Tell him to fold the sheet of paper by taking one corner, aligning that corner with the one just opposite it and creasing the fold. (After this fold the shape will be a triangle.) Provide assistance as needed.
5. Ask him to place the triangle, single point down, on his work area.
6. Tell him to fold the top two corners forward to make the floppy ears.
7. Give him a pencil, markers, and crayons, and discuss what the puppy needs, such as eyes, nose, whiskers, and mouth.
8. Give him additional sheets of paper to fold and make into different-looking dogs.
9. This three-triangle fold lends itself to creating many other animals.
10. You may also use heavier paper folded this way to have him make a scary or interesting face mask; cut out the eyes and the mouth, let the child decorate with colored markers, and staple on an elastic headband.

4.100 Matches or chooses through tactile cues like objects: hot/cold; wet/dry
Strand: 4-8 **Age:** 40-43m 3.4-3.7y

Definition
The child will use his tactile sense to match objects that are hot and cold or wet and dry only by touching or handling them. He will not use his sense of sight to differentiate the objects or forms.

Instructional Materials
Four small sponges, a brown bag.

Instructional Activities

1. Dampen two of the sponges, and place one in the bag and the other on the table.
2. Place one dry sponge in the bag and the other dry sponge on the table.
3. Tell the child to put his hand into the bag to feel something wet or dry.
4. Tell him that when he feels the wet or the dry object, he is to use his other hand to match the wet or dry item with something on the table.
5. Ask him to match the items in both his hands.
6. Discuss what "wet" and "dry" mean.

4.101   Places small pegs in holes on board
Strand: 4-6A **Age:** 42-50m 3.6-4.2y

Definition
The child will place at least six small pegs in a pegboard without assistance.

Instructional Materials
Pieces of solid *Styrofoam* 4 x 8 inches or larger, colored golf tees or wooden pegs. Draw small circles on *Styrofoam* to indicate where the tees or pegs should be placed. Colored felt-tip pen.

Instructional Activities
1. Demonstrate by pushing one tee or peg into a circle on the *Styrofoam*.
2. Tell the child to push a tee or peg into a circle on the foam.
3. Increase the difficulty by marking patterns of circles on the *Styrofoam* with a colored felt pen.
4. Tell him to push colored tees into matching colored circles on the *Styrofoam*.
5. Other shapes may be made on the *Styrofoam* pegboard.

4.102   Reproduces a two-dimensional block design
Strand: 4-6B **Age:** 42-50m 3.6-4.2y

Definition
The child will view a demonstration, and use blocks to reproduce a block design card. When she is presented with a two-dimensional block design card involving not more than seven blocks, she will copy the pattern with the blocks directly below or near the pattern card. She may also refer to the card when she is involved in manipulating the blocks to match the design.

Instructional Materials
At least 15 1-inch by 1-inch cubes in a variety of colors, purchased or made from scrap lumber, sanded and painted. Stamp pads or sponges in shallow dishes of different-colored nontoxic, washable paints to match the colored cubes, several sheets of white paper.

Instructional Activities
1. Place the cubes, stamp pads or paint sponges, and paper on a working surface.
2. Take a single cube and lightly press it on the stamp pad or paint sponge, then stamp the square on the sheet of paper.
3. Continue stamping squares, using different colors, to create block patterns on the paper.
4. Allow the paper to thoroughly dry.
5. Using the wooden blocks, reproduce the stamped block pattern.
6. Invite the child to make her own stamped block pattern and then to reconstruct the created pattern using the wooden blocks.
7. Encourage her to make different stamped block designs and give them to other family members and her friends to make the block reproductions.

4.103   Matches or chooses through tactile cues like objects that are rough and smooth
Strand: 4-8 **Age:** 45-48m 3.9-4.0y

Definition
The child will use his tactile sense to match objects that are rough or smooth only by touching or handling them. He will not use his sense of sight to differentiate the objects or forms.

Instructional Materials
24 index cards (5 x 8 inches), nontoxic glue or tape, a collection of rough and smooth items (not larger than 5 x 8 inches). Attach the following with glue or tape: Set of Rough Cards: Cards 1 and 2--piece of sandpaper, Cards 3 and 4--sand or gravel, Cards 5 and 6--piece of corrugated paper, Cards 7 and 8--cornmeal, Cards 9 and 10--bristles from a brush, Cards 11 and 12--piece of screen. Set of Smooth Cards: Cards 1 and 2--piece of velvet, Cards 3 and 4--piece of satin, Cards 5 and 6--piece of polished wood, Cards 7 and 8--piece of slick paper, Cards 9 and 10--cotton balls, Cards 11 and 12--piece of fur. A blindfold.

Instructional Activities

Note: The child may feel the card you hand him before he feels each of his cards.

1. Place the Rough Cards 1, 3, 5, 7, 9 and 11 in a stack on the table. Place the Smooth Cards 1, 3, 5, 7, 9 and 11 in a stack on the table. Shuffle the two sets together. Place Rough Cards 2, 4, 6, 8, 10 and 12 in a stack on the table. Place Smooth Set Cards 2, 4, 6, 8, 10 and 12 in a stack on the table. Shuffle the two sets together.
2. Invite the child to play a game of Touch and Tell.
3. Show him a card from the Rough set, and ask him to feel the texture and describe how it feels.
4. Show him a card from the Smooth set, and ask him to feel the texture and describe how it feels.
5. Explain how to play Touch and Tell. One player wears a blindfold, and each player has a set of cards; some feel rough, some feel smooth, and some feel rougher and smoother than others.
6. Place the blindfold on him.
7. Hand him a card, and ask him to feel it.
8. Tell him to feel the first card in his stack.
9. If the cards match, set them aside.
10. If the cards do not match, the child should place the top card on the bottom of his stack and feel the next card; continue until a match is found.

See #4.100.

4.104 Matches or chooses through tactile cues like objects that are sticky and nonsticky

Strand: 4-8 **Age:** 45-48m 3.9-4.0y

Definition

The child will use her tactile sense to match objects that are sticky or non-sticky only by touching or handling them. She will not use her sense of sight to differentiate between the objects or forms.

Instructional Materials

Tape that is sticky on one side (masking or transparent), salt, sugar, small dishes.

Instructional Activities

1. Sprinkle a tablespoon of salt into one dish and a tablespoon of sugar into another dish, and place them on the table.
2. Place the tape with the sticky side out around the fingers of one of the child's hands.
3. Tell her that there is salt in one dish and sugar in the other.
4. Tell her to use her taped fingers to pick up the salt.
5. Demonstrate, if necessary.
6. Place tape with the sticky side out around the fingers of her other hand.
7. Point to the dish with the sugar in it.
8. Tell her to use her newly taped fingers to pick up the sugar.
9. Discuss what happened, remove the tape, and encourage her to feel the texture of the salt and then the texture of the sugar.
10. Place the tape with the sticky side down around the fingers of her hand.
11. Tell her to pick up the salt with her newly taped fingers.
12. Discuss what happened.
13. Place the tape with the sticky side up around the fingers of her other hand.
14. Ask her to try to pick up the salt with her newly taped fingers.
15. Discuss what happened, which fingers picked up the salt, why the sticky tape picked up the salt and the smooth-sided tape did not.
16. Put tape on her hand, sticky side out, and let her try to pick up as many things as she can with her sticky hand.
17. Discuss which things she could pick up, which she could not, and why.

See #4.100.

4.105 Matches or chooses through tactile cues like objects that are long and short

Strand: 4-8 **Age:** 45-48m 3.9-4.0y

Definition

When he is presented with five objects that vary in length from a few inches to 10 inches, the child will sort the objects as long or short based only on tactile cues.

Instructional Materials

10 long objects, 10 short objects, paper bag.

Instructional Activities

1. Place five long objects and five short objects in a paper bag.
2. Place the remaining objects in a box on the table.
3. Invite the child to sit at the table next to the box.
4. Pull a long object from the box.

5. Ask the child whether it is long or short.
6. Ask him to put his hand into the bag and find a long object.
7. If he is incorrect and takes out a short object, tell him to put the object back in the bag and allow him to try again.
8. Repeat the activity by varying the long and short objects.

See #4.100.

4.106 Matches or chooses through tactile cues like objects that are hard and soft

Strand: 4-8   **Age:** 48-51m 4.0-4.3y

Definition

The child will use his tactile sense to match objects that are hard and soft only by touching or handling them. He will not use his sense of sight to differentiate the objects or forms.

Instructional Materials

Sheets (8 ½ x 11 inches) of poster board or colored cardboard, black marker, nontoxic glue, a collection of small hard and soft items. (Examples: hard --pieces of wood, buttons, plastic poker chips, screw, washer, seashells, seeds, rock chips; soft--cotton ball, foam, sponge piece, marshmallows, feather). A box, a hole punch, yarn. Blindfold.

Instructional Activities

1. Place the cardboard sheets, marker, glue, and the collection of hard and soft pieces of material in the box on the table.
2. Invite the child to the work area.
3. Explain that he is going to make Feely Picture Cards.
4. Give him the box of hard and soft items.
5. Ask him to feel the various items and discuss the concept of hard and soft.
6. Give him a sheet of cardboard and tell him it is to be a picture card of Hard Feelies.
7. Write the word "Hard" at the top of the cardboard.
8. Ask him to close his eyes or place a blindfold on him.
9. Ask him to feel the items and to find a hard object in the box to make the first picture card of Hard Feelies.
10. After he finds a hard object by feeling, allow him to open his eyes.
11. Help him glue his selected hard item to the sheet of cardboard.

12. Give him the box of hard and soft items. Review the discussion of the concepts of hard and soft.
13. Give him another sheet of cardboard, and tell him this is to be a picture card of Soft Feelies.
14. Write the word "Soft" at the top of the cardboard.
15. Ask him to close his eyes or place a blindfold on him.
16. Ask him to feel to find a soft object in the box to make the first picture card of Soft Feelies.
17. After he has found a soft object by feeling, allow him to open his eyes.
18. Help him glue his selected soft item to the sheet of paper.
19. Continue developing the Feely Hard and Feely Soft Picture Cards.
20. Ask him to stack all the Feely Hard Picture Cards together, and use a hole punch and yarn to attach them to make a Feely Hard Picture Book.
21. Ask him to stack all the Feely Soft Picture Cards together, and use a hole punch and yarn to attach them to make a Feely Soft Picture Book.

See #4.100.

4.107 (Removed, see page xii)

4.108 Matches or chooses through tactile cues like objects that are thin and fat

Strand: 4-8   **Age:** 48-53m 4.0-4.5y

Definition

The child will use his tactile sense to match objects that are thin or fat by only touching or handling them. He will not use his sense of sight to differentiate the objects or forms.

Instructional Materials

An assortment of thin and fat items, making sure to include a cracker and an apple. Two pictures made out of cutouts from magazines, one depicting thin items, including a cracker, and the other one fat items, including an apple.

Instructional Activities

1. Place the two pictures on the table.
2. Show the child the pictures on the table and discuss them, making sure that the physical characteristics of thin and fat are included in the discussion.
3. Ask the child to place one of his hands behind his back.

4. Tell him you will to place an item in his hand, and by feeling it he is to match it with a picture on the table.

5. Place a cracker in his hand, let him feel it, and then ask him to point to the picture on the table that shows the same shape.

6. Discuss the thin shape of a cracker.

7. Ask him to put one of his hands behind his back.

8. Place the apple in his hand, let him feel it, and then ask him to point to the picture on the table that shows the same shape.

9. Discuss the fat shape of the apple.

10. Place the cracker next to the picture of a cracker and the apple next to the picture of the apple.

11. Discuss the dimensions of the cracker, making sure he understands the term "thin."

12. Discuss the dimensions of the apple, making sure he understands the term "fat."

13. Compare the thin cracker with the fat apple.

14. Place another thin item, such as a comb, on the table and discuss its dimensions. After discussing it, ask him to put the item next to the picture that best describes the way it looks.

15. Place another fat item, such as a lemon, on the table and discuss its dimensions. After discussing it ask him to put the item next to the picture that best describes the way it looks.

16. Ask him to put his hands behind his back.

17. Tell him you will put an item in his hands, and that by feeling, he is to tell whether it belongs in the "thin" or the "fat" category.

See #4.100.

4.109   (Removed, see page xii)

4.110   Spreads paste/glue on one side of paper and turns over to stick it to another paper

Strand: 4-6D   **Age:** 30-40m 2.6-3.4y

Definition

When she is asked, the child will spread paste or glue on one side of a sheet paper that is at least 4 inches by 6 inches in size, and then she will attach the pasted sheet to another sheet of paper. It is not important that she align the two sheets of paper. She will turn the pasted side over to adhere it to another sheet.

Instructional Materials

Construction paper, nontoxic paste or glue, a tongue depressor. Crayons, ribbons, pipe cleaners (for glasses).

Instructional Activities

1. Draw and cut out the following from construction paper: a large oval for a face, two ovals for eyes, a triangle for a nose, a half-circle for a mouth, two ear shapes, a half-circle the same size as the top of the oval face for hair.

2. Fold a large sheet of construction paper once crosswise.

3. Open the paper and draw a square on the left side of the sheet, leaving the right side blank.

4. Give each child a sheet of folded paper, paste or glue, and a tongue depressor.

5. Tell her to spread the paste or glue with her finger or a stick on one side of the fold.

6. Tell her to close the paper so that the two sides stick.

7. Draw and cut out two construction paper squares from another piece of paper.

8. Give her the two squares and ask her to paste one square onto the other one.

9. After she has practiced adhering the squares together, give her the assorted construction paper shapes.

10. Ask her to find the big oval and tell her it is a face.

11. Ask her to find the two small ovals and to tell you what they are to be used for.

12. After she has identified them as eyes, tell her to put them on the face and paste or glue them down.

13. Ask her to find and tell you what part of the face the triangle represents.

14. When she identifies the triangle as the nose, tell her to put it on the face and paste or glue it down.

15. Continue with the mouth, ears, and hair.

16. Encourage her to add extra things to the face, such as freckles, glasses, or a hair ribbon.

17. Display the face she created.

4.111   Draws a picture of a person

Strand: 4-6A   **Age:** 48-60m 4.0-5.0y

Definition

When asked to draw a person, the child will draw her own person, which will include at least eight of the following recognizable body parts: a head, body, eyes, nose, mouth, hair, arms, shoulders, legs, hands, and feet. She will draw her person using a pencil, a marker or a crayon. If she wishes, she may add additional features to her person.

Instructional Materials

Paper, crayons, markers, and a pencil.

Instructional Activities

1. Place the drawing materials on the table.
2. Give the child the piece of paper and ask her to pick a writing tool.
3. Take a piece of paper and a writing utensil for yourself.
4. Tell the child that you are going to draw a picture of a person together with her.
5. Draw a circle for the head and tell the child to draw a head on her paper.
6. Draw another circle for the body and ask the child to do the same.
7. Ask the child what other body parts the person needs.
8. Follow her directions as she names body parts by adding those features to your person, while at the same time you have the child add the same body parts to her drawing.
9. If she neglects to name a body part, you suggest the missing features.
10. Continue until the drawing of the person is complete.
11. Continue the activity by taking turns naming and drawing body parts for another drawing of a person.

4.112 Strings small beads reproducing color and shape sequence/pattern

Strand: 4-7C **Age:** 48-60m 4.0-5.0y

Definition

When the child is presented with a bead-stringing set and a bead pattern for him to copy, he will demonstrate his ability to reproduce the bead pattern by stringing the beads to match the visual model. The bead pattern will represent different colors and bead shapes, and will include at least ten beads.

Instructional Materials

Bead pattern cards purchased at a school supply store or several different bead patterns drawn on 3-inch by 8-inch cards. Box of beads and a hard-tipped string or shoelace with a knot tied at one end.

Instructional Activities

1. Place the box of beads and string on a table. Take a string, a bead pattern card and the beads needed to follow the first pattern.

Demonstrate placing the beads on the string according to the pattern on the card.
2. Take the beads off the string.
3. Tell the child to take his turn.
4. Ask him to put one bead on and then match it to the pattern to check whether he is correct.
5. If he makes an error, show how to correct it.
6. Allow him to continue until he strings the beads successfully.
9. Increase the difficulty by adding different colors, more beads on the pattern cards, and by giving him more beads than are needed for a pattern.
See #4.98.

4.113 Cuts out small square/triangle with scissors

Strand: 4-7D **Age:** 48-62m 4.0-5.2y

Definition

When he is given a sheet of paper with a square at least 3 inches on each side, the child will use scissors to cut the square out without assistance, staying within ½ inch of the lines. When he is given a sheet of paper with a triangle at least 3 inches on each side, he will cut the triangle out without assistance, within ½ inch of the lines.

Instructional Materials

/*\ **Safety Note:** Provide scissors appropriate for the child. Remind the child of safety regarding scissors.
Several sheets of colored construction paper, marking pens, child-size safety scissors, nontoxic glue, string, tape. Bits and pieces of items to use for decoration such as pieces of yarn, stickers, pieces of fabric, ribbon.

Instructional Activities

1. Draw a circle, a square, a rectangle and a triangle on the colored construction paper. Place the paper, the scissors, decorating materials, and glue on the work area.
2. Discuss shapes with the child, talking about different ways we use and make shapes.
3. Give him the construction paper and the scissors, and ask him to cut out the shapes.
4. Tell him to choose some yarn bits, ribbon, stickers, or fabric pieces, to decorate his cutout shape.
5. Give him time to decorate his shape.
6. Attach a piece of yarn or string to the shape, and hang it by a vent or open window and let him watch the fancy shapes turn.
See #4.96.

4.114 (Moved to Cognitive, skill 1.308)

4.115 Matches or chooses through tactile cues like objects that are circular, triangular, rectangular, and square

Strand: 4-8 **Age:** 53-60m 4.5-5.0y

Definition

The child will use his tactile sense to match or choose two-dimensional and three-dimensional shapes that are square, circular, triangular, and rectangular, only by touching or handling them. He will not use his sense of sight to differentiate the various shapes.

Instructional Materials

Crackers shaped like a circle, a rectangle, a triangle. (You may find these different shaped crackers available in one box.) A blindfold, a napkin.

Instructional Activities

1. Place a napkin on the table; on the napkin put the three different shapes of crackers.
2. Put the blindfold on the child.
3. Give him one of the crackers to feel. Ask him to feel the cracker, and then to find a cracker on the napkin that is its same shape.
4. If he is correct tell the child he may eat the cracker.
5. If he needs assistance, remove his blindfold, and ask him to correct his error.
6. Repeat and continue with the other cracker shapes.

See #4.100.

4.116 Traces around own hand

Strand: 4-6A **Age:** 53-62m 4.5-5.2y

Definition

The child will trace around her own hand. She will trace her non-dominant hand. Her first drawing will be an outline with fingers closed, thumb extended. Her second drawing will be with thumb extended and fingers apart.

Instructional Materials

Heavy cardboard or large piece of paper, pitcher of water, bowl, paper towels. Drawing paper, nontoxic paint and a pencil or a medium point marker. Nontoxic clay that will harden, can be painted and will not break easily. Rolling pin.

Instructional Activities

1. Lay a heavy piece of cardboard or large piece of paper on a table. Set a pitcher of water and a small bowl nearby. Keep paper towels handy.
2. Give the child the lump of clay and ask her to flatten it. To do this she should place the ball on the table and pat it with the heel of her hand. A rolling pin may also be used. Have her flatten the clay to make a circle large enough to place her hand in the center.
3. Ask her to put her hand, palm side down, in the center of the clay and to press firmly. (If necessary, moisten the clay with water to soften it for use and to stick pieces together.)
4. Ask her to remove her hand; her hand print should be visible in the clay.
5. Trim the edges of the clay, stick an open paper clip in the back of the plaque for hanging.
6. After the clay hand print plaque is dry, provide nontoxic paint and let the child paint the whole plaque one color or the hand print one color and the outside edge another.
7. These plaques can be used as gifts for parents on Mother's Day, Father's Day, or Christmas, or for display.
8. Give the child an opportunity to feel the hand print and trace around the outside of the hand.
9. Give her a sheet of paper, ask her to pick up a pencil and place her other hand on the paper, palm side down, and draw around that hand with her fingers open.
10. Let her use crayons or paint to make the drawn hand print into a pretty glove.

4.117 Matches or chooses through tactile cues like objects that are light and heavy

Strand: 4-8 **Age:** 57-60m 4.9-5.0y

Definition

The child will use her tactile sense to match objects that are light or heavy only by handling them. She will not use her sense of sight to differentiate the objects or forms.

Instructional Materials

Four bean bags that look alike on the outside filled with materials of varying weights, such as nuts and bolts, beans, cereal, and cotton balls. Two boxes. A large rock and a feather. Scale if available.

Instructional Activities

Note: Optional--use a scale to determine accuracy.

1. Fill Bean Bag 1 with a heavy substance such as nuts and bolts or washers. Fill Bean Bag 2 with a medium-heavy substance such as beans. Fill Bean Bag 3 with a semi-light substance such as dry cereal. Fill Bean Bag 4 with a light substance such as cotton balls. Place the bean bags on the table. Place the two boxes on the table. Put the rock in one box and the feather in the other box.
2. Ask the child to come to the table. Explain to the child that the box with the large rock is where heavy items will go and the box with the feather is where the lighter items will go.
3. Ask her to pick up two of the bean bags, one in each hand. Discuss the weight of each bean bag.
4. Ask her to place the heaviest (making sure she understands the meaning of heaviest) bean bag in the box with the large rock.
5. Ask her to place the lightest (making sure she understands the meaning of lightest) bean bag in the box with the feather.
6. Ask her to pick up the remaining two bean bags and repeat the procedure, placing the heavy bean bag in the box with the large rock and the lighter bean bag in the box with the feather.
7. Remove the bean bags from the boxes and mix them up.
8. Have the child pick up one bean bag at a time and identify whether it is heavy or light.
9. Ask her to throw the heavy bean bags in the box with the large rock and the light bean bags in the box with the feather.
10. If she misses, allow her another opportunity.
11. Continue with the other bean bags.
12. After she has had a chances to throw the bean bags, ask her to talk about the difference in throwing a heavy bean bag and a lightweight bean bag.

4.118 Identifies objects through the sense of touch

Strand: 4-8 **Age:** 57-60m 4.9-5.0y

Definition

When he is presented with objects of different properties, the child will identify the objects by touching them. He will not use his visual sense to identify the objects.

Instructional Materials

A cloth bag with a pull string. At least five common objects to put in the bag, such as a marble, toothbrush, rock, small doll with hair, and crayon.

Instructional Activities

1. Have the child join you at the table. Explain that you have taken some items that he is familiar with that you have placed in your cloth bag.
2. Tell him you want him to reach into the bag without looking and to find one item that he will feel while it is inside the bag.
3. Ask him to describe how the item feels.
4. Encourage him to guess what the item is without looking at it. Once he has guessed, remove the item to see if he was correct.
5. If he was correct, remove the item from the bag. If it was not correct return the item.
6. Let another child take a turn and continue until all the items have been identified.

4.119 Cuts out pictures following general shape

Strand: 4-7D **Age:** 58-61m 4.10-5.1y

Definition

When she is shown how to cut out a general shape that is not less than 6 inches in length and width and is outlined with a line not more than ¼ inch wide, the child will cut out the general shape of the picture without physical assistance.

Instructional Materials

⚠️**Safety Note:** Provide scissors appropriate for the child. Remind the child of safety regarding scissors.

Construction paper in different colors, a black medium marker, scissors in the correct size for child, tape, string.

Instructional Activities

1. Cut at least five 8-inch circles from the colored construction paper, and on each circle draw a curved line: begin the line from the edge of the circle, drawing gradual curves until you reach the center of the circle. Remember to make the continuous drawn curves far enough apart so they will hang as a spring coil after they are cut.
2. Cut at least five 8-inch squares from the colored construction paper and on each square draw a straight line: begin the line from the edge of the square, draw a right

angle corner, then a straight line, draw a right angle corner, continuing until you reach the center of the square. Make the continuous drawn lines far enough apart so they will hang as an elongated springing box after they are cut.

3. Give the child a pair of scissors and a pre-drawn colored circle.

4. Using a pre-drawn colored circle, demonstrate how to cut on the line, starting at the edge. After the lines have been cut, take the end of the spiral and gently pull it, tape a string to the end, and hang it up as a decoration.

5. Ask the child to cut her spiral decoration, and then help her tape a string to the end and hang it up.

6. Repeat the above, using the squares of colored construction paper.

7. Be sure to hang up all her finished products for display.

See #4.113.

4.120 Cuts cloth with scissors

Strand: 4-7D **Age:** 66-72m 5.6-6.0y

Definition

When the child is presented with a cotton flat-weave cloth, she will use sufficiently sharp scissors to make a cut at least 6 inches long.

Instructional Materials

/***Safety Note:** Provide scissors appropriate for the child. Remind the child of safety regarding scissors.

At least six 8-inch square felt pieces in three different colors. Nontoxic fabric glue, child-size scissors, markers.

Instructional Activities

Note: Remind the child about scissor safety.

1. On the felt squares, draw a two-finger mitten (thumb and baby finger separated from the three middle fingers) measured to fit the size of the child's hand. Place the felt squares and the other materials on the table.

2. Explain to the child that she is going to cut the felt to make puppets.

3. Show her the lines drawn on the felt and ask her to cut on the lines.

4. After she has cut two pieces of felt in same colors, show her how to glue the edges together, leaving the bottom of the mitten puppet open.

5. When the glue has dried, place the felt puppet on the child's hand.

6. Allow her time to manipulate and play with the puppet. The thumb and baby finger act as arms for the puppet.

7. Discuss with her what character she would like her puppet to be.

8. After she decides, provide her with markers and ask her to make the face and clothing on the puppet.

9. Encourage her to cut the other pieces of felt to make different puppets.

10. Conclude the puppet-making activity by developing a short play using the puppet characters.

4.121 Makes fine visual discriminations, matches letters that look very similar

Strand: 4-6A **Age:** 60-72m 5.0-6.0y

Definition

The child will recognize all the letters in a row that are the same. The sequence of letters for him to match will be: 1) uppercase open letters, 2) uppercase round letters, 3) lowercase open letters, 4) lowercase round letters. The child does not need to provide the letter name or the letter sound.

Instructional Materials

A worksheet with six printed letters on the left side of the paper. The same letters printed on the right side of the paper but arranged in a different order. Large pencil or crayon.

Instructional Activities

1. Ask the child to come to the table. Give him the worksheet and use the first letter as a demonstration. Give him a crayon or a large pencil.

2. Show the child the first letter on the left side of the paper.

3. Ask him to point to the same letter on the right side of the paper.

4. When he has made a match, ask him to draw a line from one letter to the other.

5. Instruct him to look at each letter in the left list and to draw a line to the identical letter in the right list.

4.122   Draws a picture of at least three objects

Strand: 4-6A   **Age:** 60-72m 5.0-6.0y

Definition

The child will draw a recognizable picture that includes at least three different objects. She will be prompted only if the objects she draws are not recognizable or if she does not respond.

Instructional Materials

Art Paper and drawing tools such as crayons, pencils, markers.

Instructional Activities

1. Provide the child with paper and drawing tools.
2. Read a short descriptive paragraph or story that has different visualization opportunities such as the examples that follow.

I See a Dream

    I see white clouds sailing in the sky.
    I see a round moon peeping over the hill.
    I see a house with a big door.
    I see a tree with flowers and leaves.
    I see a flower, tall and big.
    I see a bird flying to a nest.
    I see a puppy chasing her tail.
    I see a baby sound asleep.
    I see a girl and boy playing.
    (The following story has drawings that help tell the story.)

I Found An Egg

    One day in spring, I was taking a walk
    I looked down and guess what I found
    A huge egg that was just lying on the ground.
    (Draw an oval that looks like an egg.)
    The very next day, when I looked outside
    The egg had changed a bit, I say.
    A tiny fluff of fur was growing out this way.
    (Draw a tuft of fur at one end of the egg)
    Early the next morning
    There was another thing new
    A long and lovely ear had sprouted and grew
    (Draw a rabbit-like ear at the other end of the egg)
    One more day and another surprise
    Not just one ear, but two so close
    This egg was growing the very most
    (Draw another rabbit-like ear next to the other)
    I couldn't believe when there were eyes
    And then a wiggle nose
    Plus a mouth arose.
    And finally some brisky whiskers
    Oh so wise!
    (Draw eyes, nose, mouth and whiskers under the ears)
    Why that egg was so funny
    More than I could believe
    'Cause it grew
    To become a Bunny, don't you see!

3. Tell the child to draw images from the story.
4. Talk about the child's drawing.
5. Hang the pictures where they can be enjoyed by everyone.

4.123   Cuts out complex pictures following outlines

Strand: 4-7D   **Age:** 64-78m 5.4-6.6y

Definition

The child will cut out a complex picture, conforming to the edges of the picture. He will cut out the complex picture without any assistance.

Instructional Materials

/*\Safety Note: Provide scissors appropriate for the child. Remind the child of safety regarding scissors.
Sheets of lightweight paper, colored construction paper, a black marker, nontoxic glue and child-size scissors.

Instructional Activities

Note: Remind the child about scissor safety.
1. Place the paper, marker and scissors on a table.
2. Take a sheet of paper and demonstrate crumpling it into a ball.
3. Give the child one sheet of paper, and ask him to crumple it up in his hand.
4. Demonstrate flattening your crumpled paper.
5. Tell him to uncrumple his paper and smooth it flat.
6. After the paper has been flattened out, give him a marker, and tell him to pick out one of the unfolded lines and trace it around the paper. Encourage him to "see" a picture in the uncrumpled lines and to trace it with the marker.
7. After he has traced his picture, give him scissors to cut on the marked lines.
8. After he has cut out the object or the abstract form, mount the cutout on colored construction paper and hang it for display.

4.124 Puts together complex/interlocking puzzle

Strand: 4-6B **Age:** 64-78m 5.4-6.6y

Definition

When the child is presented with at least a 12+-piece interlocking puzzle, she will put it together.

Instructional Materials

Scraps of wallpaper in various sizes (Check wallpaper stores for outdated wallpaper books). Paste or nontoxic glue. Heavy paper that can be cut, scissors.

Instructional Activities

1. Glue the wallpaper scraps on heavy paper and let them dry.
2. Cut the paper into at least 12 puzzle pieces.
3. Lay the pieces in the correct design on a flat surface or on another piece of cardboard.
4. Show the puzzle to the child.
5. Tell her that you are going to mix up the puzzle pieces.
6. Ask her to put the puzzle together.
7. Encourage her to make other puzzles by drawing a picture, by choosing other wallpaper sheets, or by finding a favorite picture from a magazine.

4.125 Identifies look-alike words correctly

Strand: 4-6A **Age:** 65-72m 5.5-6.0y

Definition

Note: *He does not have to read the words.*
The child will match words that are visually alike. He will match words that are very different in configuration. Next he will match words that are similar in configuration. Finally, he will be asked to match words that are identical from a field of four words.

Instructional Materials

Index cards with words printed on them; the words should be in various configurations. Example: tell (tall letter, short letter, two tall letters), happy (tall letter, short letter, three letters that go below the line), what (short letter, tall letter, short letter, tall letter). Cut out the cards to cover the linear design of the words. There should be at least two of each cutout word card. Example: two cutout cards of the word "tell," two cutout cards of the word "happy," etc.

Instructional Activities

1. Place the cutout word cards in a small sack and shake it to mix up the cards. Have the child take a seat at a table or work area.
2. Show the child a card and tell him more cards like it are in the sack.
3. Tell him to draw a card from the sack and put it on the table.
4. Then ask him to draw another card from the sack and try to match the cards by the shape of the word.
5. Continue until he has drawn and matched all the cards.
6. As he becomes proficient in matching by configuration, allot a specific amount of time for him to complete the task. Setting a time will not only increase the challenge but will also encourage the child to look at the whole shape rather than just the detail.

4.126 Builds 5-block bridge

Strand: 4-6B **Age:** 66-72m 5.6-6.0y

Definition

The child will make a five-block bridge after viewing a demonstration. The bridge will have an opening between the bottom blocks of no less than ¼ inch.

Instructional Materials

A small tabletop sandbox, at least 10 one-inch blocks, small toy cars, tools to make a road. Optional material: a sheet of blue paper, small toy boats and a piece of clear plastic.

Instructional Activities

Note: Conduct the activity in an outdoor area. If needed, place the sandbox on sheets of paper, a plastic cover or a tablecloth.
Note: She may use additional blocks to close any bridge gaps
1. Place the sandbox, blocks, toy cars, tools, blue paper, plastic sheet, and toy boats on a table.
2. Show the child the sandbox and the props.
3. Discuss a scene for her to consider constructing. Talk about bridges, a river beneath it, boats on the river, a road going to the bridge and cars on the road.
4. Help her in placing the blue paper and then the plastic on top of it in the bottom of the sandbox. Identify this as the river.
5. Explain that for cars to cross from one side of the river to the other there must be a bridge.
6. Ask the child to build a bridge over the river.
7. After she constructs a bridge, talk about the need for a road.

8. Ask her to build a road to and from the bridge..
9. After she has finished the river, bridge, and road, let her place the play cars and boats in the scene.
10. It is important to encourage the child to play with the sandbox materials, allowing her to change the arrangement of the roads and to add other props.

4.127   (Removed, see page xii)

4.128 Holds paper with one hand while drawing with the other hand
Strand: 4-6A   **Age:** 36-48m 3.0-4.0y

Definition
When given a piece of paper and a crayon to draw with, the child will take the crayon in her dominant hand and will use her non-dominant hand to hold the paper while drawing.

Instructional Materials
Paper, crayons, markers, and a pencil.

Instructional Activities
1. Place the drawing materials on the table.
2. Give the child a piece of paper and let him chose a writing utensil.
3. Ask him to draw a picture.
4. If he does not spontaneously hold the paper steady, comment on the moving paper and ask him if it is easy to draw with his paper moving.
5. Suggest that he hold the paper steady with his other hand.
6. Demonstrate how to do this by joining the activity and drawing a picture too. Verbalize what you are doing. For example, "I am going to put the crayon in this hand and now I am going to hold the paper with my other hand."
7. Continue the activity by providing the child with additional paper to draw on.

4.129 Cuts out a circle with scissors
Strand: 4-7D   **Age:** 42-48m 3.6-4.0y

Definition
When she is given a sheet of paper with a circle, at least 6 inches in diameter, the child will use scissors to cut the circle out without assistance, staying within ½ inch of the lines.

Instructional Materials
/*\Safety Note: Provide scissors appropriate for the child. Remind the child of safety regarding scissors.
Several sheets of colored construction paper, marking pens, child-size safety scissors, nontoxic glue, string, tape. Bits and pieces of yarn, stickers, pieces of fabric, ribbon, sequins.

Instructional Activities
1. Draw a circle on the colored construction paper.
2. Discuss the shape and talk about other things in the environment that are also round.
3. Give her the construction paper and scissors and ask her to cut out a circle.
4. Tell her to choose some yarn pieces, ribbon, stickers, and fabric pieces to decorate her circle.
5. Give her time to decorate her shape.
6. Attach a piece of yarn or string to the shape, and hang it by a vent or open window and let her watch the fancy shapes move in the breeze.
See #4.96.

4.130 Places a paper clip on paper
Strand: 4-6D   **Age:** 48-60m 4.0-5.0y

Definition
When provided with paper and paperclips, the child will place a paperclip on a single sheet of paper, or a few sheets of paper, without tearing the paper.

Instructional Materials
Various colors of construction paper, crayons, markers, scissors, and paper clips.

Instructional Activities
1. Place the paper and the materials on a table. Tell the child that you need him to draw some pictures for his mother and some for his father (or any other important people in his life, like grandparents, friends, etc.)
2. First ask him to draw two or three pictures for his mother.
3. After he finishes the picture ask him to tell you about what he has drawn.
4. When he finishes describing the pictures, ask him to paper clip them together.
5. Provide him with a piece of paper that says "Mom," along with a paper clip. Ask him to paperclip the paper that says "Mom" on the pile of pictures he has made for his mother so he knows whom the pictures belong to.

6. Repeat this activity, but have him draw pictures for his father this time.
7. Have him share the pictures with his parents when he goes home.

4.131 Holds pencil/crayon using a static tripod grasp

Strand: 4-6A **Age:** 42-48m 3.6-4.0y

Definition

The child will hold the pencil/crayon near the sharpened part using a static tripod grasp. The fingers make a rough approximation of a more mature, adult-like grasp. The sharpened part of the pencil is positioned with the thumb on the side and the middle, ring, and index fingers resting on top of the pencil. The child's wrist is straight and the hand moves as a unit.

Instructional Materials

A large sheet of paper (at least 22 x 28 inches), a chalkboard, chalk, and primary pencil or crayons.

Instructional Activities

Note: If the child exhibits any difficulty in holding the writing tool use an adapted pencil grip.
1. Place the sheet of paper on a table top and prepare the chalkboard for some large drawings. Invite the child to the table or chalkboard.
2. Give the child a writing tool (chalk or pencil).
3. Say, "Make a long line on the chalkboard/paper."
4. Continue by giving directions such as, "Draw a wavy line." "Make a cross." "Draw a jumpy line." etc.
5. Allow the child to do the activities on both the sheet of paper (horizontal) and the chalkboard (vertical).

4.132 Holds pencil/crayon using a dynamic tripod grasp to draw

Strand: 4-6A **Age:** 54-72m 4.6-6.0y

Definition

The child will hold the pencil/crayon at the sharpened end using a dynamic tripod grasp. The fingers have a more precise position like that of a mature, adult-like writing grasp. The sharpened end of the pencil is between the pads of the thumb and the middle finger with the index finger resting on top of the pencil. The ring and little fingers are flexed, forming a stable

arch. The child's wrist is slightly extended and moves as the child draws.

Instructional Materials

Sheets of paper, a chalkboard, chalk, and primary pencils or crayons.

Instructional Activities

Note: If the child exhibits any difficulties in holding the writing tool use an adapted pencil grasp.
1. Place a sheet of paper on the tabletop and prepare the chalkboard for drawing. Invite the child to the table or chalkboard.
2. Give the child a writing tool (pencil or chalk).
3. Say, "Draw a picture of a tree (or other object)."
4. Continue by giving directions of objects to add to the tree, such as, "Draw the grass around the tree." "Make a sun." "Draw a flower."
5. Allow the child to do the activities on both the sheet of paper (horizontal) and the chalkboard (vertical).

5.95   Tells own age

Strand: 5-2 **Age:** 30-36m 2.6-3.0y

Definition

When the child is asked, "How old are you?" she will answer by stating her age. She may indicate how old she is by holding up the appropriate number of fingers as she tells the number.

Instructional Materials

A piano, guitar, or ukulele. A simple song that is easy to learn and tells the age of a child. If a song is not available, make up a song to an easy familiar tune; for example:
"I Am Three" (To the tune of *Three Blind Mice*)
I am three,
I am three,
A Big, big three,
A big, big three.
Are you three, just like me?
Are you three, just like me?
A big, big three
Just like me.

Instructional Activities

1. Ask the child to come near the musical instrument for the song.
2. Ask the child how old she is. Assist her if she is unsure of her age.
3. Explain to her that she is going to learn a new song about how old she is. Tell her the song is titled, I Am Three (substitute her correct age).
4. Play and sing the song, I Am Three. Repeat the song several times.
5. Encourage the child to join in the singing.
6. Allow her to take the singing lead, and phase out your support.
7. After she is comfortable singing the song, suggest that actions be added.
8. Example:
   I am three (proudly point to self)
   I am three (proudly point to self)
   A big, big three (hold up three fingers)
   A big, big three (hold up three fingers)
   Are you three, just like me? (hold out both hands, palm sides up)
   Are you three, just like me? (hold out both hands, palm sides up)
   A big, big three (hold up three fingers)
   Just like me. (proudly point to self)
9. Sing the song with the child and do the actions.
10. Allow her to sing along and model the actions.
11. Accompany her on the instrument as she sings and acts out the song.

5.96   Plays with one or two other children

Strand: 5-5 **Age:** 30-38m 2.6-3.2y

Definition

The child will begin to exhibit adaptive behaviors and to play with other children by beginning to share and engage in a simple conversation while playing, but their play agendas may differ.

Instructional Materials

A mirror, a table with a washable top, dampened sponge and paper towels. Soap sticks or crayons. (Soap sticks/crayons are available commercially or can be made as follows: In a 1 cup measuring cup, measure 1/8 cup of water and fill the rest of the cup to the top with soap flakes. Mix with a spoon until the mixture is thick and blended. Add drops of food coloring to the soap mixture and stir. Scoop out some of the mixture and put it into one of the spaces in an ice cube tray. Press the mixture down and continuing adding the mix until the cube space is filled to the top. To make more than one color, divide the soap mix into different batches and add different colors of food coloring prior to filling a space. Place the trays in a warm, dry place for two days until hard. Pop them out of the trays and your colored crayons are ready to use.)

Instructional Activities

1. Place the sponge and paper towels on the table. Remember that you can clean up the soap with a little water.
2. Ask two or three children to come to the table.
3. Give each one the same color soap crayon.
4. Demonstrate drawing with the soap crayons, washing the lines off with the sponge and drying the table.
5. Tell them they may draw anything they wish on the tabletop.
6. Observe each child as he draws on the table with the soap crayons.
7. Provide them with different colored crayons. Prompt and encourage them to draw a picture together on the tabletop.
8. Next, allow them time to play together with the crayons without prompting them to see if they will share and engage with one another.

5.97 Exchanges items with another child during play

Strand: 5-5 **Age:** 32-38m 2.8-3.2y

Definition

The child will trade a toy with another child. They do not have to talk, and the other child should go along with the trade. The children may engage in independent play with the exchanged toys. They may or may not play together with the exchanged toys.

Instructional Materials

/*\ **Safety Note:** Provide scissors appropriate for the child. Remind the child of safety regarding scissors.

A knee-length hose (sock/stocking) for each child, tissue paper or newspaper, rubber bands, string, plain-colored dots and strip stickers, child-safe scissors.

Instructional Activities

1. Place the material on a table. Invite the children to come to the table.
2. Tell them that each of them will make a toy animal he can pull.
3. Provide each child with a knee-length hose and the tissue paper or newspaper, and demonstrate how to stuff the hose (stocking) with the paper to make an animal body. Help the children tie the hose with rubber bands or string in several locations to make a lumpy sectional creature.
4. Let each of them use the dot and strip stickers to create facial features on the animals.
5. Secure the end of the hose with a rubber band or string, attach a long enough string to the animal's collar to allow each child to pull his animal.
6. After they have an opportunity to pull their animals, establish a starting line and an ending line.
7. Explain that they must pull their animals from the starting line to the ending line. This can be in the form of a parade or a racing format.
8. After the children have a chance to parade or race their animals, ask them to trade animals for another parade or race, making sure that they begin at the starting line and stop at ending line. Tell them when they reach the ending line, they are to give their traded animal back and in return, they will get their own animal back.
9. Invite them to repeat the parade with their own animal and then trade for another animal to walk.

5.98 Engages in cooperative play with other children

Strand: 5-5 **Age:** 36-48m 3.0-4.0y

Definition

When a child is playing cooperatively with other children, she should be involved with the two essential elements of cooperative play which include: (1) The goals should be similar; (2) There should be positive interdependence among the children.

Instructional Materials

Blindfolds or scarves to cover the eyes of the children.

Instructional Activities

1. Locate an area large enough for the children to move around wearing blindfolds.
2. Explain to the children that they are going to wear blindfolds and that they must walk around the area, trying to grasp the hands of two other children.
3. Demonstrate taking the hands of two different children.
4. Place a blindfold on each child, and say "Go."
5. After everyone is linked up, ask them to remove their blindfolds and untangle themselves without dropping hands.
6. Make sure the group works together to untangle the knots.
7. Assist as needed.
8. Repeat the game, and encourage them to twist and turn as they grasp hands.

5.99 Avoids hazards and common dangers

Strand: 5-8 **Age:** 34-41m 2.10-3.5y

Definition

When the child is shown items that are dangerous, such as matches, knives, medicine bottles, sharp-pointed instruments, or cleaning materials, he will demonstrate his understanding of the item's potential danger. He may express this by saying, "Bad," "No," "Hurt," "An ouch," "Stay away," or he may respond by non-verbal behavior such as backing away or shaking his head.

Instructional Materials

Several pictures of dangerous objects mounted on tag board. A sign on tag board that reads "No! Go! Show!" and award buttons that say "No! Go! Show!"

Instructional Activities

1. Place the pictures face-down on a table. Invite the children to the table.
2. Discuss the meaning of the word "dangerous," how a person should act when discovering something dangerous, what to do when you do not know if something is dangerous. Ask the children to name things that are dangerous, discuss the ramifications of what can happen if a person plays with the dangerous item (e.g., burns, cuts, sickness, someone can get hurt very badly).
3. Encourage the children to contribute to the discussion to be sure they understand the meaning of dangerous and the common objects to stay away from.
4. Show the children the sign that reads "No! Go! Show!" Read the sign, and explain that if a child is not sure whether or not an object is dangerous or if a dangerous object is easily accessible, he should not touch it, but he should think and say, "No! Go! Show!" (Go = move or Go away from the dangerous object; Show = find an adult and Show them the item without touching it.)
5. Tell the children that you are going to show some pictures of dangerous objects and that you want them to tell you what it is, why it is dangerous, and what they should say instead of touching the item.
6. Show a picture and say, "What is this?", then, "Why is it dangerous?" Then ask, "What should you say?"
7. After the activity, reward the children with a "No! Go! Show!" button.
8. Allow each child to bring in pictures of dangerous objects, and encourage them to be the leader who asks the questions.

5.100   (Removed, see page xii)

5.101   Sits quietly when listening to stories, music, television, movies, etc.

Strand: 5-4   **Age:** 36-40m 3.0-3.4y

Definition

The child will quietly listen to an audio, visual, or audio/visual presentation. During the presentation he will remain seated and quiet, except to answer questions or to make comments pertinent to the presentation and at appropriate times. The length of attending time will depend on different variables such as (1) The child's age, (2) His interest in the
presentation, (3) The time of day, (4) Others involved in the activity, (5) Peer acceptance, (6) The antecedent that occurred to prompt the presentation, (7) The reward offered for attending.

Instructional Materials

Masking tape, a story the child has not heard.

Instructional Activities

1. Ask the child to find a comfortable seat on the floor, or if there is more than one child, seat them in a semicircle.
2. Put a small piece of masking tape on the child's knees.
3. Ask him to hide the tape with his hands (model correct placement of his hands).
4. Discuss the title of the story and what it is about.
5. Read the story and let the child look at the pictures.
6. Check his hands while reading the story to see if, for the most part, he keeps the tape covered.
7. Reward him if he hid the tape most of the time (with his hands), or if he can answer questions about the story that shows he listened well.

5.102   (Removed, see page xii)

5.103   Requests aid for spills

Strand: 5-6   **Age:** 36-40m 3.0-3.4y

Definition

When the child spills, he will ask for help to clean up the spilled material using the proper sponge/towel, etc. An adult will provide assistance as needed.

Instructional Materials

Props for the child to play restaurant. Examples: table, chairs, dishes, menus, apron, silverware, plastic glasses, tray, towels, writing tablet, pencil.

Instructional Activities

1. Set up the restaurant situation. Talk about going to a restaurant, what you do, what happens, what you can order, and how you pay.
2. Let children participate in the selection of the cast (customers, waiter/waitress, cashier, cook) to play restaurant.
3. Using the props, dress up the characters.

4. Set the stage by telling the customers to walk into the restaurant. Tell the waitress to show them where to sit and give them a menu.
5. Encourage them to continue the scene without any prompting.
6. After they have become comfortable playing restaurant, give them some suggestions for role-playing. Examples: What will you do if the restaurant is out of what you order? What will you do if you spill water on the table? What will you do if you break a dish? What will you do if you finish eating before others?
7. You can easily modify this role-playing to a different food setting, such as a cafeteria, a fast food restaurant, a picnic, or home.

5.104 Names a friend or a pet
Strand: 5-2 **Age:** 36-42m 3.0-3.6y

Definition
The child is presented with the question, "Do you have a friend [or pet]? What kind of pet is it?" and then, "What is the name of your friend [or pet]?" She will be given ample time to respond, and if she has more than one friend [or pet], she will be encouraged to tell the names of each one.

Instructional Materials
Song to the tune of *Skip to My Lou*; write a verse that involves the child's pet's name. Example:
Annie's on the pillow, mew, mew, mew.
Annie's on the pillow, mew, mew, mew.
Annie's on the pillow, mew, mew, mew.
That's what she likes to do.
To the tune of *Skip to My Lou*.; write a verse that involves one of the child's friends.
Example:
Billy is my friend, coo, coo, coo.
Billy is my friend, coo, coo, coo.
Billy is my friend, coo, coo, coo.
That's what he likes to do.
If possible, have a musical instrument available to play the tune such as a piano, autoharp, keyboard.

Instructional Activities
1. Place the instrument in easy access to the child. Invite the child to join you at the musical instrument.
2. Hum the tune of *Skip to My Lou* several times, and invite the child to join in humming the tune.
3. Explain to her that you are going to make up words to the tune, made-up words that use

the name of a pet such as: Annie on the Pillow.
4. Discuss with her the name of her pet, or a pet she is familiar with. Using the name of this pet, make up words to the tune of *Skip to My Lou*.
5. Sing the song several times, and invite her to join you in singing the song.
6. Repeat the above procedure, using the name of a friend and then using the name of one of the child's friends.
7. To modify this activity, add additional verses to the song that tell other things the pet does or other things her friends do.

5.105 Responds to simple questions
Strand: 5-7 **Age:** 36-42m 3.0-3.6y

Definition
When the child is presented with a question, he will answer/respond correctly.

Instructional Materials
What Am I? Riddles. The content of these riddles should include objects or persons. Example: "I am round, red, and good to eat. What am I?"

Instructional Activities
1. Invite the child to come to the Riddle Circle.
2. Explain that you are going to describe something. Tell him to raise his hand if he knows what it is.
3. Say the first What Am I Riddle: "I am round, red, and good to eat. What am I?"
4. Pause for him to think about an answer and to raise his hand.
5. Ask him for the answer.
6. After he says "apple," ask additional questions such as, "What shape is an apple?" "What color is an apple?" or "What do we do with apples?"
7. If he responds with a remark that is meant to attract attention, that uses inappropriate language, or that is intended to ridicule or hurt another, he should be ignored, corrected, or given a chance to respond again.
8. Repeat with another What Am I Riddle.
9. Give him an opportunity to be the one who asks the riddles.

5.106 (Removed, see page xii)

5.107 Practices safe procedures when riding in a car
Strand: 5-8 **Age:** 36-48m 3.0-4.0y

Definition
/\Important Safety Note: This definition is not exhaustive; see your state's motor vehicle safety code for complete car-safety procedures. Also, prior to the child independently demonstrating this skill, remind parents and all drivers of their responsibility to properly place infants/young children in approved car seats (based on age and weight).*

When he is riding in a car, the child will always properly be in a car seat (based on age and weight) or wear a seat belt, refrain from putting his arms or hands out of car windows, not play with an object that can be dangerous or is distracting to the driver, not play with the car door locks or windows, and will follow directions he is given.

Instructional Materials
Note: Often seat belts are available from the highway patrol, various state and local safety departments, automobile salvage locations, or parent groups.
Obtain a seat belt that is the same as those found in a car/vehicle.

Instructional Activities
Note: There are child-oriented car safety programs available from various safety sources that will either send instructional material or will make a classroom visit.
1. Affix the seat belt to a chair.
2. Ask a child to sit in the chair.
3. Help the child hold the ends of belt in each hand.
4. Demonstrate how to attach the buckle.
5. Assist the child in closing the buckle.
6. Repeat several times.
7. Say, "Now you do it."
8. Give help as needed.
9. To motivate the children in this activity, use a space blast-off approach. Say, for example, "Buckle up for blast-off," and then "One, two, three, blast-off!"
10. Remind the child that planes do not take off until everyone has buckled up, that rockets do not take off until everyone is buckled, and that cars should not start until everyone has buckled up.
11. If at all possible, charge the child with the responsibility of making sure that everyone in the car he is riding in has buckled up.

5.108 Names siblings
Strand: 5-2 **Age:** 32-42m 2.8-3.6y

Definition
The child names her siblings when she is presented with the question, "Do you have any brothers? How many brothers do you have?" and then "What are your brothers' names?" Then she is presented with the following questions, "Do you have any sisters? How many sisters do you have?" and then, "What are your sisters' names?" She is allowed ample time to respond. If the child has multiple siblings, accept the names in any order.

Instructional Materials
/\Safety Note:* Provide scissors appropriate for the child. Remind the child of safety regarding scissors.
Empty paper towel tubes and wrapping paper tubes, different colored sheets of construction paper, child-safe scissors, crayons, nontoxic glue.

Instructional Activities
1. Cut several different size circles from colored construction paper to fit vertically in a row on the roll tube as faces.
2. Tell the child she is going to make a different kind of family picture.
3. Discuss the members of her family such as what their names are, who is oldest, who is youngest.
4. If the child has a larger family, suggest that she select a larger tube.
5. Explain that she should use the larger circles for older members of the family and smaller circles for younger members of the family.
6. Give her a paper tube, a circle for each family member, crayons, and glue.
7. Tell her to draw each family member's face on a circle.
8. Ask her to glue each circle face on the paper tube.
9. Tell them to say the name of each person as she glues the picture onto the paper tube.

5.109 Categorizes children/adults in correct sex group

Strand: 5-2 **Age:** 36-44m 3.0-3.8y

Definition

When the child is asked, he will be able to identify members of his family, and other familiar people, by sex. For example, he will be able to tell that his mother and sisters are girls and that his father and brothers are boys.

Instructional Materials

A photograph of the child's family members, organized as follows: Cut the faces from the photographs, and glue a piece of felt to the backs of the faces. From pieces of felt, make cutouts of male and female adult, child, and infant bodies without faces, or from magazines or catalogs, cutout bodies and then glue felt on the backs. A felt board.

At the top of the board, place a female body and a male body. On the felt board, place the bodies without faces and the photograph or magazine faces.

Instructional Activities

1. Ask the child to choose a face and to place it on the appropriate boy or girl body.
2. After he has placed the head on the body, ask him if the completed figure is a girl or a boy.
3. Tell him to continue putting faces on bodies, and if the completed person is a boy, to place him below the boy on the felt board. If the person is a girl, tell him to place her below the girl on the felt board.
4. Encourage him to give names to the created people.

5.110 Looks at person when speaking/spoken to

Strand: 5-5 **Age:** 36-44m 3.0-3.8y

Definition

In either a group situation or a one-to-one conversation, the child will look at the person who is speaking. When greeting someone, she will look at their face at least part of the time. She may or may not make direct eye contact.

Instructional Materials

A blindfold.

Instructional Activities

1. Include several children in this activity. Place the blindfold on the table.

2. Explain to the children they are going to play a game called I Hear You.
3. Assign the children to stand in different locations around the room and have one child stand in the center of the room. The child standing in the center is "It" and will have to identify who spoke or made a noise.
4. Blindfold the child (the person who is "It") in the center of the room.
5. Explain to the children that they are to stand around the room and take turns making a sound or saying something.
6. Tell the blindfolded child that she is to point to the person who spoke or made a noise.
7. Have her remove her blindfold to look at the person who spoke or made a noise.
8. The person who spoke or made a noise now become the person who is "It" and puts on the blindfold.
9. Make sure that each child is allowed to have a turn making a noise and being "It."
10. To enhance the excitement of the game encourage the children to try to disguise their noise-making or verbalization.

5.111 Remains calm if goals cannot be reached

Strand: 5-5 **Age:** 36-44m 3.0-3.8y

Definition

The child will accept a situation when the goals cannot be reached. He will accept this disappointment in a calm manner. If the goals change, he will accept the new situation, begin an activity to achieve the new goal, and display an adaptive attitude.

Instructional Materials

Create an obstacle course with different items, such as: tables, carpet squares, pillows, boxes, etc. Masking tape to show the starting and ending lines. A timer.

Instructional Activities

Note: Limit the amount of different obstacle materials for young children or children who have limited motor skills. If a timer is not available or is difficult to control, time him by starting and stopping a musical selection.

1. Explain to the child that you have placed different objects on the floor for him to walk on, crawl through, and jump on.
2. Demonstrate how you want him to move through the course.

3. Tell him to start at the beginning of the course and do what you tell him, for example, "Step on the carpet, jump on the pillow, crawl under the table and sit in the box."

4. Allow him to explore the obstacle course until he feels comfortable with each movement.

5. Explain to him that you will set the timer (time depends on the age and motor skills of the child) and will say, "Go." Tell him when the timer goes off that he should be at the end of the course.

6. Set the timer and say "Go." Encourage him as he races against the clock.

7. If he reaches the end before the timer goes off, congratulate him.

8. If he does not reach the end before the timer sounds, discuss with him how he can improve his time and reset the timer so that he can achieve his goal.

9. Helping him accept the goal when it is not achieved is vital to his emotional growth and development.

10. Some suggestions for addressing specific behaviors are:

Behavior--He becomes overly emotional (cries, pouts, sulks).

Strategy--(1) Ignore the reaction; (2) Discuss disappointments, and explain how others feel when a person cannot accept changes. It is best to choose a time when he is in good spirits for this discussion, not while he is reacting.

Behavior-- He refuses to accept a new solution.

Strategy--(1) Ignore the reaction; (2) If the new solution can be implemented immediately, proceed with the modification, with or without him. (When you must change an activity or event with a child and the change is not going to occur immediately, it is important to explain that a change will be occurring and you can pre-stress him before it does occur); (3) Involve him in the change or solution to create a situation in which he participates in the decision-making process.

Behavior-- He maintains a positive attitude about the happening.

Strategy--(1) Reinforce him for his attitude. (2) Let him help others understand the problem and the solution to it.

Behavior-- He whines because the goal cannot be reached.

Strategy--(1) Do not let him see that his whining bothers you; leave the room if necessary. (2) Recommend to him to that he smile when he talks, because smiling will make his voice sound better.

5.112 Shares toys/equipment with another

Strand: 5-5   **Age:** 36-44m 3.0-3.8y

Definition

The child will share her toys/equipment with another when asked. She will share her toy/equipment with another without being asked. When she has shared her toy/equipment, she will also establish ownership, limit sharing time, and display the ability to request the toy or equipment back.

Instructional Materials

Aluminum foil, child-safe scissors, nontoxic glue, assorted decorative scraps (material scraps, construction paper scraps, colored dot stickers, pipe cleaners, etc.) A paper sack or a box for each child.

Instructional Activities

/*\Safety Note: Take special precautions and carefully supervise the children when they are working with the aluminum foil to avoid anyone getting cut on the edges. Provide scissors appropriate for the child. Remind the child of safety regarding scissors.

1. Place the material on a table. Invite the children to the table and tell them each of them will make two aluminum animals.

2. Demonstrate how to make an aluminum animal by tearing off a sheet of aluminum foil. Crush the foil in your hand and shape it into an animal or a bird. Using the scraps, add legs, eyes, ears, nose, mouth, or beak.

3. Give each child a sheet of foil, and ask her to take it and crush the foil in her hand. Provide assistance as needed.

4. Allow each child time to decorate her creation.

5. Give each child another sheet of foil, and ask her to take it and crush the foil in her hand. Provide assistance as needed.

6. Allow time for the child to decorate her second creation.

7. After each child has made two animals or birds, explain that each one may choose one of the two to keep for her very own and then must share the other one.

8. Give each child a sack or a box to put her own animal in and instruct her to place the other animal on the table.

9. Allow the children to play with the "to share" animals on the table. Suggest an activity such as an animal parade, a zoo visit, or a jungle trail.

10. If a child exhibits a change of heart and is not ready to share, remind her that she has a special animal that is her very own inside her sack or box.

5.113   Shows independence from an adult

Strand: 5-5   **Age:** 42-54m 3.6-4.6y

Definition

The child will independently engage in an activity/task without adult assistance. He does not need to complete the activity but must demonstrate a comprehensive independent skill level. Example: Puts on his sweater correctly, but does not zip it up. Puts his toys in his toy box, but does not put the toy box away. Plays pretend with a friend, without asking an adult how to do it.

Instructional Materials

/*\Safety Note: Provide scissors appropriate for the child. Remind the child of safety regarding scissors.

A learning center, remembering that learning centers are places where: (1) A child can operate and learn on an independent level; (2) Multi-level experiences are included to assure success; (3) A child is offered choices in the required tasks to allow for independent self-selection in how he wants to learn; (4) The activities are presented in a motivating manner, making it easy to become involved, and follow the directions independently. The learning center topics may include drawing and painting, sounds, pretend play, stacking, cutting, listening, gadgets. Select a topic for the learning center and collect the necessary materials. Example:

Topic: Writing Center.

Materials: Pencils, markers, paper, child-safe scissors, shapes, templates, gadgets, cookie cutters, coins.

Directions: Provide a model of a cookie cutter that has been drawn around, and provide a picture of things that have been drawn around. (To avoid the child's creating a "trace-around" just like the models, remove the cookie cutter and items that were used to make the examples.) Provision for Activity Conclusion: Provide a place for the child to display his completed project.

Instructional Activities

1. Place all the pre-collected and pre-planned materials in the learning center.

2. Invite the child to come to the center, and explain that this is a place for him to trace many different things; point out the material he may use, show him the model, and make sure that he is aware of where he may exhibit his completed work.

3. Leave him to self-explore and decide independently what he is going to use to experience tracing.

4. If he appears to be unsure about what to do or if he withdraws from the activity or becomes discouraged, go to the center and reinforce his efforts. Provide some "think-about" suggestions; say, for example, "If you trace around this tree, do you think it would look nice beside the house you've drawn?" Solve any material problems and encourage him to continue.

5. At the conclusion of his work, make sure to praise his product, as well as his ability to work independently.

6. It is important to change the Learning Center topic and material often.

5.114   Stays with group during an activity

Strand: 5-5   **Age:** 36-44m 3.0-3.8y

Definition

The child will stay with her designated group during an activity, until told otherwise. When she is involved in an outside activity (visiting a museum, attending a presentation, going to a park, etc.), she will stay with the group to which she was assigned, unless told otherwise. When asked to select a group, she will remain with that group until she is reassigned or is given an opportunity to re-select.

Instructional Materials

Drawn and cut out shapes of six hollow tree trunks and three squirrels. Safety pins.

Instructional Activities

1. Locate a large area to play a running game.

2. Divide the children into three groups of three children each. The three children in groups one and two should have a hollow tree trunk pinned (safely) to them. The three children in group three should have a squirrel pinned to them.

3. When you pin on the shapes, explain group membership.

4. Make sure the children understand the name of their group and the importance of staying with their assigned group.

5. Ask the three children in group one and the three children in group two (hollow tree trunks) to join hands to make two hollow tree trunks.

6. Ask the children in group three (squirrels) to stand around the trees.

7. Tell the children that only one squirrel may be in a tree trunk at a time.

8. Explain to them that each time you clap your hands, all the squirrels must find a tree.

9. The homeless squirrels must attempt to get to a tree during the change.

10. Clap your hands again, and tell the squirrels to change trees, giving the treeless squirrel a chance at a tree.

11. Discuss with the tree groups the importance of staying with their groups.

12. Allow the children to take turns being squirrels and trees.

5.115　Speaks clearly without mumbling
Strand: 5-7　**Age:** 36-48m　3.0-4.0y

Definition
When he is speaking, the child will speak clearly and distinctly so others can understand him.

Instructional Materials
Stickers the child would like, purchased from retail stores, or make "Good Speaking Stickers" from white adhesive labels and colored markers. (The children may also enjoy making these stickers.)

Instructional Activities
1. Have the stickers available for reinforcement.

2. Set up periods throughout the day and during different days of the week when other teachers, children, the principal, or the nurse may visit the class.

3. Tell the child when the visitors will be coming into the class.

4. Demonstrate how to introduce himself politely and how to speak clearly so the visitor will be able to understand him.

5. Tell him if he introduces himself to the visitor and if the visitor does not have to ask him to repeat what he says, he will earn a sticker.

6. Choose a child to tell his name, something about himself, and about what the class is doing when the visitor arrives.

7. After the visitor leaves, award the Good-Speaking Stickers.

5.116　Transitions from one activity to another at the request of an adult
Strand: 5-1　**Age:** 36-48m　3.0-4.0y

Definition
When the child is actively engaged in an activity of her own choosing, she can transition to another activity at the direction of an adult. She will maintain focus on the new activity and complete the activity before moving on to something else.

Instructional Materials
Picture books, building blocks, puzzles. Art supplies for painting (paper, paints, and paint brushes).

Instructional Activities
1. Invite a group of children to play. Show them the different items they have available to play with. Put out the picture books that they can look at, the blocks that they can build with and the puzzles they can put together.

2. Let the children know that they will play for a while, but you will be calling them to come and do something else with you shortly.

3. Let the children play for a while. A few minutes before you will be ending the play period, let them know that they only have two minutes left to play.

4. When the two minutes is up, call the children to join you at the art table. Have the art materials ready on the table (paper, paints, and paint brushes).

5. Verbally reinforce all the children who transitioned to the art table.

6. If there are children who did not join you at the art table, remind them that it is time to stop playing and that they need them to come to the art table. If necessary, help them put their toys away, or in a safe place so they can continue playing later.

5.117　Performs or attempts new activity
Strand: 5-1　**Age:** 37-42m　3.1-3.6y

Definition
When the child is asked he will attempt an activity he has not previously performed; however, the new task will involve motor, cognitive, and behavioral skills that he has. He will demonstrate adaptive behaviors that indicate an effort to try the new activity, and he will attend to it for a reasonable length of time; he will also demonstrate a trial-and-error approach, will ask questions to aid in doing the activity, and will seek support or help with the material, if needed.

Instructional Materials

A large ball of yarn or strips of material that have been attached and wrapped into a ball.

Instructional Activities

1. This activity requires a lot of space, so make sure there is an adequate area for the children to move about.
2. Give the ball of yarn to one of the children.
3. Tell him to wrap the yarn around his waist as many times as needed to stay in place. Provide assistance if needed; it is important for the yarn to remain around his waist.
4. After the yarn is around him, tell him to give the ball to another child, and then that child is to wrap the yarn around his waist as many times as needed for it to stay in place.
5. After the yarn is around the second child, tell him to give the ball to another child who is to wrap the yarn around his waist as many times as needed for it to stay in place.
6. Continue until all the children have been intertwined in yarn.
7. Reverse the process.
8. The last player should begin to rewind the ball (provide assistance if needed to get started), pass it to the child next to him, and so on until the wound ball is back at child one.
9. Allow the children to work together in various ways to wind and unwind themselves.
10. Repeat this activity, because each time they do it, it is a new experience for them.
11. During this activity, the following are suggested actions based on occurring behaviors:

Behavior--Is uncooperative in the setting. Disrupts others by annoying or pushing. Does not stay with or try to complete the activity within a normal time limit.

Strategy--To avoid frustration, make sure that he can accomplish part of the activity with at least some success. The best intervention for aggression is, if possible, to anticipate the action and remove him from the situation for a short period of time. Request a high probability behavior instead of a low probability behavior. Example: Low probability--"This is a turning game"; High probability--"In this game you get to do your favorite thing: turn and twist."

Withdrawn Behavior--Does not participate. Is anxious or fearful for no reason. Shows unhappiness or cries.

Strategy-- Involve him in the activity with one other child before introducing him to a larger group. Avoid reproaching or rushing him to participate. Reinforce him consistently for any simple effort, particularly individual efforts that are non-solicited. Use verbal reinforcement that he understands.

Dependent Behavior--Needs a great deal of support and attention from others. Uses only one way to do a task, does not apply trial-and-error methods. Appears inactive or apathetic when appropriate for him.

Strategy--Begin with very simple activities that require him to make decisions between two choices. Review an activity familiar to him that he is successful at. Reinforce his actions. Provide several trials in varied situations for learning acceptable behavior, but do not tell him how to behave.

5.118 Takes turns

Strand: 5-5 **Age:** 37-42m 3.1-3.6y

Definition

The child will respond to a demonstration or verbal reminder to take turns during a structured game, when playing with others, or while waiting to use material. While she waits for her turn, she will demonstrate appropriate behavior and refrain from such behaviors as aggression, poor sportsmanship, pouting, or seeking attention.

Instructional Materials

/*\Safety Note: Provide scissors appropriate for the child. Remind the child of safety regarding scissors.

Animal pictures, cut out from magazines, catalogs, and calendars (one per child). Lightweight cardboard, scissors, pins, nontoxic glue.

Instructional Activities

1. Cut out the animal pictures and attach the pictures to a lightweight cardboard square or circle. The mounted animal pictures should be an appropriate size to be pinned on the child's shirt.
2. Ask the children to sit facing you.
3. Hold up one of the animal cards.
4. Tell the children they must take turns naming the animal on the card.
5. Tell them you will call on one child at a time and that they must take turns and wait until you call their name.

6. Show the children an animal card and say, for example, "David, name this animal."

7. If he answers correctly, pin the animal card on him.

8. Continue until all the children have animal cards.

9. Play a fun game that requires taking turns, and call on each child in turn by her animal card name.

10. The following are some possible child behaviors and some intervention suggestions:

Behavior--A child shouts out the name of the animal, even if you called on another child. She refuses to wait her turn.

Strategy--(1) Make sure she understands what taking turns means, explain the concept, and then role-play taking a turn; (2) Make sure every child who is waiting her turn is rewarded. (3) Use an "I" message, such as "Nancy, I know how anxious you are to answer, but your talking when it is not your turn upsets me because it spoils the game. Please stop." (4) Remove her from the setting.

Behavior--When reminded to take her turn, she pouts and refuses to play the game.

Strategy--(1) Make sure she understands what taking turns means, explain the concept, and then role-play taking a turn. (2) Be ready to advise and help her if she has an interaction problem. A child cannot be expected to know how to overcome all obstacles. Suggestions or a helping hand when she needs it may be all that is necessary to involve her in the game and assist her in learning to take turns. However, wait until she really needs help, or she soon will learn that pouting and withdrawing will get her the assistance she needs. When a child becomes dependent on others, she often learns to doubt her own abilities and finds it easier to wait for help. (3) Explain to her that if she chooses not to play the game, you are sorry because you do not want her to miss out on any fun, but suggest that perhaps she would like to watch for awhile. Tell her when she is ready to join again, to let you know, and she will be welcome. Wait until she indicates she is ready to play and review with her that playing the game means taking turns. (4) Request a high probability behavior instead of a low probability behavior; for example: Low probability--"You do not have to play"; high probability--"It is okay if you do not play, but you are so good at naming things; we will miss you."

Behavior-- She acts bossy and is negative to other players. For example, she tells everyone how to play, makes fun of children who give a wrong answer, inserts other ways to play the game, inappropriately corrects responses given.

Strategy--(1) Make sure that she knows how to play the game, can name some of the animals, and understands what taking turns means. Occasionally a child would rather be in trouble for not making an effort than to run the risk of being called a name by her peers for trying and failing; (2) Create an atmosphere for cooperation through encouragement. Once she feels that she is understood she is more inclined to listen and to make an effort to reach a solution to a problem. To encourage a child, follow these recommendations: (1) Talk to her about how you think she might be feeling. Continue the discussion to determine if what you think she is feeling is actually right. Say, for example, "Sometimes when we play a new game we feel like we cannot play it, right?" (2) Discuss times when you felt that same way. Say, for example, "I know how you feel; when I played Hide and Seek for the first time I just knew I couldn't do it right"; (3) Ask her if she would be willing to work with you on a solution to this problem. Say, for example, "Carolyn, let me show you how to play the game." (4) Discuss with her some things that she might do the next time she feels like not trying when she is asked to play a new game. All this should be done in an attitude of friendliness, caring, a desire to encourage, and respect.

5.119 **Eats most foods in a tidy manner**

Strand: 5-6 **Age:** 37-46m 3.1-3.10y

Definition

When the child is given food in a bowl or a small plate, he will use a spoon, a fork (regular or child size), and a cup (with a handle) with little spilling.

Instructional Materials

/***Safety Note:** Be aware of special diets and allergies before doing these activities.

A large mirror, a placemat, a plate, utensils, a napkin, a "scoop" food such as applesauce and a "spear" food such as cheese.

Instructional Activities

1. Place the dishes and utensils on a placemat. Place the scoop food and the spear food on the dishes. In front of this setting, place the large mirror.
2. Have the child look in the mirror and notice that his face and mouth are clean.
3. Show him his clean, tidy placemat.
4. Instruct him to take a bite of food using the utensils and to put the utensils back on the plate when he is thorough.
5. Have him watch himself eating in the mirror and remind him to use the napkin to wipe his face and hands periodically during the meal.
6. Reinforce him for using his napkin and keeping his eating area tidy.
7. Culminate the activity with a trip to a restaurant for all tidy eaters.

5.120 Performs new activities voluntarily
Strand: 5-1 **Age:** 40-46m 3.4-3.10y

Definition

When the child is presented with "Who wants to [name of a new activity]," she will volunteer to do it, or when she is presented with a new activity, she will want to do it. When she is presented with a group of new activities, she will explore and perform at least one of them, as well as exhibit behaviors that adapt to the new task.

Instructional Materials

Nontoxic paint, a large paintbrush, large sheets of paper, another painting tool such as a rubber spatula, a large feather, or cotton swabs.

Instructional Activities

1. Place the large sheet of paper on a table with the nontoxic paint, the paintbrush, and the alternative painting instruments.
2. Encourage the child to paint a picture, using the paintbrush.
3. Change the paper and remove the paintbrush.
4. Tell her that she is to paint another picture, only this time she must paint it a new way.
5. Tell her to use one of the other items instead of a brush.
6. Continue providing her with sheets of paper and allow her to find different painting instruments.
7. If she exhibits inappropriate behaviors when she tries to use the different painting instruments, give her the paintbrush to use for painting. It is not important for her to perform a new activity at any specific time.

She may need additional experiences, more opportunities for retaining information, and chances to work independently. As she matures and develops, she will become more adept at new tasks.
See #5.155

5.121 Says "Thank You" when appropriate. Says "Please" with requests
Strand: 5-7 **Age:** 40-52m 3.4-4.4y

Definition

When the child is given an object he requested, or receives a compliment or a service, he will say "thank you" voluntarily. When he requests an object or a service, he will say "please" without being prompted.

Instructional Materials

A list of directions that would be fun for the child. Examples: Go shake hands with Johnny. Gallop to the door and gallop back to your chair. Get a cup, fill it with water, and give it to Mary. Go to the mirror and make a funny face. Put chalk on your nose and try to write on the chalkboard.

Instructional Activities

1. Invite the children to sit at the table.
2. Give the child a direction to follow, such as, "Go shake hands with Johnny."
3. Tell him that he must say, "Please, may I?" before he may get up from his seat.
4. Tell him he must wait until you say "yes" or "no."
5. Tell him to respond to your answer by saying "thank you" and then following the direction if your answer was "yes."
6. Have the child remain seated if he does not say "please" or "thank you."
7. Reward him for completing the task.
8. Make sure that every child has an opportunity to participate.

5.122 Assists with simple adult tasks
Strand: 5-5 **Age:** 41-48m 3.5-4.0y

Definition

The child will assist with simple adult chores. Her involvement will depend on her cognitive abilities, motor skills, attention span, interest, and her level of responsible behaviors. She will be allowed to select a simple adult task that she wishes to do; however, the options presented to her should be within her capabilities and at the discretion of the adult.

Instructional Materials

A large sheet of chart paper, markers.

Instructional Activities

Note: Pictures that depict the tasks can replace the words. Write a title on the chart, for example, <u>Helping Hands</u>, <u>Willing Workers</u>, <u>Cheery Chores</u>, or <u>Jolly Jobs</u>.

1. On the chart paper list all the household tasks in which the child can act as an aid or assistant. Example: (1) Water plants; (2) Clean tabletops; (3) Put away material; (4) Cooking assistant; (5) Pass out papers; (6) Distribute refreshments; (7) Sort material. Opposite each task allow space to write a child's name.
2. Show the children the chart, discuss the various tasks listed, demonstrate if necessary, and ask for volunteers.
3. Explain to the volunteers the importance of their assistance, the responsibility that goes with the assignment, and how much they are appreciated.
4. Provide them with instructions, time to do the jobs, assistance, encouragement, and reinforcement.
5. Change the jobs on the chart as needed, and encourage them to volunteer for various tasks.

5.123 Comes to an activity when asked by a responsible person

Strand: 5-5 **Age:** 41-48m 3.5-4.0y

Definition

The child will come to an activity when he is asked; however, if he chooses to not be involved, he will decline appropriately. If the activity is in his best interest (his safety or health), he will be instructed to come to it (e.g., fire drill) immediately.

Instructional Materials

/*\Safety Note: Provide scissors appropriate for the child. Remind the child of safety regarding scissors.
Large sheets of paper, removable tape, non-toxic paint, scissors, brushes.

Instructional Activities

1. Cut strips of removable tape, and place the strips in a design on the large sheet of paper. After the strips are in place, paint the whole sheet of paper with one color paint. After the paint dries, remove the tape and display the tape design picture.
2. Show the child the tape design picture.

3. Tell him how you made it.
4. After he views the picture, put it away.
5. Ask him to go to the table or easel, and use the tape, scissors, and paint to make a tape design picture.
6. If he does not go to the table or easel, ask him again.
7. If he still chooses not to engage in the activity, review the steps to it and show him the finished tape design picture once again.
8. Give him any necessary assistance as he creates his picture.
9. Allow him an opportunity to do another picture.
10. Display his completed pictures.

5.124 Waits for turn at least two times

Strand: 5-5 **Age:** 42-54m 3.6-4.6y

Definition

The child will respond to a demonstration or verbal reminder to take turns during a structured game, when playing with others, or waiting to use material. While waiting for her turn, she will demonstrate appropriate behavior and refrain from behaviors such as aggression, poor sportsmanship, pouting, seeking attention, wanting power. She will wait at least two times before having her turn.

Instructional Activities

See #5.118 for instructional materials and activities. This skill is almost identical to #5.118 except the child has to wait at least two times before having her turn.

5.125 Says "Hello" and "Good-Bye" at correct times

Strand: 5-7 **Age:** 36-48m 3.0-4.0y

Definition

When the child arrives at a location, he will respond to and will give the correct verbal greeting (e.g., "Hello," "Hi," or "Hi, how are you?") to the persons in attendance. When he leaves a location, he will respond to and make the correct verbal farewell (e.g., "Good-Bye," "Bye," "Good-Bye, it was good to see you.") to those in attendance. Prompting may be necessary; however, it should be faded as early as possible. Likewise, if others arrive at or leave his location, the child will say "hello" or "good-bye" appropriately.

Instructional Materials

A series of metered poems in which the first line begins with a location (e.g., "Just around the corner," "Down below the step," or "Up above the pillow," and with a second line continuing: "There just might [verb]," "You just might [verb]," "We just might [verb]," or "He just might [verb]."
Example:
Just Around the Corner
Just around the corner,
There just might blow
A plump, purple kite
That says, "Hello."
Just Around the Corner
Just around the corner,
There just might fly
A stingy bumblebee.
Hurry, say "Good-bye."
A large sheet of drawing paper, drawing markers.

Instructional Activities

1. Place the large sheet of drawing paper on the bulletin board. Invite the children to join you near the drawing paper.
2. Explain that you are going to recite a poem and draw a picture about a plump, purple kite.
3. Recite the first poem, Just Around the Corner.
"Just around the corner,
There just might blow
A plump, purple kite. (Draw a plump purple kite on the drawing paper.)
That says 'Hello!'" (Write the word Hello in a cloud above the drawn kite.)
4. Ask the children to listen while you recite the poem again.
5. In a suspenseful manner say, "Just around the corner, There just might blow..."
6. Point to the purple kite you drew and say, "A plump, purple kite that says..." (Point to the child) "Hello!"
7. Repeat, and ask the child to say as many of the words in the poem as he knows, with emphasis on "Hello."
8. Repeat again, phasing out to allow the child to lead.
9. Invite him to point to the kite at the correct time and to point to another child for the "Hello."
10. Discuss the word "Hello," what it means, who the plump, purple kite was greeting, to whom you say hello.

11. Recite the second poem, Just Around the Corner.
"Just around the corner,
There just might fly
A stingy bumblebee." (Draw a bumblebee with a pronounced stinger on the chart paper.)
"Hurry, say Good-Bye!" (Write the word "Good-Bye" in a cloud above the bumblebee.)
12. Ask the child to listen to the poem again.
13. In a suspenseful manner say, "Just around the corner, there just might fly..."
14. Point to the bee and say, "A stingy bumblebee. Hurry, say..." (Point to the child) "Good-Bye!"
15. Repeat, and ask him to say as many of the words in the poem as he knows, with emphasis on "Good-Bye!"
16. Repeat again, phasing out to allow the child to be main speaker.
17. Invite him to point to the bumblebee at the correct time and to point to another child for the "Good-Bye."
18. Discuss the word "Good-Bye," what it means, why the hurry to say "good-bye" to the bumble-bee, when we say "good-bye," and to whom you say "good-bye."
19. After he has learned the Just Around the Corner--Hello and Just Around the Corner--Good-Bye poems, recite them together, using the illustrations as props.
20. Use this method for writing poems (first line location--"Just around the corner," second line ending in verb--"There just might fly" to involve the child in writing other poems.

5.126 Tries again when a change or disappointment occurs

Strand: 5-1 **Age:** 42-46m 3.6-3.10y

Definition

The child will try an activity again after a proper length of time has lapsed. During this recovery period, she will be reassured and reinforced for her efforts, ability, approximation, and patience.

Instructional Materials

At least 4 yards of 3/4-inch wide white plastic belting purchased from a fabric store. Brass paper fasteners, a paper hole punch, nontoxic fabric paint. A small box, a container.

Instructional Activities

1. Cut the plastic belting into 10-inch lengths and use the paper punch to punch a hole 3/4 inch from each end of the 10-inch lengths. Use

the fabric paint to paint the strips different colors.
2. Demonstrate to the child how to link the strips together by looping one strip with another and then putting a fastener into the holes to secure. Loop another strip through the completed one and repeat the process.
3. Provide the child with the strips and the fasteners and allow her to link them together and experience progression.
4. After she completes the task, ask her to take the strips apart, place them in a container, and put the fasteners in a box.

5.127   Quiets down after active period
Strand: 5-4   **Age:** 42-46m 3.6-3.10y

Definition
After active play, the child will sit down, remain seated, stop talking loudly, refrain from physical play, keep his hands and feet to himself, and present a relaxed manner.

Instructional Materials
A soothing, relaxing musical selection by a composer such as Bach or Beethoven. Equipment to play music.

Instructional Activities
1. Prepare the musical selection so it is ready to play.
2. Ask the children to go to their seats after playtime.
3. Speak in a whisper or a soothing tone.
4. Reinforce the children who follow the directions and go to their seats.
5. Ask each child to inhale deeply, fully expanding his chest, to exhale and drop the trunk of his body forward at the waist.
6. Have each child make his chin touch his chest with his arms dangling between his knees.
7. Reinforce by saying, "Now our room is a toy store full of rag dolls."
8. Play the music.
9. Walk around and lift arms to check each child's limpness or relaxation.
10. Repeat several times.
11. Discuss how each child can use this relaxation method when he is excited, angry, or tired from sitting.

5.128   Claims ownership of own possessions
Strand: 5-4   **Age:** 36-48m 3.0-4.0y

Definition
The child will declare ownership of items and will defend her own possessions. If an adult or peer tries to take away a possession that belongs to her, she will resist. She will physically resist by holding onto the item or grabbing it back. She will verbally resist by saying such things as, "It is mine," "It belongs to me," or "Give my ball back."

Instructional Materials
A favorite toy belonging to each child. Assign her to bring it to the assessment. Basket or box to put toys in.

Instructional Activities
1. Ask each child to put their favorite toy in a basket or box on the floor. Ask the children to sit in a circle around the basket.
2. Hold up a toy and say, for example, "Let us see, this must be Sally's car." Ask, "Is this Sally's car?"
3. Encourage her to answer "Yes" or "No."
4. Wait for the correct owner to claim her toy. If there is no response, ask correct owner, "Whose toy car is this?"
5. Continue asking questions until she claims her toy and denies that it belongs to anyone else.
6. Take another toy for the box. Continue guessing the names of children who do not own the toy to keep up the interest in the activity.
7. Encourage participation by everyone and involve all the children in the activity.
8. After you have gone through the entire box of toys, tell the children they may play with their toys. Ask them to share (stress the concept of sharing) the toys with others.
9. Vary this activity by substituting other types of possessions.

5.129   Shows an emerging sense of humor by laughing at the appropriate time
Strand: 5-7   **Age:** 42-54m 3.6-4.6y

Definition
When the child is involved with a humorous story, a comment, an event, a caper, or a funny trick, he will laugh at the appropriate time. The appropriate time

will most likely be at the end or during the humorous presentation.

Instructional Materials

Some selected humorous short poems, available from your local library. Check available references to locate funny selections. Examples: *The Purple Cow* by Gelette Burges, *After a Bath* by Aileen Fisher, or parody writing/limericks.
Example:
There was an old lady
Who liked to eat snacks:
Raisins and carrots,
Crackers and tacks.
There was an old lady
Who liked to fix stew.
No matter what she fixed
It turned out like glue.
There was an old lady
Who fed the gray hog.
What did she feed it?
Two mice and a frog.

Instructional Activities

1. Arrange the listening area with comfortable pillows, chairs, and stuffed animals for holding. Make sure there is a large enough place for physical action.
2. Invite the child to the listening area. Explain that you are going to read some silly poems.
3. Begin reading:
"There was an old lady
Who liked to eat snacks;
Raisins and carrots,
Crackers, and tacks."
4. Read the parody several times, encouraging the child to join in as he becomes familiar with the words and meter.
5. Tell him he may act out the poem as he says it. Encourage him to have fun, act silly, and laugh at the poem and his actions.
6. Read the next poem:
"There was an old lady
Who liked to fix stew.
No matter what she fixed
It turned out like glue."
7. Read the parody several times, encouraging the child to join in as he becomes familiar with the words and meter.
8. Tell him he may act out the poem as he says it. Encourage him to have fun time, act silly, and laugh at the poem and his actions.
9. Repeat the above with other poems and silly rhymes.

5.130 Sits without moving when involved in an activity

Strand: 5-4 **Age:** 43-46m 3.7-3.10y

Definition

The child will sit in a seat, on a bench, or on the floor without excessive moving or fidgeting when she is participating in or observing an activity. The time she sits without moving excessively will be determined by the entry behavior of the child, the amount of time the activity takes, the group participating, the child's interest in the activity, her background information and skill level relative to the activity. Excessive moving and fidgeting behaviors are viewed as: (1) Getting out of her seat, (2) Standing on the seat, (3) Lying on the table, (4) Poking, hitting and kicking, (5) Interfering with the activity by swinging or swaying arms, (6) Stamping feet, (7) Overtly grabbing or hugging other participants, (8) Tipping over in the chair, (9) Rolling, if on the floor, (10) Any excessive motions that interfere with the activity or others who are involved in it.

Instructional Materials

Floor mats, pieces of foam, rest rugs, or any other material that can be used as rest mats.

Instructional Activities

Note: When you give directions, speak rather slowly and deliberately and when demonstrating the relaxation movements, do them slowly and deliberately.
1. Have the rest mats available for the child.
2. Ask the child to lie on the floor face-up with her hands at her sides, legs uncrossed and flat on the floor.
3. Tell her to listen carefully as you tell her some things to do with parts of her body.
4. Say, "Shake one of your hands slowly."
5. Demonstrate a slow motion of shaking one hand. Ask her to shake her hand slowly.
6. Say, "Shake your other hand slowly."
7. Demonstrate a slow motion of shaking the other hand. Ask her to shake her other hand slowly.
8. Say, "Shake both of your hands slowly."
9. Demonstrate shaking both hands slowly. Ask her to shake her hands slowly.
10. Say, "Shake one of your arms slowly."
11. Demonstrate shaking one arm slowly. Ask her to shake one arm.
12. Say, "Shake your other arm slowly."
13. Demonstrate shaking the other arm slowly. Ask her to shake her other arm.
14. Say, "Shake both your arms slowly."

15. Demonstrate shaking both arms slowly. Ask her to shake both her arms slowly.
16. Continue with the controlled relaxing activity by asking her to shake her feet (one at a time, and then together), roll her head, etc.
17. Modify the activity by asking her to close her eyes while she does the slow, deliberate exercises.
18. Ask her to sit on a chair, hands hanging down on each side of the chair with her feet flat on the floor.
19. Explain to her that she must sit still and listen carefully as you tell her some things to do.
20. Say, "Start at the top of your head and shake it, then shake your shoulders, shake your arms, shake your body waist-up, shake your legs and then your foot, and shake all of your body." Demonstrate the relaxed shaking movements.
21. Say, "Sway with your arms above your head. Sway your head and arms. Sway your head, arms, and the top of your body." Demonstrate the relaxed swaying movements.
22. Say, "Act like a rag doll." Demonstrate the relaxed rag doll position.
23. Continue doing the relaxing sitting activities.
24. Ask the child to stand up, arms hanging down at her sides, legs straight and feet together.
25. Explain to her that she must stand still and listen carefully as you tell her some things to do.
26. Say, "Bend over at the waist, arms hanging loosely and sway from one side to another." Demonstrate the vertical hanging sway.
27. Say, "Put your arms above your head and sway from one side to the other." Demonstrate the vertical wave.
28. Say, "Put one foot forward and shake it, then put the other foot forward and shake it." Demonstrate the foot movements.
29. Say, "Put one arm forward and shake it, then put the other arm forward and shake it." Demonstrate the arm movements.
30. Continue doing the relaxing standing activities.
31. If the child exhibits behaviors that prevent her from sitting, standing, or lying still during the relaxation activities, the following is recommended:

Behavior--She moved excessively, inappropriately, and with a lack of direction.

Strategy--(1) Explain and model exactly what you expect her to do during the relaxation activities; (2) In the spirit of fun, place a limit on her movement. For example, when she is lying down, draw a wide line around her body, and explain to her that the line is like a corral and that she must not go outside her corral. When she is sitting on a chair or standing, draw a wide line around her feet and tell her that her feet are stuck in the mud and that she cannot move them; (3) Excuse her from the activity; (4) Reinforce her when she is sitting still and involved in the activity, when she is trying to sit still, and when she demonstrates less movement but still is not sitting quietly.

Behavior--She moved excessively, disrupting the activity and those who are involved in it.

Strategy--(1) Remove her from the sitting position and provide her with a period of planned physical exercise.; (2) Remove her and encourage her to observe the activity. Observational learning can facilitate a positive atmosphere, when watching is presented as an alternative to participating and the child can see how fun the activity can be.

Behavior--She throws a temper tantrum. (When a temper tantrum becomes her favorite method for problem-solving, this could indicate a behavioral concern.)

Strategy--(1) Ignore, unless she is in danger of harming herself, others, or property. In that case, silently remove her to a secure area away from other people and then ignore her; (2) Without dealing with personalities, without becoming angry, and remaining in control, move into a problem-solving mode; (3) Involve her in a physical release, such as running, throwing things at a target, pounding a soft ball, punching a ball of clay; (4) Request that she continue to have the tantrum, but tell her she may only have a tantrum at a certain location and at a certain time of the day. A child often resists being told what to do, and if you use a paradoxical task approach, she may decrease the behavior.

5.131 Follows directions and obeys an authority figure

Strand: 5-1 **Age:** 43-48m 3.7-4.0y

Definition

The child will follow directions given by an authority figure. (An authority figure is a person such as a parent, a teacher, a teacher's adult helper, a baby-sitter, community figures such as police officers or firefighters, persons involved in the education, safety, and health of the child.) The response time will depend on the child's cognitive and language development, his adaptive behaviors, experiences, and association with the authority figure.

Instructional Materials

/***Safety Note:** Provide scissors appropriate for the child. Remind the child of safety regarding scissors.

A dowel stick or a broomstick, a shoe box, sheets of construction paper in black, red, green and yellow, aluminum foil, cardboard, a pail of sand, child-safe scissors, masking tape to attach to the floor, nontoxic glue, markers, a hat that resembles a police hat (if available).

Instructional Activities

1. Use the aluminum foil to make two police badges, one to pin to a shirt and the other to go on the hat. Make a stoplight, by placing one end of a dowel stick in a pail of sand and placing the other end of the stick in a shoebox. Before attaching the shoe box to the dowel stick, cover the shoe box with black construction paper, cut out two red circles, two green circles and two yellow circles; place the red circle at the top of the box, place the yellow circle under the red circle and the green circle under the yellow circle. Place the shoe box on the end of the dowel stick, so that the red circle is on top. Set up an imaginary street with the stoplight and crosswalk made by attaching strips of masking tape to the floor.
2. Tell the child you are going to pretend to be the police officer who will help him cross a busy street, and tell him he must follow every direction you give.
3. Discuss with him who a police officer is, what an officer does, and how an officer helps people.
4. Tell him to pretend to play on the sidewalk on one side of the street.
5. Tell him that when the light turns green, he is to follow the police officer's directions to cross the street.
6. Say, "The light is green." Remind him to look both ways, stay inside the crosswalk, and walk rapidly across the street.
7. Be sure to reinforce him if he follows the police officer's directions.
8. Some suggestions for addressing specific behaviors are:

Behavior--Did not follow the directions, appeared inattentive.

Strategy--(1) Make sure that he is aware of who the person giving the directions is and why they are doing it. Example: Police--Keep you safe. Teacher--Helps you learn. Parents--Help you because they love you. TV personality--Helps you learn and have fun. (2) The activity should be something that he already has the skills to accomplish.

Behavior--Followed only part of the directions and then became distracted.

Strategy--(1) The directions should be presented to him in small units. When the directions are repeated, state them slowly, or ask the child to say the directions one at a time, or add a visual or tactile element to the verbal directions. (2) Remove any distractions prior to giving the directions. (3) Make sure the child has an idea of the beginning and the ending of the activity.

Behavior--Rushed into the activity before the person had completed the directions.

Strategy--(1) Provide short activities with brief, simple directions. (2) Help him do each direction, rewarding him upon completion of each direction.

Behavior--Once the child attends to the directions, he will not easily stop or transfer to the next direction.

Strategy--(1) Assist the child in the process of listening, waiting and responding. (2) Prepare him for another direction about to be stated.

5.132 Identifies dangerous situations/objects verbally or with gestures

Strand: 5-8 **Age:** 43-48m 3.7-4.0y

Definition

The child will identify dangerous situations such as sharp objects, hot appliances, toys on a stair-step, cleaning-fluid bottles, broken glass, medicine bottles. The child will either tell another that the identified object is dangerous, or she will point to the situation. She may or may not take action to remedy the dangerous situation.

/***Safety Note:** *This definition offers examples only; local program/family safety procedures should be reviewed to prepare a comprehensive list of dangerous situations/objects.*

Instructional Materials

Two sheets of large paper, markers, nontoxic glue. A collection of pictures that illustrate safe situations or safe objects. A collection of pictures that illustrate unsafe situations or unsafe objects. Examples: Matches burning, electric cord with wires exposed, a closed medicine bottle, a collection of pills on a low table, a toy in the walkway, toys in toy boxes, a sharp pointed object, a broken glass.

Instructional Activities

1. Place the two sheets of paper on a table, and on one sheet write the word "Safe," and on the other sheet write the word "Dangerous."
2. Invite the child to the table.
3. Explain to her that you are going to show her a picture and that she must decide if it shows a safe or dangerous situation.
4. If she says the picture is "safe," discuss with her why it is safe and glue the picture to the large sheet of paper labeled "Safe."
5. If she says the picture is "dangerous," discuss with her why it is dangerous, what she should do if she ever sees this problem, and glue the picture to the large sheet of paper labeled "Dangerous."
6. Continue with the other pictures.
7. After all the pictures have been categorized, point to and review why the objects or settings are safe or dangerous.

5.133   Cleans up spills independently

Strand: 5-6 **Age:** 44-52m 3.8-4.4y

Definition

When the child spills, he will clean it up using the proper material.

Instructional Materials

Props for the children to play restaurant. Example: table, chairs, dishes, menus, apron, silverware, plastic glasses, tray, towels, small tablet, pencil.

Instructional Activities

1. Set up the restaurant situation. Talk about going to a restaurant--what you do, what happens, what you can order, how you pay.
2. Allow the children to participate in the selection of the cast (customers, waiter or waitress, cashier, cook) to play restaurant.
3. Using the props, dress up the characters.
4. Set the stage by telling those who are customers to walk into the restaurant. Tell the waiter to show them where to sit and to give them a menu.
5. Encourage them to continue the scene without any prompting.

6. After they have become comfortable in playing restaurant, give them some suggestions for role-playing. For example, ask: "What will you do if they are out of what you order? What will you do if you spill water on the table? Show how you will use the napkins on the table to clean up a small water spill. What will you do if you break a dish? What will you do if you finish eating before others?"
7. You may easily modify this role-playing to a different food setting, such as a cafeteria, a fast food restaurant, a picnic, and home.

5.134   Tells name of city in address

Strand: 5-2 **Age:** 44-54m 3.8-4.6y

Definition

When the child is asked, "In what city do you live?" or "In what town do you live?", she will respond correctly. If she lives in a rural area, her response will probably be the town or city where she goes for shopping and services. When asking the question, say, "In what city or town do you live?" instead of, "What town or city is in your address?" If she responds by giving her name and complete address, accept this because she has probably learned by rote memory how to respond to a question about where she lives.

Instructional Materials

A map of the child's local town, usually available from the Chamber of Commerce office, tourist centers, auto rental agencies, bus route maps. Markers, a highlighting pen, stamps of buildings (if possible).

Instructional Activities

1. Spread out the city map on a large table. Ask the child to look at the map.
2. Discuss with her locations and landmarks on the map familiar to her.
3. Locate her home, and identify her house by stamping a picture of it on the map or by drawing a house at the location.
4. Identify possible routes from the child's house to the park (draw or stamp a tree) or to school (draw or stamp a school building) or any other familiar places.
5. Talk about other areas of the town or city, using the name of the city during the discussion.
6. Using the highlighting pen, trace a route that she might take to another part of the town, such as the zoo (stamp or draw an animal that

lives in the zoo), airport (stamp or draw an airplane), or lake (stamp or draw a boat).

7. Point to the child's house and ask her to identify what you are pointing at, ask her to tell you in which town or city her house is, and prompt as necessary.
8. Point to a place in her neighborhood (like her school) and ask her to identify what you are pointing at, ask her to tell you in what town or city the landmark is, and prompt as necessary.
9. Point to a place in the city, such as the airport, ask her to identify where you are pointing, and ask her to tell you in what town or city the landmark is; prompt as necessary.
10. Ask her to point to her house.
11. Ask her to tell you the name of the city where she lives.
12. If she is correct, say, "Yes, you live in [name of city]."
13. If she is incorrect, say, "No, you live in a city named [name of city]."
14. Ask her to point to [a neighborhood landmark].
15. Ask her to tell you the name of the city where she lives.
16. Follow the correct and correcting procedures as mentioned above.
17. Continue asking her questions about the locations identified on the map and ask her to name the city they are in.
18. Follow the correct and correcting procedures as mentioned above.
19. Ask her to point to part of the map that shows the whole city or town.
20. As the child is pointing to the entire area of the map, ask her the name of the city/town.

5.135 Plays with group of 3 or more children

Strand: 5-5 **Age:** 42-54m 3.6-4.6y

Definition

The child will participate in a group game with other children. The group activity may be played inside or outside, and the activity maybe active (ball or circle games) or passive (table games). At least three other children will be involved in the game/activity. The child may or may not follow all the rules.

Instructional Materials

An object to drop into another child's hand, such as a button, a walnut, a small stone.

Instructional Activities

1. Have the object ready to give to the child who is designated to be "It."
2. Ask the children to sit in a circle and to put a hand behind them, palm side up (demonstrate the position).
3. Select one child to be "It" and to stand on the outside of the circle.
4. Explain to the child who is "It" that she is to walk around the outside of the circle of children and that she is to pretend to be placing the button in each person's hand. She will need to choose a child, and really drop the button into their hand.
5. The child who receives the button must chase the child who is "It" around the circle and catch her before she reaches the chaser's place to sit.
6. If the chaser touches her before she gets back to the circle seat then she is "It" again.
7. If the child who is "It" gets back to the circle seat before she is tagged, then the chaser becomes "It."
8. During this activity, the following are suggested actions based on any occurring behaviors:

Behavior--She does not participate because of lack of understanding.
Strategy--(1) Review the rules with the child; (2) Role-play the game and walk her through the roles of being "It" and of being a circle player; (3) Allow the children to play the group game, and when the child who is not sure of the rules is either "It" or the chaser, assist her at that time; (4) If she seems comfortable, invite her to sit with you while the others play the game and verbally explain it as it is being played.
Behavior--She is stubborn, wanting to be "It" all the time, or she wants to have the button dropped in her hand each time the child who is "It" walks around the circle.
Strategy--(1) Remove her from the group game, and invite her to watch the action of the other children; (2) Verbally explain to her that when she wants to be either "It" or the chaser all the time, she makes the game difficult for everyone else; (3) Remove her, and involve her in another activity.
Behavior--She withdraws, refusing to participate by not running when she has the button or sitting down when she is "It."
Strategy--(1) Review the rules of the game to make sure she understand how to play the group game; (2) Remove her from the activity.

(3) Discuss with her how it is okay not to want to play sometimes, and also okay to be a watcher.

5.136   Shares toys with other children
Strand: 5-5   **Age:** 46-52m 3.10-4.4y

Definition
The child will share her toy or equipment with several other children when asked. She will also share her toy/equipment with others without being asked. When she has shared her toy or equipment she will establish ownership, limit sharing time, and display the ability to request the toy or equipment back.

Instructional Activities
See #5.112 for instructional materials and activities. This skill is almost identical to #5.112 except the child has to share with several other children.

5.137   Uses appropriate manners to request an object
Strand: 5-7   **Age:** 40-53m 3.4-4.5y

Definition
When the child is requesting an object or service, he will say "please" and word his request in a polite manner using acceptable language.

Instructional Materials
A list of directions the children eagerly perform. Examples: Go shake hands with Johnny. Gallop to the door, and gallop back to your chair. Get a cup, fill it with water, and give it to Mary. Go to the mirror and make a funny face. Put chalk on your nose and try to write on the chalkboard.

Instructional Activities
1. Invite the child to sit at the table.
2. Give the child a direction to follow such as: "Go shake hands with Johnny."
3. Explain he must say "Please, may I?" before he may get up from his seat.
4. Have him wait until you say "yes" or "no."
5. Have him remain seated if he does not say "please."
6. Reward him for completing the task.
7. Make sure every child has an opportunity to participate.
See #5.121.

5.138   Behaves according to desires of others
Strand: 5-4   **Age:** 48-60m 4.0-5.0y

Definition
The child will comply with an appropriate behavior when the desire of others is expressed. Examples: "Please be quiet," "Sit down," "Stand in line." She will comply with the accepted, implied behavior, in varied settings. Example: She is quiet when she is in a place where others are reading. She sits on a chair at a table when she is eating in a restaurant, or she stands in line when she is ordering food in a restaurant.

Instructional Materials
A large positive behavioral chart, made as follows. On one side of the chart put the child's name and make at least 10 squares behind her name. Decorate the corners of the chart with a sticker that represents something she likes (e.g., kittens, teddy bears, cars, dogs, flags, trains). Additional larger stickers or pictures to use as rewards.

Instructional Activities
1. Place the chart in full view of the child.
2. Tell the child that every time she does what she is asked to do, you will put (for example) a flag sticker in one of the squares behind her name. Tell her when she has earned a sticker in each of the 10 squares, she will get a special reward.
3. The reward should be something that the child enjoys and would work to receive. When you give it to her, make sure the presentation is accompanied with praise and a review of what she did to receive it.

5.139   Passes food/drink on request
Strand: 5-6   **Age:** 48-54m 4.0-4.6y

Definition
The child will pass food or drink, when requested. He will pass food without spilling.

Instructional Materials
Soap, water, towel, snacks, tray, napkin.

Instructional Activities
1. Place the tray with snacks and the napkins on the table.
2. Choose one child to be the host or hostess.
3. Have the host wash his hands with soap and water.

4. Review the host's serving and cleanup duties.
5. Give him the napkins and the snack tray.
6. Instruct him to pass the napkins to the children.
7. Direct him to pass the snack tray to them.
8. Suggest appropriate remarks he should make, such as, "Would you like to try a carrot stick?"
9. Make an effort to have him do the cleanup.
10. Rotate host responsibilities daily at snack time.
11. Reward each host with special a hat or button he may wear the remainder of day.

5.140 Performs assigned task

Strand: 5-4 **Age:** 48-55m 4.0-4.7y

Definition

When the child is presented with a task to do, she will perform the assignment to the best of her ability. She will perform the task by following directions, asking questions, requesting assistance if needed, accepting help when provided, and persisting in accomplishing the task.

Instructional Materials

A prepared list of tasks that are needed in the particular setting. Examples: (1) Put the games away; (2) Water the plants; (3) Pick up the books; (4) Sort the crayons; (5) Wipe off the tables; (6) Stack the mats.
A large sheet of paper to use as a chart, markers, and a large reward sticker.

Instructional Activities

1. On the chart paper, write the title, "Helping Hands," and then write the list of tasks that are needed. Behind each item on the list, draw a series of empty boxes.
2. Tell the children you are looking for some helping hands. Explain what it means to be a helping hand.
3. Show the chart and read the list of jobs.
4. Ask who wants to do one of the jobs.
5. Allow the child time to accomplish her selected task.
6. After she completes her task, place a sticker on the chart.
7. Prepare a daily checklist containing the child's name, the job, and a reward box.
8. Allow the child to change jobs as her motivation diminishes.
9. It is important not to put the child's name behind the selected job on the chart. Visible

comparison of job completion can be defeating and create a negative response.

5.141 Returns objects or materials to their assigned/appropriate place

Strand: 5-4 **Age:** 48-55m 4.0-4.7y

Definition

When he is asked, the child will return objects or materials to their assigned places without any verbal prompting or physical assistance.

Instructional Materials

/*\Safety Note: Provide scissors appropriate for the child. Remind the child of safety regarding scissors.
Colored poster board, scissors, a positive comment stamp (e.g., "You did it!" "Terrific!" "Good Work!" "Super!"). Small reward.

Instructional Activities

1. Cut the poster board into coupon shapes and stamp a positive comment on one side of the coupon and on the other side write the words "Super Borrower."
2. Determine what the child finds rewarding enough to work for.
3. Discuss the meaning of borrow, pointing out that borrowed items belong to someone else and that they must be taken care of, as well as returned.
4. Tell the child that each time he borrows something, uses it, and then puts it in its proper place he will receive a "Super Borrower" coupon.
5. Tell him that his Borrower coupons may be traded in for a predetermined reward.

5.142 Quiets down after active period and waits for instructions

Strand: 5-4 **Age:** 48-60m 4.0-5.0y

Definition

After active play, the child will sit down, remain seated, stop talking loudly, refrain from physical play, keep her hands and feet to herself, and present herself in a relaxed manner. She will remain quiet, waiting for further instructions.

Instructional Materials

A soothing, relaxing musical selection by a composer such as Bach or Beethoven. Equipment to play music.

Instructional Activities

1. Prepare the musical selection so it is ready to play.
2. Ask the children to go to their seats after playtime.
3. Speak in a whisper or a soothing tone.
4. Reinforce the children who follow the directions and go to their seats.
5. Ask each child to inhale deeply, fully expanding his chest, to exhale and drop the trunk of his body forward at the waist.
6. Have each child make his chin touch his chest with his arms dangling between his knees.
7. Reinforce by saying, "Now our room is a toy store full of rag dolls."
8. Play the music.
9. Walk around and lift arms to check each child's limpness or relaxation.
10. Repeat several times.
11. Discuss how each child can use this relaxation method when he is excited, angry, or tired from sitting.

See #5.127.

5.143 Verbalizes feelings to another prior to physical expression

Strand: 5-5 **Age:** 48-60m 4.0-5.0y

Definition

The child controls his temper by verbalizing his feelings rather than exhibiting behaviors such as aggression, tantrums, or withdrawal. He will find less reason to exhibit anger, frustration, or aggressive behaviors, because expressing himself with words more effectively communicates his feelings and needs.

Instructional Materials

A prepared notebook with a colorful cover for each child. Write the words All About Me on the front cover. A snapshot of the child brought from home and glued on the front of the notebook.

Instructional Activities

1. Give the notebook to the child.
2. Tell the child at end of day to think of something that happened to him during day that made him feel angry or sad. Have him make a special separate list of those things that made him proud or happy and record them in the notebook too.
3. On the first page of his book write down what made him feel angry or sad.
4. Ask him to think about how he reacted.

5. Discuss his reaction, and determine if it was the best action to take.
6. Write his reaction on the first page.
7. If his actions were inappropriate, discuss what else could have been done, and write an appropriate action in his book.
8. Repeat this procedure each day for a period of time (a week, a month).
9. Review the book with the child, focusing on his feelings and his reactions, and what he has learned about how expressing his feelings helped modulate his reactions. Also discuss the happy/proud events that he recorded.

5.144 Asks for assistance when needed

Strand: 5-5 **Age:** 48-56m 4.0-4.8y

Definition

The child will ask for assistance from another person when she needs help. The child can request the assistance of an adult or another child. When she asks for assistance, she will use courteous language.

Instructional Materials

A stick (tongue depressor, ruler, or dowel) and two cardboard circles at least 5 inches in diameter for each child. A marker, stapler, tape.

Instructional Activities

1. Staple the cardboard circles to each other, leaving a hole for inserting the stick. On each side of the circle write the word HELP. Attach the stick to the circles to be used as a handle.
2. Show the child the Help sign, and make sure she understands the meaning of the word "help."
3. Give her the sign and explain to her that she is to use it whenever she needs help.
4. Assure her that when she raises the sign requesting help, someone will be there to assist.
5. Set up a situation, and role-play using the sign and asking for help.
6. If the child uses her Help sign when she does not really need it, overuses it, uses it as an attention seeking device, or plays with it, explain to her that she may only use her Help sign [set number] times. Record each time she requests help and alert her when she has only a few left. It is important to assist her to evaluate when she really needs help and to make sure she receives positive attention. Make sure she makes an effort to reduce the number of requests for assistance.

5.145 Obeys rules

Strand: 5-5 **Age:** 48-60m 4.0-5.0y

Definition

The child will participate in a group activity with other children and he will follow the rules. The group activity may be played inside or outside and the activity may be active (ball or circle games) or passive (table games). The rules of the game will be clearly defined prior to any action.

Instructional Activities

See #5.135 for instructional materials and activities.

5.146 (Removed, see page xii)

5.147 Requests food/drink be passed at the table

Strand: 5-6 **Age:** 48-60m 4.0-5.0y

Definition

The child will ask for food or drink that is out of reach to be passed to him.

Instructional Materials

/*\Safety Note: Be aware of special diets and allergies before doing these activities.
Snacks such as cookies and milk. Dishes.

Instructional Activities

1. Place a plate of cookies, pitcher of milk, and cups on a table next to you.
2. Select four children who have mastered the table manner of requesting food and drink to be passed.
3. Seat five children at the table.
4. Tell the children they may have milk and cookies if they request them by saying, "Please pass the cookies," and "Please pass the milk."
5. Let the child who requests the milk and cookies appropriately have some milk and cookies.
6. Ignore the child who does not request the milk or cookies.
7. Refuse service to the child who tries to grab food or drink.
8. Prompt any child who needs assistance to say "Please pass the cookies" and "Please pass the milk."
9. Put the snack away after a short time.
See #5.139.

5.148 (Removed, see page xii)

5.149 Participates in conversation/discussion

Strand: 5-7 **Age:** 48-60m 4.0-5.0y

Definition

The child will participate in a discussion, both as a listener and as a contributor. He will contribute to the discussion in a polite and constructive manner.

Instructional Materials

Drawing paper, markers, crayons or paints, several pictures of flowers (seed catalogs are an excellent source for pictures). A collection of different artificial or real flowers.

Instructional Activities

1. Place the drawing materials on the table. Invite the child to the art table, and distribute the drawing material.
2. Show the child the pictures of the flowers, and discuss the color, shapes of the leaves and stems. Make a point of telling him that each flower is different.
3. Remove the pictures of the flowers.
4. After this discussion, tell each child to use the drawing paper, markers/crayons, and other materials to draw a picture of a flower.
5. Display the completed pictures on the bulletin board.
6. Ask each child to stand by his picture and tell about it. Prompt him if necessary.
7. After he describes his flower, ask him to give his flower a name and tell why he thinks his flower is special.
8. Allow each child to have a turn to discuss his drawing, name it, and tell about it.
9. Invite the children to join you in the communication, or circle time, area.
10. Tell them that you have some beautiful flowers to talk about, but that first you must explain some important things to remember about group discussions: (1) Only one person may talk at a time; (2) Listen to others when they are talking; (3) Stay on the subject; (4) A group discussion is not the time to be a show-off; (5) Everyone who contributes is important and special. Invite the child to share ideas on how to participate in a discussion.
11. Show the group the flowers (artificial or real), and begin the discussion by identifying the different kinds of flowers, the difference

in the petals, the shape and color of the flowers, and so on.

12. Encourage the children to add to the discussion.

13. Give each child a different flower and ask each one to tell the group about his flower.

14. Encourage all children to participate, and address inappropriate behavior by techniques such as ignoring attention-seeking children, using "I" messages, moving a child and physically placing him closer to an adult, and rewarding good participation.

5.150   Keeps safe distance from matches, stove, and open flame

Strand: 5-8   **Age:** 48-60m 4.0-5.0y

Definition

When the child is shown fire hazards, such as matches, a hot burner, or an open flame and candles, she will demonstrate her understanding of the danger of fire and hot items. She may exhibit this understanding by keeping a safe distance, going for help, calling an emergency telephone number, or by following procedures for a fire drill.

Instructional Activities

Most local fire departments provide fire safety instruction to educational programs. If your local fire department does not provide this service, they may be able to suggest other sources for teaching children fire safety.

5.151   Comforts playmates in distress

Strand: 5-5   **Age:** 48-60m 4.0-5.0y

Definition

The child will comfort a peer who is in distress, either physically or emotionally. He will show his caring by either a gesture or verbal comments.

Instructional Materials

A sign that reads: <u>Feeling Time</u>.

Instructional Activities

1. Place the <u>Feeling Time</u> sign in a comfortable area in the environment (area with pillows on the floor, a soft rug, comfortable chairs, room enough to hold a stuffed animal).

2. Invite the group to <u>Feeling Time</u>, a time for sharing feelings about things that have happened that day at school or at home earlier, on the playground, or with a friend.

3. Model by sharing some of your feelings.

4. Ask if anyone had any feelings (that day, at school, on the playground, with a friend) that he would like to share.

5. Prompt if necessary, asking questions such as, "What was the happiest feeling you had today?" "Did you want to yell and stamp your feet today?" "Did you feel sorry for anyone today?"

6. Allow them to remain silent if they choose.

7. Praise and encourage children who want to talk about their feelings.

8. Give a brief interpretation of feelings as they are shared, saying, for example: "You felt like... ," "I felt that way when... ," or "You almost cried when you felt sad."

9. Seek group support for the child who is upset by having other children share similar experiences or by asking, "What can we do to make Casey feel better?"

10. Assure them that although feelings may be upsetting or disturbing, having these feelings is okay and talking about them often helps.

5.152   Uses basic playground equipment safely

Strand: 5-8   **Age:** 48-60m 4.0-5.0y

Definition

The child will demonstrate using playground equipment safely, not only for herself, but without endangering others. The playground equipment involved should be the basic items available to most children on a playground.

Instructional Materials

/*\Safety Note: Provide scissors appropriate for the child. Remind the child of safety regarding scissors.

Material to make a chest banner (one that fits diagonally from the child's shoulder to waist), wide ribbon, markers, words written with gold letters, nontoxic glue, pins, scissors.

Instructional Activities

1. Using a marker or ornate letters write: Slide Safety Specialist, Swing Safety Specialist, or Bar Safety Specialist on the wide ribbon.

2. Select a child to become the Slide Safety Specialist.

3. Explain to her that she is going to be the Slide Safety Specialist.

4. Tell her that to become this special person, she must know all the safe things to do on a slide.

5. After she has discovered all the safe things to do, she must tell others how to be safe on the slide.
6. After the child learns the safety issues and is prepared to tell others, place the ribbon diagonally across her chest and attach.
7. Invite all the other children to gather around the slide to hear the Slide Specialist's presentation.
8. Continue the above specialist's role with all the other playground equipment.

5.153 Avoids or maintains distance from dangerous situations/objects
Strand: 5-8 **Age:** 49-54m 4.1-4.6y

Definition
When the child encounters a dangerous situation or object, he will avoid or immediately move away from the setting or item. He will also report the situation to a responsible adult. He will also point out dangers that confront others.

Instructional Materials
Small posters depicting dangerous situations, masking tape, sheet of red construction paper.

Instructional Activities
1. Tape two straight lines on the floor, one to be used as the starting line and the other the finish line.
2. Discuss each situation on the posters.
3. Instruct the children to take a position on the starting line facing you and closest to the posters.
4. Hold up one of the danger posters and have all the children walk backwards away from poster toward the finish line.
5. Hold up a red sheet of paper to indicate "Stop!"
6. Continue until each child has walked backwards to the finish line.
See #5.132.

5.154 Remains calm in changing/disappointing situation
Strand: 5-1 **Age:** 49-55m 4.1-4.7y

Definition
The child will accept a situation that is disappointing or has caused a change. When the situation changes due to circumstances beyond her control (e.g., because of rain, the trip to the park was canceled), and the child is told the reason, she will remain calm,

accept that the situation will be altered or modified, and display adaptive behaviors.

Instructional Materials
/***Safety Note:** Be extremely careful when the child is around heat. Do not let her handle hot pans or cookware.
If the planned changes require additional materials (storybook, food treat, musical selection), make sure the materials are available.

Instructional Activities
Note: Present this as a game with an exaggerated emphasis on the element of surprise.
1. Tell the child that something unusual and exciting may happen sometime during the day.
2. As the child is involved in a task, interrupt her gently and tell her it is time for a treat.
3. Tell her to enjoy the treat.
4. Encourage her to return to her task, help her assess where she left off, and discuss the next step.
5. Later, interrupt her again by giving her an item that is related to what she is doing. For example, if she is coloring a picture, give her at least two more different colored markers or crayons.
6. Conduct the interruptions, changes, and any disappointments in the spirit of fun and with humor.
7. See #5.111 for some suggestions for addressing specific behaviors.

5.155 Volunteers for tasks
Strand: 5-4 **Age:** 49-56m 4.1-4.8y

Definition
When the child is presented with "Who wants to (do a specific task)?", he will volunteer, or when he presented with a new activity, he will want to do it. When he is presented with a group of activities, he will volunteer to perform at least one of them, and will exhibit behaviors that adapt to the new task.

Instructional Materials
Several tasks that need doing in the setting-- housekeeping or helping tasks. Select easy tasks at first, such as passing out papers, collecting the crayons, putting the storybooks away.

Instructional Activities
1. Ask the child to listen carefully.
2. Tell the children that you have a task that needs to be done.

3. For example, tell them you need a volunteer to collect the crayons.
4. Ask for a volunteer.
5. Praise the child who volunteers and ask the rest of the children to clap for him.
6. Reward the volunteer with a special treat or activity when he completes the task.
7. Repeat with the next needed task.
8. Gradually increase the difficulty of the tasks, making sure the children are aware that assistance is available.

See #5.120.

5.156 Cooperates with request for quiet
Strand: 5-4 **Age:** 49-58m 4.1-4.10y

Definition
When the child is requested to be quiet, she will become quiet. "Quiet" is defined as sitting still, waiting to talk, or using a quiet voice (whisper), refraining from tapping, pounding, or thumping, and keeping her hands and feet to herself. The request to be quiet is made verbally or with a predetermined visual or auditory signal.

Instructional Materials
/*\Safety Note: Provide scissors appropriate for the child. Remind the child of safety regarding scissors.
Some pieces of felt, markers, beans, pieces of yarn, scissors.

Instructional Activities
1. Using the material, make a bean bag in the shape of a mouse's head.
2. Tell the child that when she is quiet and working hard, Mr. Mouse will visit her.
3. Tell her she may keep Mr. Mouse to remind her that she is "as quiet as a mouse."
4. Explain that Mr. Mouse will go back to his home when she no longer needs to be quiet.
5. When the child needs to be quiet, bring out Mr. Mouse.

5.157 Conforms to group decisions
Strand: 5-4 **Age:** 49-58m 4.1-4.10y

Definition
In a group of at least three children, all the group members, except for the child, decide that something should be done a certain way. The one child may initially protest the decision, but he does what the other group members do (as long as it does not conflict with health/safety rules he has been taught).

Instructional Materials
Two storybooks new to the children.

Instructional Activities
1. Invite the children to join you in the storytelling area. Tell the children you have two new storybooks to read to them, but there is time for only one.
2. Tell them a brief synopsis of the two stories.
3. Tell them they must vote for the story they want to hear the most.
4. Hold up each book and have them vote.
5. Before you read the chosen story, explain that all the children should listen and try to enjoy the story, even if it was not their choice.
6. The following are some typical child behaviors:
Behavior--The child is unreasonable and unfair. He wants one story, will not participate in voting, will not vote, and will not listen to the story decided on.
Strategy--(1) Make sure he understands the concept of others' rights and the majority rule. (2) Model being fair and just. Be careful to show no favoritism, be impartial when you settle disputes, never penalize a whole group for a fault when only one child is responsible. Expect the child to interact with the group fairly. (3) Invite him to go to a designated "I Wonder" chair during story time. Tell him the "I Wonder" chair is a spot where he can wonder about how he should have acted. Remind the others that the child in the "I Wonder" chair may not be disturbed. When you tell a child to go to the chair, simply say, "Jason, please go sit in the 'I Wonder' Chair." Assist him to the chair, if necessary. (4) Ask him a direct question. For example, say, "Nelson, we only have time for one story; how do you think we should pick one?"
Behavior-- He socially withdraws from others. He actively avoids any group involvement
Strategy--(1) Help him learn to accept feelings of anger, fear, and embarrassment by acknowledging that these feelings are natural and okay; (2) Provide him with many opportunities to have a positive experience with groups; (3) Model accepting behavior, being cheerful and being a good sport allow him to view good behavior. Display a willingness to follow a majority rule and to get along with the group standards; (4) Reward any interaction that he does exhibit; (5) Teach social skills such as: (a) how to give and receive positive interaction, (b) how to

make friends by offering to include the person in an activity, being interested in what the other person is saying, and offering help and assistance, (c) how to have effective communication skills, both in talking to others and listening to them.

Behavior--He is directive and bossy. He gives instructions to the group about which book to choose, how to vote, what they are going to do, and how they are going to do it.

Strategy--(1) Make sure the child understands the concept of voting. Instead of calling for a show of hands for the voting, give each child two small sheets of different colored paper (e.g., red and blue). Place a red sheet on one book and a blue sheet on the other book. Hold up the book with the red sheet of paper, and tell the children that if they want to choose that book, they must put a red sheet of paper into the voting box when it is passed to them. Repeat the instructions for voting for the book with the blue sheet. Or lay the two books on the table, give each child a token (e.g., paper clip, small rock, chip) and ask him to place it on the book he wants to hear. Making a more secret ballot or a voting process that the children view as fun often helps clarify what is happening and why; (2) Tell him he must listen until the timer goes off (set the timer, determining the number of minutes according to his behavior), and then explain to him that he may only talk until the timer goes off (set the timer, determining the number of minutes according to his active behavior); (3) He often becomes overly bossy because he is not sure how to act in the group decision-making process. Create an atmosphere for cooperation through encouragement. Once the child feels he is understood he may be more inclined to listen and to make an effort to reach a solution to a problem.

7. Much of the inappropriate behavior that occurs in a group settings are due to the children's lack of ability and opportunities to learn to operate in this setting. Working with a group to make decisions and plans is much different than playing a game, throwing a ball to a friend, or looking at a book.

5.158 Treats other's property with respect
Strand: 5-4 **Age:** 49-58m 4.1-4.10y
Definition
When she handles property that belongs to someone else, the child will take proper care of it so that it is not damaged, destroyed, or unusable. She will treat property that belongs to others as if it were her own.

Instructional Materials
A large sheet of poster board, a marker.

Instructional Activities
1. In a designated area, arrange a table, a chair, and some shelves. Make a sign on the poster board that reads Toys On Loan.
2. Ask each child to bring a toy from home that she would be willing to share with her classmates.
3. Have each child share her toy and then place it on a shelf in the Toys on Loan area.
4. Record her name and the toy in order to return it to the proper owner.
5. Tell the children that during free time or another designated time they will each be allowed to go and check out a toy.
6. Explain to them that when they check out a toy they must treat it as if it were their own.
7. Talk about being responsible and how to take care of things that belong to someone else.
8. Tell them that when the toy is returned, you will check it for cleanliness, dents, scrapes, or broken parts.
9. As the child's responsible behavior improves, vary the toys in the Toys on Loan area, moving from large unbreakable things to smaller delicate items.

5.159 Sits in seat, stands in a line without excess moving during an activity
Strand: 5-4 **Age:** 49-60m 4.1-5.0y
Definition
The child will sit in a seat or stand in a line without excessive moving or fidgeting when he is observing or participating in an activity. The time he sits or stands without moving excessively will be determined by his entry behavior, the amount of time the activity takes, the group participating, the child's interest in the activity, his background information and skill level relative to the activity. Excessive moving and fidgeting behaviors are viewed as: (1) getting out of his seat, (2) standing on the seat, (3)

sitting on the floor, (4) poking, hitting and kicking, (5) interfering with the activity by swinging or swaying arms, (6) stamping feet, (7) overtly grabbing or hugging other participants, (8) tipping over in the chair, (9) rolling on the floor, (10) any excessive motions that interfere with the activity or with the others involved.

Instructional Activities

See #5.130 for instructional materials and activities.

5.160   Tells or gestures to adult about any danger/injury

Strand: 5-8   **Age:** 49-60m 4.1-5.0y

Definition

When the child witnesses another person involved in a dangerous setting or injured in some way, she will quickly report the incident to an appropriate person, or she will motion to someone to indicate that assistance is needed.

Instructional Materials

A police officer hat and badge. Dress-up props (hats, jackets, etc.) Material to make safety badges or buttons.

Instructional Activities

1. Using the materials, make a safety badge for each child.
2. Pick three children to act out a scene about someone being lost or injured.
3. Assign one child to be the police offer. Provide them with the police officer hat and badge.
4. Assign another child to be the person who is lost or injured. Let them dress-up as they wish.
5. Assign the third child to be the person who finds the lost or injured child. Let them wear dress-up clothing too.
6. Have them act out the following scene. Someone is walking when they hear a child yelling for help. They find a child who is injured. Just then, a police officer comes by. The person who discovered the injured child calls out to the police officer to come and help. The police officer comes and helps the injured child.
7. Propose other scenarios by asking questions like: What would happen if there were no police officers around? Who would they call for help? What would they do if they saw a child who was lost and crying for their

parents? What would they do if a stranger offered them candy if they would go with them? What if a stranger asked you to help them find a lost dog or cat?
8. Help the child act out these scenarios.
9. Give a safety badge to the child if she knows what she should do in any of these situations.
10. Switch roles and repeat.

See #5.132.

5.161   Performs activities in presence of or when led by new person

Strand: 5-1   **Age:** 50-55m 4.2-4.7y

Definition

The child will demonstrate confidence and will perform an activity in front of or in conjunction with a new person. He will adapt his actions and behaviors when he is involved with the new person. A new person may be defined either as an observer or as a participant in the environment.

Instructional Materials

A new person to invite to the class.

Instructional Activities

Note: Stress the importance of having nothing to do with strangers in certain situations. Make sure that the child understands the difference between meeting new people in a controlled or planned situation and contact with strangers. If the child seems confused or has any questions in telling difference between the two types of contacts, place the emphasis on how he is to react when a stranger approaches him.

1. Invite the new person to the class, and ask him to prepare a new activity for the child.
2. Ask the child to perform a familiar task for the visitor.
3. Involve the new person in the child's performance.
4. Tell the child that the visitor will show him a new activity.
5. Excuse yourself from the group.
6. Return to the group after the visitor has shown him a new activity.
7. Discuss the activity with the child, making sure he has an opportunity to explain what the visitor did and how he was involved.
8. Continue to expose the child to the visitor, and gradually involve him and the visitor in activities.
9. Some suggestions for addressing specific behaviors are:

Behavior--He became shy, self-conscious and preferred not to be the center of attention in front of the new person.

Strategy--(1) Ignore the reaction; (2) Involve him in a joint activity with other children, the new person, and others in the setting; (3) Provide him with a signal (a sign to hold up, a special word to say, or a hand signal) to use when he is ready to participate or perform; (4) Ask him to do a task for the new person, such as to bring the person something, show the person around, or give the person a message.

Behavior--Acts out and shows off.

Strategy--(1) Thank the child for his performance (interrupt, if necessary), and suggest that he go to a cooling down area; (2) Tell him firmly to stop the behavior. Remember to deal with his behavior, never with the child's personality. (3) Involve him in a totally different activity.

Behavior-- He needed support and help to do the known presentation.

Strategy--(1) Reinforce him and provide the requested assistance; (2) Give him a chance to review and rehearse his performance; (3) Provide props and other cues to enable him to do his performance.

Behavior-- He demonstrated maturity by "reading" his environment and the new person before he performs.

Strategy--(1) Reinforce him for evaluating the situation before reacting. (2) Assist him in his evaluation process by introducing him to the new person, asking him when he is ready to respond, using statements that generate high probability behavior (for example, "Alex is very good at singing *The Eensy, Weensy Spider*, and he does it with actions.")

5.162 Uses napkin to wipe hands, mouth during and after meal

Strand: 5-6 **Age:** 50-57m 4.2-4.9y

Definition

The child will use a napkin to wipe her hands and mouth during and after the meal. She may need to be reminded.

Instructional Materials

Construction paper (at least 12 inches by 18 inches) in various colors, markers, grid paper, stickers, small rewards. (The squares on the grid paper must be large enough for a sticker to fit.)

Instructional Activities

1. Place the colored construction paper, markers, and the grid paper on a table. Explain to the child that she is to take a sheet of construction paper and decorate it any way she chooses because it will be her placemat.
2. After she completes her placemat, place the grid sheet on the side of her placemat.
3. Tell her that wiping her hands and mouth with a napkin will earn her a sticker on the grid paper.
4. Observe her eating during lunchtime.
5. Place a sticker in a box on the child's grid each time she uses her napkin appropriately.
6. Count the stickers earned daily or weekly for each child. Remember that many children cannot wait a week to earn a reward; therefore, the reinforcement should come as often as necessary.
7. Designate a "Special Award Time."
8. Let the child who earned the most stickers sit at the head of the table at the special time.
9. Decorate the head of table with a special placemat, bouquet of flowers, or a special napkin.
10. Vary the activity by working on different table manners.

5.163 Bargains with other children

Strand: 5-5 **Age:** 50-66m 4.2-5.6y

Definition

The child will exchange items after a discussion of the exchange. Example: "If you let me swing, you may ride my bike." The agreement may include the following elements: (1) Items to be exchanged or activities to exchange, (2) Criteria involved (time, location, person).

Instructional Materials

Some tangible items such as toys, school supplies, treats, snacks.

Instructional Activities

1. Place the items in a container, and allow each child to draw an item from the container.
2. Tell the child he must decide whether he wants to keep the item he draws or trade or bargain with another child for the item he drew.
3. If he decides to make a trade, he must find a child who has an item he wants and attempt to negotiate a bargain.
4. Tell him to trade or bargain for the item he wants.

5. Provide suggestions to get them started.
6. Replace the tangible items with non-tangible ones, such as games to play or activities to do together.
7. Repeat the procedure.

See #5.112, #5.136.

5.164 Tells month of birth

Strand: 5-2 **Age:** 48-58m 4.0-4.10y

Definition

When the child is asked, she will tell the month of her birthday. Some prompting may be necessary. Examples: "Halloween is in the same month," "Remember, it is in the same month when we build snowmen," or "January, February ..." (pause to allow her to say March.)

Instructional Materials

Check of the records to locate the child's birthday.

Instructional Activities

1. Ask the child to join you and be ready to play the Birthday Game.
2. Explain to the child that you will ask her to stand and tell her birthday.
3. Tell her to listen and say, "Apples, Pears, Peaches, Plums, tell me when your birthday comes!"
4. Pause to allow her to say her birthday.
5. Tell her the date of her birthday if she is incorrect.
6. Repeat the rhyme and allow her to state her birthday.
7. If more than one child is involved, say the name of one of the children, or point to one of them and say the rhyme.

5.165 Tells street name and town in address

Strand: 5-2 **Age:** 48-66m 4.0-5.6y

Definition

When the child is presented with the question, "In what city do you live?" or "In what town do you live?" he will respond correctly. If he lives in a rural area, his response will probably be the town or city where he goes for shopping and services. When you asking the question, it is important to ask, "In what city or town do you live?" instead of "In what town or city is your address?" When he is presented with the verbal question, "On what street do you live?" he will respond correctly. After he has named the street and city or town where he lives ask, "On what street and in what city/town do you live?" If he responds by stating his name and complete address, accept this because he has probably learned to respond to a question about where he lives by rote memory.

Instructional Materials

/*\Safety Note: Provide scissors appropriate for the child. Remind the child of safety regarding scissors.

Several sheets of 8-by 10-inch construction paper, scissors, nontoxic glue, pencil, markers, crayons.

Instructional Activities

1. Using a sheet of construction paper, cut out a typical street sign. Place the paper and drawing materials on a work area.
2. Instruct the child to draw a picture of his house on a sheet of construction paper.
3. Display the completed picture on a bulletin board.
4. Explain that every house is on a street and that the street has a name.
5. Glue the pre-cut street sign near the picture of the child's house.
6. Discuss the street sign, making sure that he can associate the paper sign with the one on his street.
7. Ask him on what street he lives, and write the name of it as he responds. If he does not know the name of his street, tell him its name as you write it on the street sign.
8. Continue by explaining that many streets make up a city and that the city has a name.
9. Ask him in what city that he lives.
10. Tell him the name of his street and the name of the city where he lives is part of his address.
11. Discuss with him why we have addresses.
12. Say, for example, "The name of your street is [Elm], and the name of the city you live in is [Baltimore]."
13. Ask him, "What is the name of the street where you live?"
14. Ask him, "What is the name of the city where you live?"
15. Let him add things to his picture.

See #5.134.

5.166 (Removed, see page xii)

5.167 Uses appropriate pitch/volume when speaking

Strand: 5-7 **Age:** 48-60m 4.0-5.0y

Definition

When he is speaking, the child will use appropriate intonation, inflection, and volume. He may increase or decrease voice pitch to emphasize a part of a verbal description, or he may increase or decrease the volume to be heard or for effect.

Instructional Materials

A folk tale or a fairy story that has different characters and that gives an opportunity for verbal expression. Adapt the selected folk tale or fair story into a dramatization. This dramatization may be for actors or puppets.
Example: *The Lion and The Mouse* by Aseop.
Characters needed: a lion, a mouse, a dog, a cat.
Lion: "Roar!" (loud and fierce)
Mouse: "Squeak." (tiny and weak)
Lion: (after catching the mouse) "I will eat you." (gruffly)
Mouse: "Please do not eat me, and someday you will be glad." (tiny and weakly)
Lion: "Ha, Ha!" (loud laugh) "Okay, little mouse, go on your way."
Lion: (walks along and is caught in a net) "Help, Help!!" (scared, mad)
Dog: "Hello, lion. I will help you." (he tries to pull the net loose with his teeth) "Growl, growl. I am sorry. I cannot help you."
Lion: "Help, Help!!" (scared, mad)
Cat: "Hello lion. I will help you." (he tries to pull the net loose with sharp claws) "Meow, meow. I am sorry. I cannot help you."
Lion: "Help, Help!!" (weakly) "Sob, sob." (crying)
Mouse: "Hello lion. Remember me? I will help you." (mouse begins to gnaw the rope until soon the lion is free).
Lion: "I am free. I am free!" (happily) "Thank you. Thank you!"
Mouse: "We will always be friends."
Props necessary if the production is to be dramatized. If the production is to be a puppet theater, secure the necessary puppets, backdrops.

Instructional Activities

1. Set up the stage for the production.
2. Tell the fairy story or the folk tale to the child, being sure to use inflections in the dialogue.
3. Repeat the fairy tale or folk story and discuss.
4. Repeat once more, encouraging the child to join in the dialogue.

5. Explain to him that you are going to act out this story. Assign roles, giving the role of the lion to the child who needs to increase intensity, the role of the mouse to the child who needs to modify pitch, etc.
6. Provide the different characters with the necessary props.
7. Begin the production by giving an introduction: (1) Give the title of the story; (2) Introduce each character and ask them to speak. For example, say, "Here is Mr. Lion." (lion roars); (3) Set the stage by saying, " One day Mr. Lion was walking in the woods and saw a mouse. The mouse would be a good bite."
8. Begin the production by cueing as follows:
Say, "The lion roared."
Pause for the lion to roar.
Say, "The little mouse squeaked."
Pause for the mouse to squeak.
Say, "The lion catches the mouse and says, 'I will eat you.'"
Pause for the lion to say, "I will eat you."
9. Continue the dialogue as described above.
10. At the conclusion of the production, allow different children to be different characters.

5.168 Stays on topic during a conversation

Strand: 5-7 **Age:** 53-60m 4.5-5.0y

Definition

The child will participate in a topic or discussion, using appropriate vocabulary, allowing others to contribute, and maintaining the topic for a reasonable length of time or until closure.

Instructional Materials

/*\Safety Note: Provide scissors appropriate for the child. Remind the child of safety regarding scissors.
A Styrofoam ball, a dowel stick, aluminum foil, child-safe scissors.

Instructional Activities

1. Make a microphone by covering the Styrofoam ball with aluminum foil and placing the ball on the end of the dowel stick. Use the scissors in a closed position in a twisting motion to make a hole in the ball.
2. Select a topic, such as toys, pets, trips, family, or friends, and give the microphone to one child.
3. Ask her to talk to the group about the selected topic.

4. Explain to her that she may ask the other children questions about her topic, and the other children may ask her questions.
5. Make sure the speaker understands that she is to stay on topic and that she is to encourage the others to stay on topic.
6. Ask her to turn the microphone over to another child, and select a new topic.
7. Make sure that each child has an opportunity to be the speaker.

5.169 Tells father's and mother's first and last names

Strand: 5-2 **Age:** 54-62m 4.6-5.2y

Definition

When the child is asked, "What is your father's first and last name?" he will be able to respond. When he is asked, "What is your mother's first and last name?" he will be able to respond. The person who asks the questions will be aware of the proper names used by the child's parents and of his family situation (e.g., single-parent family), and will respond accordingly. Any discussion about the use of different names, acceptable nicknames, names of endearment, and names of identification (Daddy Paul) will be avoided.

Instructional Materials

/*\Safety Note: Provide scissors appropriate for the child. Remind the child of safety regarding scissors.
Empty paper towel roll tubes, construction paper in different colors, nontoxic glue or paste and scissors.

Instructional Activities

1. Cut several circles from the construction paper.
2. Explain to the child that he is going to make a family tree.
3. Talk about the names of the members of the child's family.
4. Write the names of his father and his mother on each of two circles.
5. Read the names out loud, and ask the child to tell you if the names are correct.
6. Give him the circles with his parent's names, and ask him to draw the family member's face on the circle.
7. Glue the circles vertically on the paper towel roll tube to make it a family tree.
8. Tell him to say the name of each person as he glues the picture onto paper roll tube.

9. Repeat the procedure by writing the names of his brothers and sisters on the other circles and let the child complete his family tree.

5.170 Recites emergency telephone number (911) and when to use it

Strand: 5-8 **Age:** 54-66m 4.6-5.6y

Definition

/*\Safety Note: *Check the emergency number or numbers used in your area.*
When asked, the child will state the universal emergency telephone number (911) and will demonstrate an understanding of when to use the number. She will understand the number is not to be used falsely.

Instructional Materials

A toy telephone or a non-working telephone. At least six scenarios of which three are emergencies and three are not. Examples: (1) Two children are playing, when suddenly one of them collapses and does not move or talk; (2) Two children are playing, and they begin to argue about what game to play. One pushes the other one, and she falls down; (3) A masked man is breaking into the door of a house where three children are playing; (4) A child opens the back door of a house and sees the garage on fire; (5) One child accidentally opened the door of a birdcage and a bird is flying about the room; (6) Two children are playing on a ladder, and one of them is halfway up and afraid to move. Props to stage the scenarios, for example: chairs, a ladder, a screen to act as a door, a basket or a box that can serve as a bird cage, a mask, table to hold telephone.

Instructional Activities

1. Make provisions for a large area to stage the scenarios.
2. Explain to the children that they are going to act out some plays.
3. Tell them the plays are about deciding what to do in case of an emergency. If necessary, explain what an emergency is.
4. Point to the telephone on the table, and tell them to use it to call the emergency number if they think it is an emergency.
5. Review the emergency number, and ask each child to repeat it.
6. Select two children to act out Scenario One (Two children are playing, when suddenly one collapses and does not move or talk.)

Also select several children to act as the emergency team if they are called.

7. Determine the roles of the each child.
8. Set the stage for the action.
9. Let the children act out the scenario creatively. When the one child collapses and the other child realizes she cannot talk or respond, observe whether she calls the emergency number.
10. If she does not call it, discuss the situation and help her recognize this situation is an emergency that warrants calling the emergency number.
11. Repeat the action, having her call the emergency number and having the emergency team come to the scene.
12. Continue with the other scenarios, helping the children understand the concept of emergencies that require calling for assistance.
13. You may modify this activity by allowing the children to develop their own scenarios and act them out.

5.171 Accepts an altered routine when requested

Strand: 5-1 **Age:** 48-72m 4.0-6.0y

Definition

When the child is presented with a change in his schedule or routine, he will accept the modification by displaying adaptable behavior. The change in the schedule or routine may be permanent or temporary.

Instructional Materials

Different activities for fun, such as: (1) Puzzles; (2) Pegboards; (3) Art activities; (4) Blocks; (5) Stack toys; (6) Books; (7) Small toys. A timer.

Instructional Activities

1. Set up the different fun activities in different areas in the room.
2. Invite the child to walk around the room to look at each area with its various fun activities. Tell him he may choose the area where he wants to go first.
3. Tell him when he gets to the area, he may choose an activity to do.
4. Tell him he may do the activity he chose until he hears a bell ring, then he must leave that area and go to another, choose another activity, and play with it until the bell rings again.
5. Set the timer for five to eight minutes.

6. If necessary, structure the activity by telling him to move to a certain area. Reward him verbally for stopping immediately, moving to new activity quietly, and starting another activity immediately.
7. To modify this activity change the activities in the areas often.
8. Some suggestions for addressing specific behaviors during this activity are:

Behavior--He refused to participate.

Strategy--(1) Make sure he understands the rules of the game; (2) Ask him to join you at one of the areas and at one of the activities. Let him lead when both of you interact with the activity. Make a fun game out of the moving to another area; (3) Give him an opportunity to observe before he is asked to participate if the activity is new to him; (4) Use the "I" message. (Tell him how you are feeling about what he is doing without establishing any blame. The steps to the "I" message include: (a) how you feel, for example, "I feel sad," (b) identify the child's behavior that makes you feel the way you do, for example, say, "when you say you do not want to play. . ."; (3) Make a reinforcement statement that involves the child, for example, "because I know you would have a good time." Use "I" messages instead of "You" messages because "You" messages tend to place blame on the child. (Examples: "You should want to have a good time. You make me angry because you will not play.) A "You" message addresses the character of the child; an "I" message addresses his behavior.

Behavior--He demonstrates aggressive behavior (throws things, disrupts the activities in an area.)

Strategy--(1) Remove him from the situation; (2) The solution to aggressive behavior is not the important issue, but instead, the process by which the aggression is resolved. Consistency, dealing only with the behavior, providing support, making sure that he understands that there are times when he does not make decisions and also times when he does make his own decisions are a few of the ingredients in the process of extinguishing aggressive behavior and encouraging self-control.

Behavior--Seeks attention on how to do each activity and when to move to another area.

Strategy-- (1) Verbally assure him he can do the task when he asks for help. For example, say, "You are so good at putting puzzles together. This one should be super-easy for a champion puzzle person like you;" (2) Provide the attention, but only as an assistance, such as (a) taking turns with him in doing the task, (b) giving verbal prompts as he interacts with the task, (c) spending only so many minutes with him, (d) breaking the tasks down into smaller elements (e.g., giving him only two pieces of a puzzle at a time, making sure that the pieces you provide will fit in), (e) starting him out and giving him a sheet of paper to hold up when he needs more help; (3) Provide him with directions on completing the activity, and tell him you are going to leave so he can practice. Assure him you will be back to check on how he is doing. Make sure that you check back, briefly provide assistance, reinforce him for what he has done, and leave.

5.172 Independently tries out new activities

Strand: 5-1   **Age:** 48-60m 4.0-5.0y

Definition

When the child is asked, she will attempt a task she has not previously performed; however, the new task should involve motor, cognitive, and behavioral components that are familiar to her. She will adapt her behaviors and demonstrate an effort to try the new task, will attend to the task for a reasonable length of time, will demonstrate a trial-and-error approach, will ask questions to aid her in doing the activity, and will seek support and help with the materials, if needed.

Instructional Materials

Musical instruments familiar to the child that she has used. At least two musical instruments that she has not used and that will provide a new musical activity for her. Examples of musical instruments to make: (1) Wooden Scraper--Secure a 1-inch diameter wooden dowel about 24 inches long. Cut notches in the wooden dowel and place a ½-inch wooden dowel, no more than 6 inches long beside the notched dowel. Play the new scraper by taking the ½-inch un-notched dowel and scraping it on notched dowel. (2) Coconut Clonker--Secure a coconut, remove the rough outer fibers by rubbing it vigorously with a scouring pad. Saw the coconut in half. Remove the meat from the inside of the coconut and wash it thoroughly. (The meat on the inside of the coconut makes a wonderful treat.) Play the new clonker by using a dowel stick or a drum stick to tap on half of the coconut shell, by hitting the two halves together, or by hitting one half of the shell on a

flat surface. The shells hit together sound like horses galloping.
A rhythm band musical selection to play, equipment to play selection.

Instructional Activities

1. Place the new instruments on a table and prepare to play the accompanying music.
2. Ask the child to come to the table. Explain that there are two new rhythm band instruments on the table.
3. Begin the musical selection, and invite the child to choose a new instrument and play along with the music.
4. Give her an opportunity to experiment with the new instruments, to determine the best way to play them, and to match the music.
5. Replay the music as needed.
6. During this activity, the following are suggested actions based on any occurring behaviors:

Behavior-- She is uncooperative, looks at the new instruments and ignores them.
Strategy--(1) Place one of the child's favorite instruments on which she has been successful next to the new one on the table; (2) Select one of the new instruments, play it, and then encourage her to join you; (3) Request a high probability behavior instead of a low probability behavior. Example: Low probability, "These are new musical instruments"; high probability, "The scraper and the clapper are new and just for you because you are such a good rhythm band player;" (4) Forcing her to participate is not appropriate; allow her to discover on her own. To insist on her doing it may affect her self-esteem, may discourage her from trying, and may cause her to become hesitant and fearful.
Behavior--She shows anger and aggression (stamps feet, abuses the new instruments).
Strategy--(1) Avoid rushing her to participate; (2) Reinforce her consistently for any simple effort, particularly individual efforts that are non-solicited. Use verbal reinforcement that she can understand; (3) Remove the new activities from the setting; (4) Distract the child by providing her with a toy or an activity that she enjoys and is successful with.
Behavior--She shows dependency (wants help, plays helpless, desires attention).
Strategy--(1) Review an activity familiar to her that she is successful at, and reinforce her actions; (2) Provide a limited amount of help with the new activity, phase out, and re-enter

briefly when the child exhibits a lack of independence; (3) Break the skill into small steps, and assist the child with beginning the first step.

Behavior--She is verbally inappropriate (whining, name-calling).

Strategy--(1) Use an active listening approach, beginning with, "You are really upset with me. What is wrong?" Her response may lead to the underlying reason for her being upset. For instance, she may say, "You never help me do anything; you always help Mark." If and when she expresses her real feelings, and puts them into words, the name-calling will seem unimportant; (2) Ignore her verbal outbursts, even if you must leave the room. (3) Ask her to smile when she talks because it will make her voice sound much better.

7. Provide many trials in varied situations for her to learn acceptable behavior, but do not tell her how to behave.

5.173   Remains in designated play areas

Strand: 5-8   **Age:** 55-60m 4.7-5.0y

Definition

When the child is made aware of the boundaries of the play area, he will remain in that area without supervision.

Instructional Materials

A long, brightly colored rope, large enough to make an activity circle in a recreation area or playground, a timer.

Instructional Activities

1. Place the rope in a circle in the middle of a room.
2. Invite the child to the circle.
3. Introduce the "Magic Circle" to the child.
4. Explain to him that he should remain within the circle as the designated play area.
5. In the center of the circle, place reinforcing games and objects.
6. Make time spent in the "Magic Circle" contingent upon not violating the boundaries.
7. Use a timer and designated seat to for the child to go to when they need to think about the rules. Remind the child that there is no negotiating when is comes to safety and that there will be a consequence a child who violates the "Magic Circle" boundaries.
8. Withdraw yourself as monitor of the perimeter, using gradual steps.

5.174   Stays with the group and refrains from following unknown people

Strand: 5-8   **Age:** 55-60m 4.7-5.0y

Definition

When the child is involved in an outside activity (visiting a museum, attending a presentation, going to a park), she will stay with the group to which she was assigned. She will refrain from following an unknown person or group of people.

Instructional Activities

See #5.114 for instructional materials and activities.

5.175   Performs undesirable task when changed to be viewed as desirable

Strand: 5-4   **Age:** 55-62m 4.7-5.2y

Definition

When the child is presented with a task to do that he does not want to do, he will change his attitude once the same task is presented in a motivating way that makes it seem more desirable/like a game. Example: The child is asked to pick up the paper from the floor. He reacts with one of the following behaviors: (1) Picks up the paper on the floor; (2) Picks up one piece of paper and quits; (3) Shoves the paper on the floor under another child's seat; (4) Picks up the paper only when verbally prompted; (5) Puts his head down and ignores the request; (6) Verbally refuses to pick up the paper. But when the request to pick up the paper on the floor is presented in a game format, he views the task as fun and something he would like to do. Example: He is asked to pick up the paper from the floor, wad it into a ball, and shoot it into the wastebasket. And for every wad that hits the basket from 2 feet away, he gets a point. The child with the most points wins.

Instructional Materials

A prepared list of tasks the children do not like to do and a list of tasks they do like to do. Example: Unfavorable tasks--(1) Pick up all the paper off the floor; (2) Wash off the tops of tables; (3) Sort supplies, such as crayons; (4) Clean out the toy box. Favorable tasks--(1) Pass out papers or supplies to other children; (2) Finger-paint or paint at the easel; (3) Draw and color a picture with their choice of crayons, markers, or colored pencils; (4) Play with a favorite toy. Match the unfavorable and favorable tasks together with an "if" and "then you." Example: (1) If you--Pick up all the paper off the floor. Then you will be able to--Pass out papers or supplies to other children; (2) If you--Wash off the tops of the tables. Then you will be able to--Finger-paint on the table; (3) If you--Sort the crayons, markers, and colored pencils. Then you will be able to--Draw and color a picture and choose crayons, markers, or colored pencils to use; (4) If you--Clean out the toy box. Then you will be able to--Play with your favorite toy. The equipment necessary to do the unfavorable and favorable tasks, such as water and sponge.

Instructional Activities

Note: These undesirable/desirable task assignments could be part of the morning planning session. Depending on the tasks, the assignments could be for a certain activity during the day, whole day, or the entire week. Do not forget that young children need short assignments and immediate rewards.

1. Invite the children to the conference area. Discuss with the children how some tasks are more fun to do than others. Explain that often we must do jobs we do not like to do in order to participate in the jobs we do like.
2. Encourage the children to talk about ways that undesirable tasks can be made more desirable or more fun.
3. Ask them to name some tasks they do not like to do and some tasks they like to do.
4. Make a list of the disliked and liked tasks.
5. Tell the children each of them must sign up to do one of the undesirable tasks and when he completes it, he may do the desirable task that goes with it. Provide an example, "If you sign up today to pick up the paper from the floor, you will also be today's child to pass out papers and pencils."

5.176 Refuses ride and/or gifts presented by stranger

Strand: 5-8 **Age:** 55-62m 4.7-5.2y

Definition

/*\Caution Alert: *Because of increasing family and community concerns regarding this issue, there are materials available and professional groups that make presentations. It is recommended that these groups be contacted. They should provide prevention and follow-up techniques. Contact your local PTA group, School District Office, Police Department, State Educational Agency, etc.*

5.177 Follows defined rules whether or not an authority figure is present

Strand: 5-4 **Age:** 56-62m 4.8-5.2y

Definition

The child will follow at least two rules that were given to him earlier without any verbal prompting in the present situation. The authority figure is either not present or is present but may or may not be aware of the child's actions. The intent is for the child to follow predefined rules because he is developing behaviors that involve self-discipline, responsibility, and cooperation, rather than behaviors based on consequences (pleasure or pain).

Instructional Materials

A bag of assorted candies (some with a flower in the center) or treats. A basket or a baking sheet to spread the candies on, paper clips and a pointed object (nail, straight pin).

Instructional Activities

/*\Safety Alert: Be especially careful for the child's safety as you work around the hot oven.

1. Place the basket of candies, the baking sheet, paper clips and pointed object on the table.
2. Explain to the child that he is going to make a candy ornament that can hang in a window to catch the sun.
3. Tell him he is going to make three ornaments first. After his ornaments have been baked, he may decide which ones he likes best or how he wants to change them and then he may make more.
4. Show him how to place the candies together, making sure they are touching and encourage him to use one that has a flower in the middle. (As the flower center candies bake, the flower will expand.)
5. Also explain to him that there should be rules to go along with this activity. Ask him which rules he thinks would be best. Together develop not more than three rules. Examples: (1) The candies are for making an ornament and may not be eaten. (The candies may be used as a reward for following the rules, but they may only be eaten after the ornaments are finished and the rules have been followed); (2) Raise your hand when you have the candies ready to bake; (3) When you are making your candy ornament, do not bother others.
6. Tell him when he gets his candies placed the way he wishes, you will then put the baking sheet in the oven to bake.

7. Tell him you must leave to get the oven ready and remind him not to forget the rules he helped decide on. Preheat the oven at 300 degrees.
8. After the oven is ready, wait until the child raises his hand before you collect his baking sheet. Bake at 300 degrees for 10 minutes.
9. Remove the baking sheet and allow the melted candy ornaments to cool a few minutes.
10. Tell the child that you will put a hole near the edge of each candy for a hanger.
11. Use the pencil or straight pin to make a hole for him. (Poke the holes in the candy before it hardens.)
12. After the candy has hardened, show the child how you make a hanger by opening a paper clip and inserting one end into the candy hole.
13. To hang, attach a string to the other end of the paper clip.
14. After the ornaments are made, discuss the rules and whether they were obeyed, and give the child a hard candy treat for following the rules. (Ignore tattling and reinforce positive things he said about another child.)
15. Give him an opportunity to create more ornaments, reviewing or changing the rules, if necessary.
16. These ornaments will last several years, and they make lovely gifts.

5.178 Identifies fire drill signal and follows teacher's directions during the fire drill

Strand: 5-8 **Age:** 36-60m 3.0-5.0y

Definition

The child will practice following the teacher's directions during a fire drill. By following the directions, the child will get out of the building when the fire alarm sounds.

Instructional Materials

/***Safety Note:** It is important to prepare the child before a fire drill so that when the alarm sounds, she will not be frightened, disoriented or panicky. A brief demonstration of the sound of the alarm and letting the child know when the first few fire drills will happen is recommended. After the child is aware of the sound and routine, it is recommended that you conduct unannounced drills.

Regular fire alarm bell, or if not accessible, a bell to ring for a role-playing experience.

Instructional Activities

Note: Local fire departments will come to your school to review with your children what they should do in case of a fire. The fire department personnel can explain about, "Stop, drop, and roll," and have your children take turns demonstrating this skill.

1. Place the fire alarm bell out of sight of the children.
2. Discuss and review the safety procedures for a fire drill.
3. Instruct the children to be seated.
4. Explain to them that they are going to have a practice fire drill.
5. Select a child to act as the teacher during the practice.
6. Ask the selected child to explain the rules of a fire drill to the other children.
7. Ring the alarm.
8. Allow the "teacher child" to conduct the fire drill, assisting only when necessary.
9. Give other children an opportunity to play the role of the teacher and practice the fire drill several times.

5.179 Recites telephone number

Strand: 5-2 **Age:** 48-66m 4.0-5.6y

Definition

When the child is asked, "What is your telephone number?" he will respond with the correct numbers. It is necessary for him to include only the local numbers (not necessarily the area code). Example: He should respond by saying the numbers in order (e.g., 8364932).

Instructional Materials

A play telephone, a piece of poster board, a marker.

Instructional Activities

1. Write the child's telephone number on a single piece of poster board. Show him the play telephone, and give him time to play with it.
2. Show the child his telephone number.
3. Point to and say the numbers as he watches.
4. Ask him to repeat the numbers or to say his number, if possible.
5. Demonstrate how to press the numbers on the play telephone while looking at the card.
6. Give him a chance to try pressing/dialing the numbers while he reads from the card.

7. Continue until he can press the numbers into the telephone without looking at the card.
8. Ask him to say the numbers out loud while pressing/dialing them.
9. Once he can press/dial the numbers and verbalize his phone number, let him call home and talk to a parent.
10. Without using either a play or real telephone, ask the child what his telephone number is; use the phones for assistance if needed.

5.180   Creates own activities
Strand: 5-1   **Age:** 58-64m 4.10-5.4y

Definition
When the child is presented with a topic, material, resources, games, or presentations, she will create her own activity. These activities may be for an individual child or for a group. The child will demonstrate appropriate and adaptive behavior when she is involved with her created activity.

Instructional Materials
Nontoxic washable water paints, a paintbrush, a sponge, paper towels, poster board.

Instructional Activities
1. Place the water paints, brush, sponge, and paper towels near the poster board.
2. Tell the child she may decorate the poster board anyway she chooses.
3. Allow 15 to 20 minutes for the project.
4. Praise her completed project, or her part if the project is not completed.
5. During this activity the following are suggested actions based on any occurring behaviors:
Behavior-- She shows a lack of initiative, looks at the board and the paints but does not act.
Strategy--(1) Ignore and refrain from doing her thinking for her. When a child depends on someone to tell her what to do or to do things for her, there is little opportunity for her to do for herself; (2) Provide her with help only when she has tried and was not successful; (3) Although it is difficult, allow her to make her own mistakes and to live with her product.
Behavior--She sulks after asking for and not receiving help in doing her picture.
Strategy--(1) Ignore her, and if she persists, continue to ignore her, showing a positive non-verbal expression such as smiling; (2) When she is not in a sulking mood, discuss how other children react to someone who

sulks; (3) Lower the task level by giving her a sheet of paper to practice what she wants to put on the poster board.
Behavior--She is unsatisfied and reacts. She begins to paint the picture, does not like what she does, takes a single color and scribbles the work out, throws the brush.
Strategy--(1) In a matter-of-fact manner, use a wet sponge and clean off the board or use a fresh board. Explain that the board is ready for her to try again; (2) Lower the task level by giving her a sheet of paper to practice what she wants to put on the board; (3) Remove the material from her, explain to her that you feel she does not want to paint today and that perhaps she will feel more like it at another time (use an "I" message or an "I understand how she feels" message.); (4) Assist her by giving her verbal ideas and suggestions for a picture.

5.181   Tells house number, street, and town
Strand: 5-2   **Age:** 54-66m 4.6-5.6y

Definition
When the child is presented with the question, "In what city do you live?" or "In what town do you live?" he will respond correctly. If he lives in a rural area, his response will probably be the town/city where he goes for shopping and services. When you ask the question, it is important to say "In what city/town do you live?" instead of "In what town/city is your address?" When the child is presented with the question, "On what street do you live?" he will respond correctly. After he has named the street and city/town where he lives, ask, "On what street and in what city/town do you live?" When he is presented with the verbal question, "What is your house number?" he will respond correctly. After he has named his house number ask, "What is your house number, the name of the street on which you live, and the city/town where you live?" If he responds by stating his name and complete address, accept this because he has probably learned where he lives by rote. Make sure he understands that his house number, street address, and city/town make up his address.

Instructional Materials
/*\Safety Note: Provide scissors appropriate for the child. Remind the child of safety regarding scissors.
Several sheets of 8 x 10-inch construction paper, scissors, pencil, markers, crayons.

Instructional Activities

1. Using a sheet of construction paper, cut out a typical street sign. Place the paper and the drawing material on a work area.
2. Instruct the child to draw a picture of his home on a sheet of construction paper.
3. Display the completed picture on a bulletin board.
4. Explain that every house has a number on it.
5. Ask him what his house number is, and write the number as he responds. If he does not know his house number, tell him the number as you write it on his house.
6. Explain that every house is on a street and that the street has a name.
7. Place the pre-cut street sign near the picture of his house.
8. Discuss what a street sign is, making sure he can associate the paper sign with the one on his street.
9. Ask him the name of the street on which he lives, and write the name as he responds. If he does not know the name of his street, tell him the name as you write it on the street sign.
10. Continue by explaining that many streets make up a town/city and that the town/city has a name.
11. Ask him what town/city that he lives in.
12. Tell him that his house number, the name of his street, and the name of the city where he lives are all part of his address.
13. Talk about the importance of knowing your address.
14. Say, "Your house number is _____ . (pause for his response) The name of your street is _____ . (pause for his response) The name of the city you live in is _____ ."
15. Ask him, "What is your house number?"
16. Ask him, "What is the name of the street on which you live?"
17. Ask him, "What is the name of the city in which you live?"
18. Let him add things to his picture.
See #5.134, 5.165

5.182 Displays good sportsmanship, win or lose

Strand: 5-5 **Age:** 54-66m 4.6-5.6y

Definition

The child will demonstrate being a good loser and a gracious winner.

Instructional Materials

A bottle with a narrow opening, a box of toothpicks.

Instructional Activities

1. Place the bottle and the toothpicks on the table.
2. Invite the children to come to the table, and place the bottle within easy reach of them. Give each child 10 toothpicks.
3. Explain to the children that each one will have a turn, and when it is her turn, she is to put one toothpick on top of the bottle.
4. The next child will place a toothpick on top of that toothpick and so on.
5. When a child places a toothpick on top of other toothpicks on the bottle and the pile falls down, the child who created the fall must take all the toothpicks that tumbled down.
6. The child who places all her toothpicks first is named the winner.
7. Talk to them about how they will feel if they cause the pile to fall. Discuss with them how they will feel if they are the winner.

5.183 Expresses feelings in controlled manner

Strand: 5-5 **Age:** 60-72m 5.0-6.0y

Definition

The child controls his temper by verbalizing his feelings rather than exhibiting behaviors such as aggression, tantrums, withdrawal. Maturity and increased vocabulary are the vehicles for talking about feelings that control tempers that often lead to inappropriate behaviors. When he has a bank of words he can use to express his feelings and feels comfortable using these terms, he will find less reason to exhibit unusual behaviors because words will work for him. He will also find he is more acceptable in his social interaction.

Instructional Materials

See #5.143 for instructional materials and activities.

5.184 Waits appropriately for attention in group situation

Strand: 5-5 **Age:** 60-66m 5.0-5.6y

Definition

In a group situation, the child will request assistance not more than twice, and after she is recognized, she will wait quietly for attention. She will follow the established rules for seeking attention or help, such as raising her hand and waiting to be called on.

Instructional Materials

See #5.144 for instructional materials and activities.

5.185   Acts upon helpful criticism presented by authority

Strand: 5-4   **Age:** 60-66m 5.0-5.6y

Definition

The child will modify his performance so that it is more like what the authority figure has in mind/suggested. The authority figure will communicate to the child ways to change his behavior by demonstration, explanation, suggestion, and modeling. The modification of his behavior may occur immediately after the recommendations or the next time he has an opportunity to react.

Instructional Materials

A simple non-threatening task the child can easily perform such as simple puzzles or pegboards.

Instructional Activities

1. Place the pegboards and the puzzles on a table in the work area. Ask the child to come to the worktable. Tell him you want to finish the puzzle and will need his help.
2. Choose a puzzle piece and place it incorrectly in the puzzle. Ask the child if it is correct.
3. Accept his correction gratefully and move the puzzle piece immediately.
4. Explain that people can always learn more and they need other people to help them learn.
5. Continue placing puzzle pieces, some incorrectly, until puzzle is complete.
6. Reverse roles and repeat. Encourage the child to place some pieces incorrectly to see if you can catch and correct him.
7. Couple your criticism with some positive statement about his work.

5.186   Remains quiet when others are talking

Strand: 5-7   **Age:** 54-72m 4.6-6.0y

Definition

The child will remain quiet when other people are talking. If it is necessary for her to interrupt, she will first excuse herself.

Instructional Materials

/*\Safety Note: Be aware of special diets and allergies before doing these activities.
A small play microphone purchased or made. Tokens or food.

Instructional Activities

1. Ask the children to sit in a circle.
2. Explain that only the child holding the microphone may speak and that all others must be quiet and listen.
3. Have one child (at a time) take the microphone and present her favorite story or talk about something that has occurred while the others listen.
4. Reward the good listeners with praise, food, or tokens.
5. Remove the children who interrupt constantly to an area where they cannot be seen by the others.
6. Repeat the activity often until the children no longer need a microphone and are good listeners without being reminded.

5.187   Understands and practices good safety procedures when boarding a bus, riding on a bus and leaving a bus

Strand: 5-8   **Age:** 60-66m 5.0-5.6y

Definition

/*\Safety Note: *Most preschoolers, except possibly those with special needs, will not have the opportunity of riding a bus to preschool. But this is an important readiness skill for attending elementary school, and preschoolers will probably have the opportunity of using a bus on field trips.*
The child will demonstrate safe procedures when entering a bus that includes using the bus steps and handrail. He will demonstrate safe procedures when riding on the bus, that include sitting in a seat at all times, keeping his hands to himself, not throwing objects, keeping hands and objects inside the bus, and following directions from the bus driver or any other person in charge. He will demonstrate safe procedures when disembarking from the bus, which

includes using the bus steps, handrail, and moving away from the bus immediately.

Instructional Materials

Access to a school bus not being used during school time, or make arrangements to visit a school bus before it leaves in the afternoon, or request for the bus to remain in the morning after its route. Invitation for the driver or bus monitor to discuss and demonstrate the safety procedures for getting off and on a bus, the rules that are enforced when riding on a bus, and any other behaviors that are expected.

Instructional Activities

1. Obtain access to school bus not being used during class period. Ask the children to stand around the door of the bus for the demonstration on entering. The following instructional strategies relate to safe procedures when boarding a bus, riding on a bus, and exiting a bus.
2. Line the children up at the appropriate boarding location.
3. Model each step: (1) Walk from boarding area to bus steps; (2) Walk up the steps using the handrail; (3) Walk down the aisle to an unoccupied seat; (4) Sit down in a seat and secure a seat belt (if available); (5) Reverse the process to teach disembarking from the bus.
4. Ask each child to do what you did.
5. Observe each child's performance.
6. For children who need additional instruction on boarding a bus, riding on a bus, and disembarking from the bus, the following are recommendations: (1) Talk the child through the process. Say, for example, "Put your foot on the first step, and place your other foot beside it. Put your hand on the handrail. Put your foot on the next step, and place your other foot beside it. Move your hand up on the handrail. Turn and walk down the aisle until you find an empty seat. Sit down in the seat. Fasten your seat belt. Follow instructions from the driver or the bus captain. When the bus has stopped, unfasten your seat belt. Walk down the aisle. Put your foot on the first step, and place your foot beside it. Move your hand up on the handrail. Put your foot on the last step, and place your foot beside it. Move your hand down on the handrail. Step out of the bus and walk immediately out of the way of the bus when it moves." Continue this talk-through, gradually leaving out the parts in which he demonstrates success. (Depending on the size of the child and the size of the

steps, it may often be easier for him not to use alternate feet when he is first learning to use the steps of the bus); (2) Place a chalk outline of a footprint or a paper pattern on the steps, down the aisle, and into a seat for the child to follow; (3) Place a mark on the handrail where the child should place his hand as he boards and exits the bus; (4) Use a direction-chanting approach. Say, for example, "Look! Look! Go! Go! Take a step. Put, put hand on the rail. Look! Look! Go! Go! Take another step. Move! Move! Hand on the rail. Walk! Walk! Down the aisle. Sit! Sit! In a seat." Reverse the chant for the bus exit. (Clapping enhances this technique); (5) Create teams of two children, making the leader the one who is successful in bus safety. Ask the second child to do exactly what the leader does; (6) After he experiences the bus safety activity several times, ask him to tell you how to do it; (7) Physically move him through the steps by using hand-over assistance and leg cueing; (8) Reinforce success immediately, by awarding a certificate or some other tangible item to each child who completes the process successfully on three to five separate days; (9) Review the safety bus issues often, particularly if there are changes in bus rules; (10) Allow the bus driver or the bus monitor to demonstrate bus safety rules often.

5.188 Looks both ways before crossing a street/road in which there is no traffic light and there may or may not be a stop sign
Strand: 5-8 **Age:** 60-66m 5.0-5.6y

Definition
The child will look both ways before she crosses a street or a road where there is no traffic light. These streets and roads are found in neighborhoods, rural communities, apartment complexes, retail and office areas, and educational campuses. Crosswalks and stop signs may or may not be available. She will go to a corner or a crosswalk to cross, if available.

Instructional Materials
/*\Safety Note: Provide scissors appropriate for the child. Remind the child of safety regarding scissors, and clearly emphasize all necessary safety instructions regarding car traffic and crossing the street.

Masking tape to attach to the floor, construction paper, scissors, boxes to be made into cars or buses, markers, colored paper, foil and other materials to make the boxes into street vehicles.

Instructional Activities

Note: A large area, perhaps a section of the playground, is needed to make this activity effective.

1. Invite the children to use the boxes to make cars, trucks, buses, or motorcycles.
2. Ask them to assist you to use the tape to outline streets (without traffic signals), rural roads, sidewalks, driveways, and crosswalks.
3. Give them an opportunity to play on the scene.
4. The children may enjoy driving the vehicles, acting as police officers or traffic control officers, bus drivers, pedestrians, and vendors.
5. Set the stage for teaching safety procedures around streets and cars such as: (1) Look both ways before crossing a street or road; (2) Cross streets in the crosswalks; (3) Watch for cars backing out of driveways.
6. It is very, very important for you to stress to the child that if a car is coming, she should NEVER try to race against it or attempt to beat it across the street.

5.189   Apologizes when reminded

Strand: 5-5   **Age:** 42-54m 3.6-4.6y

Definition

When it is appropriate (e.g., the child accidentally breaks something, bumps into someone, hurts another), he will apologize by saying at least, "I am sorry." He may need to be reminded to apologize and what to say.

Instructional Materials

A chant-like poem that deals with apologizing, especially the issue of when to apologize. Example:
To apologize, means to say:
I am sorry,
Please excuse,
I just forgot,
I should not have used.
To apologize, means to say:
I feel so bad,
I am just a tease,
I must have slipped,
Forgive me please.
Obtain a rhythm instrument, such as a tambourine, a drum, or a tone block.

Instructional Activities

1. Place the rhythm instrument on a table.
2. Discuss what the word "apologize" means.
3. Talk about times when it is appropriate to apologize.
4. Ask the child what he would say to apologize.
5. Say the <u>Apologize</u> chant, using the following accents and the musical instrument to keep a beat:
To apologize, means to SAY:
I am SORRY,
Please excuse,
I just FORGOT,
I should not have used.
To apologize, means to SAY:
I feel so BAD.
I am JUST a tease,
I must have slipped,
FORGIVE me please.
6. Say the apologize chant several times, using an expressive chanting form.
7. Invite the child to join in whenever he wishes.
8. Continue repeating the chant until he seems comfortable joining in.
9. Ask him to say just the first line, "To apologize, means to SAY."
10. Say the next four lines in accented chant form, "I am SORRY, Please excuse, I just FORGOT, I should not have used."
11. Ask him to say the next line, "To apologize, means to SAY."
12. Say the next four lines, in accented chant form.
13. As he becomes more familiar with the chant, switch roles, and you say the lead sentence, "To apologize, means to SAY," and ask him to echo with the next four lines.
14. Phase out of the chant by assigning one child to say the lead sentence and the others to say the echo sentences.
15. To expand this activity, invite the children to create four additional lines to the chant.

5.190   Plays group games following rules

Strand: 5-1   **Age:** 60-72m 5.0-6.0y

Definition

The child will participate in a group game with other children and she will follow the game rules. The group activity may be played inside or outside, and the activity may be active (ball or circle game) or passive (table game). The rules of the game will be clearly defined prior to any action.

Instructional Activities

See #5.135 for instructional materials and activities.

5.191 Plays simple competitive table games

Strand: 5-5 **Age:** 60-72m 5.0-6.0y

Definition

The child will participate in a competitive table game with other children, and he will follow the game rules. The rules of the game will be clearly defined prior to any action.

Instructional Materials

/*\Safety Note: Provide scissors appropriate for the child. Remind the child of safety regarding scissors.

Ten pieces of different colored construction paper, cut to make 40 to 50 cards, 3 x 4-inch cards (four to five cards of each color), scissors, a marker, a box to hold the cards.

Instructional Activities

Note: This table card game may be played by using other concepts than color matching, such as numbers, shapes, spatial positions, letters.

1. Cut out the playing cards, and on one side of one card, write the word "ZING" and add a zingy design. On each of the other cards, on one side put a big black dot.
2. Invite the children to the table to play a card game called <u>Zing</u>.
3. Shuffle the cards.
4. Deal each child six cards, black dot down.
5. Place the rest of the cards in a box.
6. Draw a card from the box, and say the color of the card (e.g., red), and show the children the card.
7. Every child who has a red card turns it over.
8. If a child has more than one red card, he may turn only one of them over.
9. Place the drawn card back in the box.
10. Continue by choosing another card, name the color of the card, and put it back in the box.
11. Draw cards until a child has turned over all his cards or until a child has turned over the card with "ZING" on it.
12. The child who turns over the ZING card becomes the caller for the next game.

13. During this activity, the following are suggested actions based on any occurring behaviors.

<u>Behavior</u>--He does not participate because of lack of understanding.

<u>Strategy</u>--(1) Review the rules with him; (2) Role-play the game and walk him through the rules; (3) If he is comfortable, invite him to sit with you while the others play the game, and explain the game as it is being played.

<u>Behavior</u>--He is stubborn, wanting to be the caller all the time.

<u>Strategy</u>--(1) Remove him from the group game and invite him to watch; (2) Explain to him verbally that when he wants to be the caller all the time, he spoils the game for everyone else; (3) Remove him and involve him in another activity.

<u>Behavior</u>--He withdraws, refusing to participate.

<u>Strategy</u>--(1) Review the rules of the game to make sure that he understands how to play the group game; (2) Remove him from the activity; (3) Discuss with him how it is okay not to want to play sometimes and okay to be a watcher.

<u>Behavior</u>--He is argumentative and disruptive.

<u>Strategy</u>--(Set up some child-oriented table games at various tables. Allow the children to choose the game they would like to play and to sit at that table. Sit at the table with the child you are working with. Tell him you are going to give out chips for taking turns and not arguing. Distribute the chips as the children play, telling them why they received each chip. Have the children count their chips when the game is over. Tell them if they receive a preset number of chips they may choose the next game they want to play.

See #5.135.

5.192 Maintains appropriate distance when talking to another

Strand: 5-7 **Age:** 60-72m 5.0-6.0y

Definition

When the child speaks to another person, she will maintain an appropriate social distance (at least 1 to 2 feet). She will sense when she is too close from cues, such as the listener's backing away, turning her head, pushing the talker, or leaving the situation.

Instructional Materials

A hand puppet for each child. A fist puppet or sock puppet make effective puppets for this activity. Make a fist puppet by asking the child to make a fist with her thumb tucked under her fingers. Her fist will be the puppet's head, and the thumb will be the puppet's mouth. Ask her to move her thumb up, down, and sideways to show how the mouth talks. Use a washable marker to draw eyes and a nose on the child's fist to represent the puppet's head. To enhance the puppet's mouth, outline it with lipstick. To make a sock puppet, find an old sock. Ask the child to place her hand in the sock, putting her fingers and thumb on the seam of the sock. Have the child spread her fingers and thumb apart and push about an inch of the toe end of the sock into her hand to make a mouth. Use a marker to draw other facial features on the puppet. The puppet can be an animal or a child. Ask the child to place her hand in the sock with her thumb on the bottom part of the mouth and her fingers in the top part.

Instructional Activities

1. Place the puppets on the table. Give the children an opportunity to play with the puppets.
2. Select two children to play out the scenario.
3. Set the stage for them by saying, "These two puppets are talking about [a specific topic of interest to the children]." Allow the children to begin the dramatization.
4. Explain to one child that she should move her puppet closer and closer to the other one.
5. Encourage the children to have the puppets continue their discussion as they move closer.
6. When the puppet is "in the face" of the other puppet, ask the "puppet" how she feels about being so close.
7. Discuss the importance of not getting too close to a person when you talk to her. Ask her how she feels when a person is too close and how she thinks the other person feels.
8. Ask two children to recreate the puppet scene, and continue the discussion.

5.193 (Moved to Cognitive, skill 1.309)

5.194 (Removed, see page xii)

5.195 Recognizes items described as dangerous
Strand: 5-8 **Age:** 61-72m 5.1-6.0y

Definition
When she is asked, the child will identify dangerous items. When she is asked, she will tell the results of mishandling or playing with dangerous items.

Instructional Materials
At least 10 square sheets of cardboard: on five sheets, glue a picture of a dangerous item or situation and on the other five sheets, glue pictures of harmless objects. A die, masking tape.

Instructional Activities
1. Tape the cardboard/picture sheets to the floor, forming a looped path.
2. Explain to the children that they are going to play a game called, Danger Ahead.
3. Establish a starting point and a finish, marking each with masking tape.
4. Roll the die.
5. Count the number on the die (e.g., four), and count the same number of pictures (four).
6. If picture number four represents a dangerous item or situation, you must go back to the starting point.
7. If picture number four represents a safe item or situation, stand on that picture until it is your turn to roll the die again.
8. Explain to the children they are to roll the die and advance the number of spaces indicated on die.
9. Tell the child if she lands on a harmless item, she may remain there.
10. Tell her if she lands on a dangerous item, she must return to the beginning point.
11. The winner is the first child to reach the finish line.
See #5.132.

5.196 (Removed, see page xii)

5.197 Adjusts behavior to fit rules and routines of different situations
Strand: 5-1 **Age:** 48-60m 4.0-5.0y

Definition
When the child is in a different situation (an assembly at school, a friend's house, a restaurant, a cafeteria, a store, a library, a museum, a church service), she will exhibit behaviors that are

appropriate to that setting. She will learn the appropriate behaviors in the setting by observation or by being told the rules and routines.

Instructional Materials

Chart paper, a marker.

Instructional Activities

1. Place the chart paper in view of the child.
2. List or illustrate the behavior rules on the chart paper. (It would be nice to have enough rules to cover all situations that may occur; however, the reality does not allow for this. The best solution is to select two or three simple rules that can be enforced and are viewed as necessary.) Read the rules, discuss their meaning, and the reasons for them.
3. Enforcing these rules should be consistent, and new rules should not be introduced until the essential ones have been learned.
4. When the child is involved in a different or unique situation (trip to a zoo, playing in a park), you may need to make and enforce new rules. Before you involve the child in a different situation that requires her to adapt her behaviors, be sure to have a plan. First, make it clear what behavior is acceptable and what is not. Tell her what will happen if unacceptable behavior occurs. Make sure that she thoroughly understands the rules and the consequences.
5. When new rules are needed because of a change in environment or situations, review the rules, discuss the reason for them and clarify what is expected.
6. Choose a child to role-play the behaviors based on the understanding of rules. It is important to explain, demonstrate, and practice until the behaviors are internalized.
7. Choose another child to role-play appropriate behaviors for obeying the rules.
8. Choose a child to role-play the behaviors she should use when another child breaks the rules.
9. Vary by role-playing situations that require new rules because of a change in environments or situations.
10. If there is a need to change any rules, repeat the process outlined above.

5.198   (Removed, see page xii)

5.199   Leaves provoking situation

Strand: 5-4   **Age:** 60-78m 5.0-6.6y

Definition

The child will voluntarily remove himself from a provoking situation. The irritating situation could be caused by a single person, a group action, an activity, an interruption, or an unexpected event.

Instructional Materials

A set of 3- by 5-inch index cards for each child. Each set of cards should contain one card that says "Yes" and one that says "No." At least five sentences (one per card) that describe a behavior which the adult will read to the children. Example: (1) Sentence One--Johnny and David got into an argument, and Johnny hit David. (2) Sentence Two--Susan, Jane, and Patty were building with blocks: Susan pushed a block and it fell on Jane, and Jane walked away. (3) Sentence Three--Several boys were playing on the bars, Bret yelled at Mark, and Mark slapped him. (4) Sentence Four--Dana pushed two girls in the water fountain line, and the two girls ignored her. (5) Sentence Five--Jimmy drew on Jay's paper, and Jay thought it would be best to let the teacher know what Jimmy did. Transparent tape, tongue depressors, a stapler.

Instructional Activities

1. Give the child a set of cards and tape. Tell her to put a tongue depressor on the back of each of her cards. Tape the depressors in place.
2. Tell the child you are going to read some sentences.
3. Tell her to hold up the Yes card if she agrees with the behavior and the No card if she does not agree.
4. Read Sentence One and say, "Hold up the Yes card if you think Johnny should have hit David. Hold up the No card if you think Johnny was wrong in hitting David."
5. Discuss Sentence One and encourage alternate ways of handling this provoking situation.
6. Read Sentence Two and say, "Hold up the Yes card if you think Jane should have walked away. Hold up the No card if you think Jane should have not walked away."
7. Discuss Sentence Two and encourage alternate ways of handling this provoking situation.
8. Continue with Sentences Three through Five.
9. An alternate to discussing ways of handling the situation, is to use role-playing.

5.200   Tells month and day of birth

Strand: 5-2 **Age:** 64-72m 5.4-6.0y

Definition

When the child is asked, he will tell the date and month of his birthday. Some prompting may be necessary.

Instructional Activities

See #5.164 for instructional materials and activities.

5.201   Keeps napkin in lap

Strand: 5-6 **Age:** 64-72m 5.4-6.0y

Definition

The child will keep her napkin in her lap except when in use.

Instructional Materials

/*\Safety Note: Provide scissors appropriate for the child. Remind the child of safety regarding scissors. Be aware of special diets and allergies before doing these activities.
Masking tape, scissors, a cloth napkin and a paper napkin available at lunch or snack time.

Instructional Activities

1. Have these items available during lunch or snack time.
2. Seat the children at the table at lunch or snack time.
3. Unroll the masking tape so the sticky side is out.
4. Attach a piece of masking tape to the clothing in the child's lap and then stick a cloth napkin to the tape.
5. Instruct the child to keep her napkin in her lap when she is not using it.
6. Ask her to take the napkin from her lap and wipe her face.
7. After she has used her napkin, instruct her to place it back in her lap.
8. Praise her for keeping her napkin in her lap.
9. Gradually reduce the tape size a little at a time until a very small piece is left holding the napkin in place.
10. After the child becomes accustomed to using the napkin and replacing it in her lap, replace the cloth napkin with a paper one.

5.202   (Removed, see page xii)

5.203   Makes appropriate request for food items in public

Strand: 5-6 **Age:** 64-72m 5.4-6.0y

Definition

The child will order (request) food appropriately when she is in public. She may make her request of a family member, a waitress, or a friend. She may need to ask for help if she does not have the necessary reading skills.

Instructional Materials

/*\Safety Note: Be aware of special diets and allergies before doing these activities.
A restaurant order pad, menus with pictures (collected from restaurants), plastic water glasses, silverware, placemats, and napkins. Small edible treat for each child.

Instructional Activities

1. Place the silverware, placemats, and napkins on a table.
2. Tell the children that they are going to pretend to eat out.
3. Invite each of them to sit at a placemat (provide assistance if needed).
4. Select a child to be the waiter, and give her a pad for taking food orders.
5. Tell her to give her guests menus.
6. Give them time to look at the menus and decide what they will order.
7. Tell the waiter to go to the table and take the order.
8. Ask them to watch as you model ordering.
9. Remind the children that their orders will be taken only if they are sitting and speaking politely.
10. Reward each "customer" with a small edible treat as their order.

5.204   Says "Excuse me" appropriately

Strand: 5-7 **Age:** 64-72m 5.4-6.0y

Definition

When it is important for him to interrupt an ongoing conversation, the child will say, "Excuse me" before he begins any verbal interaction. When he accidentally bumps into someone, needs to get around someone, or must walk in front of someone, he will say, "Excuse me."

Instructional Materials

A timer, and a short verbal selection, such as a short story, a poem, or a topic to talk about.

Instructional Activities

1. Establish a comfortable listening and talking area.
2. Tell the child that you are going to begin talking about a specific topic.
3. Say, for example, "Beginning now, if you try to interrupt me while I am talking, I will ignore you unless you say, 'Excuse me' when you interrupt."
4. Praise the child if he says, "Excuse me" before interrupting or waits until you are finished speaking.
5. Consistently follow through. If he interrupts without saying, "Excuse me," ignore him; if he does say, "Excuse me," praise him.

See #5.121.

5.205 Waits to be acknowledged before speaking

Strand: 5-7 **Age:** 64-72m 5.4-6.0y

Definition

When part of a group, the child will wait to be acknowledged before she speaks. She may request recognition by a non-verbal signal such as raising her hand, or she may need to wait for her turn to speak.

Instructional Materials

A minute timer.

Instructional Activities

1. Place the timer in the child's view. Explain to the child that she is not to interrupt you while you are talking, unless she says, "Excuse me."
2. Tell her that beginning immediately, if she tries to interrupt you while you are speaking without saying, "Excuse me," you will ignore her, and that if she continues trying to interrupt, you will set the timer for two minutes.
3. Make sure she understands that she must sit quietly for two minutes and when the timer goes off, you will talk to her.
4. Praise the child if she waits to be acknowledged before speaking.
5. Follow through consistently after giving the verbal directions.

See #5.186.

5.206 Answers telephone and carries on simple conversation

Strand: 5-7 **Age:** 64-72m 5.4-6.0y

Definition

The child will answer the telephone when it rings, and he will say, "Hello." If the person calling asks to speak to another person, the child will call the correct person to the telephone. If the caller asks the child how he is, he will respond appropriately.

Instructional Materials

Play telephones or disconnected telephones, one per child.

Instructional Activities

1. Place the telephones on the table, one for each child.
2. Seat the children around the telephone(s) and allow each child to have a turn.
3. Ring the telephone.
4. Instruct the child to answer his telephone when it rings.
5. Discuss and demonstrate how to answer the telephone and telephone manners.
6. Call the child's phone and converse for a few minutes.
7. Let him call another phone and visit.

5.207 Walks on sidewalk, does not go into street

Strand: 5-8 **Age:** 64-78m 5.4-6.6y

Definition

The child will not go into a street, unless she is in the crosswalk to cross the street or walking from one corner of the street to the other corner.

Instructional Materials

A "Sidewalk Safety License" for each child. The License should read: "[child's name] walks safely, stays on the sidewalks. [Child's name] will only cross the street at the crosswalks and at the corners."

A gold seal makes this license look very official; seals are available from commercial sources or can be made from circles cut with a pinking shears from gold paper or from white paper sprayed with gold paint.

Instructional Activities

1. Place the completed licenses on a table for an official presentation.
2. Discuss with the children how cars must stay on streets, roads, highways, and freeways.

3. Take the children for a walk, staying on the sidewalks.

4. Explain that cars stay on roads and people stay on sidewalks and out of streets.

5. Ask the children to line up.

6. Take them on a walk along the sidewalk, explaining your stops at alleys or driveways to make sure there are no cars coming.

7. During the walk, include a street crossing.

8. Ask the children what safe thing they must do before they cross the street. The responses will vary, depending on the type of traffic signals.

9. When the children return to school, review the need to stay on sidewalks and why walking or playing in the street is forbidden.

10. Present the Sidewalk Safety licenses to the children.

5.208   Sacrifices immediate desires for delayed reward

Strand: 5-4   **Age:** 65-72m 5.5-6.0y

Definition

The child is given the choice of being given an immediate smaller reward (e.g., one pencil, a short story read to him, five minutes free time of his choice) or a later larger reward (e.g., a package of pencils, a longer story read to him, 15 minutes of free time of his choice), and he selects the later reward.

Instructional Materials

Several tokens (plastic counters, buttons, stickers), several items to be used as a reward. Make sure that the reward is something that the child wants and will work for.

Instructional Activities

1. Determine a task to assign the child for which he can earn tokens. Place a number value on the treats, for example; little toy cars are worth four tokens, little toy trucks are worth six tokens, little baby dolls are worth eight tokens.

2. Give the child the directions for the task.

3. Tell him he will receive a token (show him the token) for each part of the task that he does.

4. Observe him as he does the task, and give him a token for accomplishment and/or effort.

5. Continue until he has earned at least four tokens.

6. Show him the rewards that he can buy with his four tokens, and also the rewards he can buy if he earns more tokens.

7. Ask him if he wants to use his tokens to buy something now.

8. If he decides to earn more tokens, let him continue the task or present him with a new activity.

9. Let him trade his tokens whenever he wishes so they become meaningful, and so he understands he will always receive a reward in exchange.

10. Continue as long as he wishes to add tokens to his bank. It is best to have him cash in his tokens at the end of the day to allow a new task, new tokens, and new rewards for the next day.

5.209   Displays behavior appropriate for the situation/place

Strand: 5-4   **Age:** 65-72m 5.5-6.0y

Definition

When the child is in a particular situation or place, she will act appropriately. Examples: (1) If she is at the park, she will take turns, play with the others, play fair, stay with her group, and be ready to leave when the group leaves; (2) If the child is in a school setting, she will follow directions, listen carefully, work cooperatively, stand up for her own rights, and try her best. Appropriate behavior is behavior that does not interfere with others or their property, and is also such that the child has a good time and cooperates with others to help them have a good time. Appropriate behavior helps the child and others contribute to the situation, connect with the happenings, and demonstrate capability. In evaluating a child's behavior, remember that value systems differ, and criteria for appropriate behavior varies with individuals, backgrounds, and experiences.

Instructional Materials

At least three open-ended short stories that deal with different situations and behaviors in various settings. Stories are available at most libraries, and reference books provide a correlation between behaviors and titles. Example: Looking up the behavior "bossy," you will find a listing of children's books that address the concept of being bossy. If open-ended prepared stories are not available, write your own or use the following examples:
Story One--<u>All Wet</u>
One day Uncle Pete asked Mary and Allan to help him wash his car.
Uncle Pete drove his car into the carport.
He had a pail of water, sponges, and a hose.
Uncle Pete washed the top of the car with the sponge.

Mary used the hose to wash the sides, and Allan worked on the windows.

Everyone was working very hard.

Suddenly Mary pointed the hose right at Allan.

Allan cried, "Do not get me wet, Mary!"

Mary held the hose so Allan got soaking wet.

Mary laughed and called Allan a fish.

Allan was not very happy with Mary.

Then Mary pointed the hose right at Uncle Pete. And...

(Picture Card One in the activity above may be used to accompany Story One in the Assessment Procedure.)

Story Two--<u>Left Out</u>

Janet, Susan, and Beth were going to the playground.

When they got to the playground, Anne was there.

Anne asked the girls if she could play with them.

Janet said, "No, you cannot play with us because you do not know how to play our game."

"What game are we playing?" asked Susan and Beth.

"I have not decided, but whatever we play, Anne cannot play because she is dumb," answered Janet.

Anne begins to leave the group, and she starts to cry.

"See, she is a cry baby," said Janet.

"I would be unhappy, too, if someone called me dumb," said Susan and Beth.

Susan and Beth...

(Picture Card Two in the activity above could be used to accompany Story Two in the Assessment Procedure.)

Story Three--<u>Smashed</u>

Today was William's birthday, and he was going to have a party.

He was so excited because all his friends were coming.

Sam, Tom, Alice, Greg, Peggy, Frank, Sharon, and Victor would all be at his party.

He had picked out the games that they would play.

He had picked out the ice cream and cake.

At two o'clock his friends started to arrive.

Everyone had a gift for William.

First they played <u>Tap the Bear</u> and then <u>Poor Kitty</u>.

Soon it was time for everyone to put on a party hat and go to the birthday table.

There was a dish of ice cream for each person.

Mom brought in William's birthday cake with six candles on it.

She lit the candles, and after William made a wish, he blew them all out.

Mom was getting ready to cut everyone a piece of cake, when suddenly Frank put both his hands on top of the cake and pushed as hard as he could.

The cake was smashed flat.

William...

(Picture Card Three in the activity above could be used to accompany Story Three in the Assessment Procedure.)

Instructional Activities

1. Invite the children to join the "Talking Circle." Begin a group discussion by asking how many have helped someone wash a car. Discuss what you use to wash a car and how you do it. Tell the children that you are going to read a story about washing a car, and ask them to listen carefully.
2. Read Story One.
3. Ask the children how they think the story ends, and accept the various endings.
4. Discuss Mary's actions and why they think she got Allan wet. Talk about what Allan and Uncle Pete could have done. Ask if Mary had also made others wet what they would have done. Ask them to tell how they would feel if what happened to Allan happened to them. If possible, have the group agree on an ending.
5. Continue the same procedure with Stories Two and Three.
6. Due to the attention spans of the children, you may want to use Stories Two and Three at a different Talking Circle session.

5.210 Acts according to social rules in work and play situations

Strand: 5-4 **Age:** 65-72m 5.5-6.0y

Definition

When the child is working or playing, he will act according to acceptable social rules. Examples: (1) If he is at the park, he will take turns, play with others, play fair, stay with his group, be ready to leave when the group leaves; (2) If he is in a school setting, he will follow the identified rules; (3) If he is a public restaurant, he will behave according to social rules of the place; for instance, if he should sit down and wait to give his order, then wait to be served, he will adhere to this socially acceptable behavior.

Appropriate social behavior is behavior that does not interfere with others or their property. This behavior should help the child and others contribute to the situation, connect with the happenings, and demonstrate capability. In evaluating a child's social behavior, remember that value systems differ, and criteria for appropriate behavior varies with individuals, backgrounds, and experiences.

Instructional Materials

At least three open-ended short stories that deal with different social rules and expected behaviors. You can obtain these stories from the public library; check reference books for a correlation between behaviors and titles. Example: By looking up the behavior "impulsive," you will find a listing of children's books that address the concept of being impulsive. If open-ended prepared stories are not available, write them yourself or use the examples that follow.

Story One--<u>A Visit to an Art Museum</u>

Victoria Weiser had a day off from her work.
She decided to take her niece, Judith, and two of her friends to the art museum.
Victoria and Judith picked up Glenn and Abe on their way to the museum.
In the car, Victoria explained what an art museum was and what you should do when you are visiting one.
At last they got to the museum, so they went in.
There were many people walking around looking at all the pictures on the wall.
The people were also looking at interesting things in the cases.
Judith asked Victoria many questions.
Suddenly Victoria looked for Glenn and Abe.
They were gone. Victoria had told them earlier that it was important to stay together.
Then Judith heard some people talking around the corner, so she went to look.
There were Glenn and Abe, wrestling on the floor. They were nearly under one of the cases that had a pretty vase in it.
Victoria said...
(Picture Card One in the activity above may be used to accompany Story One in the Assessment Procedure.)

Story Two--<u>No Brush</u>

It was Audrey's and Rebecca's turn to paint a picture at the easels.
Audrey had waited so long for her turn.
She had thought and thought about the picture she wanted to paint.
Audrey and Rebecca went to the easels.
Rebecca took all the brushes from Audrey's paint jars, and put them in her pockets. She even put her foot on one.
Rebecca also took all the brushes from the paint jars at her easel.

Audrey was very disappointed when she discovered that she did not have any brushes.
Then she looked at Rebecca and saw all the brushes.
She asked Rebecca for her brushes.
Rebecca said, "I need them all, so you may not have any."
Audrey...
(Picture Card Two in the activity above may be used to accompany Story One in the Assessment Procedure.)

Story Three--<u>My Turn</u>

James was sitting on the big pillow looking at his favorite animal book.
He liked this book best of all because it had pictures of farm animals.
He knew a lot about farm animals.
Every summer he went to visit on a farm.
Just as he turned the page to look at the horses, Paul grabbed the book and started to pull it away.
This made James angry, so he hung on tightly to the book.
Each of the boys tugged and tugged.
Suddenly they heard a page rip.
And then...
(Picture Card Three in the activity above may be used to accompany Story One in the Assessment Procedure.)

Instructional Activities

1. Invite the children to join the "Talking Circle." Begin the group discussion by asking the child how many of them have been to a museum. Discuss what you do and see at a museum. Tell them you are going to read a story about three children who went to an art museum. Tell them to listen carefully.
2. Read Story One.
3. Ask them how they think the story ends, and accept the various endings.
4. Discuss the actions and ask why the boys started to wrestle on the floor. Talk about what the boys should have done. Determine what Victoria will do and why. Ask them to tell how they would feel if they had been at the art museum. If possible, have the group agree on an ending. Ask the children to draw a picture of the ending to this story.
5. Continue the same procedure with Stories Two and Three.
6. Due to childrens' attention spans, use Stories Two and Three at a different Talking Circle session.

See #5.209.

5.211 Controls temper well, verbalizes feelings in appropriate manner

Strand: 5-4 **Age:** 40-72m 3.4-6.0y

Definition

The child controls her temper by verbalizing her feelings instead of exhibiting behaviors such as aggression, tantrums, and withdrawal. Maturity and increased vocabulary become the vehicles for talking about feelings that control her temper that otherwise leads to inappropriate behaviors. When the child has a vocabulary that she can use to express her feelings and when she feels comfortable in using these terms, she will find less reason to exhibit unusual behaviors because words will work for her. She will also find she is more acceptable in her social interactions.

Instructional Activities

See #5.143 for instructional materials ad activities.

5.212 Contributes to ideas of group

Strand: 5-5 **Age:** 65-72m 5.5-6.0y

Definition

The child contributes suggestions, recommendations, ideas, and direction to a group. This group may be peers, adults, or a combination of both. The subject of the group may vary from playing a game to improved behaviors to making plans to go on a trip to choosing a gift for a family member.

Instructional Materials

A picture that lends itself to interpretations. Find such pictures in magazines, picture books, or art prints. One of the best sources for interpretive pictures is your local library, where prints of paintings are available for checkout. Examples: *One of the Family* by Frederick George Cotman, *Mother and Children* by Pierre Auguste Renoir, or *The Boating Party* by Mary Cassatt.

Instructional Activities

1. Place the picture in full view of the children.
2. Call attention to the selected picture (e.g., *Mother and Children*) by asking an interpretation question. As an example, ask, "Where do you think this mother and her two little girls are? What time of year do you think it is? Which little girl is the oldest? Why do you think one girl brought her doll?"
3. Ask a child to take a turn to tell a story about the picture.
4. After a few stories have been shared, call attention to different parts of the picture that

may have been misinterpreted. If one of the children mentioned the "puff the little girl is holding," it may indicate that a winter fur muff is an unfamiliar object. Lead the discussion to center on any other unfamiliar objects in the picture. If the activity is misunderstood, lead the discussion to involve the details in the picture that may lead to a different meaning.
5. During the picture discussion, encourage the children to take turns talking, to listen when another child discusses the picture, to accept what others say, and to feel free to add ideas.

5.213 Explains outcomes/consequences of not following rules

Strand: 5-5 **Age:** 65-72m 5.5-6.0y

Definition

The child will be able to explain to another child what will happen if a rule is broken. If there are sequences to what occurs when a rule is broken (e.g., warning first, a second chance, put head down, go to your room), she will be able to relate the correct order.

Instructional Materials

A prepared set of rules and consequences that apply to the child's situation. The rules should be reasonable, written positively, brief and to the point, observable, and enforceable. The consequences should be related as much as possible to the misbehavior, enforceable, not liked by the child, but not harmful. The consequence should occur as soon as possible after the rule has been broken. The child should also understand the concept of choice to enable her to select between rules and outcomes. Be sure to include the positive consequences that will occur when the rules are obeyed.

Instructional Activities

1. If appropriate, write the rules on a chart or draw pictures that represent the rules. If appropriate, write the consequences on a chart, or draw pictures that represent the rules on another chart.
2. Invite the children to the listening area. Explain the rules to them.
3. It is important to present the rules in the mode of "You are expected to obey the rules because they will help us all work together."
4. Make sure they have a complete understanding of the rules as well as the reason for them.

5. Role-play both following the rules and breaking the rules.
6. Ask a child to explain the rules to another child. Correct or prompt as necessary.
7. Explain the consequences of breaking a rule.
8. It is important that you present the consequences as if they will never happen, because the rules are expected.
9. Make sure the children have a complete understanding of the rules as well as the reasons for them.
10. Role-play what will happen if a rule is broken.
11. Ask a child to explain to another child what will happen if a rule is broken. Correct or prompt as necessary.

5.214   (Removed, see page xii)

5.215   Makes own decision concerning activities with minimal adult supervision
Strand: 5-4   **Age:** 65-78m 5.5-6.6y

Definition
When the child is involved with an activity and has at least two alternatives, he will independently select one of the alternatives with minimal adult supervision. If the selected alternative is not appropriate or is not effective, he may change to another choice with only minimal adult supervision. Example: The child has been asked to make a colored sand painting. He has a mixture of colored sand on a large sheet of newspaper. With white glue, he has made a design on a sheet of construction paper and he begins sprinkling the colored sand on top of his glue drawing. Before he completes his first sand picture, he takes another sheet of paper and starts drawing another picture with the glue because he has decided he wants to use different colors of sand. He controls the colors he wants to use in his sand painting.

Assessment Materials
An assortment of construction manipulatives, such as interlocking cubes, snap shapes, wooden connecting pieces, pattern snap blocks, etc. (If commercial construction manipulatives are not available, make manipulatives for the activity as follows: Collect different size straws including fat straws, thin straws, long ones, and short ones, paper clips. Open some of the paper clips, bend some of the clips, twist them and pinch them.)

Instructional Materials
Two slips of paper per child, with a child-based activity pictured on each slip of paper. Examples: Slip One--Puzzle, Slip Two--Blocks, Slip Three--Pegboards, Slip Four--Coloring Book, Slip Five--Modeling Clay, Slip Six--Plants Being Watered, Slip Seven--Sponge and Table, Slip Eight--Broom and Floor, Slip Nine--Paint Jars and Sponge, Slip Ten--Paintbrushes, Water, Paper Towels.

Instructional Activities
1. Place all the slips of paper in a box. Tell the child that he is to draw two slips from the box.
2. Ask him to look at the pictures. Explain the pictured task, if necessary.
3. Tell him he may do only one of the two activities.
4. Allow time for him to decide and do the activity he chooses.
5. After he completes the selected activity, let him do the activity on the other slip if he chooses, or let him draw two more slips.
6. It is important to change the pictured tasks often.

5.216   Understands the dangers of streets/roads and moving vehicles
Strand: 5-8   **Age:** 65-78m 5.5-6.6y

Definition
When she is asked, the child will be able to tell the dangers related to streets or roads and vehicles. She will describe safety rules relating to crossing streets, not running into streets, traffic lights, cars backing out of driveways, buses pulling away from curbs, riding tricycles or bicycles in the proper places, playing in alleys, playing on rural roads, understanding universal signs, and walking safely in parking lots and around cars.

Instructional Materials
/***Safety Note:** Provide scissors appropriate for the child. Remind the child of safety regarding scissors.
Masking tape to attach to the floor, a ball, a large dowel, large flower pot, one or two shoe boxes, red, green and yellow construction paper, scissors, boxes to make into cars and buses, markers, aluminum foil and other materials to make the boxes into street vehicles.

Instructional Activities

1. A large area, such as a section of the playground, is needed for this activity to be effective. To make a traffic signal, place the large dowel stick in a solid base, such as a large flowerpot. From the red, yellow, and green construction paper, cut three 6- to 8-inch circles; glue the red circle on one side of the shoe box, a yellow circle on another side, the green circle on another, and a walk signal on the other. Place the shoebox on top of the dowel. By turning the dowel, you can change the traffic light. You can make two traffic lights to add additional safety situations.

2. Invite the children to use the boxes to make them into cars, trucks, buses, and motorcycles.

3. Ask them to assist, as you use masking tape to outline streets, sidewalks, driveways, and crosswalks on the playground or surface.

4. Place the traffic light on the appropriate street corner and the vehicles on the street.

5. Give the children an opportunity to play on the street scene.

6. Children may wish to drive the vehicles, to act as police officers or traffic control officers, bus drivers, pedestrians, or vendors.

7. Set the stage for teaching safety procedures around streets and cars, such as: (1) Crossing the street with the green light or the walk light, while still watching for cars that may not stop when the light is red; (2) Children playing catch when a ball rolls into the street; (3) Getting into a car that is parked against the curb; (4) Getting off a bus and moving immediately to the sidewalk; (5) Crossing streets in the crosswalks; (6) Watching for cars backing out of driveways.

8. Invite the children to discuss the dangers of streets and moving cars, and encourage them to develop safety scenarios.

9. You may expand this activity to include setting up parking lots and then demonstrating parking lot safety procedures.

10. You may easily modify this activity by making the traffic light stop signs and change the design to represent a small community or a rural environment.

5.217 Waits until the designated time to leave the table

Strand: 5-6 **Age:** 66-72m 5.6-6.0y

Definition

The child will remain at the table until the identified time to leave. This time could be when he is excused, when others are finished, or at a designated time.

Instructional Materials

Musical instrument such as a piano or bells. A game that deals with having good table manners. If a game is not readily available, make one up, or use the example that follows.: "Good Manners" (to the tune of "*The Farmer in the Dell*.")
Good manners when we eat,
Good manners when we eat,
Hi-ho and cheery-oh,
Good manners when we eat.
The napkin is to wipe,
the napkin is to wipe,
Hi-ho and cheery-oh,
the napkin is to wipe.
Please pass the plate to me,
Please pass the plate to me,
Hi-ho and cheery-oh,
Please pass the plate to me.
I will clean my drippy spill,
I will clean my drippy spill,
Hi-ho and cheery-oh,
I will clean my drippy spill.
Excuse me please I am through,
Excuse me please I am through,
Hi-ho and cheery-oh,
Excuse me please I am through.
Good manners when we eat,
Good manners when we eat,
Hi-ho and cheery-oh,
Good manners when we eat.

Instructional Activities

Note: As the children become involved in new and different social manners, you can easily add the new manners to the action song.

1. Explain to the children that they are going to learn a new Manners Song to the tune of *The Farmer in the Dell*.

2. Hum or play the tune, *Farmer in the Dell*.

3. Introduce the manners song by singing the first two lines.

4. Ask the child to sing the two lines with you.

5. Repeat the two lines several times.

6. Continue, using the remaining lines.

7. After the children learn the song, add the dramatizations.

"Good manners when we eat, Good manners
   when we eat,
 Hi-ho and cheery-oh, Good manners when we
   eat.
 The napkin is to wipe, the napkin is to wipe,"
   (pretend to wipe face with napkin.)
 "Hi-ho and cheery-oh, the napkin is to wipe."
   (pretend to wipe face with napkin.)
 "Please pass the plate to me, Please pass the
   plate to me," (dramatize passing a plate)
 "Hi-ho and cheery-oh, Please pass the plate to
   me" (dramatize passing a plate)
 "I will clean my drippy spill, I will clean my
   drippy spill,"(pretend to wipe up a spill)
 "Hi-ho and cheery-oh, I will clean my drippy
   spill." (pretend to wipe up a spill)
 "Excuse me please I am through, Excuse me
   please I am through," (pretend to get up from
   a table)
 "Hi-ho and cheery-oh, Excuse me please I am
   through." (pretend to get up from a table.)
 "Good manners when we eat, Good manners
   when we eat,
 Hi-ho and cheery-oh, Good manners when we
   eat."

5.218   Initiates topics in conversation appropriate for the situation

Strand: 5-7   **Age:** 66-72m 5.6-6.0y

Definition

The child will initiate a topic or a discussion, using vocabulary and content appropriate for the situation. She will allow others to contribute and will maintain the topic for a reasonable length of time or until closure.

Instructional Activities

See #5.168 for instructional materials and
   activities.

5.219   Accepts friendly teasing

Strand: 5-4   **Age:** 66-78m 5.6-6.6y

Definition

When the child is being teased, he will accept it without becoming angry or displaying any emotional outbursts. His response may be verbal or non-verbal. He should have the ability to determine if the teasing is friendly or if it is done with malice. Accepting friendly teasing will also depend on other variables, such as who is doing the teasing, what the teasing topic is, when, and where it is occurring.

Instructional Materials

An embarrassing moment or a funny mistake
you made to share with the children.

Instructional Activities

1. Invite the children to join the "Sharing Circle."
   Ask the children to think about a time when
   they made a funny mistake.
2. Start the discussion with an example from
   your life.
3. Allow the children to engage in friendly
   conversation about this event.
4. Invite the children to share a funny mistake
   they made.
5. Reinforce them for sharing but do not require
   participation.
6. Point out that while people try hard to do
   things, they often fall short of their goal.
7. Emphasize that when we can laugh at our
   errors and others' errors in nice way, it helps
   us accept our limitations and yet keep trying.
8. Discuss how the child might be teased, and
   allow friendly teasing. If the child appears to
   be upset about the teasing, immediately stop
   the action.
9. Encourage other children to share and discuss
   how they might have been teased.

5.220   Plays and works without disrupting work of others

Strand: 5-4   **Age:** 66-78m 5.6-6.6y

Definition

The child will play or work without disrupting others. She will not disrupt by talking, touching, doing non-verbal antics, or making unnecessary noises.

Instructional Materials

Enough small blocks for each child involved to
be able to build something, a timer, small
rewards.

Instructional Activities

1. Place all the blocks in the middle of the table
   or floor.
2. Arrange the children in groups of two.
3. Ask the children to share the blocks with a
   partner.
4. Tell them that the team that is able to build
   without interfering or disturbing others will
   receive a reward at the end of five minutes.
5. Set the timer for five minutes, reward, and
   praise the children who worked quietly
   throughout the session.

6. Gradually increase the time spent on the building task.

5.221   Offers help to others voluntarily

Strand: 5-5   **Age:** 66-78m 5.6-6.6y

Definition

Without being asked, the child will offer help to others. His assistance may be in the area of academic work, physical help, behavioral support for peers, or he may volunteer to help an adult.

Instructional Materials

Sheets of legal size white paper (one sheet for every two children), a ruler, writing instruments.

Instructional Activities

1. Divide the sheet of paper into two sections. On one section, prepare a work activity at the child's entry level (e.g., a maze, a connect-the-dots, or a color activity), and on the other section, prepare another work activity at the child's entry level, but different than section one.
2. Ask the children to form partners or assign partners.
3. Give each set of partners one sheet of paper with the two sections to complete.
4. Tell the first child to do the first section, and the second child to do the second section.
5. Explain to them that they may help each other. Tell them to raise their hands when they are finished.
6. Reward the children who work cooperatively and help each other.
7. Check each child's work when he finishes, and if he made errors, provide directions for correcting them. Then give the children a chance to help each other correct errors.

5.222   Plays difficult games requiring knowledge of rules

Strand: 5-5   **Age:** 66-78m 5.6-6.6y

Definition

The child will participate in a group game that requires attention and knowledge of the rules. The group activity may be played inside or outside, and the activity may be active (ball or circle games) or passive (table games). The rules of the game will be clearly defined prior to any action.

Instructional Materials

Two pairs of shoes, two pairs of gloves or mittens, two shirts that button, two hats. Masking tape to be placed on the floor.

Instructional Activities

1. Place a strip of tape on the floor to mark the starting line. A short distance from the strip of tape, place a taped X, and by the X put the two pairs of shoes; a short distance from the shoes place another taped X, and put the two pairs of gloves by that X; another short distance from the gloves place another tape X, and put the two shirts by that X; and a short distance from the shirts, place another taped X, and put the two hats by that X.
2. Divide the children into two teams.
3. Ask each team to form a single line.
4. Tell the first child for each team to stand on the taped starting line.
5. Explain the rules of the relay to the teams: The first child on each team should hop to the first X, take off her shoes, and put on one of the pairs of shoes. She should then take off these shoes, put on her own and hop to the next X. When she arrives at the second X, she should put on the gloves, take them off, and hop to the next X. When she arrives at the third X, she should put on the shirt, button it up, then take it off, and hop to the next X. When she arrives at the fourth X, she should put on the hat, take it off, and hop back to the starting line.
6. As soon as the first child from each team begins to hop to the second X, the next team member follows the same path.
7. The relay game continues until each child has a turn at each X.
8. The team that completes all the X's first is the winner.
9. To make this relay more challenging, add more clothing to the "track," add more individual activities to do at each X (e.g., a comb for combing hair), or allow the child to run instead of hop to the various X's.
10. During this activity, the following are suggested actions based on any occurring behaviors:

Behavior--She does not participate because of lack of understanding.

Strategy--(1) Review the rules with her; (2) Role-play the game and walk her through the X's; (3) Allow her to play the group game, and when she is not sure of the rules, stop and explain; (4) If she is comfortable, invite her to sit with you while the others play the game, and explain the game as it is being played.

Behavior--She is stubborn, wanting to be on the track all the time.

Strategy--(1) Remove her from the group game and invite her to watch the action of the others; (2) Explain verbally to her that when she wants to be in the race all the time, she spoils the game for everyone else; (3) Remove her, and involve her in another activity.

Behavior-- She withdraws, refusing to participate by not taking her turn.

Strategy--(1) Review the rules of the game to make sure she understands how to play the group game; (2) Remove her from the activity; (3) Discuss with her how it is all right not to want to play sometimes and okay to be a watcher.

See #5.135.

5.223   Behaves in a courteous manner towards others

Strand: 5-5   **Age:** 60-78m 5.0-6.6y

Definition

The child will demonstrate behaviors that are courteous to his peers and to adults. The manners he exhibits must have meaning to himself as a person. They should relate to a sense of self-assurance that will make him feel comfortable with others. If his manners are not related to this self-assurance, he will be viewed as awkward, clumsy, and insincere.

Instructional Materials

A large piece of tag board, sheets of paper large enough for each child to write his name, markers, a box. A crown, a banner, or a pin to be worn by the "Personality of the Day."

Instructional Activities

1. Place a box on the table.
2. Tell the children they are going to elect someone in the group to be the "Personality of the Day." (If their attention spans allow, this could be of the week instead of the day.) You may need to explain or change the term personality to "King or Queen of the Day," "Special Child of the Day," and so on.
3. Give each child a sheet of paper and ask him to write his name on the sheet.
4. Place the sheets of paper in the box.
5. Shake the box.
6. Make a big production out of drawing a name from the box.
7. Crown the child whose name is drawn.

8. Take a picture of the child elected, and mount it in the center of a large piece of tag board.
9. Explain to the rest of the children that you will help them write nice things about the honored child.
10. Collect these "nice" statements throughout the day (or week).
11. Give the privileged child the chart with his picture and statements written by the other children to keep.

5.224   Chews and swallows to empty mouth before speaking

Strand: 5-6   **Age:** 66-78m 5.6-6.6y

Definition

When eating, the child will not speak until she has chewed and swallowed her food.

Instructional Materials

/*\Safety Note: Be aware of special diets and allergies before doing these activities.

A hand puppet for each child. A fist puppet or sock puppet make effective puppets for this activity. Make a fist puppet by asking the child to make a fist with her thumb tucked under her fingers. Her fist will be the puppet's head, and the thumb will be the puppet's mouth. Ask her to move her thumb up, down, and sideways to show how the mouth talks. Use a washable marker to draw eyes and a nose on the child's fist to represent the puppet's head. To enhance the puppet's mouth, outline it with lipstick. To make a sock puppet, find an old sock. Ask the child to place her hand in the sock, putting her fingers and thumb on the seam of the sock. Have the child spread her fingers and thumb apart and push about an inch of the toe end of the sock into her hand to make a mouth. Use a marker to draw other facial features on the puppet. The puppet can be an animal or a child. Ask the child to place her hand in the sock with her thumb on the bottom part of the mouth and her fingers in the top part.

A collection of snacks (e.g., crackers, fruit, marshmallows, dry cereal, cheese) that require the child to chew.

Instructional Activities

1. Place the hand puppet and the snacks on a table.
2. Put on one of the hand puppets.
3. Take one of the snacks, put it in your mouth, and eat it.

4. While you are chewing and swallowing, place your fingers over the puppet's mouth to indicate that she cannot talk.
5. When you have swallowed the food, remove your fingers and let the puppet talk.
6. Give the child a hand puppet and a snack.
7. While she is chewing the snack, her puppet must keep her lips closed and must not talk.
8. Explain that her puppet may not talk until she has chewed the snack and swallowed it.
9. Praise her and her puppet for politely chewing and quietly swallowing before speaking.
10. This activity may be modified to involve two children and two puppets.

5.225 Pauses to allow others to speak
Strand: 5-7 **Age:** 60-78m 5.0-6.6y

Definition
The child will pause when one or more other persons are talking. If it is necessary for him to interrupt, he will excuse himself.

Instructional Activities
See #5.186 for instructional materials and activities.

5.226 (Removed, see page xii)

5.227 (Moved to Cognitive, skill 1.310)

5.228 Tells birthplace by state and town
Strand: 5-2 **Age:** 68-78m 5.8-6.6y

Definition
When the child is asked, he will say the town where he was born. When he is asked, he will say the state where he was born. He may say the town and state together when he is asked in what town he was born.

Instructional Materials
The name of each child's birthplace.

Instructional Activities
1. Invite the children to join you at the interest area.
2. Announce to the children, "I was born in [name your birthplace]."
3. Point to each child and say, "You were born in [name his birthplace]."
4. Ask each child to repeat what you said.
5. Continue until each child repeats the sentence.

6. Increase the activity by asking each one, "Where were you born?"

5.229 Takes dirty dishes to designated area
Strand: 5-6 **Age:** 68-78m 5.8-6.6y

Definition
When the child is finished with her meal or has been excused, she will take her plate, silverware, plastic glass, and bowl from the table to the designated place for dirty dishes. She will deliver the soiled eating utensils, when reminded, and then without verbal prompting or physical assistance.

Instructional Materials
At least five different colored dot stickers or washable markers, reward stickers.

Instructional Activities
1. Select a time when the child will be eating, using dishes, silverware, and napkins. This could be lunch time or juice/snack time. Place a red sticker on top of her plate and her plastic glass, cup, or carton, and place a green sticker on her silverware. Identify the two locations where she is to take her dirty dishes when she is finished, and place a corresponding color sticker at the specific area.
2. As the child receives her food and drink, explain that when she finishes and is excused, she is to bring her empty and dirty dishes to various places.
3. Explain to her that she must find the correct place to put her dirty dishes by matching the colored stickers.
4. Point to the red sticker on her plate, and point to the red sticker at the designated area for soiled plates.
5. Continue with the rest of the color cueing.
6. As each child is excused, observe her complete the matching process and assist as needed.
7. Increase the number of different places to take the soiled items by having a different color/location for plates, cups/plastic glasses, trash, and silverware.
8. Gradually phase out the color coding.

5.230   Chews and swallows quietly with lips closed

Strand: 5-6 **Age:** 68-78m 5.8-6.6y

Definition

When he is eating, the child will put the proper amount of food in his mouth and will chew and swallow with his lips closed.

Instructional Materials

/*\Safety Note: Be aware of special diets and allergies before doing these activities.
Provide a hand puppet for each child. A fist puppet or a sock puppet are effective puppets for this activity. The puppet may be an animal or a child. Ask the child to put his hand in the sock with his thumb in the bottom part of the mouth and his fingers in the top part. Have a collection of snacks (crackers, fruit, marshmallows, cereal, cheese) that require chewing.

Instructional Activities

1. Place the hand puppet and the snacks on a table.
2. Put on one of the hand puppets.
3. Take one of the snacks, put it in your mouth, and eat it.
4. While you are chewing, make sure that the puppets lip's are closed.
5. To make sure the puppet keeps his lips closed and does not talk, place your fingers or ask the child to place his fingers over the puppet's lips to keep him from talking.
6. When you have swallowed the food, remove your fingers and let your puppet talk.
7. Give the child a hand puppet and a snack.
8. While he is chewing, make sure that his puppet's lips stay closed.
9. Explain that his puppet must keep his lips closed while he is chewing and he may not talk until he has finished chewing the snack quietly.
10. Praise the child and the puppet for chewing politely.
11. You may modify this activity to involve two children and two puppets.
See #5.224.

5.231   Uses appropriate/non-vulgar language

Strand: 5-7 **Age:** 68-78m 5.8-6.6y

Definition

The child will use appropriate language for a given situation, based on his age, developmental vocabulary, and culture. He will not use vulgar language or exhibit obscene gestures.

Instructional Materials

A behavioral recording process. Examples: a chart or a check list.

Instructional Activities

1. Make sure the recording chart or check list is available if there is an issue with a child using vulgar language, swearing, or using obscene gestures.
2. Intervention should be based on the frequency of use, the reason for use, understanding the meanings of the word, experiences, and manners of releasing frustration.
3. Intervention strategies should include: (1) Ignoring; (2) Accepting and discussing the words, to include the definition, how the word is used, implications when the word is used, how the word affects others, and words that could be used instead of the vulgar terms; (3) Reward appropriate vocabulary; for high-frequency users, a diminishing quota procedure is effective; (4) Give him a firm message that swearing is not acceptable; (5) Excuse him from the room when he uses vulgar language.

5.232   Reads and follows directions on safety signs

Strand: 5-8 **Age:** 70-78m 5.10-6.6y

Definition

The child will recognize and understand the universal safety signs that are appropriate for his group and environment. These universal safety signs include but are not limited to: telling where to cross the street, where to exit, school crossing signs, when to stop, where restrooms are located, where a railroad crossing is, that danger is ahead, and where a telephone is located.

Instructional Materials

Stamps that represent the universal signs, a stamp pad. Sheets of paper to stamp the signs on. Poster paints in red, yellow, blue, and green.

Instructional Activities

1. On a table, place the poster paint containers (the recommended colors are red, yellow, blue, and green), and the sheets of paper.
2. Using the stamps, stamp a Universal Sign on a sheet of paper. Discuss with the child what the sign means, where you would see it, and what you should do when you see the sign.
3. Continue with the other stamps (stamp on a sheet of paper and discuss).
4. Reverse the activity by asking the child to find the stamp that shows a sign that says this is the way out of this room in case of an emergency.
5. After he stamps the Exit sign, ask him to describe his sign and what it means.
6. Continue with the other stamps. (Tell the child to find a sign, to stamp it, and tell about it.)
7. This activity can be enhanced by describing a scenario and asking the child to stamp the sign he would see. Say, for example, "You are standing on the street corner. The traffic light is red. You are waiting for [stamp the sign]."
8. Discuss with him what he should do when he sees the sign. Continue using other scenarios related to other signs.

5.233 Engages in rough-and-tumble play

Strand: 5-5 **Age:** 48-60m 4.0-5.0y

Definition

The child engages with a small group of children, interacting in a playful manner. The play is physical and fast, and the children may be loud.

Instructional Materials

A large parachute.

Instructional Activities

1. Gather the children around the parachute and have them hold on to the material with both hands while sitting on their bottoms.
2. Explain to the children that the parachute can go up and down or side to side.
3. Practice moving the parachute up and down, as well as side to side.
4. Ask the children to take turns deciding whether the parachute should go up and down or side to side and then have everyone perform the movement the child has chosen.
5. Next, introduce the concepts of fast and slow. Demonstrate the new concepts when moving the parachute either up and down or side to side.
6. Again take turns having the children decide whether the parachute should go up and down or side to side, but this time include whether the movement will be fast or slow.
7. When the children are comfortable with the different movements and speeds, take turns selecting two or three children to go under the parachute while you move the parachute up and down, fast or slow, again allowing the children to take turns choosing the motion and the speed.

6.94 Pulls shoes off completely, including undoing laces, straps (*Velcro*), and buckles
Strand: 6-2B **Age:** 30-42m 2.6-3.6y

Definition
The child will take off both of her shoes, including undoing laces, straps (Velcro) and buckles (when asked or voluntarily - children should be urged to keep their shoes on, unless otherwise instructed/asked).

Instructional Materials
A bell.

Instructional Activities
1. Select a large area where the children may sit on chairs in a circle and still have ample space in the center of the circle.
2. Tell the children that they are to sit on the chairs.
3. Tell them they are to take off their shoes when you ring the bell.
4. Collect all the shoes and set them on the floor in the middle of the circle.
5. Tell them when they hear the bell they are to race for their own shoes and put them on as fast as they can.
6. The winner is the child who puts on her shoes first.

6.95 Indicates by words or gestures a need to go to the toilet
Strand: 6-6 **Age:** 30-42m 2.6-3.6y

Definition
The child will indicate by using words or gestures that he needs to be excused to use the bathroom.

Instructional Materials
A piece of poster board, markers and stickers.

Instructional Activities
1. List the names of each child on the poster board, leaving space for stickers next to their name. This will be the reward chart.
2. Explain to each child the classroom process for going to the bathroom.
3. Be sure to include why it is important for everyone to have a way to indicate that they need to go to the bathroom that you understand.
4. Have each child practice a "walk-through," making sure that they understand the process and you understand what they will be saying or how they will gesture to indicate their need to go to the bathroom.

5. Each time a child indicates through words or gestures that they need to be excused to go to the bathroom, and they go to the bathroom, reward them with a sticker on the poster board reward chart.

6.96 Unzips and unsnaps clothing
Strand: 6-2B **Age:** 32-40m 2.8-3.4y

Definition
The child will unzip or unsnap clothing that she is wearing. The child will pull the zipper completely down to release the item of clothing. The child will gently pull the snaps to open the article of clothing.

Instructional Materials
Cloth doll, such as a *Raggedy Ann*-type doll. Doll clothes with zippers and snaps. Key ring.

Instructional Activities
1. Use medium to large *Raggedy Ann*-type doll.
2. Secure doll clothes with zippers and snaps.
3. Show the child how to dress and undress doll.
4. Point out similarities between Raggedy Ann's and the child's clothes as she plays.
5. Watch the child as she undresses the doll.
6. If the child has difficulty unzipping the clothing, place a key ring through hole in zipper tab.
7. Demonstrate how to pull zipper down and back up.
8. Ask the child to pull zipper down.
9. Give the child physical assistance if necessary.
10. Make a game by moving your hand slowly up and down the zipper and having the child follow your moving hand with his hand up and down the zipper.
11. Let the child act as assistant or model to another child when she has accomplished task.
12. Allow the child to use the doll and doll clothes during independent playtime.
13. If the child needs help with unsnapping, provide hand-over-hand assistance as you verbally describe the process to her.

6.97 Pulls pants up completely from floor to waist
Strand: 6-2A **Age:** 30-38m 2.6-3.2y

Definition
Note: *Training in dressing/undressing is a real-life skill experience that occurs more frequently in a home setting, rather than an educational setting. However, certain aspects could and should be reinforced in the*

child's educational setting. It is important when addressing dressing/undressing skills in the educational situation that program policies be adhered to.
The child will pull up a pair of large pants. He will pull these pants up from his ankles to his waist.

Instructional Materials

Two sets of clothing outfits that include two pairs of pants, two front-buttoning shirts, two pairs of shoes, two hats, two pairs of gloves. Two containers that close (e.g., briefcase, box, sack). Masking tape.

Instructional Activities

1. Divide the clothing into two sets, put one set in one container and the other set in the other container.
2. Attach two strips of masking tape to the floor to mark a starting line and a dressing line, at least 10 feet in front of the start.
3. Place the containers with the clothing inside on the dressing line in front of each child.
4. Select two children to run a Clothing Race.
5. Tell the two children that when you say "Go," they are to run to the container, open it, and put on everything that is inside.
6. Wearing all the clothing, they must run back to the starting line, and return to the container.
7. When they return they are to take off the clothes, put them back into the container, and return to the starting point.
8. The first child to return is the winner.
9. Allow other children to have a turn to participate in the Clothing Race.

6.98 Wipes around nose using tissue if reminded

Strand: 6-9 **Age:** 36-38m 3.0-3.2y

Definition

The child will wipe around her nose when asked-- using a tissue. The child may voluntarily get a tissue or the tissue may be given to her.

Assessment Materials

A box of tissue.

Instructional Materials

/*\Safety Note: Provide scissors appropriate for the child. Remind the child of safety regarding scissors.
Construction paper, markers, tissues, scissors and glue.

Instructional Activities

1. Cut some of the construction paper in a face-shaped ovals.
2. Place the other materials on the worktable.
3. Next, help the child trace around one of their hands on a piece of construction paper.
4. Have the child cut out the hand shape, or help them cut out the hand.
5. Provide the child with the oval pattern. Explain that she should use the markers and draw a face on the oval.
6. After the child has completed the face, explain that the face has a cold and its nose is running.
7. Discuss what the "face" should do about its nose.
8. Provide the child with the tissues and ask her to take one, wipe the nose of "face."
9. Now have the child position the tissue over the nose and mouth they have drawn, and then place their cut-out hand on top of the tissue.
10. Have the child help you stable the tissue and hand in place over the nose and mouth.
11. Display the face and use it as a reminder when the child needs to wipe her nose.

6.99 Swallows food in mouth before taking another bite

Strand: 6-3A **Age:** 36-41m 3.0-3.5y

Definition

When he is eating, the child will place the proper amount of food into his mouth and will chew and swallow it before taking another bite.

Instructional Materials

/*\Safety Note: Be aware of special diets and allergies before doing these activities.
A hand puppet for each child. A fist puppet or a sock puppet make effective puppets for this activity. To make a fist puppet, ask the child to make a fist with his thumb tucked under his fingers. His fist will be the puppet's head, and his thumb will be the puppet's mouth. Ask the child to move his thumb up and down to show how the mouth talks. Use a marker to draw eyes and a nose on the child's fist to represent the puppet's head. To enhance the puppet's mouth, outline it with lipstick. To make a sock puppet, have the child place his hand in the sock, placing his fingers on the seam of the sock. Spread the fingers and thumb a part and push about an inch of the toe end of the sock into his hand to make a mouth. Use a marker to draw

other facial features on the puppet. The puppet can be an animal or a child. A collection of snacks (crackers, fruit, marshmallows, dry cereal, cheese squares) that requires chewing to eat.

Instructional Activities

1. Place the hand puppet and the snacks on a table.
2. Put on one of the hand puppets.
3. Take one of the snacks, put it in your mouth, and eat it.
4. While you are chewing and swallowing, place your fingers over the puppet's mouth to indicate he may not talk now.
5. When you have swallowed the food, remove your fingers from the puppet's mouth and ask the puppet if he is ready for another snack.
6. Say, "You are a good puppet; you waited to take another bite until you swallowed the last bite, and you waited to talk until your mouth was empty."
7. Give the child a hand puppet and a snack.
8. While he chews the snack, he must keep his puppet's lips closed or make him pretend to chew.
9. Explain that his puppet must chew the snack and swallow it before he may have another snack.
10. Praise the child and the puppet for politely chewing and quietly swallowing.

6.100   Puts on appropriate clothing depending on the weather

Strand: 6-2A   **Age:** 42-54m 3.6-4.6y

Definition

When the child is getting ready to go outside (depending on the weather) she will put on her jacket or coat without being asked.

Instructional Materials

A doll and clothing for the doll.

Instructional Activities

1. Present the doll and the clothing to the child. Discuss the various pieces of clothing making sure that the child understands when the different pieces should be worn.
2. Present to the child a scenario pertaining to the doll. For example: the doll is going to take a walk to the park. It is chilly outside and it might rain. What clothing should the doll wear?
3. Ask the child to dress the doll appropriately.

4. Continue until all the clothing has been identified and used to dress the doll.
5. Encourage the child to make up stories about the doll, the clothing and the specific use of the clothing.

6.101   Puts toothpaste on toothbrush and wets

Strand: 6-8   **Age:** 36-48m 3.0-4.0y

Definition

The program-based components for this skill are not covered because oral hygiene is a skill usually dealt with at home - rather than in an educational setting. If oral hygiene is dealt with in the educational program, it is important to check with local agencies to determine appropriate policies.

Instructional Materials

A dental demonstration kit and water. (By contacting a Dental Office they may be able to provide you with a demonstration kit or they will refer you to a dental resource in your community.) Two sheets of paper for each child, with the outline of a toothbrush drawn on each. Toothpaste.

Instructional Activities

1. Invite the children to the story telling area.
2. Read a story/poem about teeth to the children.
3. After reading the story discuss why we should take care of our teeth, what we can do keep our teeth healthy, etc.
4. Demonstrate the best ways to brush our teeth, the use of floss and rinsing after brushing.
5. Introduce the papers with the outlines of a toothbrush drawn on it.
6. Demonstrate squeezing the tube of toothpaste onto the outline.
7. Use the cue word, "squeeze."
8. Place the child's hand on tube and guide his hand as he tries to put toothpaste on his outline.
9. Ask him to try filling his next outline alone.
10. Verbally prompt him if necessary.

6.102   (Removed, see page xii)

6.103   (Removed, see page xii)

6.104 Cleans up spilled liquid

Strand: 6-3B **Age:** 36-48m 3.0-4.0y

Definition

When the child spills, she will clean it up with the proper material, with someone else providing assistance as needed.

Instructional Materials

Several small containers to hold the different colored finger paints. Newspapers, smocks (e.g., men's old T-shirts), slick paper, paper towels, sponge, water.

Instructional Activities

1. Invite the children to the table to do a finger painting activity.
2. Wet the paper all over with the sponge.
3. Place a spoonful of paint on the wet paper.
4. Tell the children to spread the paint with their hands.
5. Encourage them to use other parts of their hands (e.g., fingers, thumb, fist) to draw in the paint.
6. Give them time to experiment and explore with the finger paint.
7. Make sure the children understand that they can erase their picture any time they wish.
8. After each child has completed her finger paint picture, place it on newspapers to dry, and instruct her to use a sponge, water, and paper towels to clean up the spills on the table.
See #5.103, #5.133.

6.105 Puts hands through both armholes of front-opening clothing

Strand: 6-2A **Age:** 36-42m 3.0-3.6y

Definition

The child will put his hands through both armholes of a front-opening blouse/shirt/jacket/etc. The garment should be opened, not requiring the child to open the item before putting it on. The child should put one arm through an armhole at a time.

Instructional Materials

/*\Safety Note: Provide scissors appropriate for the child. Remind the child of safety regarding scissors.

Secure enough interfacing fabric (available at most fabric shops) to cover the child's front and back, neck to knees. Washable crayons (if washable crayons are used on interfacing, the colors will wash out and the costume can be

used over and over), scissors, yarn or string and a paper punch.

Instructional Activities

1. Cut a rectangular piece of fabric large enough to cover the child's front and back and long enough to reach from his neck to his knees. In the center of the piece of material, cut a slot for his head. Use the paper punch and punch holes in each side of the costume and lace or tie each side together with the yarn/string. Be sure to allow an opening on each side for the child's arms to fit through.
2. Invite the child to assist you in making the costume. Once the yarn is started in the punched holes, the child should be encouraged to complete the "sewing".
3. After the costume is finished, provide the child with the washable crayons to use to decorate the garments. The decorations should be relative to the dramatization that the group is planning.
4. Make a slit up the front of the costume.
5. Provide each child with a finished costume and ask him to put it on, placing one arm in a sleeve at a time.
6. Remember that the costume may be washed and reused.

6.106 Pushes arm into second sleeve and pulls clothing to shoulders

Strand: 6-2A **Age:** 36-42m 3.0-3.6y

Definition

The child will put her hands through both armholes of a front-opening blouse/shirt/jacket/etc. and pull the garment to her shoulders. The garment should be opened, not requiring the child to open the item before putting it on. The child should put one arm through an armhole and then the other arm through the other armhole before pulling the sweater/shirt to her shoulders. The child may or may not use her predominate hand first in putting on the piece of clothing.

Instructional Materials

Two complete sets of clothing, which includes two pairs of pants, two front-buttoning shirts, two pairs of shoes, two hats, two pairs of gloves. Two containers that close (e.g., suitcase, box). Masking tape.

Instructional Activities

1. Divide the clothing into two sets, put one set in one container and the other set in the other container.

2. Attach two strips of masking tape to the floor to mark a starting line and a dressing line at least 10 feet in front of the start.
3. Place the containers with the clothing inside on the dressing line in front of each child.
4. Select two children to run a "Clothing Race."
5. Tell the two children that when you say, "Go," they are to run to the container, open it, and put on everything that is inside.
6. Wearing all the clothing, they must run back to the starting line, and return to the container.
7. When they return they are to take off the clothes, put them back into the container, and return to the starting point.
8. The first child to return is the winner.
9. Allow other children to have a turn to participate in the "Clothing Race."
10. Invite the children to remove the clothes from the trunk, and to select the ones they want to put on. Encourage them to be creative. After they dress, invite them to make up a play and to role-play their part.

See #6.105.

6.107   Assists in washing body when bathed by an adult

Strand: 6-5   **Age:** 40-54m 3.4-4.6y

Definition

The program-based components for this skill are not covered because bathing is a skill usually dealt with at home - rather than in an educational setting. If bathing is dealt with in the educational program, it is important to check with local agencies to determine appropriate policies.

6.108   Assists in drying body when finished with bath

Strand: 6-5   **Age:** 36-43m 3.0-3.7y

Definition

The program-based components for this skill are not covered because bathing is a skill usually dealt with at home - rather than in an educational setting. If bathing is dealt with in the educational program, it is important to check with local agencies to determine appropriate policies.

6.109   Turns water off when requested/on own

Strand: 6-5   **Age:** 36-44m 3.0-3.8y

Definition

The child will turn off running water when he is through using it (classroom sink, drinking fountain, sink in restrooms, etc.) He will turn if off when asked to or on his own.

Instructional Materials

A bell, or a squeaky toy, beside the sink or water faucet. A tongue depressor, 3 x 5-inch cards and markers. Glue or stapler.

Instructional Activities

1. Place the bell/squeaky toy, tongue depressor, card and markers on a table.
2. Invite the child to the worktable and allow him to assist in making a sign. On the card print the word "off" in big letters with a colorful marker. Make sure that the child hears the word, understands what it means and uses it correctly.
3. Attach the card to the tongue depressor (staples and glue work well).
4. Place the "off" sign on top of the bell/squeaky toy.
5. Ask the child to join you at the sink, and explain why water faucets should be turned off after using them.
6. Demonstrate how to turn the faucets on and off.
7. Allow the child to turn the water on and off.
8. Explain to the child that sometimes we forget to turn the water off and the squeaky toy is here to help us remember.
9. Turn the water on and then turn the water off; after turning the water off, pick up the bell or squeeze the toy to make a noise.
10. Tell the child every time he turns the water off, the squeaky toy/bell wants to make a noise.
11. Ask the child to turn the water on, then turn it off and ring the bell/push the squeaky toy.
12. The noise device may act as a reminder that the water has been turned off.

6.110 Puts comb/brush in hair

Strand: 6-5 **Age:** 36-44m 3.0-3.8y

Definition

The child places a comb or a brush in her hair; the comb/brush does not necessarily have to be used to actually "comb or brush" the hair.

Instructional Materials

Used wigs (make sure to first wash and disinfect any used wigs) or a doll. A comb, brush and a mirror.

Instructional Activities

1. Place the wigs, comb, brush and mirror in the "dress-up" area.
2. During dramatic playtime, encourage the children to dress-up, put on fun wigs, etc.
3. Demonstrate how to make interesting hair-styles using a comb and brush.
4. Encourage the child to comb/brush a wig before adding it to her dramatic costume.
5. Allow the child to admire herself in front of a mirror.

6.111 Puts on T-shirt with front/back in correct position

Strand: 6-2A **Age:** 36-44m 3.0-3.8y

Definition

The child will put on a T-shirt making sure that the front and back are in the correct position.

Instructional Activities

See #6.106 for instructional materials and activities.

6.112 Puts sock on completely

Strand: 6-2A **Age:** 36-44m 3.0-3.8y

Definition

The child will put on her sock and pull it on completely from the toe, to heel, to ankle.

Instructional Materials

A large sock, dolls, socks that fit the doll.

Instructional Activities

1. Show the child the large sock. Make sure that the child understands the heel, toe and top of the sock.
2. Take a hold of the sock at the top making sure that the heel is toward you.
3. Place your toes inside the toe of the sock and pull it up.
4. Make any necessary adjustments.

5. Invite the child to take a large sock and repeat the above steps. Provide assistance as needed.
6. For additional practice, allow the child to put socks on the feet of the doll in the dress-up area.

6.113 Directs spoon/fork into mouth without spilling

Strand: 6-3A **Age:** 30-42m 2.6-3.6y

Definition

The child will grasp a spoon or a fork, fill it, move the spoon or fork to his mouth and insert it with no spilling. He may grasp the utensil with either a supinate (palm of hand directly forward and thumb away from body) or palmar (grip controlled by palm down, fingers direct). He generally loads the spoon/fork with the right amount of food.

Instructional Materials

/*\Safety Note: Be aware of special diets and allergies before doing these activities.
A spoon and a fork for each child, a bowl of yogurt, slices of apples, masking tape, a collection of newspapers.

Instructional Activities

1. Place a strip of masking tape on the floor to indicate a starting point and an ending spot. Lay newspapers on the floor between the two strips of tape to catch spills. Set the spoon(s), the fork(s), the bowl of yogurt and the apple slices on a table near the starting tape.
2. Explain to the children that they are going to have a Yogurt Walk.
3. Ask them to watch carefully.
4. Go to the starting tape, take a spoon, and dip it into the yogurt until you have a scoop on the spoon.
5. Make sure the children are aware of the Yogurt Walk steps.
6. Say, "Watch me very carefully. I am going to walk to the stop line, and I am going to try not to spill any yogurt. If I spill the yogurt, I must go back, get some more, and try again. Here I go."
7. Repeat the Yogurt Walk steps until the children become motivated and understand the activity.
8. Ask for a child volunteer.
9. Review with him what he is to do.
10. Encourage the other children to cheer the Yogurt Walker.
11. Give each child a chance to participate.

12. You can modify this activity by forming teams and changing the Yogurt Walk to a Yogurt Race.
13. Next, explain to the children that they are going to have an Apple Walk.
14. Ask them to watch carefully.
15. Go to the starting tape, take a fork, and spear an apple slice onto the fork.
16. Make sure the children are aware of the Apple Walk steps.
17. Say, "Watch me very carefully. I am going to walk to the stop line, and I am going to try not to lose my apple slice. If I lose my apple slice, I have to go back, get some more, and try again. Here I go."
18. Repeat the Apple Walk steps until the children become motivated and understand the activity.
19. Ask for a child volunteer.
20. Review with him what he is to do.
21. Encourage the other children to cheer the "Apple Walker."
22. Give each child a chance to participate.
23. You can modify this activity by forming teams and changing the Apple Walk to an Apple Race.
24. To increase the difficulty, select a smaller or softer food to be speared.

6.114 Serves self at table, pouring and scooping with no spilling
Strand: 6-3A **Age:** 36-48m 3.0-4.0y

Definition
The child will serve herself at the table. She will pour liquid into a glass or cup, use a spoon to scoop food from a serving dish, and take a finger food (e.g., slice of bread) from a plate. She will ask for food and drink to be passed to her.

Instructional Materials
/*\Safety Note: Be aware of special diet needs or allergies.
Food such as yogurt, cookies, milk, plates, cups or glasses.

Instructional Activities
Note: You can easily modify this snack time activity by using different foods and different serving containers.
1. Place a plate of cookies, a bowl of yogurt, a pitcher of milk, and the dishes on a table next to you.
2. Invite at least three children to the table.
3. Ask one of them to serve milk to herself and the others.

4. Demonstrate how to pour one glass of milk.
5. Give her the pitcher, and ask her to serve the milk.
6. Ask another child to serve yogurt to herself and the others.
7. Demonstrate how to spoon the yogurt out of the serving dish onto a plate.
8. Give her the spoon, and ask her to serve the yogurt.
9. Ask another child to serve a cookie to herself and the others. Demonstrate how to hold the plate and take off a cookie.
10. Provide the children with any necessary assistance to ensure this snack time activity is a positive experience.

6.115 Puts shoes on the correct feet
Strand: 6-2A **Age:** 30-42m 2.6-3.6y

Definition
Note: *It is not necessary that the child understand the concepts of right and left.*
The child will put on his shoes by matching the right shoe to his right foot and his left shoe to his left foot.

Instructional Materials
Chairs.

Instructional Activities
1. Have the child sit on the floor or a low chair so his feet are on the floor.
2. Let the child bring his foot over his other knee and bring the shoe to his foot. Let him put his toes into the shoe and bring the shoe over the heel. Assist as needed.
3. Repeat with the other foot. Assist as needed.
4. Let the child practice with loose shoes.
5. Let the child begin with open back or slip on type shoes.
6. Remove or loosen the shoelaces and bring the tongue of the shoe out so the child can put his foot easily into the shoe.
7. Place the shoes on the floor and let the child work his foot into the shoe while he is in sitting or in supported standing position.
8. Let the child see what you are doing and how you are putting his shoe on his foot if he is unable to do so by himself.

6.116 Places outer-wear clothing in assigned location

Strand: 6-2B **Age:** 36-58m 3.0-4.10y

Definition

The child will hang her jacket/coat/sweater/head-gear (hat/scarf, etc.) on a designated hook or in a designated place.

Instructional Materials

Provide the child with markers, labels, and fun stickers.

Instructional Activities

Note: If the child's name is to be placed on the label, that should be done before the child decorates the labels. If the child is capable of putting her own name on the label, ask her to do that before she decorates.

1. Place the markers and fun stickers on a worktable.
2. Explain to the children that they are going to make their own label to be placed next to their coat hook.
3. Make sure that each child is aware of what a coat hook is, what it is used for and how it is her very special place.
4. After the child has used the markers and favorite stickers to create her label, allow her to place it next to her assigned hook.

6.117 Drinks from water fountain when turned on by adult

Strand: 6-3B **Age:** 37-42m 3.1-3.6y

Definition

The child will drink from a water fountain when it is turned on by an adult. He must be able to reach the fountain independently; however, steps may be provided.

Instructional Materials

The poem, *Drinking Fountain*, by Marchette Chute. This poem is in most children's poetry anthologies. Available drinking fountain.

Instructional Activities

1. Invite the children to gather around the drinking fountain. Read the poem.

The Drinking Fountain by Marchette Chute
  When I climb up
  To get a drink,
  It doesn't work
  The way you'd think.
  I turn it up,
  The water goes,

  And hits me right
  Upon the nose.
  I turn it down
  To make it small,
  And don't get any
  Drink at all.

2. After you read the poem several times, ask a child to climb up to the drinking fountain, as you read the first verse.
3. Turn the water up high so it will hit him on the nose, as you read the second verse.
4. Turn the water down low, so the stream is impossible for drinking, as you read the last verse.
5. Continue this dramatization until every child has had a chance to participate.

6.118 Pulls off front-opening clothing over wrist, forearm and elbow with assistance

Strand: 6-2B **Age:** 28-38m 2.4-3.2y

Definition

The child will take off her front-opening clothing (sweater, shirt, jacket) by pulling it over her wrist, forearm and elbow with assistance, if needed.

Instructional Materials

Collected old clothes, such as costumes, hats, scarves, and props. An old suitcase or trunk for storage.

Instructional Activities

1. Place the collected clothes in the trunk.
2. Invite the children to remove the clothes from the trunk, and to select the ones they want to put on. Encourage them to be creative.
3. After they dress, invite them to change clothes and observe them as they remove their costumes.

6.119 Pulls pants down from waist to feet

Strand: 6-2B **Age:** 30-40m 2.6-3.4y

Definition

Note: *Training in dressing or undressing is a real-life skill experience that occurs in a non-educational setting. However, certain aspects could and should be reinforced in the child's educational setting. It is important that program policies be adhered to when teaching dressing/undressing skills in the educational setting.*
The child will pull his pants down from waist to floor.

Instructional Activities

See #6.118 for instructional materials and
activities.

6.120　(Removed, see page xii)

6.121　Removes pull-over clothing from both arms and starts over head

Strand: 6-2B　**Age:** 38-42m　3.2-3.6y

Definition

Note: *Training in dressing or undressing is a real-life
skill experience that occurs in a non-educational
setting. However, certain aspects could and should be
reinforced in the child's educational setting. It is
important that program policies be adhered to when
teaching dressing/undressing skills in the educational
setting.*
*The child will take-off a piece of clothing that is not a
front-opening garment. The child will take the pull-
over clothing (sweater, T-shirt, etc.) off his arms and
begin to pull the article over his head.*

Instructional Materials

Mirror and chair. Stretchy ski hat and a large
shirt.

Instructional Activities

1. Place the child in front of a mirror while
   sitting on a chair.
2. Model arm raising exercises and have child
   imitate so she is warmed up for task.
3. Place stretchy ski hat over her head.
4. Ask her to raise her arms up and remove the
   hat.
5. Repeat.
6. Place large shirt over child's head at eye level.
7. Say, "Where is Mary? Show me your eyes," or
   "Peek-a-boo, I see you," to encourage her to
   remove the shirt by taking it off over her
   head.
8. Place your hands over the child's and guide
   her through the task if she has difficulty.
9. Increase the difficulty by the placing shirt
   around child's neck and asking her to remove
   it.

6.122　Refills a glass using a container with a handle and a spout

Strand: 6-3B　**Age:** 38-46m　3.2-3.10y

Definition

*Using a container with handle and a pouring spout
that holds less than 8 ounces of a liquid (water, juice,
milk), the child will refill a glass. Some spilling may
occur at first.*

Instructional Materials

A container with a handle and a spout, juice and
a glass or cup for each child. Paper towels,
sponges available.

Instructional Activities

1. Seat the children at the table.
2. Tell them they are going to have a party.
3. Ask one child to be the host.
4. Set out the container of juice and the cups.
5. Ask the host child to pour the juice for the
   others.
6. Place half a cup of juice in the container and
   have her pour it into a cup.
7. Continue until she has poured juice into each
   cup.
8. Let all the children drink the juice and chat
   with each other.
9. Choose another child to be the host at another
   juice time.

6.123　Blows into tissue with some assistance

Strand: 6-9　**Age:** 38-46m　3.2-3.10y

Definition

*The child will blow his nose into a tissue. The child
may voluntarily get a tissue or have the tissue given
to him. He may need assistance holding or
positioning the tissue.*

Instructional Materials

A box of tissue, a wastebasket.

Instructional Activities

Note: Changing the color of the tissues often will
be motivational for the children, as well as a
procedure for controlling overuse.
1. Place the box of tissue in an accessible location
   for the children.
2. Talk about where the box of tissue is located
   and what to do with the soiled tissues.
3. Encourage the child to blow his nose when he
   is sniffing, sneezing, or he is attempting to
   pick his nose.

6.124 (Removed, see page xii)

6.125 (Removed, see page xii)

6.126 (Removed, see page xii)

6.127   Closes the front snap on an article of clothing

Strand: 6-2A   **Age:** 36-48m 3.0-4.0y

Definition

The child will close the front snaps to an article of clothing. The child will grasp the clothing that surrounds one of the snaps, match the two parts and press until the snaps interlock.

Instructional Materials

A jacket with large snaps.

Instructional Activities

1. Secure a jacket with large snaps for the child.
2. Demonstrate how the snaps close.
3. Show the child how the jacket would look if it was snapped wrong.
4. Have the child practice closing the snaps without the jacket on.
5. Demonstrate how to close the snaps using her thumb on one side and forefinger on the other. Show the need to "line up" the two parts of the snap before pressing them together.
6. Have the child put on her jacket and repeat the process.

6.128 (Removed, see page xii)

6.129   Takes pull-over clothing off completely

Strand: 6-2B   **Age:** 40-48m 3.4-4.0y

Definition

Note: *Training in dressing or undressing is a real-life skill experience that occurs in a non- educational setting. However, certain aspects could and should be reinforced in the child's educational setting. It is important that program policies be adhered to when teaching dressing/undressing skills in the educational setting.*
The child will take-off a piece of clothing that is not a front-opening garment. The child will take the pull-over clothing (sweater, T-shirt, etc.) off completely.

Some assistance may be needed, however the goal is to strive for independence.

Instructional Materials

Collected old clothes, such as costumes, hats, scarves, and props. An old suitcase or trunk for storage.

Instructional Activities

1. Place the collected clothes in the trunk.
2. Invite the children to remove the clothes from the trunk, and to select the ones they want to put on. Encourage them to be creative.
3. After they put on the dress-ups, invite them to play and have fun in the costumes.
4. After they finish playing, have them take the clothing off and put it away.
5. Offer assistance with removing the clothing, if needed.

See #6.121.

6.130   Takes front-opening clothing off completely

Strand: 6-2B   **Age:** 40-48m 3.4-4.0y

Definition

The child will completely takeoff his front-open clothing (sweater, shirt, jacket), with assistance if needed. The assistance needs to be phased out as soon as possible.

Instructional Materials

/*\ **Safety Note:** Be aware of special diets and allergies before doing these activities.
Coats, jackets, and sweaters. Cookies and juice.

Instructional Activities

1. Tell the children they have been invited to party and should put on coats and get ready to leave.
2. Have each child walk around room and pretend they arrived at party.
3. Ask the children to unfasten and take off their coats.
4. Tell the children when they have taken their coats off they may sit down and have cookies and juice as part of the party.

See #6.118.

6.131   Goes to toilet at regular intervals without asking

Strand: 6-6   **Age:** 30-44m 2.6-3.8y

Definition

The child will go to the bathroom at the scheduled classroom times.

Instructional Materials

A regular schedule for Bathroom Breaks.

Instructional Activities

1. Make sure that the children understand that Bathroom Breaks are meant for them to go to the bathroom in order to attempt to relieve themselves, and to wash hands.
2. Before Bathroom Breaks, remind them of what they are supposed to do.
3. After reminding them, gradually ask them to explain the reason for Bathroom Breaks.

6.132　Brushes teeth with horizontal and vertical motion

Strand: 6-8　**Age:** 40-52m　3.4-4.4y

Definition

The program-based components for this skill are not covered because oral hygiene is a skill usually dealt with at home - rather than in an educational setting. If oral hygiene is dealt with in the educational program, it is important to check with local agencies to determine appropriate policies.

Most communities have people who work in the dental care field who are available to visit educational settings.

These resource people bring materials for demonstration on correct ways to brush teeth, and kits that include toothbrushes, toothpaste, dental floss and parent information packets.

These dental visitors are also prepared to talk about proper care of teeth, preventive dental care, the importance of a good diet, and visiting a dentist. Often they will bring models of teeth for the children to practice on, and they will leave a dental educational unit for further exploration and practice.

6.133　Unbuttons clothing

Strand: 6-2B　**Age:** 40-52m　3.4-4.4y

Definition

Note: *Training in dressing or undressing is a real-life skill experience that occurs in a non-educational setting. However, certain aspects could and should be reinforced in the child's educational setting. It is important that program policies be adhered to when teaching dressing/undressing skills in the educational setting.*

The child will unbutton her clothing. The clothing, to begin with, should be front-opening.

Instructional Materials

Coffee can with a slit in the lid. Several buttons of different sizes.

Instructional Activities

1. Gather several buttons.
2. Prepare the coffee can by slitting the plastic lid in center a bit larger than largest button.
3. Present the children with several different sizes of buttons.
4. Instruct the children to push the buttons through the slit in top of the can.
5. Give each child several turns pushing the buttons through the slit.

6.134　Hangs/disposes of towel after using

Strand: 6-5　**Age:** 42-48m　3.6-4.0y

Definition

The child will hang the towel on the appropriate hook or bar. The child will throw the disposal towel in the appropriate waste container.

Instructional Materials

Paper towels, a trash can, a fun sticker, small prize.

Instructional Activities

1. Have the children sit in their chairs.
2. Drop paper towels on floor around the room.
3. Place a trash can near you.
4. Tell the children to get the paper towels and drop them in the trash can.
5. Have them wash and dry their hands when they are done picking up the towels.
6. Tell them that they should also bring the wet paper towels to the trash can.
7. Remind the children to put used paper towels in trash can after they dry their hands.

6.135　Spits toothpaste out

Strand: 6-8　**Age:** 36-48m　3.0-4.0y

Definition

The program-based components for this skill are not covered because oral hygiene is a skill usually dealt with at home - rather than in an educational setting. If oral hygiene is dealt with in the educational program, it is important to check with local agencies to determine appropriate policies.

Most communities have people who work in the dental care field who are available to visit educational settings.

These resource people bring materials for demonstration on correct ways to brush teeth, and kits that include toothbrushes, toothpaste, dental floss and parent information packets.

These dental visitors are also prepared to talk about proper care of teeth, preventive dental care, the importance of a good diet, and visiting a dentist. Often they will bring models of teeth for the children to practice on, and they will leave a dental educational unit for further exploration and practice.

6.136 Rinses toothbrush

Strand: 6-8 **Age:** 42-48m 3.6-4.0y

Definition

The program-based components for this skill are not covered because oral hygiene is a skill usually dealt with at home - rather than in an educational setting. If oral hygiene is dealt with in the educational program, it is important to check with local agencies to determine appropriate policies.

Most communities have people who work in the dental care field who are available to visit educational settings.

These resource people bring materials for demonstration on correct ways to brush teeth, and kits that include toothbrushes, toothpaste, dental floss and parent information packets.

These dental visitors are also prepared to talk about proper care of teeth, preventive dental care, the importance of a good diet, and visiting a dentist. Often they will bring models of teeth for the children to practice on, and they will leave a dental educational unit for further exploration and practice.

6.137 Wipes mouth and hands dry after brushing teeth

Strand: 6-8 **Age:** 42-48m 3.6-4.0y

Definition

The program-based components for this skill are not covered because oral hygiene is a skill usually dealt with at home - rather than in an educational setting. If oral hygiene is dealt with in the educational program, it is important to check with local agencies to determine appropriate policies.

Most communities have people who work in the dental care field who are available to visit educational settings.

These resource people bring materials for demonstration on correct ways to brush teeth, and kits that include toothbrushes, toothpaste, dental floss and parent information packets.

These dental visitors are also prepared to talk about proper care of teeth, preventive dental care, the importance of a good diet, and visiting a dentist. Often they will bring models of teeth for the children to practice on, and they will leave a dental educational unit for further exploration and practice.

6.138 Allows hair to be washed

Strand: 6-5 **Age:** 42-50m 3.6-4.2y

Definition

The program-based components for this skill are not covered because hair washing is a skill usually dealt with at home - rather than in an educational setting. If hair washing is dealt with in the educational program, it is important to check with local agencies to determine appropriate policies.

Instructional Materials

Locate an action poem about washing hair; these poems are available from your local library. If an action poem is not available, the following is an example:

Washing Hair
Washing hair
With gentle soap
Rubbing, scrubbing, soapy suds
Rinse-a-do, rinse away, rubadee-dub
Rubadee-dub, rinse away
Shake, toss and turn
Squeaky clean
Squeaky clean

Instructional Activities

1. Invite the child to the story telling area. Explain to the children that you are going to read them a poem about washing your hair.
2. Read the poem Washing Hair to the children.
3. Discuss washing your hair, what happens, who does it, how it feels, etc.
4. After the discussion, read the poem once again.
5. Tell the children you are going to read the poem again and invite them to say the parts they know.
6. Repeat until the children are familiar with the poem Washing Hair.
7. Add actions to the poem, such as:
Washing Hair
   Washing hair (Tip head back)
   With gentle soap (pour on shampoo)
   Rubbing, scrubbing, soapy suds (using finger tips, rub, scrub head)
   Rinse-a-do, rinse away, rubadee-dub (tip head back, run open fingers through hair)
   Rubadee-dub, rinse away (run open fingers through hair)
   Shake, toss and turn (shake head, tossing hair with fingers)
   Squeaky clean (happy smile, move head as if showing off clean hair)
   Squeaky clean (happy smile, move head as if showing off clean hair)

6.139 Washes and dries hands without assistance

Strand: 6-5　**Age:** 30-42m 2.6-3.6y

Definition

The child will wash her hands by rubbing soap all over her wet hands. She will rinse the soap off by placing her hands under running water. Finally, she will get a towel and dry her hands thoroughly, both the palms and the tops of her hands. She completes the task independently.

Instructional Materials

Locate a finger-play pertaining to washing hands or the following may be used:

Wash My Hands

I wash my hands like this (demonstrate washing hands)

I wash my hands like this (demonstrate washing hands)

Soap (hold up one hand in fist position) and water (hold up the other hand in fist position), soap (hold up one hand in fist position) and water (hold up the other hand in fist position).

Clean (open both hands to indicate clean hands and pat the air), clean (open both hands to indicate clean hands and pat the air), clean (open both hands to indicate clean hands and pat the air).

Or

Wash Right Hand-Wash Left Hand

This is my clean hand (show hand).

I will raise it up high (raise hand up high).

This is my dirty hand (show hand)

I will touch the sky. (raise hand up high)

Clean hand (show clean hand), dirty hand (show dirty hand).

Roll them around (roll hands)

Clean hand (show clean hand), dirty hand (show dirty hand).

Wash, wash, wash (washing hand motions).

Instructional Activities

1. Invite the children to the story telling area. Tell them you have a fun finger play for them to do.
2. Say the finger play, including the accompanying motions.
3. Repeat the finger play with motions.
4. Invite the children to join you in saying the finger play and doing the motions.
5. Continue until the children have learned the finger play and the motions.
6. Discuss with the children the importance of washing hands, when they should wash their hands and review how to wash their hands properly.

7. Repeat the finger play and the motions.
8. Invite a child to be the finger play leader.

6.140　Puts on clothing in the correct front and back position

Strand: 6-2A　**Age:** 44-50m 3.8-4.2y

Definition

The child will put on clothing (like a T-shirt) making sure that the front and back are in the correct position.

Instructional Materials

Old shirts and jackets that open in the front. Non-opening garments (T-shirts, sweaters, elastic waist pants, etc.)

Instructional Activities

1. Obtain some shirts and jackets that open in the front.
2. Show the child where labels appear on their jackets and shirts.
3. Place the clothing in a pile and have the child sort the pile so the fronts face up.
4. Give the child a pile of non-opening garments and have her sort these so the labels are on the bottom.
5. Help the child correct any mistakes, and remind her that the labels are typically in the front or back of the clothing.
6. Make a game out of the sorting by seeing who can sort the fastest.

See #6.111.

6.141　Pinches tissue off end of nose

Strand: 6-9　**Age:** 44-52m 3.8-4.4y

Definition

The child will wipe around his nose using a tissue. The child will pinch the tissue when he reaches the end of his nose. The child may voluntarily get a tissue or the tissue will be given to him.

Instructional Activities

See #6.98 for instructional materials and activities.

6.142　Tears toilet tissue appropriately and flushes toilet after use

Strand: 6-6　**Age:** 44-56m 3.8-4.8y

Definition

The program-based components for this skill are not covered because toileting is a skill usually dealt with at home - rather than in an educational setting. If toileting is dealt with in the educational program, it is important to check with local agencies to determine appropriate policies.

6.143 Tightens shoelaces with a vertical or horizontal pull

Strand: 6-2A **Age:** 45-50m 3.9-4.2y

Definition
The child will tighten his shoelaces by pulling the laces. The child needs to pull both laces at the same time and can use a vertical or horizontal pull.

Instructional Materials
A shoe with laces or a lacing frame.

Instructional Activities
1. Provide the child with the laced shoe or the lacing frame.
2. Ask the child to position himself behind the shoe or the frame. Demonstrate how to tighten laces on the shoe or on the board. Assist the child by using a hand-over approach; gradually phase out the physical help.

6.144 Tucks in or straightens front-opening clothing

Strand: 6-2A **Age:** 54-66m 4.6-5.6y

Definition
The child will push a front-opening shirt/blouse into pants/skirt and straighten the front of the garment.

Instructional Materials
Collected old clothes, such as blouses and shirts. Marker.

Instructional Activities
1. Secure a collection of old blouses and shirts that will fit the children.
2. Use a marker to draw "tuck-in" and "mid-front" lines on the garments.
3. Give the children the clothing and have them select a blouse or shirt.
4. Have the children put on the garment and tuck it in via the marks, and have them straighten the clothing properly by looking at the marks.
5. Praise those children who get the marks lined up.

6.145 Dries face with towel when requested/on own

Strand: 6-5 **Age:** 36-48m 3.0-4.0y

Definition
The program-based components for this skill are not covered because washing/bathing involve skills usually dealt with at home - rather than in an educational setting. If washing/bathing is dealt with in the educational program, it is important to check with local agencies to determine appropriate policies.

6.146 Applies soap to cloth

Strand: 6-5 **Age:** 46-54m 3.10-4.6y

Definition
The program-based components for this skill are not covered because washing/bathing involve skills usually dealt with at home - rather than in an educational setting. If washing/bathing is dealt with in the educational program, it is important to check with local agencies to determine appropriate policies.

6.147 Prepares simple foods for eating

Strand: 6-3A **Age:** 42-56m 3.6-4.8y

Definition
When she is presented with appropriate food, the child will demonstrate the skills necessary to prepare it for consumption. The preparation required could include peeling a banana, pouring a liquid, spreading a soft spread, cracking and peeling an egg, or inserting a straw. With the proper selection of foods for her to prepare, she will be exposed to sensory experiences. Example: Sensory--See how food changes (e.g., hard-boiled egg), the smell of food, how food feels (e.g., banana with the peel on it and after peel is removed), and the sounds of food (e.g., crunchy pretzels dipped in peanut butter).

Instructional Materials
/*\Safety Note: Be aware of special diets needs and allergies before doing these activities, and caution the children about sharp egg shells.
At least two hard-boiled eggs per child, plus one for the instructor. Bowl for each child. Paper towels.

Instructional Activities
1. Boil the eggs until they are hard-boiled and chill.
2. Give each child two eggs in a bowl and a paper towel.

3. Using your egg, demonstrate how to remove the shell on the egg by rolling it on the table sideways and cracking the shell.
4. Peel the egg in your fingers and put the peeled egg in a bowl and the shell on the paper towel.
5. Have the children begin peeling their eggs. If necessary, place your hand over the child's hand to help her peel her first egg.
6. Ask her to peel the second egg herself.
7. Repeat the hand-over-hand method if she is having difficulty peeling her egg.
8. Tell the children they may eat their eggs.
9. You can vary this activity by cutting the eggs after peeling and adding mayonnaise for egg salad.
10. To teach cutting and cleaning other ingredients (e.g., celery, pickles, onions) may be added.

6.148   Returns toothbrush, paste to designated container/location
Strand: 6-8   **Age:** 46-56m 3.10-4.8y

Definition

The program-based components for this skill are not covered because oral hygiene is a skill usually dealt with at home - rather than in an educational setting. If oral hygiene is dealt with in the educational program, it is important to check with local agencies to determine appropriate policies.
Most communities have people who work in the dental care field who are available to visit educational settings.
These resource people bring materials for demonstration on correct ways to brush teeth, and kits that include toothbrushes, toothpaste, dental floss and parent information packets.
These dental visitors are also prepared to talk about proper care of teeth, preventive dental care, the importance of a good diet, and visiting a dentist. Often they will bring models of teeth for the children to practice on, and they will leave a dental educational unit for further exploration and practice.

6.149   Eats different types of foods
Strand: 6-3A   **Age:** 48-54m 4.0-4.6y

Definition

When he is presented with different types of foods, the child will eat them appropriately. The foods should include foods that are crispy, sticky, chewy, liquid and solid.

Instructional Materials

/*\Safety Note: Be aware of special diets needs and allergies before doing these activities.
Different textured foods, liquids, eating utensils.

Instructional Activities

1. Plan a Tasting Party game by placing the collected foods and liquids and the eating utensils on a table.
2. Explain to the children that at a Tasting Party everyone tries all the foods.
3. Discuss each food including its name, its texture, its smell, and how to eat it.
4. Place one of the foods that you just discussed on a tray.
5. Pass around the tray of food, and ask each child take a sample of the food.
6. Ask all the children to taste each item.
7. Discuss what the food tastes like, what it felt like to eat, and ask the children if they remember the name of the food.
8. Continue the same process described above with other foods.
9. Place the leftover food on the table, and invite the children to select what they want.

6.150   Puts proper amount of food in mouth and chews with lips closed
Strand: 6-3A   **Age:** 48-54m 4.0-4.6y

Definition

When eating, the child will place the proper amount of food into her mouth and will chew and swallow with her lips closed.

Instructional Activities

See #6.99 for instructional materials and activities.

6.151   Buttons front-opening clothing
Strand: 6-2A   **Age:** 36-54m 3.0-4.6y

Definition

Note: *Training in dressing or undressing is a real-life skill experience that occurs in a non-educational setting. However certain aspects could and should be reinforced in the child's educational setting. It is important that local policies be adhered to when teaching dressing/undressing skills in the educational setting.*
The child will button front-opening clothing.

Instructional Materials

Button boards. You can make a button board by sewing large buttons to a piece of fabric with string, leaving about a half an inch of string between the string and the fabric. This will give enough space between the button and the fabric so the child can pass the button through the buttonhole easily. Attach the fabric to a board. Dolls and doll clothing with large buttons. Front-opening clothing with large buttons.

Instructional Activities

1. Take the button board and pass the button halfway through the hole and let the child pull the button completely through the hole.
2. Let the child practice dressing dolls with clothing that has large buttons.
3. Let the child button front opening clothing with large buttons. Use a practice smock or a sleeveless vest with large buttons.
4. Use buttons with loops instead of buttonholes.

6.152   Replaces top on toothpaste
Strand: 6-8 **Age:** 48-54m 4.0-4.6y

Definition
The program-based components for this skill are not covered because oral hygiene is a skill usually dealt with at home - rather than in an educational setting. If oral hygiene is dealt with in the educational program, it is important to check with local agencies to determine appropriate policies.

Instructional Materials
Salt, water, baking soda, peppermint flavoring, blender, measuring cup, measuring spoons, small plastic container for each child, paper towels.

Instructional Activities
1. Place all the material on a table.
2. Discuss with the children the importance of using toothpaste. Talk about how much toothpaste to put on the toothbrush, why we rinse out our mouths after brushing our teeth, and the importance of putting the top back on the toothpaste.
3. Explain to them that they are going to help make toothpaste.
4. Measure 2 tablespoons salt and place it in the blender.
5. Turn on the blender to the "mix" setting, and run it until the salt has a powdery form.
6. Ask a child to measure ½ cup water and pour it into the blender.
7. Turn the blender on "blend."
8. Ask a child to pour baking soda from a 16-ounce box into the blender.
9. Blend the mixture.
10. Add ¼ teaspoon peppermint flavoring.

11. Blend the total mixture.
12. Place a small amount of the toothpaste in each child's plastic container.
13. Review with them the importance of toothpaste, why we use it, and how to use it.
14. Talk about the importance of replacing the top on the toothpaste tube at home to keep the toothpaste fresh and clean.
15. Leave the containers of toothpaste out over night. In the morning, have the children examine the toothpaste to see how it dried out and is no longer useable.

6.153   Holds container with one hand while sucking liquid through a straw
Strand: 6-3B **Age:** 38-48m 3.2-4.0y

Definition
When the child is given a straw in a container, she will suck the liquid through the straw. She will need to hold the container with one hand and the straw with her other hand.

Instructional Materials
/*\Safety Note: Be aware of special diets needs and food allergies before doing these activities.
Straws, cups, and a pitcher. Milk, juice, or water.

Instructional Activities
1. Place the straws and cups on the table. Invite the child to take a straw and a cup.
2. Have the child take a turn pouring a small amount of the liquid from the pitcher into her cup.
3. Tell her to put the straw into her cup and to drink the liquid.
4. If she finishes, offer her more liquid to drink using her straw.

6.154   Goes to toilet when necessary with infrequent accidents
Strand: 6-6 **Age:** 36-48m 3.0-4.0y

Definition
The child will indicate verbally, with a gesture, or by using a tangible object that he needs to be excused from the room to go to the bathroom.

Instructional Materials
Have available a tangible object that the child can use to indicate he has left the room to go to the bathroom. Examples: (1) A stuffed animal that in one position means that no one has left the room to go to the bathroom and that in another position means that someone has left;

(2) A small flag that in an upright position means someone has left and that when in a down position means that no one has left to go to the bathroom; (3) A colored tag on a string: the string or tag has been placed on a hook to indicate someone went to the bathroom, and when that person returns he takes the string or the tag down; (4) A small board that is colored red on one side and the other side is blue, the board is kept on a cup hook. When a child needs to leave the room he places the board so that the red side is showing, this indicates to other children that some one has left (particularly important if the classroom rule is that only one person may be excused at one time); (5) Giving a hand signal and waiting for approval; (6) Raising their hand and asking permission to go to the bathroom; (7) Verbally requesting to go to the bathroom, etc.

Instructional Activities

1. Explain to each child the classroom process for going to the bathroom.
2. Be sure to include why it is important to have this rule, as well as a demonstration "walk-through" to make sure that each child understands the process.

6.155 Washes and rinses body areas

Strand: 6-5 **Age:** 48-56m 4.0-4.8y

Definition

The program-based components for this skill are not covered because washing/bathing involve skills usually dealt with at home - rather than in an educational setting. If washing/bathing is dealt with in the educational program, it is important to check with local agencies to determine appropriate policies. See the Introduction for information specific for children with special needs.

6.156 Runs comb/brush through hair

Strand: 6-5 **Age:** 56-72m 4.8-6.0y

Definition

The child places a comb or a brush in his hair. The child will hold the comb in an up-right position so that the teeth will go between hair strands. The child will put enough pressure on the brush so that the bristles will go between the hair strands.

Instructional Materials

Used wigs (make sure to wash and disinfect any wigs before using). A comb, brush and a mirror.

Instructional Activities

1. Place the wigs, comb, brush and mirror in the "dress-up" area.
2. During dramatic playtime, encourage the children to dress-up, put on fun wigs, costumes, etc.
3. Demonstrate how to make interesting hairstyles using a comb and brush.
4. Encourage the child to comb/brush a wig before adding it to his dramatic costume.
5. Allow the child to admire himself in front of a mirror.

6.157 Adjusts water temperature to warm when shown by an adult

Strand: 6-5 **Age:** 36-48m 3.0-4.0y

Definition

The child will understand how to adjust cold water and hot water in a sink. The child will be able to turn the cold and hot faucets to the correct positions so the water will be the desired temperature, when shown by an adult.

Instructional Materials

White poster board or 3 x 5-inch cards, red and blue markers and tape.

Instructional Activities

1. Discuss with the children hot and cold water, making sure that the children are aware of how dangerous hot water can be. Include in the discussion that there are hot and cold water faucets and how to adjust the temperatures to get warm water.
2. After the discussion, provide the children with two cards or two pieces of poster board.
3. Explain to the children that the color red indicates hot and the color blue indicates cold.
4. Ask the child to make a red dot on one of the cards and a blue dot on the other card. If the children have the skills, they may write the word "hot" (red marker) on one card and the word "cold" (blue marker) on the other card or write the letter H (red marker) on one card and the letter C (blue marker) on the other card.
5. After the labeling has been done, ask each child to go to the classroom sink and tape her red card on the hot water faucet and tape her blue card on the cold water faucet. If the hot and cold water are adjusted by a single faucet, turning it to the left or right, ask the child to tape her card in the correct direction.

6.158 Undresses daily at designated times without being reminded

Strand: 6-2B **Age:** 48-56m 4.0-4.8y

Definition

Note: *Training in dressing or undressing is a real-life skill experience that occurs in a non-educational setting. However, certain aspects could and should be reinforced in the child's educational setting. It is important that local policies be adhered to when teaching dressing/undressing skills in the educational setting.*

6.159 Blows into tissue independently on request

Strand: 6-9 **Age:** 48-56m 4.0-4.8y

Definition

The child will blow into a tissue when she needs to or on request. The child will hold the tissue over her nose, blow, pinch the tissue off the end of her nose, and wipe around the nose area.

Instructional Materials

A box of tissues, a wastebasket.

Instructional Activities

1. Place the box of tissues in an accessible location for the children.
2. Talk about where the box of tissue is located and what to do with the soiled tissues.
3. Explain how a tissue has germs on it and that we do not want someone else touching our used tissue because they may get our germs on their hands.

6.160 Wipes self after toileting

Strand: 6-6 **Age:** 48-66m 4.0-5.6y

Definition

The program-based components for this skill are not covered because toileting is a skill usually dealt with at home - rather than in an educational setting. If toileting is dealt with in the educational program, it is important to check with local agencies to determine appropriate policies.

6.161 Dresses independently when asked

Strand: 6-2A **Age:** 48-66m 4.0-5.6y

Definition

Note: *Training in dressing or undressing is a real-life skill experience that occurs in a non-educational setting. However, certain aspects could and should be reinforced in the child's educational setting. It is important that local policies be adhered to when teaching dressing/undressing skills in the educational setting.*

6.162 Uses towel to dry body after washing

Strand: 6-5 **Age:** 48-60m 4.0-5.0y

Definition

The program-based components for this skill are not covered because washing/bathing involve skills usually dealt with at home - rather than in an educational setting. If washing/bathing is dealt with in the educational program, it is important to check with local agencies to determine appropriate policies. See the Introduction for information specific for children with special needs.

6.163 Disposes of tissue

Strand: 6-9 **Age:** 50-56m 4.2-4.8y

Definition

The child will throw a soiled tissue away in the appropriate container.

Instructional Materials

/*\Safety Note: Provide scissors appropriate for the child. Remind the child of safety regarding scissors.

Paper sacks (lunch sacks are excellent), markers, stickers, crayons, paints, any other decorative materials. A tissue for each child, scissors and glue.

Instructional Activities

1. Place the art material on the work table.
2. Invite the children to the work area.
3. Explain to the children they are going to make their own tissue disposal bag.
4. This bag is to be kept by their work area, especially when they have a cold.
5. Explain they may decorate their bags any way they wish, however they need to attach a tissue to the bag to remind them of its use.
6. After they have completed this art project allow them to take their bag to their own area.

7. Give each child a tissue, ask them to pretend to blow their nose and dispose of the used tissue in the bag.
8. During the day, remind the children when they need to wipe their noses. Prompt the children by saying, "Blow and throw."
9. At the end of the day or whenever appropriate provide the children with an opportunity to dispose their bags and make a new one.

6.164 Drinks from water fountain without aid of adult

Strand: 6-3B **Age:** 50-60m 4.2-5.0y

Definition

The child will drink from a water fountain without any assistance from another person. The fountain may be a faucet type, a button type, or an automatic release. While she learns how to turn the fountain on, she does not have to drink from it. She must be able to reach the fountain independently, steps may be provided.

Instructional Materials

See #6.117 for instructional materials and activities, but encourage the children to turn the water on by themselves.

6.165 (Removed, see page xii)

6.166 Zips up front-opening clothing

Strand: 6-2A **Age:** 60-72m 5.0-6.0y

Definition

The child will zip up her clothing. The clothing should be front opening. The child will zip up her clothing by hooking the zipper base, holding the zipper tab and pulling up.

Instructional Materials

Coats/jackets with zippers.

Instructional Activities

1. Have the child put on a coat or jacket with a zipper.
2. Start with the zipper already fastened at the bottom.
3. Let the child practice pulling the zipper up and down.
4. Point your finger up or down, and make a game out of the child moving the zipper in the same direction.
5. Teach her how to "thread" the zipper starting at the bottom of the jacket, and how to make

sure the moving zipper is at the bottom of the track before inserting the "non" moving side of the track: (1) Have her hold the material at the base of the zipper to straighten the zipper teeth; (2) Have her hook the zipper parts together at the base; (3) Tell her to grasp the zipper tab in her dominant hand; (4) Tell her to pull the zipper up. (5) Cue her to include all three steps by saying, "Hold, hook, pull up."
6. Repeat often until child has mastered the skill.

6.167 Uses toilet properly by self with no accidents

Strand: 6-6 **Age:** 52-60m 4.4-5.0y

Definition

The program-based components for this skill are not covered because toileting is a skill usually dealt with at home - rather than in an educational setting. If toileting is dealt with in the educational program, it is important to check with local agencies to determine appropriate policies.

6.168 Washes face and ears while in bath/shower

Strand: 6-5 **Age:** 52-62m 4.4-5.2y

Definition

The program-based components for this skill are not covered because washing/bathing involve skills usually dealt with at home - rather than in an educational setting. If washing/bathing is dealt with in the educational program, it is important to check with local agencies to determine appropriate policies.

6.169 Opens container and removes foods

Strand: 6-3A **Age:** 40-54m 3.4-4.6y

Definition

The child will open at least five different kinds of containers without any assistance. Examples of the five different kinds of containers are lunch boxes, milk cartons, juice box with straw, plastic containers, plastic bag, pre-packaged food items, threaded jar or bottle tops that have already had the seal broken.

Instructional Materials

At least six different containers, each opening in a different manner. Examples: (1) Small box with a lid (shoe box, gift boxes); (2) Jars or bottles with screw-on lids (water bottle, peanut butter jars, baby food jars, mustard jars); (3) Plastic storage containers with snap tops; (4)

Plastic bags with zip-lock tops; (5) Straws wrapped in paper or plastic; (6) Boxes with interlock tabs (tea boxes, cereal boxes, cracker boxes). A timer.

Instructional Activities

1. Place the different containers on a table in a straight line, leaving about 6 inches between them.
2. Invite a child to come to the table.
3. Tell her you are going to see how fast she can open containers.
4. Demonstrate with the first box: take off the lid and lay it down by the box. Move on to the empty jar, unscrew the lid and place it beside the jar. Continue with the plastic storage container, the bag, and the straw. After you demonstrate, replace the lids, put out a new straw, and close the interlock tab.
5. Tell the child it is her turn to see how quickly she can open each of the objects on the table, beginning with the shoebox and ending with the tea box.
6. As soon as she seems comfortable with the activity, set the timer and explain how she should race against the clock.
7. To modify this activity, arrange two identical rows of different containers. Divide the children into two teams and instruct them how to have a relay race against each other opening the containers.
8. The team that opens each container and reaches the last one first is the winner.
9. You can also make this activity more elaborate by doing the following: (1) Put a food reward inside a jar; (2) Demonstrate to the child how to remove the lid; (3) Unscrew the lid so she can turn it easily; (4) Assist her physically if necessary; (5) Let her have the reward when she removes its lid.

6.170 Washes face with soap when requested/on own

Strand: 6-5 **Age:** 54-62m 4.6-5.2y

Definition

The child will wash her face independently or when requested. She will use her hands or a cloth to wet her face, she will put soap on her hands or a cloth to put on her face, she will gently rub her soapy face, and she will rinse off her face with warm water and dry on towel.

Instructional Materials

A mirror, makeup or washable paints, soap, water, a washcloth, two chairs, dress-up clothes.

Instructional Activities

1. Place the mirror and the makeup or washable paints on a table.
2. Place two chairs at the table.
3. Ask the child to sit in front of the mirror.
4. Using the makeup or paint, make a clown face on the child.
5. Invite her to dress up in funny clothes, and allow her time to do clown tricks.
6. When it is time for her to clean up, give her the washcloth, water, and soap so she can wash her face.
7. When she finishes washing her face, ask her to look in the mirror to make sure all the makeup or paint is off.

6.171 Assists while another washes hair

Strand: 6-5 **Age:** 54-62m 4.6-5.2y

Definition

The program-based components for this skill are not covered because hair washing is a skill usually dealt with at home - rather than in an educational setting. If hair washing is dealt with in the educational program, it is important to check with local agencies to determine appropriate policies.

Instructional Materials

Poem about Washing Hair. If a poem cannot be found, use the following poem:
Washing Hair
Washing hair
With gentle soap
Rubbing, scrubbing, soapy suds
Rinse-a-do, rinse away, rubadee-dub
Rubadee-dub, rinse away
Shake, toss and turn
Squeaky clean
Squeaky clean

Instructional Activities

1. Invite the child to the story telling area. Explain to the children that you are going to read them a poem about washing your hair.
2. Read the poem Washing Hair to the children.
3. Discuss washing your hair, what happens, who does it, how it feels, etc.
4. After the discussion, read the poem once again.
5. Tell the children you are going to read the poem again and invite them to say the parts they know.
6. Repeat until the children are familiar with the Washing Hair poem.
7. Add actions to the poem, such as:
Washing Hair

Washing hair (Tip head back)
With gentle soap (pour on shampoo)
Rubbing, scrubbing, soapy suds (using finger
   tips, rub, scrub head)
Rinse-a-do, rinse away, rubadee-dub (tip head
   back, run open fingers through hair)
Rubadee-dub, rinse away (run open fingers
   through hair)
Shake, toss and turn (shake head, tossing hair
   with fingers)
Squeaky clean (happy smile, move head as if
   showing off clean hair)
Squeaky clean (happy smile, move head as if
   showing off clean hair)

6.172   Opens all fasteners

Strand: 6-2B   **Age:** 54-62m 4.6-5.2y

Definition

The child will open the fasteners on any article of
clothing.

Instructional Materials

Collected old clothes, such as costumes, hats,
scarves, and props.

Instructional Activities

1. Secure a collection of clothing with fasteners
   on the front and back.
2. Tell the children you are to have a fun fashion
   show.
3. Lay the clothes out on the floor, and let the
   other children take turns fastening the clothes
   before they put them on.
4. Then have the children put the clothes on, and
   assist each other if necessary.
5. Have the children proceed with the fashion
   show.
6. Let them change costumes and practice
   unfastening the garments.
7. Help if necessary so all the children are
   successful and have fun.
See #6.96, #6.133.

6.173   (Removed, see page xii)

6.174   Spreads with a knife

Strand: 6-3A   **Age:** 48-60m 4.0-5.0y

Definition

The child will use a knife (plastic) to spread a soft
substance (e.g., butter, jam, cream cheese, apple
butter) on a piece of bread, a cracker or a slice of
toast.

Instructional Materials

/***Safety Note:** Be aware of special diets and
   allergies before doing this assessment.
   Carefully supervise use of knife.
Flour, water, cardboard, plastic knife,
magazines, cutouts, fabrics, wallpaper, pictures.
Whip the flour with a little water to obtain a
paste-like, easy to spread consistency.

Instructional Activities

1. Give each child a piece of cardboard for a
   collage backing, a plastic knife, and paste.
2. Let her choose the cutouts, fabrics, and
   wallpapers she wishes to use.
3. Demonstrate how to spread paste on back of
   the materials to be used.
4. Ask her to imitate the spreading motion with
   the her knife.
5. After the item has paste on it, have her place it
   on the cardboard.
6. Display complete collages.

6.175   Covers mouth with tissue, hand or the bend of the elbow when sneezing or coughing

Strand: 6-9   **Age:** 54-66m 4.6-5.6y

Definition

The child will use a tissue to cover his mouth when
he sneezes or coughs. The child will use the tissue to
wipe any residue from his nose and then will throw
the tissue away. If a tissue is not available, the child
will cover his mouth with his hand or aim the cough
into the bend of his elbow. The child should wash his
hands after sneezing, coughing, or blowing his nose
to prevent the spread of germs.

Instructional Materials

A bag of confetti (secured from commercial
sources, save the paper holes from a paper
punch, or cut newspaper into very small pieces),
a portable hair dryer, a flat dish (e.g., saucer).

Instructional Activities

1. Place half of the small pieces of paper in the
   flat dish and set it on a table.
2. Invite the children to join you at the table.
3. Discuss with them how germs cause colds and
   other illnesses.
4. Make sure they understand that germs are so
   tiny that you cannot see them.
5. Ask them to watch the confetti in the dish.
6. Turn on the hair dryer to the lowest speed
   possible, and hold it far enough away from

the dish of paper that the pieces will blow in a spiral.

7. After the paper has blown about, tell the children the same thing happens when they sneeze, and they should think of the pieces of paper as germs.
8. Ask them how they can prevent the sneeze germs from spreading.
9. If they do not suggest covering their mouths and noses with a tissue, prompt them and demonstrate.
10. To reinforce the use of a tissue when sneezing, place the other half of the small pieces of paper in the dish.
11. Cover the dish with a cloth. If you are using a tissue, tuck it in under the dish.
12. Turn the hair dryer on at a low speed, and hold it far enough away from the covered dish to ripple the cloth or tissue.
13. Discuss with the children why the "paper germs" did not spread.
14. Compare the demonstration with covering mouths and noses when sneezing to prevent the cold germs from flying about.

See #6.159.

6.176 Remembers to wash and dry hands after using the toilet

Strand: 6-6 **Age:** 54-72m 4.6-6.0y

Definition

The child will understand the importance of washing and drying hands before and/or after certain activities. These activities should include before eating, before handling food, after toileting, after playing with dirty material, after working with materials such as clay, etc.

Instructional Activities

See #6.139 for instructional materials and activities.

6.177 Blows nose independently

Strand: 6-9 **Age:** 48-64m 4.0-5.4y

Definition

The child will blow his nose into a tissue without being reminded. The child will hold the tissue over his nose, blow, pinch the tissue off the end of his nose and wipe around the nose area.

Instructional Activities

See #6.159 for instructional materials and activities.

6.178 Adjusts clothing before leaving bathroom

Strand: 6-6 **Age:** 48-66m 4.0-5.6y

Definition

The child will not leave the bathroom until she has her clothing adjusted. This includes all zippers up, skirts down, belts/sashes buckled/tied, shirts/blouses tucked in if appropriate, etc.

Instructional Materials

Develop at least five pictures that show clothing in an untidy manner. These pictures are available from teachers store, however they can easily be created by line drawings. Examples: (1) Picture One - Boy with pants unzipped; (2) Picture Two - a shirt tail out of pants; (3) Picture Three - Boy with a belt unbuckled and hanging around hips; (4) Picture Four - Girl with pants unbuttoned; (5) Picture Five - Girl with skirt half way up and half way down.

Instructional Activities

1. Invite the children to the table.
2. Show the children the pictures one at a time and discuss what is unkempt about the person in the picture.
3. Discuss how the child in the picture could improve her appearance.
4. During the picture viewing and the discussion, include times when our clothes may become untidy and what we can do to prevent these embarrassing situations.

6.179 (Removed, see page xii)

6.180 Carries liquid in open container, without spilling

Strand: 6-3B **Age:** 58-70m 4.10-5.10y

Definition

The child will carry a container at least three-fourths full of liquid, without spilling. He may use both hands to carry the container.

Instructional Materials

Masking tape, a container to carry water, water.

Instructional Activities

1. Place two strips of masking tape about 10 feet apart on the floor to indicate a starting line and a finish line.
2. Put a small amount of water in the container.
3. Invite one child to stand on the starting line and another to stand on the finish line.

4. Give the child at the finish line a container with a small amount of water in it.
5. Tell the child on the starting line that when you give the, "Go" signal, he is to hurry to the other child and take the container of water. Tell him to walk, not run.
6. Ask him to carry the pitcher back to the starting line.
7. If he spills, have him return to starting point to begin again.
8. Allow other children to take a turn carrying the water.
9. To make the activity more challenging, increase the amount of water in the container and the depth of the container.

6.181   Ties shoes, following step-by-step demonstration/support

Strand: 6-2A   **Age:** 60-68m 5.0-5.8y

Definition

The child will tie his shoelaces by pulling the laces, making and tightening a bow following step-by-step demonstration/support. The child will tie his shoes using the following steps: (1) Place one end of the laces in each of the child's hands, a pincer grasp is necessary; (2) Cross one lace over and then under the other lace; (3) Pull laces tight; (4) Physically assist the child, using hand-over-hand support, to make a loop with one lace; (5) Physically assist the child to make a loop with the other lace; (6) Help the child cross the loops; (7) Fold one loop over and then wrap it under and through the opening that is made at the bottom of the two loops; (8) Holding one loop in each hand with a pincer grasp, pull the loops simultaneously, forming a bow; (9) Tighten as necessary.

Instructional Materials

A shoe that ties or a lacing frame.

Instructional Activities

Note: It important for the child to have ample time to practice shoe tying, and when he becomes frustrated the task should be stopped.
1. Provide the child with the laced shoe or the lacing frame.
2. Ask the child to position himself behind the shoe or the frame.
3. Demonstrate how to tie the shoe or the board.
4. Assist the child by using a hand-over-hand approach, as well as verbal coaching.
5. Gradually phase out the physical help, but verbally explain each step if necessary.

6. Phase out all assists, and use them only when the child is experiencing difficulty.
See #6.143.

6.182   Places a front opening garment on a hanger and hangs it up

Strand: 6-2B   **Age:** 60-68m 5.0-5.8y

Definition

The child will place a front opening garment (sweater/blouse/shirt/etc.) on a hanger. The child will fasten (buttons/zips/snaps/etc.) the front opening garment after it is on the hanger.

Instructional Materials

/*\Safety Note: Provide scissors appropriate for the child. Remind the child of safety regarding scissors.
Large paper sacks (one per child) from grocery stores, markers, scissors, hangers, crayons, etc.

Instructional Activities

1. Place the art material and the grocery bags on the worktable. Invite the children to the table.
2. Give each child a big bag.
3. Assist the children in drawing a line perpendicular from the sealed end of the sack to the open end of the sack. The line should be drawn in the middle of the sack, to resemble the front-opening of a shirt/sweater, etc.
4. Explain to the children that they should cut on the drawn line.
5. Assist the children in cutting an area for the their necks and cutting holes on each side of the sack for the arms.
6. After the sacks have been cut allow the child to decorate her sweater/blouse/shirt/etc., using the markers, crayons, etc.
7. After the clothing has been decorated and "designed" have a fashion parade, so that each child may show off her creation.
8. When the children are ready to remove their shirt/sweater/etc., give each of them a coat hanger to hang up their special garment.
9. After each garment is placed on hanger, they can be used as room decoration and enjoyed by the children.

6.183 Selects and uses appropriate protective clothing per weather/settings

Strand: 6-2A **Age:** 60-70m 5.0-5.10y

Definition

The child will select the appropriate clothing for different weather conditions (rainy days, chilly times, hot weather, etc.) The child will select the appropriate clothing to wear based on the activity and setting (apron when using clay/water/cooking/etc.)

Instructional Materials

/***Safety Note:** Provide scissors appropriate for the child. Remind the child of safety regarding scissors.
Magazines, catalogs, or travel brochures. Child-safe scissors, large index size cards, glue.

Instructional Activities

1. Place the materials on a table.
2. Ask the children to look through the magazines or catalogs to cut out pictures that show weather conditions (e.g., rain, snow, wind, hot sun).
3. Ask them to cut out pictures of clothing that is appropriate for different kinds of weather (e.g., raincoats, sweaters, parkas, heavy jackets, shorts).
4. Glue the illustrations they cut out on the cards.
5. Show them the pictures of weather conditions and talk about what it would feel like if you were there, what time of year it would be, what fun things you would do, and what you should wear.
6. Show them the clothing pictures, and discuss the kind of weather you would wear these clothes in and why it would be important to wear them.
7. Lay the pictures of the clothing face-up in a row on the table.
8. Lay the pictures of weather conditions face-down in a pile on the table.
9. Tell one of the children to draw the first card, to look at the scene, describe it, and match it with the picture of the protective clothing to wear. As an example, match a picture of rain with the picture of a raincoat.
10. Allow each child to take a turn matching the weather conditions with the correct clothing to wear.

6.184 Uses paper towel from dispenser or cloth towel to dry hands in new situation

Strand: 6-5 **Age:** 40-52m 3.4-4.4y

Definition

When in a new situation, the child will either hang a hand towel or dispose of a paper towel after using it. The child will hang the towel on the appropriate hook or bar. The child will throw the disposable towel in the appropriate waste container.

Instructional Materials

A hand towel or disposable towels.

Instructional Activities

/***Safety Note:** If the facility has a hand-blow dryer, specific instructions need to be given.

1. When the occasion arises and the children are exposed to a new hand-washing situation, point out where the towels are in the bathroom.
2. Explain to the children where they are to throw the paper towels or place a cloth towel when done.
3. If at all possible use a recall comparison to assist the children in making a transfer association. Example: Say, "At our classroom sink we pull the towels out of dispenser (box) and then we throw them in the basket under the sink. At this sink we take a paper towel off the stack and throw it away in the slot next to the stack."

6.185 Put laces in shoes and laces correctly

Strand: 6-2A **Age:** 66-78m 5.6-6.6y

Definition

The child will put the laces in her shoes and correctly cross-lace (one end of the laces at a time) using alternate eyelets.

Instructional Materials

Shoes that require laces or a lacing board, a red marker and a green marker.

Instructional Activities

1. Place the shoes or lacing board, without the laces in, on a work table.
2. Place a red dot on the end of one of the laces and a green dot on the other end of the lace.
3. Explain to the children they are to take one of the laces and a shoe or lacing board and put the laces in place.
4. Ask the child to look at the red dot at one end and a green dot at the other end.

5. Tell the children when they hear the word red they are to take the lace end with the red dot and put it through the bottom eyelet.

6. Demonstrate placing the red dotted end through the eyelet.

7. Tell the children when they hear the word "green" they are to take the lace end with the green dot and put it through the other bottom eyelet.

8. Demonstrate placing the green dotted end through the other eyelet.

9. Continue saying "red-green-red-green," etc. and pointing to the correct eyelet if needed.

10. Gradually phase out the color cueing and allow the child to lace the shoe/board independently.

6.186 Cuts with a knife

Strand: 6-3A **Age:** 60-72m 5.0-6.0y

Definition

The child will use a knife (plastic or table) to cut soft foods (e.g., banana, cake, Jello). He will begin cutting with a knife by using a down and pull motion. As he becomes skilled in cutting soft foods with a down and pull motion, he should be encouraged to cut harder foods, using a down, pull, and saw motion.

Instructional Materials

A plastic or table knife for each child, cookie sheet, oven, recipe for biscuits (which will include such ingredients as: white flour, baking powder, salt, oil, milk), measuring cups, measuring spoons, spoons to stir, paper towels, napkins, hot pads.

Instructional Activities

/*\ **Safety Note:** Instruct and supervise the child regarding use of a knife, how to be careful around a hot oven, and be aware of special diet needs or allergies.

1. Place the ingredients, cookie sheet, utensils and paper towels on a table.

2. Invite the children to the table, and tell them they are going to make biscuits.

3. Make sure they have washed their hands.

4. Preheat the oven to the temperature indicated in the recipe.

5. Let the children help measure and mix the dry ingredients.

6. Ask a child to help stir in the liquids and mix the ingredients gently.

7. Using as little flour as possible on the tabletop, demonstrate how to knead and roll the dough. (The children may tend to over-handle the dough at first, so a demonstration

and explanations will help them understand how to knead lightly.)

8. Explain to them that they need to make a "log" with the dough.

9. Give each child a knife and tell him to cut a biscuit off the log about ¼ inch thick. Consider pre-scoring the log to assure success.

10. Place the cut biscuit in the lightly greased cookie sheet. Place in the preheated oven for the recommended amount of time.

11. Discuss with the children the transformation of the food as it taken from the oven. Show the children how brown the biscuits have gotten and how they raised during cooking.

12. After the biscuits have cooked and cooled, allow the children to cut them in half and to enjoy the treat.

13. Provide any assistance needed when using a knife.

14. To enhance this treat, place an easy-to-spread cheese or jam on the table, and invite them to add this to their biscuits.

See #6.174.

6.187 (Removed, see page xii)

6.188 Identifies the correct restroom to use by recognizing the sex sign in a new setting

Strand: 6-6 **Age:** 65-78m 5.5-6.6y

Definition

The child will identify the correct restroom sign when shown several different signs (boys, girls, men, women, international signs, laddies and lassies, cowboys and cowgirls). The child should also be aware that some bathrooms are unisex, hence the sign may just read "bathroom" or "restroom."

Instructional Materials

Stamps or stickers that represent the Universal signs for bathroom facilities, a stamp pad, paper.

Instructional Activities

1. Place the materials on the table.

2. Using the stamps or the stickers, place a Universal sign on a sheet of paper.

3. Discuss with her what the sign means, where she might see it, and what she should do when she sees the sign.

4. Continue with the other stamps.

5. Reverse the activity by asking her to find the stamp that shows a sign that indicates "Men's Restroom."

6. Ask her to stamp the sign and tell about it.
7. Continue with the other stamps; tell her to find a sign, stamp it, and tell about it.
8. You can enhance this activity by describing a scenario and asking the child to stamp the sign she would look for. For example, tell him, "You are in the library, when you need to go to the bathroom. You will need to look for which sign?" Continue giving other scenarios related to other signs.

6.189 Flosses teeth
Strand: 6-8 **Age:** 65-72m 5.5-6.0y

Definition
The program-based components for this skill are not covered because oral hygiene is a skill usually dealt with at home - rather than in an educational setting. If oral hygiene is dealt with in the educational program, it is important to check with local agencies to determine appropriate policies.
Most communities have people who work in the dental care field who are available to visit educational settings.
These resource people bring materials for demonstration on correct ways to brush teeth, and kits that include toothbrushes, toothpaste, dental floss and parent information packets.
These dental visitors are also prepared to talk about proper care of teeth, preventive dental care, the importance of a good diet, and visiting a dentist. Often they will bring models of teeth for the children to practice on, and they will leave a dental educational unit for further exploration and practice.

6.190 Uses proper brushing strokes to clean teeth
Strand: 6-8 **Age:** 65-78m 5.5-6.6y

Definition
The program-based components for this skill are not covered because oral hygiene is a skill usually dealt with at home - rather than in an educational setting. If oral hygiene is dealt with in the educational program, it is important to check with local agencies to determine appropriate policies.
Most communities have people who work in the dental care field who are available to visit educational settings.
These resource people bring materials for demonstration on correct ways to brush teeth, and kits that include toothbrushes, toothpaste, dental floss and parent information packets.

These dental visitors are also prepared to talk about proper care of teeth, preventive dental care, the importance of a good diet, and visiting a dentist. Often they will bring models of teeth for the children to practice on, and they will leave a dental educational unit for further exploration and practice.

6.191 Selects clean clothing, changes underclothes regularly
Strand: 6-2A **Age:** 66-72m 5.6-6.0y

Definition
The program-based components for this skill are not covered because dressing/undressing is a skill usually dealt with at home - rather than in an educational setting. If dressing/undressing is dealt with in the educational program, it is important to check with local agencies to determine appropriate policies.

6.192 Cuts with knife and fork
Strand: 6-3A **Age:** 66-78m 5.6-6.6y

Definition
The child will hold a knife and fork appropriately to cut food. She will hold a fork upside down (standard position with forefinger on top) in her non-dominant hand and a knife in her dominant hand (standard position with forefinger on top) to cut solid food. After she cuts the food, she will set the knife down and move the fork and food to her dominant hand for eating.

Instructional Materials
/*\Safety Note: Provide scissors appropriate for the child. Remind the child of safety regarding scissors, knives, cutters, sharp objects, and be aware of special diets needs and food allergies before doing these activities.
Different type of cutters, such as a scissors, cookie cutters, a knife (plastic or table), a letter opener, a pizza cutter, a rotary cutter. A collection of materials that can be cut, such as clay and paper. Pizza.

Instructional Activities
1. Place the collection of cutters and the material to be cut on a table.
2. Invite the children to the table, and ask them to experiment with the various cutting instruments and the materials to be cut.
3. After they explore and use the various cutting tools and materials, discuss with them which one was easiest to use and which tool made the best cuts.

4. At the conclusion of this activity, treat the children to a pizza, and ask one child to cut it with the pizza cutter.
See #6.174 and #6.186.

6.193   Ties shoelaces independently
Strand: 6-2A   **Age:** 66-78m 5.6-6.6y

Definition
The child will tie his shoelaces independently by pulling the laces, making and tightening a bow. The child will tie his shoes using the following steps: (1) Places one end of the laces in each of the his fingers, a pincer grasp is necessary; (2) Crosses one lace over and then under the other lace; (3) Pulls the laces tight; (4) Makes a loop with one lace; (5) Makes a loop with the other lace; (6) Crosses the loops; (7) Folds one loop over and then wraps it under and through the opening that is at the bottom of the two loops; (8) Holds one loop in each hand with a pincer grasp, pulls the loops simultaneously, forming a bow; (9) Tighten as necessary.

Instructional Materials
Shoe that ties or a lacing frame.

Instructional Activities
Note: It is important for the child to have ample time to practice shoe tying, and when he becomes frustrated the task should be stopped.
1. Wrap various sized boxes in colored paper.
2. Obtain different colored ribbon to match boxes.
3. Tell the child to choose a box and a ribbon to tie around the box.
4. Tell the child to wrap the ribbon around the box and tie it in a bow.
5. Help the child if necessary.
6. Continue until all the boxes are wrapped.
7. Put different prizes in the boxes and let the child keep a box to open for all his hard work.

6.194   Turns clothing right side out
Strand: 6-2B   **Age:** 66-78m 5.6-6.6y

Definition
The child will turn an article of clothing right side out. The child will right side a closed front garment by taking the bottom of the item and pulling it through the neck area. The child will right an open-front garment by turning the shoulders inside out and then straightening the item.

Instructional Activities
See #6.118 for instructional materials and activities. Ask the children to put the clothing away when they have finished playing. Encourage them to turn the clothing right side out.

6.195   Brushes after meals or at designated times
Strand: 6-8   **Age:** 70-78m 5.10-6.6y

Definition
The program-based components for this skill are not covered because oral hygiene is a skill usually dealt with at home - rather than in an educational setting. If oral hygiene is dealt with in the educational program, it is important to check with local agencies to determine appropriate policies.
Most communities have people who work in the dental care field who are available to visit educational settings.
These resource people bring materials for demonstration on correct ways to brush teeth, and kits that include toothbrushes, toothpaste, dental floss and parent information packets.
These dental visitors are also prepared to talk about proper care of teeth, preventive dental care, the importance of a good diet, and visiting a dentist. Often they will bring models of teeth for the children to practice on, and they will leave a dental educational unit for further exploration and practice.